Natural Moral Law in Contemporary Society

Studies in Philosophy and the
History of Philosophy

General Editor: Jude P. Dougherty

Volume 53

Natural Moral Law in Contemporary Society

Edited by Holger Zaborowski

The Catholic University of America Press
Washington, D.C.

The paper used in this publication meets the minimum requirements of American National Standards for Information Science—Permanence of Paper for Printed Library Materials, ANSI Z39.48-1984.
∞

Library of Congress Cataloging-in-Publication Data
Natural moral law in contemporary society / edited by Holger Zaborowski.
p. cm. — (Studies in philosophy and the history of philosophy ; v. 53)
Includes bibliographical references (p.) and index.
ISBN 978-0-8132-1786-4 (cloth : alk. paper)
1. Christian ethics—Catholic authors.
2. Natural law—Religious aspects—Catholic Church.
I. Zaborowski, Holger, 1974– II. Title. III. Series.
BJ1249.N395 2010
171'.2—dc22 2010007517

Contents

Holger Zaborowski, Introduction 1

1. *Joseph Cardinal Ratzinger / Benedict XVI,* That Which Holds the World Together: The Prepolitical Moral Foundations of a Free State 13
2. *Robert Sokolowski,* Discovery and Obligation in Natural Law 24
3. *David S. Oderberg,* The Metaphysical Foundations of Natural Law 44
4. *J. Budziszewski,* Natural Law as Fact, Theory, and Sign of Contradiction 76
5. *J. L. A. Garcia,* The Virtues of the Natural Moral Law 99
6. *Jean De Groot,* Teleology and Evidence: Reasoning about Human Nature 141
7. *Mary M. Keys,* Politics Pointing beyond the *Polis* and the *Politeia:* Aquinas on Natural Law and the Common Good 170
8. *V. Bradley Lewis,* Natural Right and the Problem of Public Reason 195
9. *Francis Slade,* Two Versions of Political Philosophy: Teleology and the Conceptual Genesis of the Modern State 235
10. *Luke Gormally,* The Good of Health and the Ends of Medicine 264

11. *Nelson Lund,* Montesquieu, Judicial Degeneracy, and the U.S. Supreme Court 285

12. *John Rist,* Aesthetics and Ethics: Some Common Problems of Foundationalism 315

Bibliography 337

Contributors 353

Index 355

Natural Moral Law in Contemporary Society

Holger Zaborowski

Introduction

"Natural law" is a concept that has been subject to severe criticism and debate, particularly since the rise of modernity. Critics of the concept of natural law speak of the illusionary or even ideological character of natural law. With the dismissal of a teleological view of nature in early modernity, the development of the modern scientific account of nature, and the modern emphasis on the decision-making and law-giving individual, they argue, natural law, as understood by premodern thinkers, no longer makes sense. New natural law theories or at least significant transformations of existing ones, as some thinkers argued, were necessary. Some thinkers even went further and totally dismissed the concept of "natural law." New paradigms of thinking replaced thus the more traditional paradigm in which the concept of natural moral law claims a central position: the paradigm of subjectivity and freedom, the paradigm of perspectivism and relativism, or the paradigm of intersubjectivity and discursive reasoning.

The traditional concept of natural law, however, has also been defended and reassessed in twentieth- and early twenty-first-century philosophy and theology. It has been defended in very different forms that often make use of the best of the traditional thinking about the subject while at the same time avoiding many of the shortcomings that led to the crisis of natural law theories. These different defenses of natural law and the different theories about natural law, however, do not necessarily make the retrieval of natural law any easier. There are many different natural law theories which are very often partly, or even completely, incompatible. There is another important reason why the concept of natural law is still such a problematic concept. This reason has to do less with its theoretical justification than with the question how natural law can be applied in concrete contexts and situations.

The concept of natural law thus still poses a major challenge for contemporary thinking. Whatever its critics may say, it is still difficult to see how some important moral, legal, and political questions could be solved without either the concept of natural law, or without a conceptual framework that de facto preserves the content of natural law from within a paradigm of thinking that, although differing from the classical paradigm of thinking about natural law, comes to similar conclusions. It is important to note here that modern philosophy, even where it does not explicitly speak about natural law, is not always altogether critical of natural law. It has at times reformulated rather than dismissed classical natural law theories.

The concept of natural law, therefore, remains controversial. There are many open questions that can only briefly be mentioned here. A philosophical critic may wonder if the development of modern philosophy ought not to be taken more seriously than some natural law theorists do. A Christian theologian may ask if a merely philosophical concept of natural law does not fall short of the new view, and, indeed, reality, of creation as disclosed in the Incarnation. There are many more questions that remain controversial and will require further thinking: questions concerning the relation between faith and reason in approaches to natural law; the kind of moral question with respect to which natural law can be applied; the hermeneutics of nature and of natural law; or the relation between natural and positive law or between metaphysics, ethics, and the natural sciences.

The essays of this volume deal with many of these questions and examine natural moral law, natural law theories, and the role that natural law can and should play in our contemporary society. While some essays explore the systematic metaphysical and moral aspects of natural law and foundational questions, others focus on questions related to the application of natural law in the political, medical, or legal realms, or discuss historical questions that are closely related to the crisis and defense of natural law. All contributors agree that natural law is a concept that cannot and must not be dismissed and that is in need of a careful retrieval. While there are clearly differences in emphasis among the contributors, most of them also agree that the defense of natural law, the critique of the modern dismissal of natural law, and the proper use of philosophical reasoning are all closely related.

All essays collected in this volume are revised versions of papers that were delivered at the 2005 fall lecture series of the School of Philosophy of the Catholic University of America in Washington, D.C. This lecture series was inspired by a letter written by then Joseph Cardinal Ratzinger, now Pope Benedict XVI, in which he asked the Catholic University of America, among other institutions, to reflect on, and explore the subject of natural law. The first essay of this volume—the only contribution that does not go back to the Catholic University of America lecture series—is an essay by then Cardinal Ratzinger in which he addresses the concept and significance of natural law. It can be read as an introduction to the problem and challenge of natural law and thus supplements the other essays of this volume.

In this essay, entitled "That Which Holds the World Together: The Prepolitical Moral Foundations of a Free State," then Cardinal Joseph Ratzinger reminds his readers of the moral foundations of any free democratic society. There is special need to do so today, he argues, for there are not only dangerous pathologies in religion (such as fundamentalism and religiously justified acts of terrorism), but also dangerous pathologies of reason that find expression in the atomic bomb or in some tendencies in the natural sciences and in the application of scientific knowledge. This is why Ratzinger sees a need to explore the moral foundations of the state that precede the political discourse. He finds these foundations historically expressed in "a law, or at least a legal minimum, antecedent to dogma; the sources of this law then had to lie, no longer in faith, but in nature and in human reason." Ratzinger is aware of the problems and challenges that are closely connected with the concept of natural law, but he still maintains that, at least for the Catholic Church, "natural law has remained . . . the key issue in dialogues with the secular society and with other communities of faith in order to appeal to the reason we share in common about the ethical principles of law in a secular, pluralistic society." Vis-à-vis the pathologies of religion and reason, Ratzinger suggests the solution of a "necessary relatedness between reason and faith and between reason and religion which are called to purify and help one another." On the basis of this, Ratzinger suggests, natural law can be defended and brought into the debate between Christianity and Western secular rationality and between them and other cultures. In the conclusion of his essay, Ratzinger expresses the hope that "ultimately, the essential values and norms that are in some way known or sensed by all men will take on a new brightness," that, in other words, the content of what previous generations have called natural moral law will be preserved and come to new fruition.

In "Discovery and Obligation in Natural Law," Robert Sokolowski sets the scene for a conceptual discussion of natural moral law. He introduces and discusses a number of important key distinctions such as the distinction between positive, established law and our individual conduct; the distinction between established law and a deeper law or custom; and the distinction between the deeper natural law and an agent's own, merely individual, wishes. Sokolowski then goes on to introduce two other important distinctions, the distinction between our established laws and the laws of other people and the distinction between natural law and the many established laws. These distinctions help Sokolowski to explore the domain of ethical and political prudence which, he argues, is the domain to which natural law essentially belongs. Sokolowski also introduces another distinction of a different character, the distinction between divine positive law and natural law. This distinction, he argues, is important also for the Christian approach to natural law insofar as, on his account, one should not too easily give up the claim of reason and dismiss the difference between divine positive and natural law. He then goes on to examine the difference between ends and purposes (another important distinction) and shows that natural law is disclosed in the complex interplay between natural ends and human purposes. Given that modern thinking increasingly dismissed the concept of natural ends (at least in very powerful proponents of modern thinking), Sokolowski encounters the challenge of restoring the concept of natural law without simply developing a pre- or antimodern position. Our challenge is, he argues, "to question the very distinction between modern and premodern and to move toward philosophy as transcending that difference." In the remainder of his essay, Sokolowski illustrates what this could mean and how natural law can be discovered through a concrete example, and provides an outline of how the natural law discourse can be reconciled with the modern discovery of human rights.

David Oderberg examines "The Metaphysical Foundations of Natural Law." He notices that almost all contemporary moral philosophy neglects metaphysical questions. Oderberg argues, however, that there is an "intimate connection between metaphysics and morality." Reality does not consist of mere facts; it is always already normative. This normative character, as he points out, is taken seriously by natural law theories; it finds its expression in the understanding of reality as a necessary cosmic order without which there could be no practice of morality and thus no morality at all. This is why concepts such as nature, function, and flourishing play a major role in all natural law theories. The metaphysical foundations of natural law, Oderberg argues, are not limited to this. What also needs to be considered is the wider metaphysical essentialism that he considers to be of central significance to the theory of natural law. It is essentialism that provides a secure foundation for natural law, Oderberg argues, because it not only holds that things do have a real essence, but also that the essences of things can be known. Essentialism, he further argues, is also necessary fully to understand another important, though today often neglected or dismissed, feature of reality that is presupposed by natural law. "Only a thoroughgoing essentialism," Oderberg points out, "can undergird natural teleology; without the former, the latter is understandably going to seem mysterious, obscure, perhaps an illusion of man's devising." Oderberg concludes his essay by discussing the role of human nature in natural law discourse and critically discusses the Grisez-Finnis-Boyle school of reasoning about natural law, thus showing not only the importance of reassessing the connection between metaphysics and ethics, but also of a sound philosophical metaphysics.

J. Budziszewski, in his article "Natural Law as Fact, as Theory, and as a Sign of Contradiction," takes Cardinal Ratzinger's view of natural law as a starting point and explores different aspects of natural law. In so doing, he provides an important contribution to the questions of what natural law is and supplements the foundational enterprises of Robert Sokolowski and David Oderberg. Natural law is, first of all, a factual feature of the world that has to do with how things—not just the human person—really are. In his essay, Budziszewski explores the pretheoretical human experience of natural law that is common to all people, in the experience of the call of one's conscience, for instance. The fact of natural law, however, also requires theoretical consideration, particularly in a time in which the content of natural law is no longer considered self-evident by many people. Natural law, Budziszewski argues, needs to be, and can very well be, understood as both true law and truly natural. Natural law is, therefore, also a theory about reality that tries to explain what reality is and how it is constituted. It provides us with insights into the basic structure of nature as meaningful and designed and therefore also with insights into ourselves. In this context, Budziszewski also discusses important and powerful objections against natural law, such as the accusation that natural law theories hold a naturalistic fallacy, then proves them inconsistent and not convincing, and explores what he calls "witnesses" (such as conscience and the designedness of things in general) of natural law to show how natural law is known. Natural law is, however, also a sign of contradiction. That natural law is a feature of reality is not a commonly shared view any more; it is also a very puzzling and scandalous concept. Budziszewski explores the reasons for this in the last part of his essay. One reason, he argues, lies in the Fall which explains why we do not want to hear of natural law. He concludes his essay by exploring the contemporary crisis of natural law and by drawing attention to ways of encountering and overcoming it.

In his contribution, "The Virtues of the Moral Law," J. L. A. Garcia focuses upon virtues-based moral theory as the wider theoretical framework for his discussion of the natural moral law. Garcia first examines the strengths of this theory and also discusses some alternatives and objections against it. He then further explores the moral virtues and vices with respect to conduct and develops a virtues-based, role-centered, and patient-focused account of "ought"-judgments. Garcia then continues his discussion of virtues-based moral theory by showing how this approach can help to understand the ideas of moral law and, more specifically, of natural law: moral and natural law are understood as the moral virtues' practical regulation which is rooted both in what we need and in what is in our interest as human beings. In the next part of his essay, Garcia shows how this theory can deal with apparent conflicts without the need to appeal to a moral standard that is deeper than the virtues themselves. Here, he presents a case for moral theory that is intention-sensitive and effects-independent in its deontic classification and evaluation of actions and omissions. In the conclusion of his essay, he explicates the related concept of input-drive and contrasts this approach with other approaches in ethical theory. He also further justifies his central idea that virtues need to be seen as internal to the moral law of nature.

In "Teleology and Evidence: Reasoning about Human Nature," Jean De Groot examines Aristotle's understanding of natural teleology and shows how his teleology of living things can help us to understand natural goods in human life and thus can also benefit contemporary ethical debates. She argues that natural teleology is the most plausible interpretation of empirical facts about human and nonhuman nature. In her essay, she first discusses to what extent natural teleology seems to fall short of certain standards of scientific reasoning and explores the inner logic of a teleological understanding of nature and how the social sciences could benefit from a philosophical explanatory framework such as the teleological view of nature. De Groot then goes on to show how natural teleology can be reconciled with an explanation of life from within an evolutionary perspective. Human goods, she argues, are contingent; in organisms, the basic structure of actions and ends is that one thing is for the sake of another. She then explores the meaning of this in a close reading of Aristotle's natural philosophy. In the next part of her essay, De Groot examines the specific (i.e., hypothetical) kind of necessity that can be found in teleological natural systems and among crafted objects, that is to say, in the realm of what is produced. In the concluding part of her essay, De Groot shows that reasoning that follows natural (hypothetical) necessity and thus (re)discovers natural teleology leads to knowledge about natural goods. In this part, she also discusses some concrete examples concerning human sexuality or economic issues that show the significance of natural teleology and natural law based on it.

Mary M. Keys discusses "Politics Pointing beyond the *Polis* and the *Politeia:* Aquinas on Natural Law and the Common Good" in her essay. She pursues a both historical and systematic interest. On the one hand, she examines Aquinas's reading of Aristotle and convincingly argues that "in developing his theory of natural law Aquinas is consciously laying new, deeper, and broader foundations for ethics and politics" than Aristotle. Aquinas, in other word, does not simply comment upon Aristotle's philosophy; he further develops some of Aristotle's ideas from within the framework of his own genuine philosophy. This philosophy, Keys also shows, deserves to be taken seriously by contemporary ethicists and political philosophers. For Aquinas provides an important contribution to our philosophical understanding of virtue and natural law. His thought contains many important and true insights; it "is especially significant for its openness to discovering and living out truth via both faith and reason, and to the cosmopolitan, transcendent, and religious, as well as the political dimensions of human life." Keys illustrates her reading of Aquinas by examining the life and self-understanding of dissidents in communist countries such as Václav Havel. They show, as Keys suggest, the permanent truth and depth of Aquinas's political theory and his insight into human nature.

The following essays focus on questions concerning the application of natural law in political philosophy and biomedial ethics. In his essay, V. Bradley Lewis explores "Natural Right and the Problem of Public Reason." Lewis discusses the development that political philosophy has taken in recent decades. He examines John Rawls's *A Theory of Justice* and the discussion and development of his "justificatory liberalism" and brings Rawls's philosophy into a fruitful discussion with an older tradition within Western political thought. This tradition finds its center in the concept that natural right and natural moral law are the basis of public reason, which is why some consider it incompatible with the more recent versions of political liberalism. From the perspective of the natural right tradition, Lewis first discusses the view of public reason developed by Rawls. He develops a careful critique of some of the views proposed by Rawls and observes that Rawls does not seem to consider natural law an appropriate part of public reason and seems to keep an intentional silence about it. Lewis then goes on further to examine the relationship between the natural law and public reason. He does so by discussing three rival representative versions of this relationship, the positions of Stephen Macedo, Kent Greenawalt, and John Finnis, that is to say, of an ally, an interlocutor, and a critic of Rawls. In the last part of this essay, Lewis examines these positions with respect to the classical natural right positions of Plato, Aristotle, and Thomas Aquinas; develops a definition of natural law; discusses the tension between truth and politics; and comes to the conclusion that the traditional view of natural right can indeed be reconciled with what he considers to be the most defensible elements of public reason.

Francis Slade discusses "Two Versions of Political Philosophy: Teleology and the Conceptual Genesis of the Modern State" in his contribution to this volume. Slade explores the rise and development of a new political philosophy in modernity that focuses on natural rights and no longer on natural law, develops the new concept of sovereignty, and thus also lays the conceptual ground for the modern state. What is, according to Slade, characteristic of modern political philosophy, is its repudiation of natural teleology and thus of natural ends and their ontological priority as well as the focus on human purposes and rights. On the basis of his historical and systematic analysis, Slade distinguishes between two different kinds of political philosophy, between the premodern political philosophy of the common good and the modern political philosophy of sovereignty or the state/government. While for the former, political form is found, Slade argues, for the latter it is created as it presupposes the ontology of the formless, nonpolitical "state of nature." In his interpretation of Machiavelli's and Hobbes's philosophies, Slade shows how the state is understood as something effected by thought, but not as determined by an ontologically prior end. He also explores the epistemological dimension of the turn in modern thinking and discovers a parallelism between the developments in political philosophy and in epistemology. In both disciplines thought is understood as freedom, as self-determining. What is by nature—such as natural ends—no longer plays a role then.

This development has also important implications for our understanding of the end of medicine, as Luke Gormally shows. He explores in his essay "The Good of Health and the End of Medicine" in a time in which there has been a significant controversy about questions such as what health is and how medicine ought to be understood. According to an empiricist, value-neutral concept of health, health is "to be defined in terms of statistically normal functional abilities within a particular age group of the sex of a species." In contrast to this understanding, an evaluative concept of health understands health as a human good that needs to be understood in the context of an individual or social preference. Gormally discusses proponents of these two views and provides the basis for an in-depth critique of them and the modern polarization of the empirical and the evaluative that they presuppose. The next part of this essay is devoted to the attempt to overcome the Cartesianism inherent to these two different concepts of health. The human body, Gormally argues, is not a machine, but an organism that needs to be characterized in terms of natural tendencies, that is, final causes or ends—against the modern tendency to dismiss natural ends altogether even though this makes it impossible still to understand what life is. For living beings, he points out, show a natural tendency toward happiness. Thus, Gormally suggests, we need to rediscover the concept of "the rational soul as the unique substantial form of human bodily life and the teleological understanding of this life" in order to overcome a mechanistic concept of the body. Health, then, can be understood with Thomas Aquinas as "the natural good of the human body" as an organism. The human body is therefore oriented toward the good of health as the well functioning of the organism, both on a subrational natural, and on a rational level. On this level, Gormally further argues, the proper end of the practice of medicine can be defined too. The end of medicine, Gormally argues, is to restore and to maintain the health of the body. This requires a twofold orientation on the side of the physician, the orientation toward the science and toward the art of medicine. In the concluding part of his essay, Gormally explores what this end of medicine involves in concrete terms and how this understanding of health and the end of medicine could help with respect to current questions in medical ethics.

In "Montesquieu, Judicial Degeneracy, and the U.S. Supreme Court," Nelson Lund provides a close reading of an important passage of the Declaration of Independence. The Declaration of Independence speaks of truths that are held to be self-evident, such as the truth that all human beings are created equal and that they have certain unalienable rights. Lund carefully analyses what it means that these truths are *held* to be self-evident. They are, as he argues, not self-evident truths, at least not in the way how "self-evident" is commonly understood. He shows that it has been considered useful to treat these truths as self-evident truths and concludes from this that "there may be circumstances in which they should not be treated as self-evident truths." There is, according to Lund, at least "one such circumstance . . . : The United States Supreme Court should never rely on these propositions, or any other conception of the natural moral law, to declare any statute unconstitutional." Supreme Court Justices, he argues, are not the best authorities to discover and apply the natural moral law. There are also better ways of doing so, such as rational philosophical reasoning. In order to prove this point, Lund discusses Montesquieu's insight that a depoliticization of the power of judging is both necessary and impossible, he examines the difference between the American and the English legal system and, in an in-depth discussion of a number of legal cases, he develops a substantial critique of the implicit and explicit philosophical claims of American judges and thus shows the significance of sound philosophical reasoning about the natural moral law.

The concluding essay, John Rist's "Aesthetics and Ethics: Some Common Problems of Foundationalism," explores how it is possible to avoid subjectivism and nihilism in aesthetics and ethics. Rist suggests a reappraisal of the Platonic tradition which understands the physical and moral beautiful to indicate "the Beauty—not merely the power and the goodness—of the God of Truth." After examining the understanding of beauty in the Old and New Testament, Rist turns his attention to Origin and Plotinus and their "aesthetics" *avant la lettre.* The Platonic tradition, he reminds us, understands the sensibly beautiful to depend on, or participate in, an intelligible Beauty and thus avoids the subjectivism of a great deal of modern aesthetics: "Living spiritual beauty is the source of sensible beauty, and the nature of physical beauty can be neither understood nor justified without reference to it." After examining the complex relation between Plotinus and Plato, Rist moves on to discuss the early Christian view of beauty. He focuses on Augustine's view of the beauty of God and of Christ and shows how Augustine combines Stoic, Platonic, and Christian elements in his discussion of beauty as ultimately founded in God's beauty. Rist then discusses the problems that arise when the Platonic (and Christian) aspects in the metaphysical discussion of aesthetics and ethics are dismissed. It is, in his view, the subjectivism and nihilism and the separation of aesthetics and ethics that characterize modern secular culture and that determine its understanding of art and of the task of the artist. The alternative that Rist develops on the basis of his historical account is the view that art is an ethical and spiritual phenomenon. He thus shows a way of avoiding subjectivism and nihilism without explicitly speaking of natural law. He does, however, implicitly speak of important dimensions of natural law—a clear sign that there are different ways of reassessing and retrieving the content of the natural law tradition. There is, roughly speaking, not only the Aristotelian-Thomistic, but (among even more traditions) also the Platonic-Augustinian tradition that allows for an in-depth understanding of the moral norms that are not subject to human lawmaking and judging, but the very presupposition of any attempt to make a (positive) law and to make a judgment about right and wrong.

I would like to thank the authors for their contributions, support, and patience, and Janelle Livesay, Mimi Klutstein-Meyer, and Cynthia Jolly for their assistance in preparing this volume for publication. Particular thanks are due to Patrick Rooney for proofreading the entire manuscript and for his help in the preparation of this volume.

Special thanks are also due to David J. McGonagle, director of the Catholic University of America Press; James C. Kruggel, acquisitions editor; Theresa Walker, managing editor; and Philip G. Holthaus, copy-editor of the present volume, for their assistance and advice. I would also like to express my gratitude to James J. Greene, Dean of Graduate Studies of the Catholic University of America, for granting me a Catholic University Research Grant-in-Aid to support the preparation of this volume. I would like to express my special thanks to Dean Kurt Pritzl, O.P., for asking me to edit this volume and for his continuing support, and to Dean Emeritus Jude Dougherty and David McGonagle for accepting this volume for publication in the Studies in Philosophy and the History of Philosophy series. The lecture series "Natural Moral Law in Contemporary Society" has been generously supported through funds from the Franklin J. Matchette Foundation, the Gregory Dougherty Foundation, and the Thomas and Dorothy Leavey Foundation. Best thanks are due to these foundations for making the lecture series on which this volume is based possible. The text by then Cardinal Ratzinger was first published in *Jürgen Habermas/Joseph Ratzinger, Dialektik der Säkularisierung. Über Vernunft und Religion, mit einem Vorwort herausgegeben von Florian Schuller* (Freiburg i. Br.: Verlag Herder, 2005). Its inclusion has been made possible by a generous gift that I graciously acknowledge.

Joseph Cardinal Ratzinger / Benedict XVI

1 That Which Holds the World Together

The Prepolitical Moral Foundations of a Free State

Historical developments are moving more and more quickly in today's world, and I believe that two factors in particular typify this acceleration of a process that began only slowly in the past. *First,* we have the formation of a global community in which the individual political, economic, and cultural powers become increasingly dependent on one another, touching and intersecting each other in their various existential spheres. *Second,* we have the development of human possibilities, of the power to make and to destroy, that poses the question of legal and ethical controls on power in a way that goes far beyond anything to which we have yet been accustomed. This lends great urgency to the question of how cultures that encounter one another can find ethical bases to guide their relationship along the right path, thus permitting them to build up a common structure that tames power and imposes a legally responsible order on the exercise of power.

The fact that Hans Küng's proposal of a "world ethos" interests so many people shows at any rate that this question has in fact been posed; and this remains a valid point, even if one agrees with Robert Spaemann's acute critique of this project.[1] This is because we must add a third factor to the two mentioned above. In the process of encounter and mutual penetration of cultures, ethical certainties that had hitherto provided solid foundations have largely disintegrated. The question of what

1. Robert Spaemann, "Weltethos als 'Projekt,'" *Merkur* 570, no. 71 (1996): 893–904.

the good is (especially in the given context of our world) and of why one must do the good even when this entails harm to one's own self—this fundamental question goes generally unanswered.

It seems to me obvious that science as such cannot give birth to such an ethos. In other words, a renewed ethical consciousness does not come about as the product of academic debates. On the other hand, it is equally indisputable that the fundamental transformation of the understanding of the world and of man that has come about thanks to the growth in scientific knowledge has played a major role in the collapse of the old moral certainties. And this means that science does have a responsibility vis-à-vis man qua man. In particular, it is the responsibility of philosophy to accompany critically the development of the individual academic disciplines, shedding a critical light on premature conclusions and apparent "certainties" about what man is, whence he comes, and what the goal of his existence is. To make the same point in different words: philosophy must sift the nonscientific element out of the scientific results with which it is often entangled, thus keeping open our awareness of the totality and of the broader dimensions of the reality of human existence—for science can never show us more than partial aspects of this existence.

1. POWER AND LAW

It is the specific task of politics to apply the criterion of the law to power, thereby structuring the use of power in a meaningful manner. It is not the law of the stronger, but the strength of the law that must hold sway. Power as structured by law, and at the service of the law, is the antithesis of violence, which is a lawless power that opposes the law. This is why it is important for every society to overcome any suspicion that is cast on the law and its regulations, for it is only in this way that arbitrariness can be excluded and freedom can be experienced as a freedom shared in common with others. Freedom without law is anarchy, and hence the destruction of freedom. Suspicion of the law, revolt against the law, will always arise when law itself appears to be no longer the expression of a justice that is at the service of all, but rather the product of arbitrariness and legislative arrogance on the part of those who have the power for it.

This is why the task of applying the criterion of the law to power leads to a further question: How does law come into being, and what must be the characteristics of law if it is to be the vehicle of justice rather than the privilege of those who have the power to make the law? It is, on the one hand, the question of the genesis of the law, but, on the other hand, the question of its own inherent criteria. The problem that law must be not the instrument of the power of a few, but the expression of the common interest of all, seems—at first sight—to have been resolved through the instruments whereby a democratic will is formed in society, since all collaborate in the genesis of the law. This means that it is everyone's law; it can and must be respected, precisely because it is everyone's law. And as a sheer matter of fact, the guarantee of a shared collaboration in the elaboration of the law and in the just administration of power is the basic argument that speaks in favor of democracy as the most appropriate form of political order.

And yet it seems to me that one question remains unanswered. Since total consensus among men is very hard to achieve, the process of forming a democratic will relies necessarily either on an act of delegation or else on a majority decision; depending on the importance of the question at issue, the proportion of the majority that is required may differ. But majorities too can be blind or unjust, as history teaches us very plainly. When a majority (even if it is an utterly preponderant majority) oppresses a religious or a racial minority by means of unjust laws, can we still speak in this instance of justice, or, indeed, of law? In other words, the majority principle always leaves open the questions of the ethical foundations of the law. This is the question of whether there is something that never can become law but always remains injustice; or, to reverse this formulation, of whether there is something that is of its nature inalienably law, something that is antecedent to every majority decision and must be respected by all such decisions.

The modern period has formulated a number of such normative elements in the various declarations of human rights and has withdrawn these from subjection to the vagaries of majorities. It is of course possible for the contemporary consciousness to be content with the inherent obviousness of these values. But even such a self-limitation of the act of question has a philosophical character! There are, then, let us say, self-subsistent values that flow from the essence of what it is to be a man, and are therefore inviolable: no other man can infringe them. We will have to return later to the question of the extent to which this idea can be sustained, above all because the obviousness of these values is by no means acknowledged in every culture. Islam has defined its own catalogue of human rights, which differs from the Western catalogue. And if my information is correct, although it is true that today's China is defined by a cultural form, namely, Marxism, that arose in the West, it is asking whether "human rights" are merely a typically Western invention—and one that must be looked at critically.

2. NEW FORMS OF POWER AND NEW QUESTIONS ABOUT HOW THESE ARE TO BE MASTERED

When we are speaking of the relationship between power and law and about the sources of law, we must also look more closely at the phenomenon of power itself. I do not propose to try to define the essence of "power" as such. Instead, I should like to sketch the challenges that emerge from the new forms of power that have developed in the last fifty years.

The first phase of the period after the Second World War was dominated by fear of the new destructive power that the invention of the atomic bomb had placed in the hands of men. Man suddenly realized that he was capable of destroying both himself and his planet. This prompted the question: What political mechanisms are necessary in order to prevent this destruction? How can such mechanisms be discovered and made effective? How can we mobilize the ethical energies that give birth to political forms of this kind and make them work? Then, for a long period, it was the competition between the opposing power blocs, and the fear that the destruction of the other side would lead to one's own destruction, that preserved us de facto from the terrors of a nuclear war. The mutual limitation of power and the fear for one's own survival proved powerful enough to save the world.

By now, however, we are afraid, not so much of a large-scale war, as of the omnipresent terror that can make itself felt and can strike anywhere. We now see that mankind does not need a large-scale war in order to make the world uninhabitable. The anonymous powers of terror, which can be present anywhere, are strong enough to pursue everyone into the sphere of everyday life. And all the time, there is the specter of criminal elements gaining access to weapons of mass destruction and unleashing chaos in the world, independent of the established political structures. This has shifted the question about law and ethos. We now ask what are the sources on which *terror* draws. How can we succeed in eliminating, from within, this new sickness of mankind? It is shocking to see here that, at least in part, terror offers a moral legitimation for its actions. Bin Laden's messages portray terror as the response of the powerless and oppressed peoples to the arrogance of the mighty and as the righteous punishment for their arrogance and for their blasphemous high-handedness and cruelty. Clearly, for people in certain social and political situations, such motivations are persuasive. In part, terrorist actions are portrayed as the defense of religious tradition against the godlessness of Western society.

At this point, another question arises, to which we must return later. If one of the sources of terrorism is religious fanaticism—and this is in fact the case—*is then religion a healing and saving force? Or is it not rather an archaic and dangerous force* that builds up false universalisms, thereby leading to intolerance and acts of terrorism? Must not religion, therefore, be placed under the guardianship of reason, and its boundaries carefully marked off? This, of course, prompts yet another question: Who can do this? And how does one do it? But the general question remains: Ought we to consider the gradual abolishment of religion, the overcoming of religion, to be necessary progress on the part of mankind, so that it may find the path to freedom and to universal tolerance? Or is this view mistaken?

In the meantime, yet another form of power has taken center stage. At first glance, it appears to be wholly beneficial and entirely praiseworthy. In reality, however, it can become a new kind of threat to man. Man is now capable of making human beings, of producing them in test tubes (so to speak). Man becomes a product, and this entails a total alteration of man's relationship to his own self. He is no longer a gift of nature or of the Creator God; he is his own product. Man has descended into the very well-springs of power, to the sources of his own existence. The temptation to construct the "right" man at long last, the temptation to experiment with human beings, the temptation to see them as rubbish to be discarded—all this is no mere fantasy of moralists opposed to "progress." If we have noted the urgent question of whether religion is truly a positive force, so we must now *doubt the reliability of reason*. For in the last analysis, even the atomic bomb is a product of reason; in the last analysis, the breeding and selection of human beings is something thought up by reason. Does this then mean that it is reason that ought to be placed under guardianship? But by whom or by what? Or should perhaps religion and reason restrict each other and remind each other where their limits are, thereby encouraging a positive path? Once again, we are confronted with the question how—in a global society with its mechanisms of power and its uncontrolled forces and its varying views of what constitutes law and morality—an effective ethical conviction can be found with sufficient motivation and vigor to answer the challenges I have outlined here and to help us meet these tests.

3. PRESUPPOSITIONS OF THE LAW: LAW—NATURE—REASON

Our first step is to look at historical situations comparable to our own, insofar as there is anything genuinely comparable. In any case, it is worth taking a very brief glance at ancient Greece, which also experienced an Enlightenment in which a divinely based law lost its obviousness, and it became necessary to look for deeper justifications of the law. This led to the idea that in the face of a positive law that can in reality be injustice, there must be a law that derives from the nature, from the very being, of man himself. And this law must be discovered, so that it can act as a corrective to the positive law.

Closer to our own times, we have the double rupture of the European consciousness that occurred at the beginning of the modern period and made necessary a new fundamental reflection on both the contents and the source of law. First, we have the exodus from the boundaries of the European world, the Christian world, that happened when America was discovered. Now Europeans encountered peoples who did not belong to the Christian structures of faith and law, which had hitherto been the source of law for everyone and which had given this structure its form. There was no legal fellowship with these peoples. But did this mean that they were outside the law, as some asserted at that time (and as was frequently the case in practice)? Or is there a law that transcends all legal systems, a law that is binding on men qua men in their mutual relationships and that tells them what to do? In this situation, Francisco de Vitoria developed the already existing idea of the *ius gentium*, the "law of the nations"; the word *gentes* also carries the association of "pagans," "non-Christians." This designates that law that is antecedent to the Christian legal form and is charged with ordering the right relations among all peoples.

The second rupture in the Christian world took place within Christianity itself through the division in faith that led to the disintegration of the one fellowship of Christians into a number of distinct fellowships, some of which were directly hostile to each other. Once again, it was necessary to elaborate a law, or at least a legal minimum, antecedent to dogma; the sources of this law then had to lie, no longer in faith, but in nature and in human reason. Hugo Grotius, Samuel von Pufendorf, and others developed the idea of the natural law, which transcends the confessional borders of faith by establishing reason as the instrument whereby law can be posited in common.

The natural law has remained (especially in the Catholic Church) the key issue in dialogues with the secular society and with other communities of faith in order to appeal to the reason we share in common and to seek the basis for a consensus about the ethical principles of law in a secular, pluralistic society. Unfortunately, this instrument has become blunt. Accordingly, I do not intend to appeal to it for support in this conversation. The idea of the natural law presupposed a concept of nature in which nature and reason overlap, since nature itself is rational. With the victory of the theory of evolution, this view of nature has capsized: nowadays, we think that nature as such is not rational, even if there is rational behavior in nature. This is the diagnosis that is presented to us, and there seem to be few voices today that are raised to contradict it.[2] This means that, of the various dimensions of the concept of nature on which the earlier concept of the natural law was based, only one remains.

2. This philosophy of evolution, which still remains dominant despite corrections on individual points, is most consistently and impressively expressed by J. Monod, *Chance and Necessity: An Essay on the Natural Philosophy of Modern Biology* (New York: Knopf, 1971). On the distinction between the de facto results of the investigations of the natural sciences and the philosophy that accompanies these, R. Junker and S. Scherer, eds., *Evolution: Ein kritisches Lehrbuch*, 4th ed. (Giessen: Weyel, 1998), is helpful. On the debate with the philosophy that accompanies the theory of evolution, see my *Glaube—Wahrheit—Toleranz* (Freiburg im Breisgau: Herder, 2003), 535–47, trans. by Henry Taylor as *Truth and Tolerance: Christianity and World Religions* (San Francisco: Ignatius Press, 2004).

Ulpian summed this up in the early third century after Christ in the well-known words: "Ius naturae est, quod natura omnia animalia docet."[3] But this is not an adequate answer to our question, since we are interested, not in that which concerns all the *animalia,* but in those specifically human tasks that the reason of man has created and that cannot be resolved without reason. One final element of the natural law that claimed (at least in the modern period) that it was ultimately a rational law has remained, namely, *human rights.* These are incomprehensible without the presupposition that man qua man, thanks simply to his membership in the species "man," is the subject of rights and that his being bears within itself values and norms that must be discovered—but not invented. Today, we ought perhaps to amplify the doctrine of human rights with a doctrine of human obligations and of human limitations. This could help us to grasp anew the relevance of the question of whether there might exist a rationality of nature, and hence a rational law for man and for his existence in the world. And this dialogue would necessarily be intercultural today, both in its structure and in its interpretation. For Christians, this dialogue would speak of the creation and the Creator. In the Indian world, this would correspond to the concept of "dharma," the inner law that regulates all Being; in the Chinese tradition, it would correspond to the idea of the structures ordained by heaven.

4. THE INTERCULTURAL DIMENSION AND ITS CONSEQUENCES

Before I attempt to draw conclusions, I should like to widen the perspective I have indicated up to this point. If we are to discuss the basic

3. "The law of nature is that which nature teaches all sentient beings." On the three dimensions of the medieval natural law (the dynamism of Being as a whole; the orientation of that nature which is common to men and animals [Ulpian]; and the specific orientation of the rational nature of man), see the information in the article by P. Delhaye, "Naturrecht," in *Lexikon für Theologie and Kirche,* 2nd ed., vol. 7, cols. 821–25. The concept of natural law found at the beginning of the *Decretum Gratiani* is noteworthy: "Humanum genus duobus regitur, naturali videlicet iure, et moribus. Ius naturale est, quod in lege et Evangelio continetur, quo quisque iubetur, alii facere, quod sibi vult fieri, et prohibetur, alii inferre, quod sibi nolit fieri" (The human race is governed by two things, namely, the natural law and customs. The natural law is that which is contained in the law and in the gospel, whereby each one is commanded to do to another what he wishes to be done to himself and is forbidden to inflict on another what he does not wish to be done to himself).

questions of human existence today, the intercultural dimension seems to me absolutely essential—for such a discussion cannot be carried on exclusively either within the Christian realm or within the Western rational tradition. Both of these regard themselves as universal, and they may perhaps be universal *de iure*. De facto, however, they are obliged to acknowledge that they are accepted only by parts of mankind, and that they are comprehensible only in parts of mankind—although the number of competitors is of course much smaller than an initial glance might suggest.

The most important point in this context is that there no longer exists any uniformity within the individual cultural spheres, since they are all marked by profound tensions within their own cultural tradition. This is very obvious in the West. Although the secular culture is largely dominated by the strict rationality of which Jürgen Habermas has given us an impressive picture, a rationality that understands itself to be the element that binds people together, the Christian understanding of reality continues to be a powerful force. The closeness and the tension between these two poles varies: sometimes they are willing to learn from each other, but sometimes they reject each other to a greater or lesser degree.

The Islamic cultural sphere too is marked by similar tensions. There is a broad spectrum between the fanatical absolutism of a Bin Laden and attitudes that are open to a tolerant rationality. The third great cultural sphere, that of India—or, more precisely, the cultural spheres of Hinduism and Buddhism—is likewise marked by similar tensions, although these take a less dramatic form (at least to our eyes). These cultures too experience the confrontation with the claims of Western rationality and the questions posed by the Christian faith, since both Western rationality and the Christian faith are present there; they assimilate one or the other in various ways, while still trying to preserve their own identity. We can round off the picture by mentioning the tribal cultures of Africa and the tribal cultures of Latin America that have been summoned to new life by various Christian theologies of liberation. In many ways, these seem to call Western rationality into question; and this means that they also call into question the universal claim of Christian revelation.

What are the consequences of all this? The first point, I believe, is that although the two great cultures of the West, that is, the culture of the Christian faith and that of secular rationality, are an important contributory factor (each in its own way) throughout the world and in all cultures, nevertheless they are de facto not universal. This means that the question put by Jürgen Habermas's colleague in Tehran seems to me not devoid of significance—namely, the question of whether a comparative study of cultures and the sociology of religion suggest that European secularization is an exceptional development and one that needs to be corrected. I would not necessarily reduce this question to the mood of Carl Schmitt, Martin Heidegger, and Lévi-Strauss, that is, to a situation in which Europeans have grown weary of rationality.

At any rate, it is a fact that our secular rationality may seem very obvious to our reason, which has been formed in the West; but qua rationality, it comes up against its limitations when it attempts to demonstrate itself. The proof for it is in reality linked to specific cultural contexts, and it must acknowledge that it cannot as such be reproduced in the whole of mankind. This also means that it cannot be completely operative in the whole of mankind. In other words, the rational or ethical or religious formula that would embrace the whole world and unite all persons does not exist; or, at least, it is unattainable at the present moment. This is why the so-called world ethos remains an abstraction.

5. CONCLUSIONS

What, then, ought we to do? With regard to the practical consequences, I am in broad agreement with Jürgen Habermas's remarks about a post-secular society, about the willingness to learn from each other, and about self-limitation on both sides. At the end of my lecture, I should like to summarize my own view in two theses.

1. We have seen that there exist *pathologies in religion* that are extremely dangerous and that make it necessary to see the divine light of reason as a "controlling organ." Religion must continually allow itself to be purified and structured by reason; and this was the view of the Church Fathers too.[4] However, we have also seen in the course of our reflections that there are also *pathologies of reason*, although mankind in general is not as conscious of this fact today.

4. I have attempted to set this out in greater detail in my book *Glaube—Wahrheit—Toleranz* (see n. 2 above). See also M. Fiedrowicz, *Apologie im frühen Christentum*, 2nd ed. (Paderborn: Ferdinand Schoeningh, 2001).

There is a hubris of reason that is no less dangerous. Indeed, bearing in mind its potential effects, it poses an even greater threat—it suffices here to think of the atomic bomb or of man as a "product." This is why reason too must be warned to keep within its proper limits, and it must learn a willingness to listen to the great religious traditions of mankind. If it cuts itself completely adrift and rejects this willingness to learn, this relatedness, reason becomes destructive.

Kurt Hübner has recently formulated a similar demand. He writes that such a thesis does not entail a "return to faith"; rather, it means "that we free ourselves from the blindness typical of our age, that is, the idea that faith has nothing more to say to contemporary man because it contradicts his humanistic idea of reason, Enlightenment, and freedom."[5] Accordingly, I would speak of a necessary relatedness between reason and faith and between reason and religion, which are called to purify and help one another. They need each other, and they must acknowledge this mutual need.

2. This basic principle must take on concrete form in practice in the intercultural context of the present day. There can be no doubt that the two main partners in this mutual relatedness are the Christian faith and Western secular rationality; one can and must affirm this, without thereby succumbing to a false Eurocentrism. These two determine the situation of the world to an extent not matched by another cultural force; but this does not mean that one could dismiss the other cultures as a kind of *quantité négligeable*. For a Western hubris of that kind, there would be a high price to pay—and, indeed, we are already paying a part of it. It is important that both great components of the Western culture learn to *listen* and to accept a genuine relatedness to these other cultures too. It is important to include the other cultures in the attempt at a polyphonic relatedness, in which they themselves are receptive to the essential complementarity of reason and faith, so that a universal process of purifications (in the plural!) can proceed. Ultimately, the essential values and norms that are in some way known or sensed by all men will take on a new brightness in such a process, so that which holds the world together can once again become an effective force in mankind.

5. Kurt Hübner, *Das Christentum im Wettstreit der Religionen* (Tübingen: Mohr Siebeck, 2003), 148.

Robert Sokolowski

2 Discovery and Obligation in Natural Law

The lecture series that begins today was prepared as a response to a request from Cardinal Ratzinger, a request made when he was prefect of the Congregation for the Doctrine of the Faith. In a letter to the president of the Catholic University of America, dated October 2004, Cardinal Ratzinger observed that the Catholic Church was "increasingly concerned by the contemporary difficulty in finding a common denominator among the moral principles held by all people." He said that the Congregation "has undertaken a study aimed at assessing the presence of essential contents of the natural law in contemporary society." He remarked that, despite the Universal Declaration of Human Rights in 1948, "there has been an obscuring of natural moral truths regarding, for example, respect for human life and the transmission of life within marriage, human love, family rights, social justice and freedom, which for centuries were unquestioned ethical principles for the life of society." The letter spells out some of the reasons why this obscuring has occurred and says that a "renewed understanding of creation" would be helpful in responding to the problem, in conversation with both other Christian groups and with non-Christian communities. He quoted John Paul II as saying that it is not a matter of the Church imposing her view on nonbelievers, but of "interpreting and defending the values rooted in the very nature of the human person."

The letter said that the Congregation was expanding this study to include the work of universities, with the goal of identifying "currents and points of agreement which may be productive in renewing an understanding of natural law." It specifically asked the Catholic University of America, among other institutions, to contribute to this effort, and this lecture series is part of the university's reply.

Since the series is sponsored by the School of Philosophy, our lectures will focus on the philosophical side of the question and on the relationship between the philosophical and theological aspects, as opposed to aspects such as the historical, sociological, legal, catechetical, and ecumenical, all of which are mentioned in the letter as areas that should be addressed in this project.

A SERIES OF DISTINCTIONS

There are two kinds of question one can raise in regard to natural law; one is to determine its content (What does it prohibit? What does it enjoin? What are its precepts?), and the other is to speak about natural law as such (What exactly is it? How is it different from other kinds of law? In what way does it command or enjoin at all?). In my paper, I will address mainly the second type of question. We can get at the notion of natural law by working out a network of distinctions.

(1) The first of these distinctions deals, not with natural law, but with positive, established, human law. No human beings can live together without some agreed-upon rules guiding their conduct, whether these rules be explicitly formulated by legislative decisions or generated more implicitly by the slow growth of custom. Laws and customs come to be because of the need to accomplish some corporate good through corporate action. The members of the corporate body are elevated into higher accomplishments by those rules. Once there are such rules or laws, it is possible for people either to break them or to obey them; rules come to light because they can be broken or obeyed. When people obey the laws they act not just for themselves but for and with the community, and when they break the established laws they act against the community. Such corporate conduct is the normal way for human beings to act and to live; from the beginning of our lives we act with others, with family members and people around us. In the beginning we are not Hobbesian; Hobbes's state of nature is accessed only by philosophical thinking, not by experience or memory.

Some of our patterns of conduct, therefore, settle into laws or rules, and we can act contrary to them. This is the first distinction I wish to introduce: the contrast between the laws and someone's conduct in violation of the laws. We can break the rules, and we do so because we want something that seems good to us but is prohibited by the rules. We act for our own gratification in contrast with the laws. I should also mention that this breaking of the rules does not only occur when I as an individual want something that is prohibited; more often than not it is we—my companions and I—who want it. Even rule breaking is usually corporate and thus involves some public reason, but this public reason is not the same as the established public reason. When the rule breaking becomes serious its perpetrators are called criminals. So the very concept of law already involves a distinction, between those who follow the law and those who break it and act for their own gratification, between the law and the lawbreakers.

(2) The introduction of natural law involves a second distinction. We distinguish the law as it has been set down and a law or custom, a "way of being," that is in some sense "deeper" than the one that has been established. Consider how this natural law looks to the agent who thinks he sees or knows it. He understands himself to be obliged by this deeper law, but he also is obliged by the law that has been established by his community. He therefore must draw a distinction between these two kinds of law. The difference between the two kinds of law is most striking when they are in conflict, when the "deeper" law is opposed to the established law. This deeper law has been usually understood, by both Christians and pagans, as a law set down by God or by the gods; it is divine in some sense as contrasted with the human. This is the second distinction I wish to introduce.

(3) The agent who sees himself in the uncomfortable position of being obliged by two conflicting laws must draw yet another distinction. This will be the third distinction I wish to introduce. In it, we contrast the deeper law of nature and the agent's own merely individual wishes (or the wishes of his companions in this action). If the agent claims to be acting according to the deeper law, he cannot be acting simply for his own gratification. He must distinguish between the deeper law and his own wishes. The deeper, natural law, therefore, has to be positioned against two parameters: the established law and my own wishes. I have to be able to say that what I am obliged by when I propose breaking the

established law is not just what I want—in this case, one would not really speak of obligation—but the way things should be, for everyone and not just for myself. Thus, the agent who breaks the established law might be either a criminal or a moral witness. He is a criminal if he breaks the law in view of his own wishes or those of his group, and he is a witness if he breaks it in view of the deeper law of nature. It is not unusual for there to be differences of interpretation here: other people may consider him and his colleagues to be criminals, whereas he and they consider themselves to be exemplars. The fact that different people might interpret him and them differently, however, does not mean that there is no real difference between being the one and being the other.

At this point I would like to mention the encyclical *Veritatis Splendor.* In sections 90 to 94, it speaks of martyrdom as a witness to God's law, but also as a witness to the moral truth that is deeper than human law. It says, "Martyrdom rejects as false and illusory whatever 'human meaning' one might claim to attribute, even in 'exceptional' conditions, to an act morally evil in itself." It observes that Susanna, in the story in the Book of Daniel, "bears witness not only to her faith and trust in God but also to her obedience to the truth and to the absoluteness of the moral order." The encyclical also appeals to "the moral sense present in peoples and . . . the great religious and sapiential traditions of East and West, from which the interior and mysterious workings of God's spirit are not absent," and it quotes the Latin poet Juvenal as saying, "Consider it the greatest of crimes to prefer survival to honor and, out of love of physical life, to lose the very reason for living" (Summum crede nefas animam praeferre pudori et propter vitam vivendi perdere causas; *Satirae,* 8.83f.). The phenomenon of martyrdom engages the distinction between the established law and the natural law.

In speaking about the difference between the established law and the natural law, we have focused on the more vivid case, in which the two are in conflict. One can also draw this same distinction when the two laws are in agreement with one another. One might be able to see a harmony between the two, and yet be able to see that the same good action is recommended, or the same bad action is prohibited, by both the established and the natural law. We might think that it is harder to draw this distinction when the two kinds of law are in agreement than when they are in conflict, but this need not be the case. We often appreciate the congruence of the two laws. Suppose a stranger comes into a town. He gets into a brawl and kills someone. In his defense, he pleads ignorance. He says that he did not know that such killing was prohibited by the established laws of the community. He was new to the place and had not yet been instructed about the local laws.

But this defense would obviously not work, because anyone should know, and he should have known, that killing other human beings is the kind of action that is prohibited in any settled community. It is the kind of thing that should be legislated. Everyone should know this, and he, the stranger, should know it, not because he has made a survey of many societies but because of his appreciation of what it is to kill a human being. Anyone should know that murder is wrong under two aspects, under the aspect of established law and under the aspect of something deeper than established law, something that calls for an established law. There may be many kinds of actions for which the defendant's argument will hold, but if there are at least some for which his argument does not hold, it would show that the distinction between established and natural law can be recognized even when the two are not in conflict.

I have elaborated three distinctions in order to identify natural law: the distinction between the established law and the agent's own wishes, the distinction between established law and the law of nature, and the distinction between the agent's own wishes and the law of nature. All three concern the relationships between a moral community and its members. Two more distinctions are needed to round out my analysis; they will concern the relationships among communities themselves.

(4) My fourth distinction is between our established laws and the established laws of other people. This distinction arises when a community enters into contact with other communities and realizes that people can live according to very different patterns of conduct and still be human. This exposure further enlarges human reason, but of course it calls our own laws and customs into question. The shock of such cultural relativism might lead us into sophistry, in which we think that ultimately there just are many incongruous ways of life. On the other hand, it might lead us to appreciate that the differences are not all that there is; beneath the differences there is something common, the law prescribed by nature or the gods: it may never be available just by itself, but it comes to light in contrast to any particular established law.

(5) This discovery of a natural law introduces us to our fifth and final distinction, between the natural law and the many established laws. In the face of a multiplicity of legal codes and customs, with their varieties and contradictions, we come to see that there is something the same "in" all these laws but "deeper" than any of them. This access to the law of nature is different from the access experienced by the member of a community who discovers an incongruity between the community's way of life and the way things should be, but both modes of disclosure are manifestations of the same law. It would be interesting to develop this topic and to show how and why these two avenues lead to the same place. For our purposes here and now, we conclude with the claim that five distinctions are in play in bringing natural law to light. These distinctions make up the domain of political and ethical prudence. We have here a network not only of distinctions but also of dimensions within which the problematic of natural law can be formulated.

NATURE AND GRACE

I must introduce yet another distinction to this network, but this one comes from an entirely new dimension. It is not just added to the others the way they are added to one another, and so I do not want to list it as number six. I will leave it unnumbered. This distinction is special to Christianity. It is the distinction between divine positive law and natural law. Within Christian faith, divine positive law is manifested to us through revelation and natural law through reason, but natural law can also be confirmed and illuminated by revelation. This distinction comes into play in regard to Cardinal Ratzinger's letter, but it is important to have the other distinctions in mind when we deal with it. It would be a disservice to the study of natural law to let the revealed law become so dominant that it eclipsed the differences we have spelled out in the natural order itself.

An ambiguity arises in the use of the term "nature" when we enter into the distinction between what is by nature and what is by grace. In ancient philosophy, nature was contrasted with convention or legality, *physis* was contrasted with *nomos*. In Christian theology, nature is contrasted with grace. But the term nature is being used equivocally, or at best analogously, in these two settings, because what we mean by the theological term "nature" includes within itself both nature and convention as described by the philosophers. The word is defined partly by what it is opposed to. In this setting, the theological use of nature includes convention. Human conventions are part of what occurs in human nature.

To bring out the relationship between natural law and grace or revelation, let us consider a concrete example, the question of polygamy. St. Thomas Aquinas discusses bigamy and polygamy in *Scriptum super Sententias,* IV, d. 33, a. 1 (see also *Summa Theologiae,* III Supplement, q. 65, a. 1). He lists three ends of marriage: the procreation and education of children, the mutual devotion between the spouses, and the expression of the relation between Christ and the Church. The first two ends are evident by nature, but the third obviously comes to light in revelation, and Aquinas says it applies only to Christian faithful. He then says that a multiplicity of wives would neither necessarily destroy nor impede the first end, it would not destroy the second but it would seriously impede it, and it would totally destroy the third. Monogamy, therefore, is already enjoined by the law of nature because a plurality of spouses would seriously impede the devotion and peace of the married partners, but it is more strongly enjoined by the revealed relationship of Christ and the Church. In that relationship, the very idea of bigamy or polygamy is entirely unthinkable.[1] Thus, the contribution of revelation is not to introduce an obligation that had previously been unheard of, but to clarify and confirm something that had already been known in a less certain way. I would suggest that a similar confirmation and clarification occurs in regard to issues dealing with the beginning and end of life, such as infanticide, abortion, contraception, euthanasia, and embryonic stem-cell research, as well as homosexual marriage. We already know that, say, infanticide or abortion have something shameful and wrong about them, but we have a clearer grasp of this when we understand ourselves to be created and redeemed by God.[2]

1. In a discussion concerning Aquinas, Russell Hittinger observed that Thomas's claim that the first two ends of marriage might possibly be compatible with polygamy was motivated in part by his desire to come to terms with the practice of the patriarchs in the Old Testament.

2. When we move into the theological context, we seem to argue in a more deductive and probative manner than we do when we argue about issues in natural law within the more purely natural order. We start with something "above" the issue in question and "come down" on it; we conclude more forcefully to the good or bad in the issue in question. In the natural order,

When we introduce the Christian theological dimension into this moral network, we must be careful to avoid smothering the distinctions that bring out natural law and the naturally good and just in the human, worldly, "natural" order. We must maintain the natural intelligibility of the goods in question and must bring out this intelligibility on its own terms, with its own moral syntax. The revelation and grace present in the Church may make us more sensitive to this intelligibility, but it must also be argued or disclosed through itself if we wish to make it clear to those who do not accept Christian revelation. Christian revelation brings nature into a sharper light, but it does so at least in part on nature's own evidence and on its own terms. This is the interplay of faith and reason that is so characteristic of the best in Christian understanding.

HUMAN PURPOSES AND NATURAL ENDS

A resource that is very helpful in dealing with the natural evidence of moral intelligibilities is Francis Slade's distinction between purposes and ends, between human purposes and natural ends.[3] *Purposes* are what we as human beings set down; they are our intentions, what we wish for and set out to attain. It is true, as Aristotle shows in book 3 of the *Nicomachean Ethics,* that we can wish for things that can never come about, neither through our efforts nor the efforts of other people; we can wish for the impossible. We can also wish for things that we cannot achieve but that others can; in this case we wish for things that are possible but not through our own agency. And finally we can wish for things that we ourselves can indeed bring about.[4] When such wishes begin guiding our deliberation and conduct, they become purposes. *Purposes* or intentions are wishes that have kicked into action. Purposes, therefore, can exist

it is not so much a question of proving that something is good or bad as bringing its goodness or badness to light, and of refuting those who propose something bad. (The refutation proceeds by showing that what they propose is contradicted by something else that they must acknowledge as good.) The character of the agents involved in the argument is essential to such disclosure.

3. See Francis Slade, "On the Ontological Priority of Ends and Its Relevance to the Narrative Arts," in *Beauty, Art, and the Polis,* ed. Alice Ramos (Washington, D.C.: The Catholic University of America Press, 2000), 58–69; and "Ends and Purposes," in *Final Causality in Nature and Human Affairs,* ed. Richard Hassing (Washington, D.C.: The Catholic University of America Press, 1997), 83–85.

4. Aristotle, *Nicomachean Ethics* 3.2.1111b19–30.

only in human beings (and perhaps in a limited and analogous way in the higher animals, as Alasdair MacIntyre maintains).[5] There are purposes in the strict sense only when there are men. Ends, in contrast, belong to things apart from any human projection. They are the perfection of things, the way things are when they are working at their best. There are ends to trees, spiders, and butterflies, but there are also ends to human beings and even to human institutions, such as the arts of medicine and architecture, as well as the human family, grammar schools, high schools, and colleges, and also theaters and museums. There are ends for human nourishment and sexuality, as well as for human thinking. These ends are beyond or more basic than our human purposes. It is in the interplay of natural ends and human purposes that the natural law gets disclosed. Morality itself arises in this interplay.

In Slade's formulation, the natural law is the ontological priority of ends over purposes.[6] Ends bring out the full intelligibility of things. Even when we experience a defective instance of a given entity, we see it against what it could and should be. The best of an entity is always present in any experience we have of the thing, provided that we are rational in our experiencing. When we give names to things, when we enter things into language and the human conversation, when things become enlisted into syntax, they do not enter this game as merely static items; they enter into the game of language as intelligible, and their intelligibility involves not only a static formal pattern or a mathematical presence; they show up to our reason as more than a shape. They are also profiled against their best, their *telos* or their perfection, as Plato was able to glimpse and Aristotle was able to articulate when they spoke of the *idea* that was behind and in and above each thing that enters into our human conversation. Our speech goes toward the thing, but also toward the idea of the thing. When we learn our native language, the one in which we live as human beings, our mother tongue, we also learn the names for things and actions, and in doing so we are introduced to those things as

5. See Alasdair MacIntyre, *Dependent Rational Animals: Why Human Beings Need the Virtues* (Chicago and LaSalle, Ill.: Open Court, 1999), 58–61.

6. See Slade, "On the Ontological Priority of Ends and Its Relevance to the Narrative Arts." For an application of Slade's ideas, see Robert Sokolowski, "What Is Natural Law? Human Purposes and Natural Ends," *The Thomist* 68 (2004): 507–29, reprinted in *Christian Faith and Human Understanding: Studies in the Eucharist, Trinity, and the Human Person* (Washington, D.C.: The Catholic University of America Press, 2006), 214–33.

they can and should be. A sense for ends is built in to human language, but it is there not as something that language inserts—we and our language do not project the thing into its optimal condition. Rather, it is the thing itself insofar as it is captured into speech (by being named) that shows what it can be. When we define what a thing is, we also imply what it should be.

We can make this claim about language and *telos* because we know that names and language express not a mental copy of the thing, not a representation of the thing, but the thing itself with its potentialities as well as its present actuality. Names express the thing in its full actuality or *telos* as well as the snapshot we might have of it at any given moment. This is what names and speech do: they let things come to light in their completion as well as what they at the moment manifest to us. In fact, a present snapshot of a thing, shorn of the thing's dynamics, would not present the intelligibility of the thing at all. It would only present its shape. There is a natural evidencing of things, and it presents the *telos* of the thing in contrast to the purposes we may have when we enlist the thing into our service.

The advent of revelation does not annul this natural evidencing. In our discussion of moral truth we must avoid appealing too quickly to the force and apodicticity of revelation, with its ability to reason deductively to the moral obligations we have. If we were to appeal immediately to a theological argument, what we say will seem not to be anchored in the way things are on their own. What we say will seem to be a personal opinion derived from a religious and moral tradition and not from the evidence of things.

THE DISTINCTION BETWEEN MODERN AND PREMODERN THOUGHT

We have a special problem in dealing with this issue nowadays, because of what occurred in the origin of the modern age, when the natural ends of things were eliminated from the philosophical understanding of the world and man. Natural ends had been visible and prominent on the philosophical screen, but Machiavelli, Bacon, Descartes, and Hobbes collectively hit the delete button, and natural ends have been gone ever since. That is, they have been gone from philosophy and the universities attached to it, but not necessarily from the way people spontaneously understand themselves and the world. Natural ends are still there on the hard drive of humanity; we cannot talk about ourselves and the world without bringing in the *telos* of the things we name. The semantics of language and speech cannot avoid shadowing forth the good, even though mathematics may not do so. But for the philosophers, natural ends have departed with no hope of return, and the only things left to give meaning and orientation to life have been human purposes. Philosophers have been trying ever since to make sense of this new situation, trying to help us to cope with a "world without ends": by legislating for ourselves, creating values, making fundamental options, carrying on experiments in living, and existing before we have any essence.

I have taken the phrase a "world without ends" from a book by Dennis Des Chene.[7] It is the title of the final chapter in the book, where the author writes, "In this concluding chapter I consider what becomes of finality in the new world of *res extensae*. The brief answer is: nothing. . . . Not just final causes, but the directedness essential to the Aristotelian concept of change, are absent."[8] Des Chene says that the loss of finality, which I would call the deletion of the ends of things, is closely related to the quantitative interpretation of the world: "To hold that the nature of corporeal substance is constituted by extension is to deny that corporeal substance could have active powers."[9] He also says that Descartes thought that any finalities in things would have to be caused by God's will, and hence they would be unknown to us, because we have no way of knowing the mind of God. In addition, Descartes wanted to avoid postulating "little souls" in bits of matter. The upshot was the elimination of final causality and reliance on efficient causation alone in our attempt to explain things and their motions. Toward the end of the chapter, Des Chene writes: "The only morality, it would seem, to be gleaned from the natural world so understood consists in the unique admonition: do what you will."[10] Unmonitored, endless purposes are all there is.

I think Des Chene is correct in seeing a connection between the

7. Dennis Des Chene, *Physiologia: Natural Philosophy in Late Aristotelian and Cartesian Thought* (Ithaca, N.Y.: Cornell University Press, 1996).

8. Ibid., 391.

9. Ibid.

10. Ibid., 398.

quantification of material substances and the loss of ends, but there was another reason for this loss, namely, the innovation brought about by Machiavelli and then Hobbes in regard to political philosophy. In Machiavelli philosophy changed from being that which transcended politics into being that which ruled politically. Philosophy began to seek the effective truth of things and not the contemplative truth. It ceased to transcend politics, and the modern state was born, and this in turn led to the modern individual as a subject of that state. The political forms of premodern thought, the various shapes that political societies could take on, were replaced by the single form—an almost mathematical form—of the modern state, and if the various cities described by Plato and Aristotle could be seen as "man writ large," the modern autonomous individual could be seen as the "state writ small." Neither the state nor the modern individual is measured by the nature of things. What Francis Slade calls the "decontextualized rule" of the modern state has its mirror image in the "deracinated or rootless individual" who tries to live in that state.[11]

This is the problem we have to face when we approach the issue of natural law and natural reason in our day and age. We have to restore the very concept of natural ends, and while we might think that we could address this as a problem in moral philosophy and the philosophy of nature, I would suggest that political philosophy plays a greater role than we might have thought in both generating the problem and offering a solution.

The search for a rehabilitation of natural ends, furthermore, should not move too quickly to the theological context. It is important to bring out the distinction between ends and purposes on their own terms and with their own evidence. They can subsequently be brought into the domain of revelation and grace. It may be the case that the deletion of natural ends at the beginning of modernity occurred at least in part because ends were understood too simply as God's purposes, and the theological sense of divine purposes and finalities overrode the natural evidence of the ends of things. It may be that in principle the distinction between ends and purposes was already dissolved in this theological context; natural ends became the purposes of the Creator. It need not have been so;

11. Slade uses these terms in a lecture entitled "Versions of Political Philosophy," given at Fordham University on November 11, 2003. I am grateful for his permission to quote them.

in Thomistic theology and philosophy, the natures of things are not chosen by God; they are expressions of the divine ideas, which in turn are the divine essence insofar as it can be participated in by creatures. Such natures and essences, therefore, have a necessity and an intelligibility of their own, now grounded in the necessity and intelligibility of *esse per se subsistens.* It would be misleading to assimilate them simply to the kinds of purposes or intentions that are part of human actions. The nature of divine teleology must be distinguished from both natural ends and human purposes.

To illustrate what I mean when I say that we should not move too quickly into the theological order, I would like to comment on a passage from a book by Leo J. Elders, *The Ethics of St. Thomas Aquinas.*[12] I admire this book, which is a comprehensive and authoritative analysis of Aquinas, but I must differ on the point that I now raise. Elders criticizes some ideas of John Finnis who, according to Elders, denies that the precepts of natural law have their basis in man's natural inclinations. Finnis denies this because he thinks it would be illicit to deduce an "ought" from an "is." Elders goes on to say, "It is cause for wonder why authors such as Finnis shy away from an 'ought' based on the 'is,' since the 'is' is obviously the order of creation, and one can hardly think of a better way to live morally than by conforming oneself to this order."[13] It seems to me that one should not restore the validity of an "ought" by appealing first of all to creation; it would be better to show that things have their own ends, different from our purposes, and to show that when language captures things and actions, when we name things and actions, we understand them in their value-laden intelligibility and not just in their static entity. Their "is" is only artificially separated from their "ought." Creation can be brought into the argument for reinforcement, but it should not be the first step.

I would also like to quote Descartes to show how his understanding of God's "intentions" led him to reject finality as an explanation in human science. In the Fourth Meditation, he says that his own nature is "very weak and limited," whereas God's nature is "immense, incomprehensible, and infinite," and God is "capable of countless things

12. Leo J. Elders, *The Ethics of St. Thomas Aquinas* (Frankfurt: Peter Lang, 2005).
13. Ibid., 210.

whose causes are beyond my knowledge." The upshot of these recognitions, Descartes says, is the following: "For this reason alone I consider the whole genus of causes that we are accustomed to seek from the end of things [quod a fine peti solet] to be totally useless in physics; there is considerable rashness in thinking myself capable of investigating the [impenetrable] purposes [fines] of God."[14] The theological context, according to Descartes, leaves no room for the natural ends of things to evidence themselves to us.

In dealing with this problem, we should not simply try to recover the premodern state of things. Such an attempt would show that we have accepted the dichotomy between the modern and the premodern. We would become "antiqued" if we proceeded in this way. Instead, our course should be to question the very distinction between modern and premodern and to move toward philosophy as transcending that difference.

DISCOVERY AND OBLIGATION IN NATURAL LAW

I would like to offer an example of how one might argue on the basis of natural law. You might think that I should take some urgent contemporary topic, such as embryonic stem-cell research, but I will not do so, because the very importance of the issue would prevent us from reaching the contemplative detachment we need. Instead, I propose to examine a more lighthearted topic, the granting of tenure to members of a university faculty.

There is an established law or custom in place in the United States in regard to this. A new faculty member is given seven years' probation. During his sixth year he is evaluated in regard to his teaching, research, publication, service, and other factors. A complex system of documentation, references, and committee screening occurs. It is my considered opinion that this established practice is against the natural law. Seven years is too short a time to permit a newly minted faculty member to

14. René Descartes, *Meditations on First Philosophy,* trans. John Cottingham, vol. 2, *The Philosophical Writings of Descartes* (New York: Cambridge University Press, 1984), 39 [55]. I have amended the translation. Note that Descartes uses the same term, *finis,* in both cases, to name the ends of things studied in physics and to name God's purposes. The word *impenetrable* is found in the French but not in the Latin text of the *Meditations.*

prove himself adequately. The time period should be ten years, or perhaps there should be a period of three years at the beginning during which the tenure clock is not ticking, with a seven year probationary period starting after that.

How do I argue my case on the basis of natural law? I do not argue on the basis of the rights of the faculty member or of the faculty or students. Also, I do not have an intuition of natural law prior to or separate from the established custom. It just seems to me, on the basis of long experience and evaluation, that more time is needed for this purpose, but I have this moral insight in view of what a faculty member is, in view of what students are, and in view of what teaching and scholarly research are. My evaluation comes on the basis of these various natures and their ends. Furthermore, you may disagree with me. You may think that seven years are perfectly sufficient and that ten years would be too long a time to wait for making a decision about tenure, but you too will argue on the basis of the ends of teaching and research, and the arguments based on such ends are also arguments based on the common good. The common good in question is made up of the ends involved in the community in question.

The issue whether the academic probationary period should be extended is of course rather remote from the primary precepts of natural law, and that is why there can be such argument about it. If the denial of tenure were to involve, say, the dispossession of the faculty member, the issue would be much closer to the primary precepts and the argument would involve less uncertainty. The very primary precepts themselves are not arguable. The maxim that good is to be pursued and evil avoided, or that each should be given what is due to him, are not principles that we first hear about and only subsequently see as obligations. How could someone be persuaded to obey them? They are components of our conduct from the beginning of our rational lives. We awaken to them in the way we awaken to the principle of noncontradiction. What sense would it make to tell someone, "You must learn to stop contradicting yourself in your thoughts"? We might tell him to stop lying, but we can't tell him to stop thinking in violation of the principle of noncontradiction, because if he truly does not follow this principle he would not be thinking and would not get the point of what we are trying to tell him. Likewise, we cannot inform someone, "There is this thing called goodness, and you have to start wanting it." We seek the good and shun the evil as soon as we start acting; the problem is not to begin wanting the good, but to determine what is truly good and truly bad. We cannot tell someone, "You should give each person his due," because if he is not already involved in discriminating between what is due to himself and to others, he would not know what those words mean. The precepts are constitutive of human conduct; they are not particular applications made within it.

Discovery of the natural law is precisely the awareness that in a situation calling for action there is an issue of rendering something that is due to someone. The problem is to see that the precept does apply. It takes a certain amount of virtue or self-control, or at least *akrasia,* to see that here and now an issue of acting appropriately arises. A vicious person, an unjust agent, will not see that such an issue is at play. He will simply act as he wishes. The obligation in the circumstances does not come to light for him. That is why the natural law alone is not sufficient for human intercourse; the strong arm of the law is needed as well, to coerce or force the malefactor to follow the primary precept of justice, and also to strengthen the resolve of the virtuous, the self-controlled, and the weak.

The discovery of the natural law's application here and now is at the same time the dawning of an obligation. We do not first discover the law and its application and only later see that we should follow it. It surfaces as obliging us. The overtones of the word *oblige* can be used to bring out the kind of command involved in natural law. It is not that we receive decrees that we must follow. Rather, we realize that we are obliged to act in the light of this or that end, and we are obliged in the sense conveyed by the phrase "noblesse oblige." It is the thing to do, the thing to be done, the thing that is worthy of us and makes us honorable as human agents. We ourselves, after all, to the extent that we are rational agents, are the promulgators of natural law. We do oblige ourselves, but in a way different from the self-legislation described by Kant. We oblige ourselves because we are able to see the *telos* of the things we are dealing with and can recognize the ontological priority of these ends over our purposes and wishes. We become witnesses to the truth of things, that is, witnesses to what the things should be. Thus, when I campaign for the extension of academic probation, I bear witness to the truth of academic life and its *telos* and also exhibit my own virtue and prudence—or lack of them—in these matters.

When we turn to more urgent issues, such as abortion or euthanasia, the witness is much more serious and the costs associated with it are that much higher. Here again, the worst thing in such established practices is not the harm done to the victim, but the moral harm done to the perpetrator, who destroys himself and his community more severely than he damages the targets of his actions. (Hence, people who work against abortion, for example, are striving not only to protect the unborn but also to preserve ourselves and our community from a degrading practice.) No one can break any kind of law without incurring a punishment. It is unworthy of people to kill in such ways and to let these purposes override the ends that are at issue. We are obliged to preserve life, and the established laws have in the past strengthened this obligation, but our newer practices and laws break that obligation. Christian revelation and God's grace certainly reinforce the natural evidence at play here, but they do not install the evidence for the first time. The issues evidence themselves to the rational agent.

Now, assume that my proposal to change the probationary period for tenure is adopted. It will then become part of established law and custom. It will oblige us not just because of the nature of the things involved in this situation, but also because of the force of established law. It will be good and obligatory under two aspects, the natural and the conventional. The conventional order will have been brought more into line with the natural order of things, but the two dimensions remain distinct.

THE ROLE OF HUMAN RIGHTS

How do human rights fit into this picture of nature and convention? I have not mentioned the role of natural rights in my exposition, except to note at one point that I was not arguing on the basis of the rights of the untenured faculty member, or those of the students or other members of the university. I said I was arguing only on the basis of the natures of things.

But suppose that the change that I propose has not yet been introduced and that I am agitating for it. Among my arguments would be the claim that we are being unfair to the untenured faculty member. Why? Because he needs more time to show what he is capable of doing. One might also argue that the students and perhaps other faculty members have a right to have their incoming faculty evaluated in a more appropriate way.

My point is this: the issue of rights arises when we enter into polemics, when we start claiming what is due to certain people, on the basis of the natures of the things involved in this situation. Rights come into play, not at the first stage of moral reflection, when we try to understand things in view of their ends, but at a later stage, when litigation begins. At that point, people start making claims. This is how Bertrand de Jouvenel puts it: "As 'mine' and 'thine' do not matter in marriage except when divorce occurs, 'rights' become valuable in proportion to the loss of affinity between Ego and his environment."[15] Litigation causes each person to look to his own interests. Thus, natural human rights arise in the context of what we could call natural law litigation. Seeing rights in this context helps us avoid the danger of postulating innumerable natural human rights, and it also helps us determine rights in the light of the natures of things, not just as absolute claims.

Imagine, for example, that a child is born into a family in which the mother and father are lawyers and hence professionally concerned about rights. A few weeks after the birth, the parents are with the child and are talking about him. They begin to reflect on what rights the child has, and the mother says, "And you know, he also has the right to a sufficiently long probationary period for tenure." Are we in fact born with such a right? Are we also born with the right to an education up to, say, a master's degree or even a doctorate? Are we born with a right to a good night's sleep? Are we born with a right to nourishment? Are we born with a right to life?

To develop this a bit, imagine that the child hears what the parents are saying and responds, "Well, I've got a right to live, to be brought up, to get adequate nourishment and shelter, and if you provide these things to me, you in turn will have the right to get social security from me, long-term nursing care, and a decent burial, and I won't do anything to harm you when you are old and weak." The very imagination of this is ludicrous, and yet this is how Hobbes sees the relationship between parents and child, or at least between mother and child. As he puts it in *De Cive,*

15. Bertrand de Jouvenel, *The Pure Theory of Politics* (Indianapolis, Ind.: Liberty Fund, 2000 [1963]), 78.

"It is manifest that he who is newly born is in the mother's power before any others; insomuch as she may rightly, and at her own will, either breed him up or adventure him to fortune. If therefore she breed him, because the state of nature is the state of war, she is supposed to bring him up on this condition: that being grown to full age he become not her enemy; which is, that he obey her."[16] It is easy to see how these rights become prominent when we move into contestation and have to claim our rights, but in normal and healthy human relationships the *telos* of the persons in questions is more basic than the rights. The good of each person and the common good, sought in friendship, predominate over the claims we make on one another and serve to guide our prudence.

Any of these things—life, nourishment, shelter, education, probationary periods for tenure, a good night's sleep—can become something that is due to us, given the proper circumstances and based on what we and the circumstances are, but the rights are not there in us a priori as a list of enumerable claims that we have as we enter into the courtroom of this world. They are rights that can be claimed if an appropriate issue arises, but they are derived from what we are. Not everybody gets into the circumstances of applying for tenure, but if they do, certain rights come into play, even in the order of nature. Certain things will show up as good by nature and not just by convention.

However, there are certain features that practically everyone is engaged in from the beginning, just by virtue of what we are, such as being allowed to live, or being given nourishment, and being brought up as a human being, and these could be listed as natural human rights, because there is no one who is not involved in them. Even these rights, however, are based on what all of us are and what our *telos* is. They arise when the *telos* becomes engaged in questions of vindication. Thus, the more primary precepts of natural law deal with those things we can't help but be involved with and they issue in the basic human rights. The more remote precepts of natural law deal with issues that might arise but may not; they deal with aspects of our nature that are not as central to us as human beings as are the aspects related to the primary precepts.

I think that this is one way that we could work toward showing how

16. Thomas Hobbes, *De Cive,* in *Man and Citizen,* ed. Bernard Gert (New York: Doubleday, 1972), 212. For a new but less vigorous translation, see *On the Citizen,* ed. and trans. Richard Tuck and Michael Silverthorne (New York: Cambridge University Press, 1998), 108.

a morality based on rights can be integrated into a morality based on ends and the common good. These remarks show that there is something deeper to morality than human rights, namely, the natural law that we discover through our rational agency and the obligation that this discovery places upon us. Christian faith can serve to enlighten this exercise of practical understanding.

David S. Oderberg

3 The Metaphysical Foundations of Natural Law

Universal law is the law of nature. For there really is, as everyone to some extent divines, a natural justice and injustice that is binding on all men, even on those who have no association or covenant with each other.[1]

INTRODUCTION

One of the defining features of contemporary moral philosophy in nearly all its guises is the lack of serious concern for metaphysics—not as a discipline in itself, but as a necessary foundation for ethics. One should not mistake the fashionable project of "evolutionary ethics" for an attempt to tie morals to metaphysics, rather than seeing it more accurately as a program for burying ethics in the quicksand of current biological fancy. Nor should one, for instance, see in existentialism a serious concern for metaphysical underpinnings rather than what amounts to no more than a series of denials of the truths that used to undergird moral thinking.[2] Again, one sees in the various forms of liberal ethics that dominate the academy—consequentialism, contractualism, deontology—an almost

I am grateful to John Cottingham and Edward Feser for helpful comments on a draft of this paper, and to audiences at the Catholic University of America, the University of Oxford, and the University of Navarra.

1. Aristotle, *Rhetoric* 1.13.1373b5: "koinon de ton kata phusin. esti gar ti ho manteuontai pantes, phusei koinon dikaion kai adikon, kan mēdemia koinōnia pros allēlous ē mēde sunthēkē." The translation (a good one) is by W. Rhys Roberts from W. D. Ross, ed., vol. 11, *The Works of Aristotle* (Oxford: Clarendon Press, 1924).

2. Here I am thinking not of any specific existentialist, only of the movement in general, a movement that may no longer have a clear identity or focus but that persists in its influence and remains one of the hallmarks of modern ethical thought.

exclusive concern with agency and practical reason, seemingly divorced from wider ontological considerations. So-called virtue ethics, of course, has a more metaphysical cast, but it cannot serve as an ethical theory in its own right; to do so deforms the very ontology that ethics requires.

Of all ethical theories, natural law theory has, both conceptually and historically, been the most explicit about its metaphysical foundations—and for good reason. One might think that the reason is simply this: it is impossible to know how the world ought to go, more specifically how one ought to act (or what makes a state of affairs or action good, or worthwhile, praiseworthy, etc.) without prior knowledge of how the world is. For how could one otherwise know whether the ethical standards the theorist posits are in any way relevant to, or meetable by, reality as it is? At the very least, knowledge of how the world is gives us knowledge, or at least some insight into, what the possibilities are, and ethics is concerned with possibilities for action, ways in which an agent may shape the world to fit the standards set. The point is not merely one regarding knowledge of particular circumstances in a given case, but knowledge of generalities about reality as a whole and humanity in particular.

This sort of understanding of the relevance of metaphysics to natural law theory is, however, radically mistaken. For it is to take on the notorious "fact-value distinction" that has poisoned contemporary moral theory and against which the natural law theorist so firmly sets his face.[3] Natural law theory does not advocate a kind of inventory taking of the "bare facts," including the bare truths of reality in general and of humanity in particular, from which the theorist can then read off the set of moral truths. Metaphysics is not enlisted by natural law theory to provide the descriptive premises from which normative conclusions are supposed to flow. On the contrary, natural law theory sees normativity as built into the very fabric of reality in the first place. There is no such thing as (to use a phrase with opportune recent resonance) a "value-free" catalogue of the facts on which the system of morality rests. Rather, natural law theory finds in the deliverances of metaphysics the very moral order the theory embraces.

3. For a trenchant recent critique of the supposed distinction, see Christopher Martin, "The Fact/Value Distinction," in *Human Values: New Essays on Ethics and Natural Law*, ed. D. S. Oderberg and T. Chappell, 52–69 (Basingstoke, U.K./New York: Palgrave Macmillan, 2004). See also my *Moral Theory* (Oxford: Blackwell, 2000), 9–15.

There are very few other theories that take as seriously as does natural law theory the intimate connection between metaphysics and morality. A famous example is Kant's deontological system. One might be tempted also to cite Derek Parfit's heavily metaphysical version of extreme consequentialism,[4] but in the latter case although the particular cast of his ethical theory is based on his metaphysics of personal identity, Parfit is a firm adherent of the fact-value distinction: consequentialism is by no means built into the fabric of his ontology, though he might like to think so. Natural law theory stands out as the preeminent system wedded to a firm view of the nature of reality and of the possibility of reality's yielding up discoveries into the moral order by which man must live.

Nevertheless, what has come to be known as the "new" natural law theory, represented by Germain Grisez, John Finnis, Joseph Boyle, and their followers, is remarkable for the scarcity of its explicit reliance on metaphysical enquiry. This is not to say that the new natural law theory is not based on at least a partially worked-out, implicit ontology; only that it displays what I have elsewhere called an "agent-centered" approach to natural law theory, rather than a "world-centered" approach.[5] Typical of the Grisez-Finnis-Boyle view, as I will sometimes call the new natural law theory, is this comment in their important 1997 overview: "One way to argue for the first principles of practical knowledge is by considering actions and seeking their reasons. We identified this line of argument . . . as the proper method of locating the basic goods, to which the principles of practical knowledge direct actions."[6] While not denying the importance of metaphysics in general, and in particular the metaphysics of human nature, the particular cast of the Grisez-Finnis-Boyle approach is one in which the theorist begins with practical reasoning, seeking to uncover the ultimate ends that make action intelligible. Now this is of course reasonable in and of itself, but it is insufficient to give natural law theory a proper theoretical grounding. There is in this approach a hint of undiminished presupposition of the fact-value distinction, and it seems as though Grisez-Finnis-Boyle do indeed presuppose it: for in

4. D. Parfit, *Reasons and Persons* (Oxford: Oxford University Press, 1984).

5. D. S. Oderberg, "The Structure and Content of the Good," in *Human Values*, 127–65.

6. G. Grisez, J. Boyle, and J. Finnis, "Practical Principles, Moral Truth, and Ultimate Ends," *American Journal of Jurisprudence* 32 (1987): 113.

the same paper, the authors explicitly assert that their theory "departs from classical models . . . by taking full account of the fact that the moral ought cannot be derived from the is of theoretical truth—for example, of metaphysics and/or philosophical anthropology." They go on to state what looks like nothing other than the fact-value distinction, concluding: "Therefore, the ultimate principles of morality cannot be theoretical truths of metaphysics and/or philosophical anthropology."[7]

What is troubling about this position is the interpretation of theoretical and metaphysical truth implicit in it, one that derives directly from the Humean, positivistic approach to facts and values. By contrast, the proper approach to metaphysics from the natural law viewpoint is not one of seeking out an illusory inventory of value-free truths, nor merely one of systematizing the assembled data of philosophical anthropology—relevant though that is to the natural law project, as accepted by Grisez-Finnis-Boyle themselves. Nor is it only the task of seeking the deepest possible understanding of human nature, as vital as that task is, which again the new theorists readily accept. Laying the metaphysical foundations of natural law theory requires as well, and as the starting point of enquiry, the addressing of basic ontological questions about the nature of reality, nonhuman as well as human. Without a foundation of this sort, natural law theory risks floating free of substantive moorings and acquiring an excessively subjective and first-personal methodology. It is to these primary questions that I now turn.

2. COSMIC LAW AND ORDER

The name "natural law theory" does not have "law" in it for nothing. In the words of Seneca, "the world is guided by providence" and there is a "guiding hand" behind the "great work" of the universe that "proceeds from the command of eternal law" *(aeternae legis imperio).*[8] According to Cicero, quoting Cleanthes, just as someone entering a house would suppose, from the orderly arrangement of things, that a person superintended their arrangement and was obeyed *(qui praesit et cui pareatur),* a fortiori the vast movements and orderly succession of phenomena so nu-

7. "Practical Principles," 101–2, for both quotations.
8. Seneca, *De Providentia* [*On Providence*] 1.

merous and mighty must be governed by some intelligence.[9] One could multiply quotations, but the point here is not to make a claim about the overall attitude of the ancients toward the government of the universe or lack thereof, but that there is an idea of law in natural law theory, that the term "law" is not a mere linguistic superfluity or rhetorical flourish.

St. Thomas Aquinas famously defined *law* as "an ordinance of reason for the common good, made by one having charge of the community, and promulgated."[10] The notions of ordinance and promulgation are central to the natural law conception of cosmic order. An ordinance is variously an act of commandment or a thing commanded; there is no risk of ambiguity as long as we are clear in a given context whether we are speaking of the object or the act, though it is often not necessary for the purpose of argument to make the distinction. Promulgation is an act of notification or publication of a law for the sake of its subjects. How do these concepts, with which we are familiar from positive law, and which natural law theory takes as central, apply to what might be called cosmic law, or natural law writ large?

Natural law theory is based on the idea of cosmic order. Part of this order is, of course, the order in human nature to which natural law theory characteristically appeals. But the order cannot stop there. The main reason for this yoking together of human and cosmic order is that morality precisely concerns man's interaction with—reaction to, and behavior toward—the world external to human nature. Morality is not only about man's dealings with himself and with others, but his dealings with the extrahuman world of objects, events, properties, states, and so on. (Here I include artifacts as part of the extrahuman world, even though in a crucial sense artifacts are essentially linked to humans. At the same time every artifact has an aspect that is not essentially linked to humans, and so every artifact is, while human-centered in one respect, also not human-centered in another and so equally part of the extrahuman world.) Actually this is not quite accurate: it is more exact to say that mo-

9. "multo magis in tantis motionibus tantisque vicissitudinibus, tam multarum rerum atque tantarum ordinibus, in quibus nihil umquam inmensa et infinita vetustas mentita sit, statuat necesse est ab aliqua mente tantos naturae motus gubernari"; Cicero, *De Natura Deorum* [*On the Nature of the Gods*] 2.15. Aquinas mistakenly attributes Cicero's reference to Aristotle rather than Cleanthes; see *Summa Theologica* [hereafter *S.T.*] I q. 103 a. 1.

10. "quaedam rationis ordinatio ad bonum commune, ab eo qui curam communitatis habet, promulgata'"; *S.T.* I-II q. 90 a. 4.

rality is only about man's dealings with himself and others, but that it is impossible to isolate those dealings from the extrahuman human world of objects, events, and the like. Again, we can say that man deals with himself and others only through the extrahuman world. Every duty, every virtue, every right, every permission, is in some way directly or indirectly, partly or wholly, intrinsically or instrumentally, about things, events, states, processes, that are not human. For example, without an extrahuman world how could one exercise temperance? Or honesty? How could one practice vices such as lust, or avarice? Consider every virtue, and you will see that the same applies, as it does to duties, rights, and other moral notions.

Now suppose that there were no cosmic order—that things in the extrahuman world moved, behaved, and reacted in ways that could only be described as chaotic or random. Suppose, to take a toy example, that we lived in a world in which the only objects of actual or possible monetary or economic value were metals. Then suppose that gold randomly mutated into copper, silver into granite, iron into coal, and coal into nickel, and so on. Suppose that gold nuggets randomly flew into the air, so that every time you tried to pick one up you could never know, even in principle, whether it would take flight and enter into orbit around Mars. Every time you tried to make a sheet of aluminium, you never knew, in principle, whether the necessary lump of bauxite would suddenly melt before your very eyes and slide down the nearest storm drain. And so on. In such a world, the actual and possible objects of monetary value behave utterly randomly or chaotically. What then for the virtues of thrift, generosity, honesty, prudence, and their corresponding vices? How on earth could one even go about learning them, let alone trying to practice them? Now expand the objects of economic value to include paper, pork bellies, oil, and whatever economic object electrons are being used for at the moment, and you can see how exactly the same reasoning applies. If there were no ordered way in which electrons could be harnessed to give rise to derivatives, then there could be no derivatives fraud, and no such thing as a right to be compensated for such an act, or a duty to punish. In short, without order in the behavior of objects in the extrahuman world, there could be no practice of morality; and if there can be no practice of morality, there can be no morality.

So far, it might be thought that ethicists of all stripes can agree on this basic kind of order as a requirement of morality. In fact, though the kinds of random macroscopic occurrence described in the simple example above are obviously absent from our world, in a deeper sense much of contemporary moral theory is suffused with at least an implicit belief that the world is fundamentally random or chaotic in its behavior. Think of existentialist ethics (and one does not have to be a card-carrying existentialist to have an existentialist ethic) and its commitment to the thought that the job of man is somehow to make sense of, or impose order upon, a deeply chaotic and inexplicable world. Any subjectivist morality is based on the same attitude:[11] think of Hume's claim that our beliefs about intrinsic order and regularity in the universe are at bottom irrational and can only be held by an act of faith. Hume of course recognized the existence of natural regularities—his whole theory of causation is based on it—but he did not regard them as intrinsic to, in the sense of a necessary feature of, the physical world.

But then it might be objected that natural law theory goes too far if it holds to necessary order in the world: for isn't it enough if there is order as a matter of brute fact? For natural law theory it is not enough, since mere brute order is an insufficient ontological support for necessary moral truth, the thought being that morality consists of necessary truths that obtain no matter what the state of the world. If those truths are objectively grounded in the nature of things—the fundamental tenet of natural law theory—then it is simply inconceivable that the nature of things, or, to speak more neutrally, the way things go, might be hostage to fortune in the sense of being open to chaotic development. Additionally, the very practice of morality requires necessary order, for otherwise how could an agent make rational plans concerning the fulfillment of his life? If there can be no rational certitude that the cosmos exhibits the stability and predictability inherent in necessary order, in what sense could an agent be rationally guided by it in his ethical decision making? Looking at the matter in terms of theoretical economy, however, perhaps the natural law theorist does not need to appeal to necessary order, but simply to some sort of extrinsic guarantee that the cosmos will behave in a

11. Consider this typical statement from E. D. Klemke: "We must say that the universe is valueless; it is *we* who evaluate, upon the basis of our subjective preferences . . . we 'impose' such values upon the universe"; "Living without Appeal," in *The Meaning of Life,* ed. Klemke (New York: Oxford University Press, 1981), 169.

regular or ordered fashion, at least so long as there exist rational agents bound by moral law. Here I have in mind the theological principle that although God could annihilate immortal souls He is guaranteed not do so. Maybe the same is true for the universe, that although it is not intrinsically necessarily ordered, it is ordered by a kind of de facto necessity, an extrinsic guarantee that it will not descend into chaos.[12]

The more probable opinion, I would argue, is that cosmic order is intrinsically necessary, and that the opponent of natural law theory would be mistaken to turn the argument on its head by asserting that the sort of ethical system mapped out by the theory is illusory because the world really is intrinsically disordered, random, or chaotic. I take this to be the default position of natural law theory's opponents: whereas in ancient days (two hundred years ago and for all recorded time before that) it was simply obvious that the cosmos was what its etymology said, namely, ordered,[13] we moderns simply cannot take the cosmos to have the order historically attributed to it. When the evolutionist George Gaylord Simpson famously stated the dogma that "[t]he meaning of evolution is that man is the result of a purposeless and natural process that did not have him in mind,"[14] he was thinking primarily of appeals to a divine source of purpose. But the thought is supposed to be reinforced by the idea that random genetic mutation gives rise, so biology currently holds, to organic development, and if this is true of life, which gives the appearance of some sort of order, how much more is it true of everything inorganic in the universe?

Yet there is no agreed definition of randomness among mathematicians or other scientists, whether within or across disciplines. Concepts such as equiprobability, inert uniformity, indeterminacy, and more abound; some definitions are irreducibly epistemic and others are not. Yet without such agreement, how can we know whether we have found an instance of randomness? Even in quantum theory, where the "gold standard" of randomness in nature is thought to be found, there is by no

12. The difference being that the soul is immortal by metaphysical necessity, even though it could be annihilated. (This supports the view that there is a difference between logical and metaphysical necessity.) On the supposition being made here, there is no metaphysical necessity of order, only a similar extrinsic guarantee that it will be preserved.

13. kósmos = order.

14. G. G. Simpson, *The Meaning of Evolution* (New Haven, Conn.: Yale University Press, 1967), 345.

means a settled view as to whether, say, radioactive decay is genuinely indeterministic, let alone random; and it must be remembered that indeterminism does not entail randomness. For instance, one of the standard "straw man" attacks on free will consists in arguing that since the alternatives for human action are that it is either determined or random, and since free will would make it random, there cannot be free will—the assumption being that human action does not look like it displays characteristics of randomness. Yet the fallacy is in supposing that the lack of determinism given the existence of free will would mean that action was random rather than simply what it is, namely, undetermined.

Everyone, of course, agrees on what randomness is not: it is an absence of order. Maybe a negative definition is all we can give, but that does not mean it corresponds to anything possible. We can, for instance, define the term *aspatiality* as the putative property of being a material object and being unextended; but that does not mean anything could in fact have "aspatiality," that it corresponds to a possible property of anything, though we have defined it as a kind of absence. Advocates of natural randomness, say, in biology, should also beware of arguing circularly for the lack of order or regularity in the organic world from the existence of random genetic mutations, if the supposed randomness of such mutations is to be defined in terms of a lack of order or regularity. My own suspicion is that the concept of randomness is irreducibly epistemic, hence that mutations are called random only insofar as we have no theory of why and under what circumstances they occur. But that gives no succor to the advocate of real randomness, nor should biologists refrain from trying to impose some sort of theoretical order on the apparent lack of regularity in genetic mutations.

If randomness is purely epistemic, then what really exists are only relative grades of order. The very fact that quantum theory is precisely a theory (whatever its truth value), captured in a complex set of equations, tells against the very idea that it encompasses real randomness (as opposed to indeterminacy). All of our best theories of the cosmos, from the microscopic to the macroscopic, involve systems of quantitative and qualitative propositions. The very possibility of such systems implies order and regularity. But the natural law theorist can admit that there are degrees of order, changes of degree being attributable to such things as diminishing complexity and the displacement of order at one level by order at another. In the former case, the second law of thermodynamics, according to which the universe will supposedly undergo a "heat death," seems to involve a reduction of order to a very basic thermal equilibrium or uniformity. In the latter, consider a person who plays a game of marbles, versus one who throws a handful of marbles into the air. In the second case, the order and regularity of movement detectable in the first case has gone when considered from the point of view of human purpose, but there remain the underlying physical laws that govern the movement of the marbles in a way that is independent of human purpose.

The natural law theorist, then, should insist at the very least on a metaphysic of intrinsic cosmic order, and probably on its necessity as well. He might even say that the "tóhu vavóhu" of Genesis 1:2 involves no real disorder, only (as the Septuagint and Vulgate imply)[15] emptiness and invisibility, a relative lack of arrangement of things into anything remotely resembling the universe after the *hexameron.* If we now look at the macroscopic level (the primary concern of morality), though, we have overwhelming evidence of a remarkable adaptation of means to ends, parts to wholes, lower functions to higher functions, unity in multiplicity and multiplicity in unity, simplicity in complexity and vice versa, regularity, system, predictability, quantifiability, qualitative harmony and, of special importance, teleological order more than sufficient to give the lie to any notion that ours is a haphazard cosmos shot through with chaos.

What, though, does this have to do with the central natural law notions of ordinance and promulgation mentioned at the beginning of the discussion? There are three related arguments for the idea that natural law requires ordinance, and all have in common the thought that order requires an orderer, law a lawgiver. In other words, there is a deep conceptual connection between something's being ordered adjectivally and its being ordered verbally. All the arguments, moreover, point to the great similarity between natural moral law and natural law broadly conceived. The first argument assumes that true chaos is possible. The question is then how order can have arisen. It is plausible to think that where there is order, there was once chaos, since the advent of order is at least

15. Latin: "inanis et vacua"; Greek: "aoratos kai akataskeuastos," lit. "unseen and unfurnished." The Greek word "chaos" (to chaos) itself means "infinite darkness," "infinite space," "emptiness," "the void," etc., not randomness or pure disorder.

in large part a temporal process involving the development of certain arrangements of things from prior disordered states. There is, though, an old but true metaphysical axiom still mirrored in the jargon of positive law: *nemo dat quod non habet*—a thing cannot give what it does not have. Now if order is supposed to have developed from chaos, it must somehow have emerged from chaos or (what I take to amount to the same thing expressed differently) been self-imposed by a chaotic universe. But how can chaos give rise to order? For it to do so, it would have to contain an internal power or principle enabling it to impose order on itself. In what sense, then, would it truly be pure chaos? It is hard to see how pure chaos could contain any powers at all, let alone the power to impose order, not least on itself as a whole. Chaos cannot give order because chaos lacks the wherewithal to bestow it. The only alternative, then, is that order is imposed on chaos by an extrinsic principle, which is perfectly in line with our own universal experience that where order is imposed on (putative) disorder in the natural world, it is done by an extrinsic thing that has the power of bestowing that order, whether that extrinsic thing be ourselves, or animals, or ordered nonorganic entities (such as when, to take a simple example, the presence of a magnet gives ordered location to randomly scattered iron filings).

An opponent might reply that cosmic order is brute: it has never emerged from chaos because chaos has never in fact obtained. But then the question is why there is order rather than chaos. Here I appeal to the principle of sufficient reason broadly construed, not to any application of probability theory or other notions specific to order and chaos per se. Put simply, the principle states that there is a sufficient reason or adequate necessary objective explanation for the being of whatever is and for all attributes of any being.[16] Now order is a kind of being additional, or better superadded, to things that would otherwise be in a state of chaos. To put it in different terms, when considering the way things in the cosmos or the cosmos itself is disposed, we have to say that their being disposed in an orderly fashion is a further fact to their being disposed *simpliciter.* But on the supposition that order is a brute fact, one that has not emerged from or been bestowed by chaos (nor could it be, if the previous

16. I use the standard formulation taken from B. Wuellner, S.J., *Summary of Scholastic Principles* (Chicago: Loyola University Press, 1956), principle #35A.

part of the argument is correct), it requires an explanation that derives from a principle extrinsic to the cosmos (or any of the things within it). This means that order cannot be a brute fact in the sense of not having been imposed by something: it requires a sufficient reason, and if the reason is not internal to the cosmos it must be external to it, and so order could not be wholly brute, even if it has always existed. To put it in the words of natural law theory, order must have been ordained.[17]

The second argument assumes, as I have suggested earlier, that true chaos is impossible, that order is necessary to the cosmos. On this assumption we must ask why there is one kind of relative order rather than another. For even within order there is no mere difference of degree but difference of kind. There is inanimate matter, there is animate matter, there is sentient matter, and there is rational matter. But any one of the relatively lower kinds of matter, all of which are forms of order, could have existed without any of the relatively higher kinds.[18] By reasoning parallel to that just given in respect of order and chaos, there needs to be a sufficient reason for there being a certain kind of relative order. And I cannot see how the demand for an extrinsic principle is any weaker here than in the previous case. Higher order cannot be given by lower order, and if there has always been higher order, we need to know why it exists rather than relatively lower order. It is, to put it mildly, somewhat controversial to say so, but I do not think the answer to such a question

17. Note that the opponent cannot simply reverse the question to one of why, if there were chaos, it would exist rather than order, in the attempt to reduce the argument to absurdity. For chaos is not a further fact about the disposition of matter; rather, it is—at least this seems the most plausible understanding—a mere *absence* of order, not even a true privation (as though matter were naturally disposed to order, which there would be no reason to think if both chaos and order were equally possible). And a mere absence requires no explanation. Still, even if it did, perhaps this would just be grist to the natural law theorist's mill, for whether there were chaos or order there would be a need for its bestowal from an extrinsic source. The exception would be if there were chaos subsequent to order, in which case an adequate explanation could, I would argue, be found intrinsically in the mere dissipation of order, not requiring an external principle.

18. More precisely, each kind could have existed without a higher kind *except,* were there a higher kind that was not *immediately* higher, if it existed along with its nonimmediate lower kind, then the intermediate kinds would have to exist. For instance, there could have been inanimate matter without animate, animate without sentient, and sentient without rational, but if there were inanimate and sentient there would have also to be animate, if there were animate and rational there would have to be sentient, and so on. Leaving aside the possibility of a world containing only animals and rational robots, and the like, I take this to be a metaphysical truth.

even awaits further empirical discovery or abstract scientific theorizing. Rather, the problem is a purely logical and ontological one, based on the truth that something cannot bestow what it does not have. It is this which grounds the need for an extrinsic principle that imposes a given level of order, remembering always that what is at issue are kinds of order, not merely degrees (which would not give rise to the necessity for an extrinsic source).

The third argument concerns the necessity of order again, but this time not the necessity of order in respect of the cosmos as a whole, but the necessity of particular order within the cosmos, and here I am referring to the necessity of law itself. It is no accident that the term "natural law" can be applied both to moral law and to nonmoral law. Natural law theory is one part of a picture of cosmic law in general, and stresses (historically, if not so much among the new natural law theorists) the similarities as well as the differences between both kinds of law. Speaking now of contemporary ethical theory in general, there is no missing the interminable debate about normativity and how it finds a place in a world that is largely not governed by norms. Natural law theory, however, while concerned with the sources of normativity or value—to use the current jargon—is just as much concerned with what unites the moral and the nonmoral. When it comes to law, the unifying element is the compulsory nature of both moral and nonmoral law, that is, their necessity.

When it comes to nonmoral law, that is, scientific law in the narrow sense, the current debate is complicated by the fact that there is an important minority view that the laws of nature are metaphysically necessary.[19] This view has a lot going for it, and if it were true the natural law theorist could happily accept it—indeed it would be further confirmation of his overall metaphysical picture—without any impairment of the two arguments just presented. Notwithstanding this fact, the third argument assumes the dominant current view that the laws of nature, while they bestow natural necessity, are themselves metaphysically contingent. The argument, as the by-now familiar reasoning goes, is that the neces-

19. See, e.g., Brian Ellis, *Scientific Essentialism* (Cambridge: Cambridge University Press, 2001); Alexander Bird, *Nature's Metaphysics* (Oxford: Clarendon Press, 2007); Sydney Shoemaker, "Causality and Properties," in his *Identity, Cause, and Mind* (New York: Oxford University Press); and see also my *Real Essentialism* (London: Routledge, 2007), chap. 6.

sity of natural law requires an adequate explanation. The possibilities are that necessity comes from contingency, that it has always been there, or that it has been imposed from outside by a lawgiver; for to say that necessity requires an explanation just is to say that lawhood requires an explanation, necessity being of the essence of law.

It is very hard to see how necessity can come from contingency, for the usual reason that one cannot give what one does not have. It is difficult to begin to see how merely contingent relations can of themselves give rise to necessary ones. What power within contingency could bestow necessity? If it is something that already contains necessity, then necessity has not come from mere contingency. If it does not already contain necessity, then it can only contain more contingency since every actual being is either necessary or contingent. So suppose necessity has always been there, that is, that the laws of nature have not emerged from anywhere; maybe there have been different laws in the past, but laws there have always been. Then we need to know why there is any necessity of natural law rather than mere natural contingency. For natural necessity is (*pace* the earlier putting to one side of the important possibility that the laws are metaphysically necessary) a further fact over and above the mere distribution of things. There could have been a cosmos of mere regularities, though there is not. (Here I assume that the regularity theory of laws is false.)[20] Again, the explanation for this could only come from outside the cosmos: for what could there be within the cosmos to explain the fact that natural necessity has always existed? Not mere contingent beings, since this response falls on the prior point that contingency cannot give rise to necessity. But not the laws themselves either, since mere natural necessity cannot explain itself. (One cannot appeal to the nature of things, or to logical considerations, since we have put to one side the position that the laws are metaphysically necessary, which is where such considerations are relevant.) The only alternative is that the explanation is extrinsic to the universe, that is, that the laws of nature have been ordained.

Throughout the course of the discussion, I have not said anything about whether the lawgiver is personal or impersonal. I believe it is not

20. For a trenchant critique of the regularity theory, see D. M. Armstrong, *What Is Law of Nature?* (Cambridge: Cambridge University Press, 1983).

difficult to show that it must be personal, but that is a subject for another time. The main point is that natural law theory requires the extrinsic ordination of all the laws of nature, of which the natural moral laws are but a part. As to promulgation, I only want to make some brief remarks. When it comes to promulgation, the natural moral and nonmoral laws are both similar and yet importantly different. The difference lies in the fact that the natural moral law is, as St. Paul says, written on the hearts of men,[21] whereas the nonmoral laws are not.[22] Why not? Well, perhaps they could have been, but the more important point is that the moral laws are so written because the natural moral law cannot wait. It brings with it an urgency that the nonmoral law does not. The scientific laws can await discovery, and by working to discover them man contributes to the fulfillment of the moral law by pursuing the fundamental goods, in particular the good of knowledge. If the scientific laws were written on men's hearts there would be precious little to work for, and yet no higher demands would be met thereby. On the other hand, although we do not know all the answers to moral questions, and fulfill our natures by pursuing such answers, still the fundamental precepts of the natural law, at the least, must be written on our hearts since the higher demands of justice require it: such precepts simply cannot await discovery before they can be obeyed. What the promulgation of the scientific laws amounts to, by contrast, is not that they are written on the heart, but that they are, at least in part, knowable by human beings. If we seek, we can find, since the laws are written in the cosmos.

3. ESSENTIALISM

Turning now to more specific features of the natural law, we see that natural law theory takes notions of nature, function, and flourishing to be

21. Romans 2:14–15.

22. Descartes does, though, say the following in the *Discourse on Method,* Part 5: "I noticed certain laws that God has so established in nature, and whose notions he has so imprinted in our souls, that after having sufficiently reflected on them we could not doubt that they are observed precisely in all that is or happens in the world" ("[J]'ai remarqué certaines lois que Dieu a tellement établies en la nature, et dont il a imprimé de telles notions en nos âmes, qu'après y avoir fait assez de réflexion nous ne saurions douter qu'elles ne soient exactement observées en tout ce qui est ou qui se fait dans le monde.") See Adam and Tannery's *Oeuvres de Descartes* 6.41; J. Cottingham, R. Stoothoff, and D. Murdoch, eds., *The*

core concepts, as much in the new natural law theory as in the more traditional variety that I defend. But there is more to the metaphysic of natural law theory than a commitment to these concepts. Rather, they form part of an overall essentialism that is central to the theory and explains why those core concepts have the place they do. Note that I do not assert here that essentialism is entailed by the existence of cosmic law and order, or the converse. If, as "scientific essentialists" such as Brian Ellis hold, all of the laws of nature supervene on the essences of things, one might begin to mount a case that cosmic order is in fact entailed by essentialism. But for present purposes all I claim is that essentialism is one crucial part of the overall metaphysic of natural law theory, even if it is logically independent of cosmic order.

In his famous book *The Closing of the American Mind,* Allan Bloom says, during the course of his analysis of the way in which contemporary notions of self and fulfillment have departed from the tradition:

> The psychology of the self has succeeded so well that it is now the instinct of most of us to turn for a cure to our ills back within ourselves rather than to the nature of things. Socrates too thought that living according to the opinions of others was an illness. But he did not urge men to look for a source for producing their own unique opinions, or criticize them for being conformists. His measure of health was not sincerity, authenticity or any of the other necessarily vague criteria for distinguishing a healthy self. The truth is the one thing most needful; and conforming to nature is quite different from conforming to law [by which he means positive law], convention or opinion.[23]

There is no obvious reason to think that the Grisez-Finnis-Boyle approach to natural law sets itself against this view (though I raise caveats later), but there is at the same time a stress on subjectivity in one's choice making that obscures a more objectivist understanding of the way in which fulfillment is achieved. This could be a legacy of the modern, post-

---

Philosophical Writings of Descartes (Cambridge: Cambridge University Press, 1984), 2.131. The latter translation differs little from my own. I agree with John Cottingham, whom I thank for reminding me of this passage, that Descartes should not be interpreted as meaning that we have innate knowledge of the laws of physics, only an innate capacity for grasping the concepts of mathematical and logical order according to which the cosmos is structured. And this is highly plausible.

23. Allan Bloom, *The Closing of the American Mind* (New York: Simon & Schuster, 1987), 179.

Rousseauan "authenticity" approach to meaning that has such a stranglehold on contemporary culture. Maybe it is this legacy's as-yet unescaped contamination of our discourse that enables Grisez-Finnis-Boyle to assert that "being free to do as one pleases," while not a basic good, is nevertheless an intelligible instrumental good—an assertion that would itself have been unintelligible to adherents of the classical tradition.[24]

In any case, natural law theory rests upon, and requires for its own intelligibility, a thoroughgoing essentialism.[25] This is the doctrine that everything has its own essence, and is usually taken to be a variant of the substantive Principle of Identity,[26] as opposed to the truism that now passes for the principle, namely, that everything is identical with itself.[27] The only reason natural law theory is justified in appealing to human nature as central to ethics is that, since everything has a nature, so must human beings. In important ways, human beings are on one side of an unbridgeable qualitative boundary separating them from the rest of the material universe. In other ways, though, they are very much part of a cosmic continuum uniting them as much to matter as to spirit.

The sort of essentialism that provides a secure foundation for natural law theory holds not simply that everything has an essence, but that these essences are real and knowable. To say that they are real is to say that they are not mere linguistic constructs or definitions of words, but that they define the things themselves, their quiddities or natures. For them to be knowable is for them not to lie in principle beyond possible experience, or some kind of veil of perception, or beyond human cognitive power, at least in general and in part. "In general," because the real essentialist does not deny that some things might be in principle unknowable in their essence (the nature of matter or energy might be an example). "In part," because the real essentialist is happy to concede that very few real essences are grasped in their completeness. How complete a grasp is does not necessarily depend on where in the ontological hierarchy the object is located. It is as unlikely that we have a complete grasp of

24. "Practical Principles," 111.

25. The following remarks summarize some of the central ideas in my *Real Essentialism*, to which the reader should refer for the full theory.

26. Wuellner, *Summary*, principle #32A.

27. To be fair, Saul Kripke has tried to give it some substance; see his *Naming and Necessity* (Oxford: Blackwell, 1980).

the essence of a fish as it is that we have a complete grasp of the essence of God. Yet in both cases we do have at least an incomplete grasp of essence: we know that a fish is a water-dwelling vertebrate with gills in the mature case (to take a typical definition); and we know that God is pure act (to take one of many definitions). But in neither case does the definition, though real, capture everything there is to know about the natures of the things defined.

It should be clear why only real essentialism will suffice for natural law theory. If essences are anything less than real, then morality lacks the foundation of its objectivity. Natural law theory is about the natures of things, in particular human nature, and so things had better have natures. Yet it would be inexplicable at best, absurd at worst, to suppose that everything under the sun lacked a real nature except for human beings; why should that be so? One might try appealing to the fact that human beings, uniquely in the material universe, have also an immaterial element.[28] But this pushes the question over to why only beings with an immaterial element should have natures, and no obvious answer is forthcoming. Hence if human beings have a nature, then everything has a nature. If essences are unknowable, then morality is unknowable, and this is hardly something the natural law theorist will contemplate. Fortunately, for a great many things we do indeed know their essences, if only partially, though for some completely. For instance, we probably grasp—rather, the relevant experts in the cognitive community, as it were—the complete essences of a great many chemical elements and compounds, though we do not know all of their possible kinds of behavior. But for the real essentialist the natures of natural objects are ontologically distinct from the properties that emanate from them, so complete knowledge of the former does not exclude partial knowledge of the latter. It is the huge strides we have made in the knowledge of the chemical elements that has led recent "scientific essentialists" such as Ellis to focus almost exclusively on them in constructing a theory of essences.

This sort of approach is anathema to the real essentialist, however, because of its reductionism. There is evidently no hope for natural law theory if the only essences we can know are the ones belonging to the

28. I have defended the immateriality of the human soul in "Hylemorphic Dualism," in *Personal Identity*, ed. E. Paul, F. Miller, and J. Paul, 70–99 (Cambridge: Cambridge University Press, 2005), originally in *Social Philosophy and Policy* 22 (2005): 70–99.

realm of the very small.[29] The real essentialist is, therefore, an antireductionist who recognizes distinct ontological levels to which belong distinct essences. He is able at once to affirm that gold is a metal with the atomic number 79, that a fish is a water-dwelling vertebrate with gills in the mature case, and that man is a rational animal. Each of these essences is as real as the others, and there can be no room for a general reductionism that explains all putative essences in terms of one level of real essences such as the chemical or the physical.

The rejection of natural teleology is probably the most important factor in the rejection of natural law theory. It is often seen as sufficient for its refutation to assert confidently that "man is not designed for anything" and so there can be no metaphysical purchase for natural law. This sort of denial is important and must not be evaded by the natural law theorist, implicit as it is in virtually all of contemporary ethical thought. Nor do I think that one can, as it were, sneak up on the denial with a view to shooting it down by means of an overemphasis on the structure of practical reasoning. I say "overemphasis" because reflection on practical reasoning is without doubt central to the natural law enterprise. But on its own it will never convince an opponent of natural teleology that he is wrong in his rejection of a certain metaphysical picture.

The first thing to note is the confusion between purpose and design common in antiteleology. It may well be that one implies the other, but they are not the same. Natural law theory does not hold that the natural law is written only on the hearts of the theists, or theists and deists; it is written on every heart and so must be recognizable even by the person who denies any sort of transcendent source of *telos*. This is not to say that a person could justifiably recognize one without the other: just as the old saying goes that there are no atheists in foxholes, and as the Psalmist asserts, "the fool says in his heart, 'There is no God,'"[30] it may be that no one who consults his conscience in a matter of natural law, recognizing for instance that it is wrong to steal or to commit adultery, could be anything other than culpably ignorant of the need for a lawgiver. On

29. The idea of scientific essentialists such as Ellis is that the reason we cannot know macroscopic essences is not that they lie behind some veil of perception (are Lockean "somethings-we-know-not-what"), but that there is no theoretical need to postulate them at all; in other words, our best scientific theories do not require them.

30. Psalms 13/14:1.

the other hand, the specific logical connection between law and lawgiver (rather than the general arguments for the existence of a divine being) plausibly requires greater philosophical reflection than many are capable of. Hence I incline to the thought that when it comes to this in particular, a person is not necessarily guilty of an epistemic vice by recognizing the former while failing to grasp the latter: we are not always culpable for failing to see the consequences of what we know. And as to the possibility of ethical behavior, there is no need for such a recognition when a person acts according to and in knowledge of the natural law. There is this exception, that if religion itself is a basic human good—as I and the vast majority of natural law theorists believe—then it would be incoherent to suppose that a rational agent could act according to and in knowledge of that good without ipso facto recognizing the need for a transcendent source of natural *telos*. The crucial point, however, is that one can, and people often do, recognize a natural purpose or function in things without giving the slightest attention to the distinct question of whether that purpose or function is bestowed by an extrinsic principle. Hence the mantra that man is not designed for anything does not undercut the core natural law proposition that human beings have a nature and function, and that the latter can be recognized without referring it to its external source.

The second point is that in the broad sense everything has a function as well as a nature or real essence, the former being given by the latter. For "function" in its broadest sense just means the natural specific activity of some thing.[31] In this sense we can ask what the function/purpose of condensation is in the water cycle, or what the function/purpose of the strong nuclear force is in radioactive decay. To describe such functions does not require making any reference to a designer, human agent, invention, conceived objective, and the like. Nor does it involve the use of biological or quasi-biological metaphor, as when we speak, for instance, of the life cycle of a star.[32] The description, devoid of metaphor, is simply of the natural specific activity of certain entities, events, or processes, usually in the context of larger entities, events, or processes. We are,

31. The following summarizes the key ideas in my "Teleology: Inorganic and Organic," in *Conteporary Perspectives on Natural Law*, edited by A.-M. González (Aldershot, U.K.: Ashgate, 2008).

32. Thanks to John Cottingham for prompting me to make this distinction.

however, fairly selective in our use of teleological language when describing the natural world. The question "What is the function/purpose of a stone?" is evidently strange and rarely asked, though one could imagine a geologist posing it in the context of an inquiry into the formation of some mineral, for instance. But stones, like everything else, are law-governed entities and so do in fact have a natural, specific activity; the use of an attenuated functional vocabulary seems inescapable in many cases, though whether we choose to use a broad range of teleological vocabulary (terms such as "purpose," "objective," "desire," "try") is less important.

It would be an important linguistic issue were one trying to hold something like panpsychism or animism at bay, in which case withholding a broad range of teleological language when describing inanimate objects would embody a substantive metaphysical point. But for those of us sane enough not to be tempted by such views, what is significant—and this is the third crucial point—is the qualitative difference between the animate and the inanimate worlds. Withholding a wide teleological vocabulary from the latter does serve the heuristic purpose of marking the difference between immanent and transient causation, the former involving causes and effects within one and the same being, and the latter causes and effects belonging to different beings. In a previous age, when people knew what the crucial metaphysical distinctions were, broad teleological language was probably used with abandon in respect of everything. Now, however, the depredations of antiteleology make more important, at least in philosophical contexts, the withholding of certain ways of talking about the inanimate, in order to serve the heuristic purpose just mentioned.

It is to agents capable of immanent causation that function and purpose in the strict or narrow sense belong. For it is only here that the concepts of goodness and flourishing in specific activity have application. Stones and electrons might have functions but they cannot flourish, or behave better or worse, rightly or wrongly, or be harmed, satisfied, or possess any of the fundamentally normative states belonging to subjects of immanent causation, that is, living things. There is no mere continuum here, but a point at which nature is carved at its joints. Yet the normative functions of living things are as real as their nonnormative functions and the nonnormative functions of everything else in the cosmos. Natural goodness is as real as natural viscosity, natural harm as natural radioactivity. The fact-value distinction of Humean fantasy fails precisely because there is no way of describing the world accurately that omits natural normative teleology.

It is, then, only a thoroughgoing essentialism that can undergird natural teleology; without the former, the latter is understandably going to seem mysterious, obscure, perhaps an illusion of man's devising. Natural teleology provides the framework within which the appeal to specifically normative teleology, of the kind exhibited by the organic world, is plausible. Further, the normative teleology of the organic world serves as the basis for a theory of specifically human teleology, and it is this latter that forms the particular subject matter—the material object, to use an older terminology—of natural law theory in ethics.

4. HUMAN NATURE

There has been some debate over the role human nature plays in natural law theory. There are critics of the Grisez-Finnis-Boyle approach, such as Henry Veatch, Russell Hittinger, and Anthony Lisska, who charge the new natural law theory with refusing to base itself on a metaphysic of human nature.[33] They have clearly been exercised by comments such as the following. Referring to the common criticism of Aquinas that he supposedly fails to show how specific moral rules are connected with self-evident principles about what is good for us, Finnis replies: "How can this objection have become so popular? [One reason] is that the very phrase 'natural law' can lead one to suppose that the norms referred to, in any theory of natural law, are based upon judgments about nature (human and/or otherwise)."[34] And at the beginning of "Practical Principles," Grisez-Finnis-Boyle state: "What we say here differs in various ways from the theories articulated by Aristotle, Thomas Aquinas, and others."[35]

33. H. B. Veatch, "Natural Law and the 'Is'-'Ought' Question: Queries to Finnis and Grisez," in his *Swimming against the Current in Contemporary Philosophy* (Washington, D.C.: The Catholic University of America Press, 1990); R. Hittinger, *A Critique of the New Natural Law Theory* (South Bend, Ind.: University of Notre Dame Press, 1987); A. J. Lisska, *Aquinas's Theory of Natural Law: An Analytic Reconstruction* (New York: Oxford University Press, 1996).

34. J. Finnis, *Natural Law and Natural Rights* (Oxford: Clarendon Press, 1980), 35.

35. "Practical Principles," 99.

Unfortunately, Grisez-Finnis-Boyle do not go on to articulate in what exact ways their theory differs from the Thomistic-Aristotelian approach, and the matter is complicated by the fact that they also, jointly and severally, spend much time arguing that their critics have in fact misinterpreted St. Thomas and that their theory is in conformity with the Thomistic approach properly understood.[36] This unclarity notwithstanding, the critics have focused on a central issue, namely, the role of the ontology of human nature in the methodology of natural law theory.

My main concern in this paper is with metaphysics, not epistemology, but the former bears inescapably on the latter and so by clarifying metaphysical issues we can reach a proper understanding of the epistemology of natural law theory. Now it is apparent (though as we shall see not evident) that advocates of natural law theory in both its traditional and new forms agree that there is such a thing as human nature. The question is what connection should be drawn between it and natural law theory as a system of practical reasoning. Jacques Maritain represents the tradition when he says:

> What I am emphasizing is the first basic element to be recognized in natural law, namely, the ontological element; I mean the normality of functioning which is grounded on the essence of that being: man. Natural law in general . . . is the ideal formula of development of a given being; it might be compared with an algebraic equation according to which a curve develops in space, yet with man the curve has freely to conform to the equation. Let us say, then, that in its ontological aspect, natural law is an ideal order relating to human actions, a divide between the suitable and the unsuitable, the proper and the improper, which depends on human nature or essence and the unchangeable necessities rooted in it.[37]

36. See references in the bibliography to "Practical Principles," 148–51, and also the discussion with citations in Jude Chua Soo Meng, "To Close a Generation Gap: Thomists and the New Natural Law Theory," *Quodlibet: Online Journal of Christian Theology and Philosophy* 3, no. 2 (Spring 2001), http://www.quodlibet.net/meng-thomism.shtml. See also Finnis, *Natural Law,* 35–36, and elsewhere in that book. For evidence of Grisez's outright hostility to traditional Thomistic natural law theory, see Hittinger, *Critique,* 14ff. Grisez considers it as, inter alia, "rationalistic," "voluntaristic," "legalistic," "otherworldy," and "minimalist." At least some of these epithets should not strike the traditional theorist as especially shameful, but there is no doubt about how Grisez regards them.

37. J. Maritain, *Man and the State,* in *The Social and Political Philosophy of Jacques Maritain,* ed. J. W. Evans and L. R. Ward, 50 (London: Geoffrey Bless, 1956).

The question is what "depends on human nature or essence" means in this context. Jude Chua Soo Meng, replying to Lisska who cites this passage from Maritain against Finnis (as well as a similar passage from Yves Simon), defends Finnis and the Grisez-Finnis-Boyle position in general by arguing that the phrase is ambiguous in the same way that Finnis's phrase "based upon judgments about nature" is ambiguous—as between ontological and epistemological dependence. He quotes Robert George to the effect that "in the epistemological mode of inquiry, our (practical) knowledge of human good(s) is methodologically prior to our (speculative) knowledge of human nature. The latter knowledge presupposes the former: It is not, as neo-scholastics suppose, the other way round." By contrast, "in the ontological mode of inquiry, an account of the human goods will refer back to human nature: 'Why are these the ends fulfilling of human beings?' 'Because human nature is constituted as it is.' But this answer in no way entails that our knowledge of the ends as human fulfilments is derived from prior speculative knowledge of human nature."[38]

If George is interpreting the Grisez-Finnis-Boyle position correctly—and there is no reason to think he misunderstands it—the connection between the ontology of human nature and the epistemology of moral reasoning is itself ontological only, not epistemological. Human nature serves as a metaphysical foundation of natural law as a system of ethics, but without informing its methodology in any obvious way. There is, however, an even darker side to the Grisez-Finnis-Boyle position, since in a footnote in *Natural Law and Natural Rights* Finnis explicitly contradicts D. J. O'Connor who asserts that "the theory of natural law turns . . . on the idea that human nature is constituted by a unique set of properties which can be understood and summed up in a definition."[39]

Were it not for an aside such as that, one could safely assert that new and traditional natural law theorists at least agreed that there is such a thing as human nature, which can be given a real definition—presumably the time-honored one that man is a rational animal, with all that this deceptively simple formula entails. That Finnis should even con-

38. See R. P. George, "Recent Criticism of Natural Law Theory," *University of Chicago Law Review* 55 (1988): 1416–17, for both quotations (quoted in Soo Meng, "To Close a Generation Gap").

39. *Natural Law and Natural Rights*, 34 n37, quoting O'Connor, *Aquinas and Natural Law* (London: Macmillan, 1967), 15.

sider the idea that natural law theory does not turn on the possibility of such a definition certainly gives pause for reflection on just what the Grisez-Finnis-Boyle version of natural law theory is after all committed to; but all I shall do here is refer the reader to the discussion of essentialism above. It is the epistemological/ontological question that needs further consideration, since it raises serious issues of methodology and highlights the way in which the new natural law theory is expounded by its adherents.

So let us assume that all natural law theorists agree on the existence of human nature. What then? As George explains it, human nature is ontologically prior to the system of morality embodied by natural law theory, where that theory comprises our practical knowledge of the human goods and all that they entail; but it is not epistemologically prior. Strictly, this implies that we can have such practical knowledge before having any speculative knowledge of human nature. How then, according to the Grisez-Finnis-Boyle account, do we get such knowledge? Here Finnis invokes the authority of Aquinas to argue that "practical reasoning begins not by understanding this nature from the outside, as it were, by way of psychological, anthropological, or metaphysical observations and judgments defining human nature, but by experiencing one's nature, so to speak, from the inside, in the form of one's inclinations."[40]

He is referring to the discussion in the *Summa Theologica*[41] where St. Thomas says such things as:

[A]ll those things to which man has a natural inclination, are naturally apprehended by reason as good, and consequently as objects of pursuit, and their contraries as evil, and objects of avoidance. Wherefore according to the order of natural inclinations, is the order of the precepts of the natural law.[42]

[T]o the natural law belongs everything to which a man is inclined according to his nature. Now each thing is inclined naturally to an operation that is suitable to it according to its form. . . . Wherefore, since the rational soul is the proper

40. *Natural Law,* 34.

41. I-II q. 94 aa. 2–4.

42. I-II q. 94 a. 2: "omnia illa ad quae homo habet naturalem inclinationem, ratio naturaliter apprehendit ut bona, et per consequens ut opere prosequenda, et contraria eorum ut mala et vitanda. Secundum igitur ordinem inclinationum naturalium, est ordo praeceptorum legis naturae."

form of man, there is in every man a natural inclination to act according to reason: and this is to act according to virtue. . . . [But] not all virtuous acts are prescribed by the natural law: for many things are done virtuously, to which nature does not incline at first; but which, through the inquiry of reason, have been found by men to be conducive to well-living.[43]

In particular, Finnis quotes the following passage:

[W]hatever is contrary to the order of reason is, properly speaking, contrary to the nature of man, as man; while whatever is in accord with reason, is in accord with the nature of man, as man. Now man's good is to be in accord with reason, and his evil is to be against reason, as Dionysius states. . . . Therefore human virtue, which makes a man good, and his work good, is in accord with man's nature, just in so far as it accords with his reason: while vice is contrary to man's nature, just in so far as it is contrary to the order of reason.[44]

There is possibly some echo of the Grisez-Finnis-Boyle interpretation in Maritain, where, stressing the guidance of natural inclination in Aquinas's account of our knowledge of the natural law, he asserts: "When he [St. Thomas] says that human reason discovers the regulations of the natural law through the guidance of the inclinations of human nature, he means that the very mode or manner in which human reason knows natural law is not rational knowledge, but knowledge through inclination." This kind of knowledge, explains Maritain, "is not clear knowledge through concepts and conceptual judgments; it is obscure, unsystematic,

43. I-II q. 94 a. 3: "ad legem naturae pertinet omne illud ad quod homo inclinatur secundum suam naturam. Inclinatur autem unumquodque naturaliter ad operationem sibi convenientem secundum suam formam. . . . Unde cum anima rationalis sit propria forma hominis, naturalis inclinatio inest cuilibet homini ad hoc quod agat secundum rationem. Et hoc est agere secundum virtutem . . . non omnes actus virtuosi sunt de lege naturae. Multa enim secundum virtutem fiunt, ad quae natura non primo inclinat; sed per rationis inquisitionem ea homines adinvenerunt, quasi utilia ad bene vivendum."

44. I-II q. 71 a. 2: "id quod est contra ordinem rationis, proprie est contra naturam hominis inquantum est homo; quod autem est secundum rationem, est secundum naturam hominis inquantum est homo. *Bonum autem hominis est secundum rationem esse, et malum hominis est praeter rationem esse,* ut Dionysius dicit. . . . Unde virtus humana, quae *hominem facit bonum, et opus ipsius bonum reddit* [Arist. *Ethics* 2.6], intantum est secundum naturam hominis, inquantum convenit rationi, vitium autem intantum est contra naturam hominis, inquantum est contra ordinem rationis." (I have slightly altered the usually excellent Dominican translation since it does not render the full force of "intantum . . . inquantum," which I have followed Finnis in translating as "just in so far as." Finnis, however, offers a translation that in other ways is less faithful to the Latin than the Dominican one without, however, being incorrect in substance.)

vital knowledge by connaturality or congeniality, in which the intellect, in order to bear judgment, consults and listens to the inner melody that the vibrating strings of abiding tendencies make present in the subject."[45]

Note the seemingly irreducible subjective or first-personal element in Maritain's statement: for it is hard to see how one person could have vital, connatural knowledge through listening to the inner melody of another person's vibrating strings. This subjective aspect is, as I read Grisez-Finnis-Boyle, essential to their interpretation as well, both of St. Thomas and of natural law theory in general.

Yet it suffers from a serious misunderstanding of both. The general question one must ask, of a supposedly providential order in which natural law is written on the consciences of men, is this: If the ontology of human nature is not epistemically prior to the deliverances of that law, then what exactly is the former's role? To say simply that there is an "ontological connection" between human nature and morality, that the latter is impossible without the former, while true, does not answer the question of how the rational agent is supposed to have any knowledge of morality if that knowledge is mere knowledge through inclination. After all, Grisez explicitly disavows intuitionism,[46] so it is not as though knowledge through inclination amounts to irreducibly intuitive moral judgment. (Which is not to deny that there are moral intuitions and that these can form a reasonable basis for moral judgment, which I imagine most natural law theorists would accept.)

No natural law theorist should deny that knowledge through natural inclination is part of the necessary epistemological basis of the theory. But this knowledge cannot be mere knowledge through inclination. It must be knowledge of nature through inclination. This is, I submit, clear from a careful reading of the relevant passages in Aquinas. Where he says that what is contrary to reason is contrary to nature, and that what is in accord with reason is in accord with nature, so that virtue is in accord with nature just insofar as it accords with reason, and vice is contrary to nature just insofar as it is contrary to the order of reason—he means that

45. Maritain, *Man and State*, in *The Social and Political Philosophy*, 53.

46. Grisez, "A Contemporary Natural Law Ethics," in *Normative Ethics and Objective Reason*, ed. George F. McLean, chap. 11 (Washington, D.C.: Council for Research in Values and Philosophy, 1996). Hittinger, *Critique*, 164ff., argues persuasively that Grisez is in fact committed to a form of intuitionism.

virtue and vice are determined by whether actions are in accord with or contrary to the nature of man as a rational being. This is clear from the context of the passage, in which Aquinas's remarks immediately succeed the statement that "the nature of a thing is chiefly the form from which that thing derives its species. Now man derives his species from his rational soul."[47] And so "consequently" *(ideo)* whatever is contrary to the order of reason, and so on. Similarly for the other passages just cited: what St. Thomas means is not that "the way to discover what is morally right (virtue) and wrong (vice) is to ask, not what is in accordance with human nature, but what is reasonable." Nor does he imply that "the primary categories . . . are the 'good' and the 'reasonable,'" with the concept of the natural being but "a speculative appendage added by way of metaphysical reflection,"[48] a matter for ex post facto reconstruction by philosophers contemplating what Maritain calls "after-knowledge."[49]

On the contrary, the agent, by gaining knowledge of human nature as rational animality through inclination, grasps what does and does not fulfill that nature, hence what is good and bad and so a matter for pursuit or avoidance. Otherwise inclination floats free, methodologically, of any substantive information that provides the basis on which true and false inclination can be distinguished. By saying that vice is contrary to human nature just insofar as it is contrary to reasonableness, Aquinas should not be taken to affirm that we first must know what is reasonable, from which we can then conclude that something is contrary to human nature and so vicious. Rather, he means that to be contrary to human nature just is, definitionally, to be contrary to the order of reasonableness that specifically characterizes human nature as rational nature. This is the justification for asserting that error is contrary to nature, knowledge in accord with it; that genuinely aesthetic experience fulfills nature and

47. I-II q. 71 a. 2: "Sed considerandum est quod natura uniuscuiusque rei potissime est forma secundum quam res speciem sortitur. Homo autem in specie constituitur per animam rationalem."

48. Finnis, *Natural Law,* 36, for both quotations.

49. *Man and State,* in *The Social and Political Philosophy,* 53 n1. In fact, Maritain uses this term in respect of the derivation of particular principles [Aquinas's "propria principia"] of natural law from the general principles, which derivations Aquinas calls at *S.T.* I-II q. 94 a. 4 "quasi conclusiones." But the tenor of Maritain's discussion strongly suggests he has the same attitude to the justification of the general principles themselves. Aquinas's use of the term "quasi" does not in my view license the claim that the derivations are not rational inferences, albeit of the practical rather than the speculative intellect.

ugliness perverts it; that religious belief and practice contribute to human flourishing and the absence thereof diminishes it.

Nor is this sort of inquiry an irreducibly first-personal affair. How could it be for the likes of Aristotle or St. Thomas, who litter their writings with remarks such as that all men seek happiness, all men desire to know, man is a social and political animal, no man would want to live without friends, and so on ad nauseam? On what basis could such generalizations be made if there were no room in ethics for the kind of third-personal, objective, speculative knowledge about just what it is that fulfills the human species? An agent's experience of his own inclinations will not on its own yield knowledge of what is good for others unless combined with an understanding or appreciation, however attenuated, of the place of inclinations of that kind in human beings as a kind. This is by no means to assert that agents must or do engage in general in any sort of elaborate philosophical reflection when making moral judgments; nor is this the straw man target of the Grisez-Finnis-Boyle critique. The new theorists are making a methodological and theoretical point about the nature of moral justification. At least Maritain allows the philosophers "after-knowledge" with which they can rationally reconstruct the derivations of natural law principles, presumably from speculative ontological premises (though maybe this is an overinterpretation of Maritain). It is not clear that Grisez-Finnis-Boyle would even allow that.

It is knowledge of the complexity of human nature that grounds our knowledge that the multiplicity of kinds of inclination actually corresponds to a diversity of goods. If it did not, how could we be sure that the diversity of kinds of inclination was not a mere conceptual distinction as opposed to a real one? Yet we know it is real because we know that the goods that are objects of the inclinations are really distinct aspects of human nature. The same goes for our knowledge of the ways in which means are ordered to ends. Mere inclinational knowledge cannot give us certainty that, for example, the goods of property are instrumental to the goods of life and health. Nor will it enable us to form a coherent picture of the way in which goods are related to each other as parts to wholes—that, for instance, health is a part of the good of life or family part of the good of friendship.

To take another issue of great current importance, there are vast numbers of people who would affirm that the inclination to pursue life is subordinated to the inclination to pursue other goods that make life fulfilling, such that if those goods cannot be meaningfully pursued then the inclination to pursue life loses its own natural goodness. They embody this thought in the inference that since the pursuit of life is good only if the meaningful pursuit of other goods that make life fulfilling is possible, then if the latter pursuit is not possible the pursuit of life is itself not good. By this argument they seek to justify the euthanasia of those who are only "minimally alive," say because they are comatose, in a persistent nonresponsive state (known pejoratively and inaccurately as a "vegetative" state), or suffering from senility or some other illness that renders the pursuit of most or all other goods impossible. How are we to gainsay this interpretation of natural inclinations? The correct response, I would argue, is that the initial thought involves a metaphysical confusion about the relationship between life and the other goods. The correct position is not that life is good only if the other goods can be meaningfully pursued, but that the other goods can be meaningfully pursued only if life is itself good, that is, worth pursuing. Moreover, this relationship does not make life an instrument to the pursuit of the other goods, from which one might then judge that if the instrument lacked anything to work on, it itself would lose value, like a corkscrew with no possible wine bottle to open. Rather, the goodness of life is a necessary precondition for the meaningful pursuit of the other goods: if it has no value, then neither do the other goods. But from this fact there is a logical block to the inference that if the other goods are not meaningfully pursuable then life itself lacks goodness; to say otherwise would be a simple fallacy. Yet no amount of first-personal reflection on our inclinations, unsupplemented by metaphysical speculation, can yield this resolution of the issue.[50]

The heart of the problem inherent in treating metaphysics as a "speculative appendage" to primary reflection on one's inclinations as a source of moral knowledge is precisely that this attitude ignores the fundamental role of promulgation in the metaphysics of natural law. All natural law theorists agree that the natural law is promulgated to humanity. But the traditional view of this—and nothing will be found in Aquinas to say otherwise—is not that the lawgiver directly promulgates certain inclina-

50. I expose this logical fallacy more briefly in my *Moral Theory* (Oxford: Blackwell, 2000), 140–41.

tions to the heart of man, which man then happily finds to correspond to the order of things. Rather, the lawgiver promulgates the natural law by making a world with a certain order and containing natures related in certain ways, including the nature of man with his connatural capacity rationally to respond to that order of things. When the agent contemplates his natural inclinations, he grasps intellectually the way in which his heart and mind respond harmoniously—when things are working well, of course—to the antecedent order of things, where that order includes most importantly his own nature itself. It is the prior order that makes the inclinational knowledge rational. To the extent that natural inclinations put us in touch with goods, they give us access to the objective order in which those goods are embedded. It is the very directedness of these inclinations to an order not of our making that gives them any claim on our attention. That the law written in our hearts makes any demands on our rational natures is due wholly to the fact that it is a law concerning something not of our own devising. As we are not makers of the natural law but receivers of it, we cannot abrogate it; nor, in the words of St. Augustine, can iniquity itself efface it.[51]

5. CONCLUSION

It is striking how so much of contemporary ethical theory has become divorced from metaphysical inquiry. Even in the applied field, where one would expect a greater focus on the analysis of human nature, applied ethics—dominated as it is by consequentialism—either fails to bring metaphysical considerations to bear on its arguments, or carries with it a host of unexamined presuppositions concerning both private good and the common good. Yet consequentialists are happy blithely to propose various desiderata for maximization without subjecting them to critical analysis. For example, classical utilitarians, without appreciating it, presuppose a teleology of human good that places pleasure and pain at the forefront without ever seriously examining whether such an order of priority squares with what we know about the human species. When there is any analysis, it has tended to come from anticonsequentialists such as Bernard Williams, who argue persuasively that what we do know about

51. Augustine, *Confessions* 2.4: "lex scripta in cordibus hominum, quam ne ipsa quidem delet iniquitas." This is quoted by St. Thomas in I-II q. 94 a. 6, *sed contra*.

human nature is in complete discord with a consequentialist approach to ethical decision making.[52]

Natural law theory, which is forcing its way onto the agenda of analytic ethics, brings with it an entire approach to the nature of things that adherents of the theory ignore at their peril. Not only must natural law theorists take metaphysics seriously, they should—with severe caution—take a substantial interest in scientific developments to see how they give the theory empirical support. For instance, they should pay attention to the efforts of some biologists and psychologists to reclaim human nature as a fit subject for empirical inquiry.[53] Not that they should by any means uncritically accept whatever science happens to be saying at any particular time. Like all good metaphysicians, they must always cast a critical, if not skeptical, eye on scientific developments, ensuring that they separate the wheat from the chaff by testing all ideas at the tribunal of philosophical knowledge.

Natural law theorists should also be interested in what both cosmology and biology have to tell us about cosmic law and order at the macroscopic and microscopic scales. While analysis of the nature of law does not, as my discussion implies, await direct support from empirical investigations such as these, it clearly dovetails with them and there is no doubt the latter can offer indirect support to the former, including clarification of certain ideas such as the distinction between order and disorder and the way in which nature manifests itself in proper function.

The reconnection of metaphysics and ethics must be at the heart of the natural law project. Not only must natural law theory advance on the applied front, it must also deepen its conceptual foundations and locate itself within broader areas of philosophical concern. The discussion presented here, outlining as it does some of the core areas that need to be addressed, is but one small contribution to a much larger task.

52. See, e.g., J. J. C. Smart and B. Williams, *Utilitarianism: For and Against* (Cambridge: Cambridge University Press, 1973).

53. E.g., the work of Steven Pinker contains useful insights; see *The Blank Slate: The Modern Denial of Human Nature* (New York: Viking Penguin, 2002). Nevertheless, a strong health warning must be issued, not only because his genetic determinism goes way beyond anything a natural law theorist could countenance, but because, like much modern science, empirical results are mired in tendentious philosophical interpretation. The natural law theorist needs in particular to separate biological fact from Darwinian propaganda, rejecting any possibility of "Darwinian natural law" or some other quasi-scientific proposal.

J. Budziszewski

4 Natural Law as Fact, Theory, and Sign of Contradiction

Before becoming Pope Benedict XVI, Joseph Cardinal Ratzinger wrote to several Catholic universities requesting that they sponsor and encourage public talks about natural moral law and contemporary society. The reasons for his request deserve thought. "The Catholic Church," he wrote, "has become increasingly concerned by the contemporary difficulty in finding a common denominator among the moral principles held by all people, which are based on the constitution of the human person and which function as the fundamental criteria for laws affecting the rights and duties of all." For centuries unquestioned, he says, these truths of the natural law "constituted a valid starting point for the Church's dialogue with the world, with cultures and non-Christian religions." The urgency of "renewing an understanding of the natural moral law" arises, he says, from the fact that its truths are now "obscured," not only in secular dogma, but even sometimes in "the teaching that takes place in Catholic universities." He clearly believes that renewing the understanding of natural law is not a task for philosophy alone, but for philosophy in partnership with revelation, because, as he explains, it requires "a deeper understanding of the theology of creation, as this flows from the unity of God's salvific plan in Christ." To guard against misunderstanding of this important point, he quotes John Paul II to the effect that "it is not a case of imposing on nonbelievers a vision based on faith, but of interpreting and defending the values rooted in the very nature of the person," "principles upon which depend the destiny of human beings and the future of civilization."

Strong words. The cardinal, now pontiff, makes sharp observations not only about the moral confusion of the times, but also about our scholarship, which ought to help to rectify the confusion, but sometimes merely joins in the muddle. I would like to call your attention, though, to three distinct aspects under which the cardinal seems to view the natural law.

In the first place, he views it as a fact. Natural law is a feature of the world, having to do with the constitution of the human person, and behind that, with the constitution of created reality as a whole. The cardinal's expression "the constitution of the person" calls several things to our attention. One is that the human being is a person, not just a mess of chemicals and electrical impulses. Personhood is not a mystification, but a reality, and persons are meant by God to know reality, including the reality of themselves. But the expression also emphasizes that the human person is constituted in a certain way. If we lost sight of this fact, true personalism would collapse into a personalistic relativism in which we could no longer tell what counted as using a person wrongly, as a means. After all, anyone can plead the second version of Kant's categorical imperative. A woman denied an abortion might protest that she should not be reduced to a "means" to her baby's survival; a man denied assistance in killing himself might complain that he should not be reduced to a "means" to the peace of his doctors' conscience.

To say that natural law is a fact does not mean that theorizing about it is unnecessary. Calling attention to a fact is always an act of theory. Even so, we are apt to forget that before the theory must come the thing that the theory is about; natural law theorizing is about something that is already and unquestionably there. I use the word "unquestionably" with a qualification. Of course the "thereness" of natural law is questionable in a certain sense; one might maintain that it is not there. But insofar as we are serious about being Catholic philosophers, committed to an adequate view of the human person, a view that makes use of all of the resources of faith and reason as they coilluminate each other, we should already know the answer to that logically possible question. At this stage of the game it would be frivolous—a squandering of what has been given to us—to waste breath on the question of whether the human person has a constitution, just as it would be frivolous for a mineralogist to ask whether there are minerals, or an oceanographer to ask whether there is ocean. The mineralogist and the oceanographer have better questions to ask. So do we.

Only in second place, then, does the cardinal view natural law as a theory. We are to be realists. The theorist must humble himself before the fact, which in this case means the reality of human personhood. This is where those "better questions" that I mentioned come in: What do we actually know about the constitution of the human person? How are its principles "natural" and how are they "law"? How can we explain them in a way that makes them intelligible even to the people of our time? I suggest that if theory does come in second place, not in first, then it will be a different sort of theory than the kind we have become accustomed to during the last several centuries. It will not be the belly-button-searching kind that demands exhaustive investigation of whether we can know anything at all before asking what, if anything, we know. Instead it will realize that we must already know something, and know that we know it, even in order to ask how it comes about that we do know it. And so a truly adequate theory of the natural law will not always be turning into metatheory of the natural law. It will resist that tendency. It will keep its eyes focused on the data, contemplating the constitution of the human person itself, rather than turning its eyes skull-inward in a futile attempt to catch itself at the act of contemplation that it was doing a moment before. Epistemology is important, even indispensable, but it is the maidservant of ontology, not its master.

In third place, the cardinal seems to view natural law as a scandal, as a sign of contradiction. I take his remark that its truths have been "obscured" as a gentle way of saying that they have been widely repudiated. Whether or not he intended to make that point in his letter of invitation, it is certainly an aspect of his broader teaching, and it is certainly true. Natural law exasperates. It offends. It enrages. By the way, this gives us a reason—a serious reason—to consider the questions that I called frivolous a few moments ago. It would be frivolous for the oceanographer to ask on his own behalf whether there is ocean, but it would not be frivolous if he lived among people who denied water even though living on a raft. In the same way, it would be frivolous for us to ask on our own behalf whether the human person has a constitution, but it is not frivolous if we live among humans who deny the personal structure of their being.

The scandal of natural law is both chronic and acute. It is acute because of the suicidal proclivity of our time to deny the obvious, a proclivity, by the way, which itself cries out for explanation. We have reached that day that Chesterton foresaw when he wrote, "Everything will be denied. Everything will become a creed. . . . Fires will be kindled to testify that two and two make four. Swords will be drawn to prove that leaves are green in summer. . . . We shall be of those who have seen and yet have believed."[1] The circumstance of living during an acute phase of the scandal makes it especially important that we not let the wool be pulled over our own eyes. Even today there is a common ground, because humans still bear a common nature; whether people are commonly willing to stand on that ground is another matter altogether. It is a slippery common ground, wet with the dew of our evasions. Therefore we must not suppose that the definition of "common ground" is "what everyone concedes" or "what no one denies." There is nothing that everyone concedes; there is nothing that no one denies. We must be willing to be bold.

I have commented on the acuteness of the scandal in our time. But the scandal is also chronic. Natural law is a sign of contradiction, not merely incidentally because of the times, but essentially because of all times. One reason is the Fall. Our condition contradicts our constitution; our state is out of joint with our nature. The natural law scandalizes us because our actual inclinations are at war with our natural inclinations, because our hearts are riddled with desires that oppose their deepest longings, because we demand to have happiness on terms that make happiness impossible. To understand the scandal at an even deeper level, natural law is a sign of contradiction because Christ the Redeemer is a sign of contradiction. The cardinal is quite clear about this. Remember the remark that I quoted earlier, that an adequate understanding of natural law implicates "the theology of creation, as this flows from the unity of God's salvific plan in Christ." Some people would say that in making such a claim, the cardinal is no longer proposing philosophical ethics, but demanding the abdication of philosophy to theology. On the contrary, he is rejecting a false view of philosophy, a view that supposes a relationship of faith and reason that is ultimately insupportable. Yes, we can and must find ways to make ourselves comprehensible to those who do not share the insights of revelation, but this does not mean that we

1. G. K. Chesterton, *Heretics* (New York: John Lane, 1905), 305 (chap. 20).

can do so without mentioning these insights. Nature presupposes supernature, and the present disorders of nature merely stun the mind when contemplated apart from the graces of creation and redemption. For this reason, a truly adequate understanding of nature's malaise requires some hint, some glimpse, some trace of its supernatural remedy.

How awful such reflections are for those of us who crave the approval of our secular colleagues. The timid flesh crawls at the thought of their skeptical glance. Yet in the long run, there is no other way to make headway. How could we expect natural law to be plausible to those whose nature experiences only its humiliation, and not its rising again? I realize too that these remarks risk scandal of yet another kind. I mean methodological scandal, and this is unavoidable. The philosophical method of our day is minimalist. It assumes that people can consider propositions about reality only in small doses, one dry pill at a time. I suggest that at least sometimes, the very opposite is true. The reason the pill goes down so hard is that it is only a pill, for the mind, like the stomach, desires a meal. Just as some foods are digestible only in combination with other foods, so also some ideas are plausible only in combination with other ideas. In order to stand firm they must have context, as the single stone requires the arch. So let us not worry about scandal, but go ahead and do the unminimalist and unsecularist thing.

NATURAL LAW AS FACT

The rest of this essay merely elaborates the three aspects under which we must view the natural law: natural law as fact, as theory, and as sign of contradiction. First, then, as fact. As I conceded earlier, to call attention to a fact is always an act of theory. Even so, it is not the same act of theory as what we do about the fact afterward, so let us consider the pretheoretical realities that provoke natural law philosophy and with which it has to deal. For convenience I will distinguish four categories of such experiences. First come those facts, those pretheoretical realities, that provoke us to philosophize about practical reason as such; second come those that provoke us to do so in terms of natural law rather than in other terms. The former category can be subdivided into facts that provoke us to philosophize about practical reason as practical, and facts that provoke us to philosophize about it as reason. In turn, the latter category can be subdivided into facts that provoke us to philosophize about natural law as law, and facts that provoke us to philosophize about it as natural.

To begin at the beginning, the pretheoretical reality that provokes us to philosophize about practical reason as practical is that we are, so to speak, magnetized toward other things, other persons, and other states of affairs.[2] We are not just knowers, but seekers, who spontaneously incline toward certain realities other than ourselves. When I say that this inclination is spontaneous, I do not mean that it is arbitrary because that is not the way that we experience it. One way of saying this is that we do not merely experience ourselves as drawn to things; we experience the things themselves as being such as to draw us. Our word for their being so—and there is such a word in every language—is "good"; goodness is the quality of being such as to draw us. So another way to express what I am saying is that we experience certain things as good, and experience ourselves as drawn to them because of their goodness. With an air of demystification, subjectivists like Thomas Hobbes tell us that it is the other way around. They deny that we are inclined toward things because they are good. Instead, they say, we call them good because we are inclined toward them. Goodness is merely a name, and inclination does not point outside itself after all; it just is.[3] But this is not just bad theory, it is a bad description of the experience. If you ask a man "Why do you love that woman?" he does not normally reply by telling you about himself—"I just do"—but by telling you about her—"Because she is wonderful."

It might be objected that in answer to the question, some people do reply "I just do," for example in country western songs. Quite so, but country western songs are more or less explicitly about disordered loves, not ordered ones, and the perception of the disorder is internal to the experience itself: "I'm crazy for crying, crazy for trying, crazy for loving you." Even then the lover does not say that the beloved is not lovable. What he suggests is that her good is mixed with bad in such a way that by inclining toward the former, he ends up suffering the latter. "I knew you'd love me as long as you wanted / And then some day you'd leave me for somebody new."

So much for the pretheoretical reality that provokes us to philosophize

2. I borrow this striking expression from Russell Hittinger.

3. Thomas Hobbes, *Leviathan; or, The Matter, Form, and Power of a Commonwealth Ecclesiastical and Civil,* 1.6.7, 1.15.40; *Elements of Law,* 1.7.3.

about practical reason as practical; what, then, is the one that provokes us to philosophize about it as reason? Here I must apologize for my earlier metaphor of magnetism, for our inclination toward the good is only a little bit like actual magnetism. For animals, perhaps the resemblance is closer. The tom enters the field of influence of the estrous queen and is drawn in to mate, the wolf enters the field of influence of the unprotected fawn and is drawn in to devour. If an animal is inclined toward two objects at once, it pursues the more attractive. Everything is simple. For us it is not like that. We deliberate about which good to follow; the goods that attract us are not causes of action, but reasons for action. Deliberation is a strange and mysterious thing, not all like what an animal does.

It might be objected that this is untrue. The animal is drawn to the highest good as estimated by sense; we too are drawn to the highest good, but as estimated with the further help of discursive imagination. On this account, deliberation merely extends our senses by allowing us to compare in our minds goods that are sensibly present with goods that are not. The animal glances back and forth between one thing and another with the eye of the body; we do the same, but with pictures in the mind. But this poorly describes what we actually do when we deliberate. In the first place, deliberation cannot be merely an extension of sense, for we are capable of being attracted by nonsensible objects like knowledge and justice. Still stranger is that we invest even sensible goods with nonsensible meanings; a meal, for example, becomes a reminder of my love for my family. Strangest of all—because perverse—is that although we agree that it is prudent to pursue the highest good, we often fail to do so. In fact we seem capable of pursuing things that even in our own considered estimate are not worthy of pursuit. Nothing like that is even possible among the animals. In view of the fact that the only way to be attracted to something at all is to see it as somehow good, it is hard to see how it is possible even for us.[4] But let us pull back from the frontier of these mysteries and go on to the next thing to be examined.

4. My answer to the puzzle rests on the fact that in order to reach a comparative appraisal of different goods, the mind turns now to the right, now to the left, suspending consideration of each good in turn in order to contemplate the other. This very power of suspending consideration allows us to prolong the suspension, willfully short-circuiting the appraisal that is supposed to result. Like Scarlett O'Hara, we say "I'll think about that tomorrow."

The most important pretheoretical reality that provokes us to philosophize about practical reason in terms of natural law—and specifically about natural law as law—are certain experiences that we later, as theorists, attribute to conscience. Not every culture has a word for conscience, arousing a suspicion among some people that these experiences are rooted not in the constitution of the human person per se but only in the constitution of the Western person, in fact the late Western person, his superego shaped by the Judeo-Christian tradition of a divine lawgiver. On the contrary, the distinction of the late Western person is not that he has these experiences, but that he has more ample resources to understand them. The universality of the experiences themselves is most famously illustrated by Sophocles, who, without any help from the traditions of his culture, nevertheless makes his heroine Antigone proclaim that the ordinances of the tyrant Cleon are invalidated by the laws of the gods—laws unwritten and unchanging, that are not only for today or yesterday, but for always. Indeed the wisdom traditions of peoples and nations across the globe acknowledge some such law.

The plot thickens, for we are really speaking of at least three different experiences of graduated intensity. Those who fail to heed conscience in the first mode meet it again in the second; those who refuse to acknowledge it even in the second mode meet it yet more darkly in the third. Antigone testified to its cautionary mode: she experienced the performance of her duties toward her dead brother not only as good but as obligatory. This may seem unsurprising, but there is something remarkable about it. Theorists of practical reason often overlook the fact that the inclination to a thing as an object of duty is more than the inclination to it as good per se. The second mode of conscience is accusatory: it indicts us for wrong we have already done. Ordinary slips of prudence lead merely to disappointment; had I only done P or had I only not done Q, I could have enjoyed a certain good or avoided a certain bad. In hindsight, I wish that I had done differently; how stupid; how unfortunate; what a waste. Bad conscience is not that kind of disappointment. True, its occasion would seem to be the same; by doing something or failing to do something, I have unnecessarily brought about a result contrary to my desire. But the experience itself is not the same, for it is more than the awareness of a foolish mistake, or even of a lack of self-control. I am conscious rather of trespass, of breach, of transgression.

There is another difference too, for the emotional and behavioral corollaries of imprudence and bad conscience are not at all the same. In the one case I suffer mere regret, but in the other I suffer remorse. In the one case I may be angry with myself, but in the other I have the sense that I am under wrath. In the one case I probably hope to keep my foolishness a secret, but in the other I may have an urge to confess. In the one case I probably hope to escape paying the price of my foolishness, but in the other I may find myself impelled to seek atonement. I have the sense of having violated a boundary that I did not make, but that my deepest self agrees with utterly. The good that I betrayed was not merely commended by inclination, but commanded by authority. I am not only dismayed, I am accused.

No one always feels remorse for doing wrong; some people never do. Yet we see that even when remorse is absent, guilty knowledge generates objective needs for confession, atonement, reconciliation, and justification. These other Furies are the greater sisters of remorse: inflexible, inexorable, and relentless, demanding satisfaction even when mere feelings are suppressed, fade away, or never come. And so it is that conscience operates not only in the first two modes but in a harrowing third: the avenger, which punishes the soul who does wrong but who refuses to read the indictment. I say more about the revenge of conscience in the final part of my essay. For now suffice it to remark only how exact is the correspondence between the supernatural experience of the sacrament of confession, and the natural experience of bad conscience. They both exhibit the same "moments," the same stages, the same phases; it is really true that nature is a preparation for grace.

But I am getting ahead of myself, for I have not yet discussed the experiences that provoke us to philosophize about natural law as natural. Although we are speaking of more than one reality, we may view them together briefly. One of them is that a propensity for the experiences that we have already been talking about is built into our design and woven into the fabric of the normal adult mind. Of course, to speak this way is to suppose that we do have a design, that our minds do have a fabric, that the way we are is not arbitrary or meaningless. Theoretically one may deny that this is so, but at the moment, we are enumerating facts, and it is a fact that human beings of all times and places perceive their lives as having such meaning. Natural law theory holds that they are right.

By the way, the experience of our lives as having meaning cannot be accounted for on grounds of so-called natural selection (which ought to be called *accidental* selection, because "nature" is precisely what it is not about). A subjective perception of meaning, reflective of nothing in reality, has adaptive value for an organism only if there is a preexisting subjective need for meaning—and what would be the adaptive value of needing meaning? Within the context of accidental selection, that question seems to have no answer. Another provocation for philosophizing about natural law as natural is the spontaneous intuition of almost all people that moral experience is rooted in what really is. According to this intuition, a rule like the prohibition of murder reflects not a mere illusion or projection, but genuine knowledge. It expresses the actual moral character of a certain kind of act. If this is so, then in a certain sense the law is built not only into human nature but into the rest of nature too. Nature must be a kind of thing that can sustain the meanings that we find in the acts that we perform in it. And as though that were not enough, there is yet one more sense in which the law strikes us as built in. We all find in experience that when we cross the grain of the universe, the universe kicks back—and to that interesting fact I will return.

NATURAL LAW AS THEORY

Enough with the pretheoretical realities; let us turn to the theory, to our attempts to account for them. The central claim of natural law theory can be expressed in just a few sentences. Law has been defined as an ordinance of reason, for the common good, made by him who has care of the community, and promulgated.[5] Nature is an ensemble of things with particular natures, and a thing's nature may be thought of as the design imparted to it by the Creator; in traditional language, as a purpose implanted in it by the divine art, that it be moved to a determinate end.[6] The claim is that natural law is both true law, and truly expressive of nature, in these senses.

Let us consider these matters step by step, starting with the definition of law. Legal positivists define law merely as the will of the sovereign.

5. Thomas Aquinas, *Summa Theologica,* I-II q. 90, a. 4.

6. Thomas Aquinas, *Commentary on Aristotle's Physics* 2.14.

This definition simply misconstrues what is asked for. The legal positivist is answering the question, "What qualifies an enactment as belonging to our system of enactments?" His answer, by the way, is circular; he consults the sovereign to recognize the law, but then consults the law to recognize the sovereign. The natural lawyer is trying to answer the entirely different question, "What qualifies an enactment as a rule and measure of human action?" Truly human action is personal and rational rather than merely impulsive, so its norm must be personal and rational too. This norm must serve the common good, because it is a rule and measure for all, not just for some. It must be enacted by public authority, for otherwise it will not bind conscience; it will give rise not to a moral duty, but only to an inconvenient circumstance, a sanction, that cautious people will keep in mind. Finally, the norm must be promulgated, because it cannot be followed if it cannot be known. Does natural law really satisfy this definition? Evidently so; all four conditions are satisfied.

Consider the natural law forbidding murder. It is not an arbitrary whim, but a rule that the mind can grasp as right. It serves not some special interest, but the universal good. Its author has care of the universe, for He created it.[7] And it is not a secret rule, for He has so arranged His creation that every rational being knows about it. So it is that when we speak of natural "law," we are not merely dropping into metaphors. It is law. It is not merely a standard for human law, although it serves as a standard too. Nor is it merely a consideration that becomes law when humans enact it, as in the theory of Thomas Hobbes. Rather it is already law, original law. Apart from it, the decrees of the powerful are not truly law, but only enacted frauds.

One might object that although a so-called natural law might either be really natural or really law, it could not be both at once. The argument would be that nature cannot contain ordinances of reason because it is mindless; that it cannot promote the common good because it has no ends; that it cannot be regarded as an enactment of authority because

7. This statement is not intended as shorthand for an account in which nature is normative because God commands that it be normative (and could have commanded that it not be). Rather, the created good is normative because it is rooted in the uncreated Good who created it. For all we know, God could have created a different nature, but He could not have willed that we dishonor or disregard the structures of good contained in the nature that He did, in fact, create.

it "just is"; and that it cannot be regarded as promulgating anything because it isn't a text. What gives this objection its apparent force is that it slips in a "ringer." In place of the classical understanding of nature as meaningful and designed, it substitutes its own understanding of nature as blind fatality. It is talking about a different thing.

Benedict XVI has recently called attention to this ancient and dangerous mistake. In informal remarks following an address in St. Peter's Square, he quoted St. Basil the Great, who said that some, "deceived by the atheism they bear within them, imagined the universe deprived of a guide and order, at the mercy of chance." Benedict remarked, "I believe the words of this fourth-century Father are of amazing timeliness. How many are these 'some' today?"[8] His question, of course, was rhetorical; we know the answer all too well. Their number is legion. But why should we accept their view of nature? What arguments have they? Or what objections do they offer to our own?

One objection to the classical understanding of nature is that it is rubbish to talk about natural purposes because we merely imagine them. According to this way of thinking, the purposes of things aren't natural; they are merely in the eye of the beholder. But is this true? Take the power of breathing. When we say that its purpose—viewed from another angle, its meaning—is to oxygenate the blood, are we making it up? Evidently not. This purpose isn't in the eye of the beholder; it is an inference from the design of the lungs. To say that the purpose of *P* is to bring about *Q*, two conditions must be satisfied. First, *P* must actually bring about *Q*. This condition is satisfied because breathing does oxygenate the blood. Second, it must be the case that the fact that *P* brings about *Q* is necessary for explaining why there is *P* in the first place. This condition is satisfied too because apart from the oxygenation of blood there is no way to explain why the power to breath should have developed.[9] We can ascertain

8. Benedict XVI, Commentary on Psalm 135 (136): 1–9: "From Created Works One Ascends to the Greatness of God." Full text at www.zenit.org/article-14504?l=english.

9. I adapt these two conditions from Robert Koons, *Realism Regained: An Exact Theory of Causation, Teleology, and the Mind* (Oxford: Oxford University Press, 2000). The change lies in the second of the two conditions: rather than requiring that the fact that P brings about Q be part of the efficient cause of P, I say that it must be part of the explanation of P, leaving open the possibility that final cause is a fundamental and irreducible category of explanation, a possibility that Koons also now accepts (personal communication).

the purposes of the other features of our design in the same way that we ascertain the purpose of breathing.

A second objection to the classical understanding of nature is that it doesn't make any difference even if we can ascertain the purposes of natural things, because an is does not imply an ought. This dogma too is false. If the purpose of eyes is that they see, then eyes that see well are good eyes, and eyes that see poorly are poor ones. Given their purpose, this is what it means for eyes to be good.[10] Moreover, good is to be pursued; the appropriateness of pursuing it is what it means for anything to be good. Therefore, the appropriate thing to do with poor eyes is try to turn them into good ones. If it really were impossible to derive an ought from the is of the human design, then the practice of medicine would make no sense. Natural law theory has contemptuously been called "metaphysical biology." So be it; biology needs metaphysics too. But we are speaking of more than biology. In exactly the same way that we infer that the purpose of the eyes is to see and the purpose of breathing is to oxygenate the blood, we can infer the purpose of the capacity for anger, the purpose of the power of reasoning, and so on. Natural function and personal meaning are not alien to each other; they are connected. In a rightly ordered way of thinking, they turn out to be different angles of vision on the same thing.

The third objection to the classical understanding is the most radical. This time the objector holds that even if nature does generate a sort of ought, that makes no difference, because any such ought is arbitrary. Man, says the objector, is the product of a meaningless process that did not have him in mind. Had the process gone a bit differently—had our ancestors been carnivores instead of omnivores, had they laid eggs instead of borne live young, had they started watching television earlier than they did—then we would have had a different nature. As it is, we observe certain natural norms: honor your parents, care for your children, tell the truth. But the norms might have turned out to be anything: drive out your parents, eat your sons and daughters, lie about it. Call such

10. See Peter Geach on predicative vs. attributive adjectives in "Good and Evil," *Analysis* 17 (1956): 32–42. "Red" is predicative; it means the same thing no matter what kind of thing we are talking about. By contrast, "fast" is attributive; what it means depends on what kind of thing we are talking about. As Geach points out, "good" is attributive and depends on the function of the thing.

norms "natural laws" if it pleases you, the objectors say, but don't imagine that they mean anything. I think this third objection is the strongest, for nature is undoubtedly a contingent being, and one cannot ground meaning in a contingency. But on closer consideration, the objection answers itself, for contingent beings never "just are"; they must have causes. If their causes are contingent beings, then they too must have causes. To avoid endless regress, the chain of causes must end in a necessary being, and since the effects that this being produces are personal, He must be personal too. But if this is true, then natural law theory is not trying to ground meaning in a contingency after all. Nature takes meaning from supernature; creation, from its Creator; the created structures of personal goodness, from the uncreated personal Good Who is their source.

I remarked earlier that the natural law truly satisfies the promulgation condition—that it is not a secret rule, for the Creator has so arranged His creation that every rational being knows about it. This needs to be more fully spelled out. The claim here is not that everyone knows the theory of natural law. That is plainly false; not everyone has even heard the expression "natural law." However, everyone is acquainted with the thing itself. To speak in the words of Thomas Aquinas, the foundational principles of morality are "the same for all, both as to rectitude and as to knowledge."[11] To say that they are the same for all "as to rectitude" means that they are right for everyone; in other words, deliberately taking innocent human life, sleeping with my neighbor's wife, and mocking God are as wrong for me as they are for you, no matter what either of us believes. To say that they are the same for all "as to knowledge" means that at some level everyone knows them; even the murderer knows the wrong of murder, the mocker the wrong of mockery, the adulterer the wrong of adultery. He may say that he doesn't, but he does. There are no real moral skeptics; supposed skeptics are playing make-believe, and doing it badly.

To be sure, the game is played very hard, and not only by skeptics. I must not take innocent human life—but only *my* tribe is human. I must not sleep with my neighbor's wife—but I can make my neighbor's mine. I must not mock deity—but I can ascribe deity to a created thing instead of the Creator. These are the lies that we tell ourselves. In our time

11. Thomas Aquinas *Summa Theologica* I-II q. 94 a. 4.

we are finding out just how hard the game can be played, and this fact puts natural law in a new theoretical situation. It might once have been thought sufficient to say that some moral knowledge is universal. It turns out, however, that the determination to play tricks on moral knowledge is universal too. A law is written on the heart of man, but it is everywhere entangled with the evasions and subterfuges of men.

But that is a problem for the final part of my essay, on natural law as a sign of contradiction. For now, let us return to how natural law is known. There are, I think, four ways. I like to call them the "witnesses" as a memorial of St. Paul's remark to the pagans of Lystra that although in times past, God allowed the gentile nations to walk in their own ways, even then "He did not leave Himself without witness."[12] The context shows that he is not speaking of human witnesses, but of impersonal testimonies built into the very pattern of God's providence. To be sure, these witnesses are wordless. The same thing might be said of them that the Psalmist says of the heavens: "There is no speech, nor are there words; their voice is not heard; yet their voice goes out through all the earth, and their words to the end of the world."[13]

The first witness may be called conscience, but in a different sense than it bears in everyday speech. We think of conscience as one thing. The classical natural law tradition distinguished two things—I think rightly. One is *synderesis*—some prefer to call it *anamnesis*—which might be called "deep conscience." Deep conscience is the interior witness to the most general norms of practical reason, including, by the way, not only principles like "good is to be done and evil avoided," but also its proximate corollaries, well summarized by the Decalogue. The other thing is *conscientia,* which might be called "surface conscience." Surface conscience is the application of the knowledge that deep conscience provides. Like memory, that knowledge is not always in the mind "actually" but is always there latently; we are in the "habit" of knowing it, even though we may not be thinking of it, even though we may not be aware of knowing it, and even though we may indeed suppress it. The habit is natural, not acquired; it is a feature of the design of the created practical intellect.[14]

12. Acts 14:16–17 (Revised Standard Version).
13. Psalm 19:3–4 (RSV).
14. See Thomas Aquinas, *Summa Theologica,* I q. 79, a. 13.

I have just spoken of design, and must now speak of it again, for the second witness is the evident designedness of things in general. We perceive immediately that nature requires an explanation beyond itself; that the things in nature are indeed designed; and that design requires personal agency. Working out the logic of these perceptions is one of the tasks of philosophy, but the perceptions themselves are prephilosophical. St. Paul alludes to them when he says that the reality of God and of some of His qualities have been known "since the creation of the world," having been "clearly perceived in the things that have been made."[15] It might be thought that although the perception of the designedness of things is theologically interesting, it is not morally interesting. On the contrary, it does at least three things for moral knowledge. In the first place it vindicates the previous witness, deep conscience, for if deep conscience is designed as a witness to moral truth by a God who knows what He is doing, then its witness to this truth is reliable.[16] It also confirms that we have duties not only to neighbor but to God Himself, to whom we owe the very possibility of the experience of anything good. Finally, it informs us that just as deep conscience is designed, so the rest of us is designed; we are a canvass for His purposes, a parchment of His meanings.

That leads us to the third witness, the particulars of our own design. Design is obvious not just in our bodies but across the whole range of human powers and capacities. The function of fear is to warn; of minds, to deliberate and know; of anger, to prepare for the protection of endangered goods. Everything in us has a purpose; everything is for something. A power is well used when it is used for that purpose and according to that design. Nor is this just about the functions of things; as I have already suggested and as natural lawyers are coming to realize more deeply, it is also about the meanings of things. Our very bodies have a language of their own; they say things by what we do with them. Bone speaks to bone, organ to organ, skin to skin. A smile means something friendly; you cannot give that meaning to a slap in the face. You can use a kiss to betray, but only because the kiss, in itself, means something else. Conjugal sex means self-giving, making one flesh out of two.

Some of the most interesting features of our design show up not at

15. Romans 1:20 (RSV).

16. Unfortunately, the same cannot be said of *conscientia*, which is why we must distinguish between well-formed and poorly formed consciences.

the level of the individual but at the level of the species. A particularly striking example is the complementarity of the sexes: short of a divine provision for people called to celibacy, there is something missing in the man that must be provided by the woman, and something missing in the woman that must be provided by the man. Indeed, complementarity is not bypassed by the celibate but provided with a higher fulfillment. When we speak of such things as being married to the Church, we are not dealing with euphemisms but with profound realities. Design features like complementarity establish conditions for human flourishing that would not have been deducible just from the fact that we are rational animals; they require observation of our personal existence.

The fourth witness to natural law is the natural consequences for its violation. Those who cut themselves bleed. Those who betray their friends are betrayed by their friends. Those who abandon their children have no one to stroke their brows when they are old. Those who travel from bed to bed lose the capacity for intimacy and trust. Especially interesting are the noetic penalties for violation, for those who suppress their moral knowledge become even stupider than they had intended. We see that the ancient principle that God is not mocked, that whatever a man sows he also reaps,[17] is sewn into the fabric of experience. A clarification is necessary, for in calling natural consequences one of the witnesses, I should not wish to be misunderstood. Natural law theory is not "consequentialist"; the penalty for violation is not what makes the wrong act wrong. It functions rather as an announcement and form of discipline. In fact, the most intriguing thing about the natural consequences of things is that they point to the natural purposes and meanings of things. For example, the natural link between sex and pregnancy is not just a brute fact to be circumvented by latex; it declares that sex serves the meaning of self-giving and the purpose of procreation, of having and raising children in the love and fear of God.

An endless confusion of cross-purposes has been caused by the fact that different theories of natural law tend to focus on different witnesses. In hostile challenge to the Scholastic thinkers, Thomas Hobbes zeroed in on the witness of natural consequences—indeed on just one such consequence, violent death. In ways that are often overlooked, and despite

17. Gal. 6:7.

the thinness of his teleology, John Locke relied on the two witnesses of design.[18] In suggestive and provocative ways, the "new" natural law theory of Germain G. Grisez, John Finnis, and Joseph M. Boyle gives central place to the design of deep conscience, but avoids direct reliance on the other aspects of our design.[19] The classical tradition, epitomized by Thomas Aquinas, attempted to provide an integrated account of all four witnesses. Unfortunately, his good example is rarely followed.

NATURAL LAW AS SIGN OF CONTRADICTION

At last we return to the sheer scandal of natural law. By its scandal, I mean more than the fact that some things about it are very puzzling. But that fact causes difficulty too, so allow me to begin there.

There are a number of different things one can study about natural law. Some natural lawyers focus on its foundations in the common moral sense of the plain person. These are of course "dialectical" foundations, because the plain person knows all sorts of things that he doesn't know he knows. A scholar, by contrast, may know very few things, but he is perhaps more likely to know how he knows them. If natural law theory is to be made plausible to its critics, then the whole problem of latent knowledge, of how we can know something at one level, even though not knowing that we know it, needs to be more thoroughly investigated.

Other natural law thinkers focus on casuistry, on the solution of difficult moral problems. This enterprise is precariously balanced between two extremes. At one extreme is the oversimplified notion that if there really is a law written on the heart, there could not be any difficult moral problems. At the other is the overcomplexified notion that every moral problem is difficult. For young people, the most dangerous and tempt-

18. John Locke, *First Treatise of Government,* secs. 53 and 86; *Second Treatise of Government,* secs. 4–6 and 54. See J. Budziszewski, *Written on the Heart: The Case for Natural Law* (Downers Grove, Ill.: Intervarsity, 1997), 104–5, and *The Line Through the Heart: Natural Law as Fact, Theory, and Sign of Contradiction* (Wilmington, Del.: ISI Books, 2009). The author wishes to express thanks to Professor Holger Zaborowski and the Catholic University of America Press for permission to include a version of the present chapter in the latter book.

19. See Germain G. Grisez, *The Way of the Lord Jesus,* 3 vols. (Quincy, Ill.: Franciscan Press, 1983–1997); John Finnis, *Natural Law and Natural Rights* (Oxford: Oxford University Press, 1980); Germain G. Grisez, John Finnis, and Joseph M. Boyle, "Practical Principles, Moral Truth, and Ultimate Ends," *American Journal of Jurisprudence* 32 (1987): 99–151.

ing extreme is the former. They confuse what feels right at the time with the natural law, and if their feelings are confused, they become disillusioned and conclude that there is no natural law. For natural lawyers themselves, however, the most dangerous and tempting extreme is the latter. We make such circuitous paths to such obvious destinations that the destinations themselves come into doubt.

Still other natural law thinkers focus on metaphysics, on the study of what the world must be like for there to be a natural law in the first place. This project is indispensable, but it is prone to confuse the theory with the fact. We see this especially in our teaching. Which is the better way to explain the idea of natural law—to ask "Have you noticed that there are some things about right and wrong that we all really know and can't help knowing?" or to say "It's all about the convertibility of being and goodness"? I think the answer is obvious.

These scandals are avoidable. However, not all scandals are avoidable. Ultimately, the natural law is a sign of contradiction for much deeper reasons. Even in the prelapsarian state, their noetic powers intact, our first parents were tempted to "be like God, knowing good and evil"—to imagine that they could be First Causes of their own moral knowledge and their own constitution as persons. How much more are we postlapsarians liable to the temptation, our noetic powers damaged by the Fall, our wills no longer innocent but depraved. In speaking of "depravity" I am not embracing Calvinism. Calvin's mistake was to think that we are totally depraved. If we were totally depraved, then we could not be depraved at all; bereft of all good, we would lose even the good of existence. Augustine's insight is more profound. Evil is a deficiency, a perversion; the only way to get a bad thing is to take something good and mar it. In order to be marred, it must be still there. Our problem is not ugliness, then, but sullied beauty. Our tragedy is twofold, for not only are we unable by our own powers to restore our loveliness, but we are wroth with the very offer of restorative grace. Such is sin.

For natural law theory, the Fall confronts us in the fact that we don't want to hear of natural law. On the one hand, we cannot fully ignore it, because its first letters are written on our hearts. On the other hand, we resist the inscription, and the letters burn. Here begins the terrible game that I mentioned earlier. The crisis of natural law in our time owes partly to the deepening intensity of the game, but partly to the fact that we ignore it. We persist in taking pretended moral ignorance at face value, in philosophizing as though the problem of moral failure were merely cognitive. We suppose that when the opinionators of our time repudiate God, celebrate the destruction of life, and rejoice in sexual debasement, they simply do not know any better. We imagine that if only we present them with airtight arguments, they will change their minds. Not in that way will it happen. There is such a thing as motivated error. Indeed the problem is more grave still. We have not destroyed deep conscience, but suppressed it. That may sound better, but in a way it is worse. Like a man who is buried alive, conscience kicks against the walls of its tomb. The defiant intellect—which is that tomb—therefore fortifies the walls.

A single example will suffice. We can't not know the wrong of deliberately taking innocent human life. The appalling thing is that we make use of this knowledge even in order to defy it. The arguments for abortion amount to claiming either that the act is not deliberate, or that it is not a taking, or that the unborn child is not innocent, not human, or not alive. A moment, please: Not innocent? Yes, even that. There is no limit to what can be denied. Legal scholar Eileen L. McDonagh calls the unborn child a "private party" who uses "violence" to "coerce" the woman "to be pregnant against her will"; it is "objectively at fault for causing pregnancy." The woman has a "right to consent to a relationship with this intruder," and is entitled to "the use of deadly force to stop it," even if it "acquires the highly charged label of 'baby.'" "Some might suggest," she says, "that the solution to coercive pregnancy is simply for the woman to wait until the fetus is born, at which point its coercive imposition of pregnancy will cease." But "this type of reasoning is akin to suggesting that a woman being raped should wait until the rape is over rather than stopping the rapist."[20]

What is one to make of such an argument? It is hard to know whether it is more horrible or more absurd. The difficulty is not that it cannot be answered, for it can. Rather the difficulty is that in order to find it plausible in the first place, a person must already be beyond or very nearly beyond argument. The level of self-deception required is stupendous. Nor is this rare, for there are many such arguments-beyond-argument. Physi-

20. Eileen L. McDonagh, *Breaking the Abortion Deadlock: From Choice to Consent* (Oxford: Oxford University Press, 1996), 6, 11–12, 36, 176–77, 188.

cian Warren M. Hern has written a learned article explaining that pregnancy is "an illness requiring medical supervision," which "may be treated by evacuation of the uterine contents," but "has an excellent prognosis for complete, spontaneous recovery if managed under careful medical supervision." If you can believe it, the article was published in a journal called *Family Planning Perspectives.*[21]

I remarked earlier that guilty knowledge sometimes generates remorse, and always generates objective needs for confession, atonement, reconciliation, and justification. Arguments like those of Hern and McDonagh illustrate the perversion of the need for justification. However, the perversions of the other four impulses are equally deadly to truth-seeking discourse, and this fact also calls for explanation. The normal outlet of remorse is to flee from wrong; of the need for confession, to admit what one has done; of the need for atonement, to pay the debt; of the need for reconciliation, to restore the bonds one has broken; and of the need for justification, to get back in the right. But if these Furies are denied their payment in wonted coin, they exact it in whatever coin comes nearest. We flee not from wrong, but from thinking about it. We compulsively confess every detail of our transgression, except that it was wrong. We punish ourselves again and again, offering every sacrifice except the one sacrifice demanded, a contrite and broken heart. We simulate the restoration of broken intimacy by recruiting companions as guilty as ourselves. And we seek not to become just, but to justify ourselves—to concoct excuses.

Each one of these perversions makes its own contribution to the distortion of scholarship and public discourse. I have spoken of justification; how about the other four? The confessional character of some of our intellectual enterprises is unmistakable; confession actually becomes a kind of advocacy. Or consider the way that recruitment becomes seduction to intellectual evil. One might suppose that I am tendentiously labeling the practice of persuasion as enlightenment when practiced by my side, but as seduction when practiced by the other side. On the contrary, the seducers themselves are often guiltily aware of their dark motives. Everyone knows scholars like an atheist of my acquaintance who boasts

21. Warren D. Hern, M.D., "Is Pregnancy Really Normal?" *Family Planning Perspectives* 3, no. 1 (January 1971): 5–10. The full text of the article is available at the website of his abortion facility, http://www.drhern.com.

of the "fun" he had "ruining all the Catholic kids" at the liberal arts college where he taught. The verb "ruining" was precisely accurate even by his lights, for the fun lay not in liberating these innocent and impressionable young minds from what he considered error, but in deflowering and desecrating them.

Perhaps the strangest impulse to incoherency in our intellectual discourse is the perversion of the need to atone. The dishonest intellect, at some level aware of having committed the sin against the truth, attempts to make up for its transgression by mortifying itself; ultimately it denies that there is such a thing as the truth, or at least that truth can be known. "Here you shall pass among the fallen people," Virgil said to Dante, "souls who have lost the good of intellect."[22] It is not only in hell that we meet them.

Abortion is not the only issue that generates such levels of denial, nor are they found only among the professional advocates of evil. Denial is the normal response of the intellect that is tortured by its conscience but refuses to repent—"normal" in the sense that fever is the normal response to infection, or that unconsciousness is the normal response to a severe blow to the head. It is part of the system of natural consequences to which I alluded earlier—a noetic and personal, rather than a physical and biological, penalty for the violation of natural law. And it comes near to being the normal condition of our time.

An even grimmer consideration is that the inherent tendency of denial is to become deeper and deeper over time, and to express itself in graver and graver transgressions. Consider the argument that human personhood is not a category of being but a mere cluster of functional attributes, such as the ability to communicate and plan, so that those who lack these abilities are not persons. The original motive for adopting such a view may be to rationalize only one kind of killing, but inevitably it justifies others. Notice that functionalism also generates a caste system, for if personhood depends on attributes that vary in degree, then personhood itself must vary in degree. Good communicators and planners will be held to possess the highest degree of personhood; second-rate ones will be held to possess the next degree; and third-rate ones will hardly

22. Dante Alighieri, *Inferno,* trans. John Ciardi (New York: Penguin Books, 1982), canto 3, lines 16–18.

be held to be persons at all. Surely the interests of those who are more fully persons must trump the interests of those who are less, one reasons, so the range of mandated outrages grows ever broader. A functionalist might be dismayed by this implication of his premises. His dilemma is that he cannot give them up without admitting that the one cherished outrage that drove him to embark on this process of rationalization was wrong all along. If he continues to set his face against repentance, then by the very logic of the case he is compelled to be obstinate about more and more.

One might object that even if all this is true, my complaint is out of place. The objection would run like this: I seem to think that the noetic consequences of the violation of natural law pose a problem for natural law philosophers, but if I am right about those consequences, then we are speaking of people who resist argument—and if they do resist argument, then philosophy has nothing to do. But this does not follow. In the first place, we can philosophize about denial even if we cannot philosophize with those who are in denial. In the second place, there are many ways of talking with people, and philosophy is only one of them. The various modes of public discourse have always been recognized as legitimate topics for philosophy. If the noetic consequences of transgression pose obstacles to sane public discourse, then why not philosophize about the obstacles too? Why not philosophize about less-than-sane public discourse and how it might be brought back to sanity?

Historically, one reason the natural law tradition has advanced is that new crises raised new questions. For our age, the crisis is an old one made newly acute, and the questions it raises are twofold: why natural law is a sign of contradiction, and what can be done about the scandal. I am convinced that if we fail to grapple seriously with these questions, we will be derelict not only in intellect but in love. To Bernard of Clairvaux is attributed the epigram, "Some seek knowledge for the sake of knowledge: that is curiosity. Others seek knowledge that they may themselves be known: that is vanity. But there are still others who seek knowledge in order to serve and edify others, and that is charity." The times are dark, and darkening. If ever there was a time for Catholic philosophers to exercise such charity, it is now.

J. L. A. Garcia

5 The Virtues of the Natural Moral Law

1. VIRTUES-BASED MORAL THEORY

Though what is called "virtue ethics" (VE) is nowadays frequently listed as a third alternative among general normative theories, alongside so-called deontological and teleological approaches, its nature is unclear and its legitimacy as an option disputed.[1] If this approach merits parity with the other two, then VE must be more than merely the theory of virtues within a given moral theory. Here are two possibilities: VE might be distinguished by its treating virtues as *autonomous*. According to such a version of VE, the moral virtues' importance is not wholly derivative from that of the (morally) desirable, moral duty, or of moral rights.[2] A more radical version of VE treats the virtues as *fundamental*: according to it, the importance or understanding of the desirable, of duty, and of rights is based on that of virtues. In contrast, Richard Brandt, presenting himself as defending a utilitarian version of VE against William Fran-

This material was prepared for presentation at Fordham University (2004) and revised and presented at the Catholic University of America (2005) and Boston College (2006). I am grateful to Rev. Arthur Madigan, S.J., and to audiences on these occasions for comments and suggestions. Matthew Daley, James Oldfield, and Teresa Fenichel, as well as the splendid collections and reading rooms in Harvard's Widener Library, provided much appreciated assistance to my research and editing. Professor Zaborowski showed superhuman patience and generosity throughout my (still unfinished) processes of rethinking.

1. See, e.g., Martha Nussbaum, "Virtue Ethics: A Misleading Category?" *Journal of Ethics* 3 (1999): 163–201.

2. This view is suggested in Gregory Velazco y Trianosky, "Supererogation, Wrongdoing, and Vice: The Autonomy of Virtue Ethics," *Journal of Philosophy* 83 (1986): 26–40.

kena's criticisms, took virtue to be more basic than duty, *but* rested both virtue and duty on a prior account of intrinsic value.[3]

My own view goes further than Brandt's, joining other radical proponents of VE in grounding both value concepts and duty concepts in virtue concepts. We should immediately observe that treating the virtues as foundational admits at least two interpretations. Virtues may be seen as the proper focus of the *moral subject*'s attention, or, alternatively, it can be claimed that virtues are the proper focus of the *moral theorist*'s attention. These are not mutually exclusive, of course, and both have appeal. My concern here, however, is limited to one part of the latter view: Because virtues are the basis on which other moral features are assigned, they do not merely determine some states of affairs as impersonally desirable/valuable, but are also what *make* some actions right or wrong, permissible or impermissible, fulfillments or violations of duty or obligation, on an appropriate reading of "make." There is already a venerable tradition of value theory according to which claims of so-called intrinsic value are to be understood as claims about what it would be suitable, correct, appropriate, or some such, for someone to "love," want, choose, or otherwise favor, endorse, or side with. So far, however, little has been done, outside of some work of Christine Swanton's, and some of my own, to construe this suitability as virtue.[4] Still, even the neo-Moorean Michael Zimmerman now understands what he calls "intrinsic value" in moral terms, though he opts in the end for a deontic rather than an aretaic way of characterizing the crucial evaluation of the relevant attitude.[5] Thomas Hurka comes closer to what I believe, seeing our favoring of the valuable not just as morally suitable but specifically as virtuous.[6] However, he insists that the valuable is itself independently intrinsically good and that both the virtues and their goodness are derivative. I optimistically see these positions as encouraging, as evidence that philosophers are getting closer to one vital piece of virtues-based moral theory (VBMT): the analysis of claims about what is impersonally valuable (what some think to be "intrinsic" value) in terms of the virtues. As I said above, however, what chiefly con-

3. Richard Brandt, "W. K. Frankena and the Ethics of Virtue," *Monist* 64 (1981): 271–92.

4. Christine Swanton, *Virtue Ethics: A Pluralistic View* (Oxford: Oxford University Press, 2003), ch. 11.

5. Michael Zimmerman, *Nature of Intrinsic Value* (Lanham, Md.: Rowman & Littlefield, 2001).

6. Thomas Hurka, *Vice, Virtue, and Value* (Oxford: Oxford University Press, 2001).

cerns me in this essay is a second principal piece of VBMT: the analysis of acting wrongly and rightly in terms of concepts of vice and virtue. I wish to take steps toward such an analysis here and, more specifically, to connect that account to the idea that conduct can be seen as immoral in ways to which we can apply the concept of a law we can meaningfully call "natural."

Such analysis starkly contrasts with the modernist tendency to define and understand virtues simply as dispositions that normally result in (1) desirable states of affairs, in (2) agents doing their duty, or (3) both. I think that propositions expressing the content of the moral law, the natural law, are best understood in terms of the virtues. Thus, I reject the common tendency to define the virtues as derivative. Bertrand Russell took this position to be obvious while still a schoolboy, writing, "[I]t being supposed that the moral sense is able to decide as to what conduct is moral . . . and what immoral . . . the virtuous disposition or character is then that which is most prone to moral acts. . . ."[7]

VE has been said to understand character (being) as central and action (doing) as peripheral; rules as "crude map[s]" of the decisions or judgments of the virtuous agent (rather than as precise guides for her to use, or standards by which we critics may judge her acts); and right action as "benefi[cial]" to its agent individually or to her community.[8] My own preference is to construe our (largely metaphorical) talk of moral rules and laws as a way of discussing the connection of a type of action to what is virtuous and vicious. I think that this virtues-basing makes the most sense and its greatest contribution is clearest in the context of a moral theory that is also what we can call "role-centered" and "patient-focused." I will not explore these latter ideas in detail here but, because I want to draw on them later, I will say a bit about each. Role centering means that all a person's moral features—her duties, obligations, rights, virtues, and the like—are ones she has within and in virtue of certain morally determinative role relationships, such as friend, fellow, brother or sister, parent, or offspring.[9] Patient focus means that these features

7. Bertrand Russell, "On the Definition of Virtue" [a school paper written for Sidgwick's 1893 ethics course], in *Collected Papers of Bertrand Russell*, vol. 1, *Cambridge Essays 1888–1889*, ed. K. Blackwell et al. (London: Allen & Unwin, 1983), 219–21.

8. Jerome Schneewind, "Misfortunes of Virtue," *Ethics* 101 (1990): 42–63.

9. I should make it explicit that I allow for self-regarding roles (and role virtues) that

get their shape and content from the needs and welfare of the person in whose life and for whom a role is occupied. Often this person is not the agent herself, but normally it is some relevant other person, not some such abstraction as the overall best outcome or the greatest good of the greatest number. Rather, as it is the (medical) interest and welfare of her patient that determine what a physician ought to do and be, what counts as being a good physician and acting well as a physician, so too what I must or ought to do and be as your friend or confidante or partner or fellow, what it would be virtuous of me to do or be, stems from what you, what someone so situated, need and normally gain from a friend, confidante, partner, or fellow.[10] So conceived, what I ought or have to do morally derives neither from the commands of pure practical reason, nor from what advances my own preferences and wants, nor from the value of some outcome from the standpoint of the universe. Thus, it is neither a categorical nor a hypothetical imperative, if we follow Kant in regarding "ought" judgments as expressing "imperatives." What I morally ought to do in a situation is what it would be morally virtuous of me to do; what I must do morally is what it would be morally vicious of me not to do.

Some think it problematic to suppose that "laws" or any norms about what should be done can exist in "nature" or, more broadly, in a world that comprises only facts. Christine Korsgaard writes:

> It is the most striking fact about human life that we have values. We think of ways that things could be better, more perfect, and so of course different than they are; of ways that we could ourselves be better, more perfect. . . . Why should this be so? Where do we get ideas that outstrip the world of experience and seem to call it into question, to render judgment on it, to say it does not measure up, that it is not what it ought to be? . . . The fact of value is a mystery, and philosophers have been trying to solve it ever since [Plato and Socrates].[11]

are also morally determinative, holding that (to use some Kantian jargon) the "determining ground" of their virtues and duties lie chiefly in the needs, welfare, flourishing, and interest of the agent.

10. Contrast the treatment of the good physician in W. D. Ross's *The Right and the Good* (Oxford: Oxford University Press, 1930), where Ross counterintuitively maintains that it is the physician's success in doing what she wants, rather than her service to the interests of the patient qua patient, that sets the standard of what makes her good or bad in that role.

11. Christine Korsgaard, *Sources of Normativity* (Cambridge: Cambridge University Press, 1996), 1–2.

It is not obvious why she thinks this. After all, any ascription to something of some feature makes sense by excluding some conceived but, it is supposed, nonactual instantiation of a complementary feature. To think that appeal to the absent, even imagined, is surprising is to make all attribution—indeed, all predication—puzzling. Still more, it seems to be part of conscious life, and certainly of practical life, that we want and would prefer certain possibilities, comparing things as we find them with things as they might be, and using the latter as a standard in assessing the former. Action and practical thinking thus must lead to, if they do not presuppose, evaluation. It is telling that Korsgaard, a Kantian who sees deontic concepts as theoretically basic, continues, "Obligation differs from excellence [i.e., from value] in an important way. . . . The force that value exerts is attractive; [but] when we are obligated, it is compulsive. . . . Excellence is natural; but obligation . . . the work of art[ifice]."[12] The supposed mystery of value, then, is not really a mystery of things being better and worse, which she seems to think is "natural" (nonartificial), but of things being right and wrong, obligatory and forbidden. Her view, it is now plain, depends on our radically separating these two groups of ranking concepts, the evaluative (including the aretaic) and the deontic. One advantage, then, of basing obligation and forbiddenness (and permissibility), the range of the moral law, on virtue concepts is that it helps dissolve Korsgaard's purported mystery. On the virtues-based view I here suggest, "normativity" is not a surprising *explicandum* but a predictable and necessary part of the familiar world. Indeed, moral virtues and many other valuable things are rooted in our desires for actual and current but also nonactual, future occupants of certain role relationships.

I will in light of these concerns take steps toward clarifying and defending the thesis that moral wrongdoing is acting viciously, that it is to conduct oneself in accordance with decisions and intentions (and from preferences and likes and dislikes) that radically depart from being morally virtuous in relation to persons.

12. Korsgaard, *Sources,* 4.

2. SOME ADVANTAGES OF VBMT, AND SOME ALTERNATIVES

Henry Richardson persuasively insists it is a desideratum of the formulation of any norm—that is, the statement of some obligation, permission, and the like—that it be transparent, making explicit on its face not just *that* some course of action is forbidden, but also *why* it is. This renders the norm more accessible, comprehensible, and open to our efforts at interpretation and justification.[13] The virtues, however, are the most familiar and striking examples of the "thick" concepts, to use Bernard Williams's term, that underlie and provide the content of moral requirements. Judith Thomson makes a related point in her recent writings, when she sharply reminds us that nothing is ever simply good or bad but only good or bad in what she calls some "way."[14] If she is correct, and if Kant is also roughly correct when he says that an "ought" judgment tells us what it is good or bad to do or omit, then it follows that what we ought to omit—what it is morally wrong, forbidden to do—is always bad in some specific way. Again, the language of vices and virtues offers the best candidates for articulating the ways in which actions are morally bad. They provide us with a clear, nuanced, and supple vocabulary.

Christine Swanton indicates that our attitudinal responses to what is valuable and disvaluable constitute some of the principal moral virtues and vices.[15] That seems correct. So it is our attitudinal responses to the possible realization of valuable and disvaluable states of affairs, as they are at stake in a given situation, that are good or bad, and therein right or wrong making. Put another way, many of the most important virtues will consist in forms of goodwill, that is, in willing that someone have one or another significantly valuable thing. By the same token, some of the principal moral vices will consist in willing someone something disvaluable, an evil, or in willing her the good insufficiently (with too little devotion, say, or in too restricted a manner), or in failing to will her some good without adequate grounds for the omission. Cruelty is an

13. Henry Richardson, "Specifying Norms as a Way to Resolve Concrete Ethical Problems," *Philosophy and Public Affairs* 19 (1990): 279–310.

14. Judith Thomson, "On Some Ways in Which a Thing Can Be Good," in *The Good Life and the Human Good,* ed. E. Paul, F. Miller, and J. Paul (Cambridge: Cambridge University Press, 1992), 96–117.

15. Swanton, *Virtue Ethics,* part two, esp. ch. 5.

obvious example of ill will, but dishonesty and disloyalty also consist in the disorientation of the will relative to such valuable benefits to another as truth and fidelity.

Some recent thinkers, including Lawrence Blum and John McDowell, have stressed the *cognitive* aspect of virtues in helping agents to recognize morally salient features of their situation and see what is at stake more clearly.[16] Nothing I here say denies that function, though I do not see it as necessary to most moral virtues or crucial to their importance. What is central then, on the form of "virtue ethics" that I advance here, are occasions of virtuous or vicious response, where the relevant forms of responses include privations, being *un*responsive. When such responses as these become fixed, deep-seated dispositions or tendencies, each appropriately harmonized with the others, then someone has a virtuous or vicious character trait. Failure to develop such consistent dispositions can also be considered a form of vicious character, a mind fixed in its desultory lack of devotion to anything important.

Virtuous response and action are thus *conceptually* prior to virtuous character, in my view, in that acting (or otherwise responding) *V*-ly (i.e., in some way virtuously) is more basic than is being a *V* person (i.e., a person characterized by one of the virtues). Nevertheless, virtuous character may, for all that, still be prior *in the order of explanation* to virtuous action in that the reason acting *V*-ly constitutes acting virtuously is *because* having a *V* character (i.e., being a *V* person, being stably disposed to *V* responses) constitutes being a virtuous person within one of the morally determinative person-to-person role relationships, being a virtuous *R1* (to some person *P1*) or a virtuous *R2* (to *P1* or *P2*), and so on, where *R1* and *R2* stand for relevant role relationships (and *P1* and *P2* for a person in whose life such a role is occupied). The concept of responding *V*-ly (in mental attitudes) is more basic in moral theory than either acting *V*-ly or that of being a *V* person. Contrary to Plato's view that just acts are ones that make one's soul just (that "produce and maintain a harmonious psyche," according to *Republic* 443e), virtuous acts are not those that *cause* virtuous character, but ones (relevantly) *produced by* virtuous motivation (whether or not an agent's character stably disposes

16. Lawrence Blum, *Moral Perception and Particularity* (Cambridge: Cambridge University Press, 1997); John McDowell, "Virtue and Reason," *The Monist* 62 (1979): 331–50.

her to such behavior). Otherwise, unjust acts that lead to remorse and moral reform would be just acts. True, as we said above, *S*'s virtues (and virtuous acts) tend to make her good (i.e., a good *R*), but this means they *count toward* her being good: that is, they are *part* of that in which her being good (being a good *R*) would *consist.*

Jonathan Bennett thinks that we appeal to certain kinds of action descriptions—and not to motives, intentions, or virtues—to back our claims about what behavior is morally wrong.[17] However, once we delve a little deeper, we notice that we typically judge these types of action wrong by linking them to vices (or, at least, to vicious inputs). Thus, we explain that stealing and murder are wrong in that they are unjust, that lying is immoral because dishonest, that torture is cruel, adultery disloyal, and other forms of behavior weak-willed, cowardly, inconsiderate, and so on. To adapt and extend Thomson's terminology (in a way of which she would probably disapprove), these vice terms present the *way* in which each type of action is morally wrong. Actions of these types, then, are wrong in that, and insofar as, someone acts unjustly, or dishonestly, or cruelly, or in some other way viciously, in performing them. This indicates that immoral, so-called impermissible, conduct is wrong by its connection to something vicious. The question remains just how virtue and vice figure in right and wrong action.

My basic answer is that acting wrongly is acting viciously, and that we can understand someone's acting rightly (in the minimal sense of behaving permissibly) as conducting herself in a way that is not genuinely vicious in any way in the situation. There may still be something vicious *about* her action, but the agent does not really act viciously in performing it. (Even if she would have acted viciously had her knowledge or intentions been different.) Most talk of moral rules, laws, duties, and obligations should, then, be interpreted as (reduced to) talk about what types of actions are immoral *because of their opposition to (relevant) virtues.* Nonmoral rules will still have a place, nonetheless, as conventions defining a practice or as personal resolutions (making it one's rule always or never to do *A*); for religious believers, one way to construe the moral law is as divinely issued and enforced instructions underscoring and implementing these truths about virtue.

17. Jonathan Bennett, *The Act Itself* (Oxford: Oxford University Press, 1995), ch. 11.

There are, of course, other locutions than those of the form "acting *V*-ly" that relate types or instances of conduct to what is virtuous or vicious. I cannot here sort out all the relevant connections, but will make some preliminary remarks. It seems to me that talk of acting from virtue (or from *V*, where *V* is a virtue term) is ambiguous, suggesting, on the one hand, acting from a fixed and stable virtuous character (or from a *V* trait of character) and, on the other, acting from and with a virtuous (or *V*) motivation on a particular occasion. A virtuous (or *V*) action, an action that is virtuous (is *V*), is one that is virtuously motivated. Talk of an act of virtue (or, more commonly, just an act of *V*) appears to me ambiguous in that it can mean either an act that is/would be virtuously motivated or an action of a type that is only generally or likely virtuously motivated. It can be true both that, in a certain agent's situation, it would in general be kind to help a certain person, but also that this agent does not act kindly in helping her. This may cause some puzzlement, but the case of intellectual virtue shows this sort of thing can be the case. You can say that this would be a smart, even brilliant, investment or other move for me to make, while also allowing that I did not act smartly, let alone brilliantly, in making it, but rather acted quite foolishly, listening to my soothsayer, or behaving randomly, or succeeding by dumb luck. Similar things hold true of acting viciously (or acting *V*-ly, where *V* is a vice term), acting from a vice (or from *V*), a vicious (or *V*) action, an act that is vicious (or is *V*), and an act of vice (of *V*). I think one thing this shows is that acting virtuously or viciously (or *V*-ly for some particular virtue or vice term) is the most important and basic phenomenon from which the other types of virtue- or vice-inflected conduct in various ways derive. Hereafter, it shall be my focus.

Some of those who share my sympathy for increased emphasis on the virtues at the foundations of moral theory have advanced views significantly different from the one I have just sketched. I will treat a few. Michael Slote holds that a right act is one whose agent expresses a virtuous motive in its performance.[18] However, he has sometimes affirmed that an act is right if and only if it is what a virtuous agent would do. I agree with his main point, but think this formulation inadequate for reasons I will shortly make clear below. In one of her earlier works, Rosalind Hurst-

18. Michael Slote, *Morals from Motives* (Oxford: Oxford University Press, 2001), chs. 1, 8.

house maintained that a right action is what a (presumably, fully) virtuous agent would do if fully informed: "An act is right if and only if it is what a virtuous agent would do in the circumstances." Later, she emended her view slightly: "An act is right if and only if it is what a virtuous agent would characteristically (i.e., acting in character) do in the circumstances."[19]

Against Hursthouse, it has been suggested that "being such that it would be performed by a virtuous person can hardly be a right-making characteristic of an action . . . [b]ecause the explanation of why the action is right, if it is, must minimally refer to some concrete aspect of the situation where the action is performed."[20] Rightness certainly needs to be the sort of property that supervenes on actual features, not merely hypothetical ones. Still, this argument against Hursthouse's position moves too fast and has too strong a conclusion. It moves too fast because even the act-utilitarian derives an action's rightness or wrongness in part from counterfactual truths (about the results of unchosen alternatives), and deliberation is *always* about actions not yet actual.[21] Moreover, it is open to Hursthouse and similar proponents of virtue ethics to say that the reason the virtuous agent in circumstance *C* would do *A* is rooted (in part) in the actual features of *C*, which is what the argument insists upon, though neither the virtuous agent nor the actual agent's instance of the action type is itself actualized. So, we need some differentiating feature to distinguish between legitimate appeals to the counterfactual in determining rightness and Hursthouse's appeal. I will return to this to show why I think this objection to Hursthouse's position, though overstated, captures an important flaw in her approach.

Let us turn now to why the stated argument's conclusion at this point is too strong. Even if it is correct (as I think it is) to say no account of right making like Hursthouse's can be correct, this does not suffice to show that Hursthouse's account provides no help in deliberation. Tracking the virtuous agent might be a (or the) right-*identifying* feature of actions, even if it is not a (or the) right-*making* one. To show it is not even

19. Rosalind Hursthouse, "Virtue Theory and Abortion," *Philosophy and Public Affairs* 20 (1991): 223–46. Also see Hursthouse, "Normative Virtue Ethics," in *How Should One Live?* ed. R. Crisp (Oxford: Oxford University Press, 1996), 19–36.

20. Hursthouse, "What Is Wrong with Virtue Ethics?" (unpublished).

21. Note that there are serious metaphysical problems in talking of the "concrete . . . motive [or, still worse] . . . consequences" of merely contemplated actions.

right identifying, it needs to be shown either that we cannot know what the virtuous agent would do, or that there is sometimes more than one thing she would do, or that we sometimes ought to do what the virtuous agent would (even could) not do.

Following Scott Gelfand, we can call this approach, which relies on what a hypothetical agent would do, "hypothetical agent-basing." Hypothetical agent-basing, such as is found in Hursthouse's view and is allowed in some of Slote's formulations, has also been criticized from a different angle. The virtuous agent would do whatever she does because of certain features of the situation. But, then, it seems that these features "themselves, not the fact that [the action] would be chosen by a virtuous agent, [that] are what make the action right." Hursthouse's counterfactuals about the virtuous agent, then, would seem to do no explanatory work, are otiose, because "the virtue of the agent does not enter into the explanation of why the action was right." This argument is ambitious and interestingly similar to the familiar Benthamite argument that appeals to divine will are otiose because the only sort of God worth obeying would just command us to act optimifically. However, this new argument also seems to be fallacious in the same ways that the Benthamite's is. Indeed, its defender needs to show why it should not be classed with the following, obviously invalid, piece of reasoning:

> It is wrong to think the legislature's action made drunk driving illegal, because the legislature only passed the law in question because of certain preexistent negative features of drunk driving, for example, the frequency with which it results in death or injury. Therefore, it follows that it must have been drunk driving's preexistent negative features that made drunk driving illegal, quite independently of the legislature's action.

That the virtuous and the legislature (and God) act because of some positive or negative feature in the situation, something about the type of action with which they are dealing, does not entail that the feature itself independently suffices to make actions morally or legally illicit, nor illegal making (*pace* the Benthamite). So, this argument is, at best, incomplete.

Gelfand, we noted, classifies Hursthouse as holding a hypothetical-agent version of what Slote calls agent-based VE, and the later Slote as holding an actual-agent version. I think this indicates a fundamental ambiguity in any such formula as "do what the virtuous agent would do."

We may use it with a description of the virtuous agent's action that picks it out chiefly by physical details (e.g., "offer blankets to the freezing people") or one that also (or instead) includes the agent's reasons, motives, or choices (e.g., "selflessly try to help them avoid freezing [by providing them blankets]"). In the first, the actual agent may not have the virtuous agent's motivation and may thus "do the right thing for vicious reasons." On that account, she may first infect the blankets with smallpox and then give them to the freezing Indians. Of course, one can say this is a different act from the virtuous agent's, giving the freezing people disease-ridden (rather than helpful) blankets. However, it is an action of the same action type under some descriptions and of a different action type under other descriptions. The issue is which describable features of the action are morally significant (e.g., for its permissibility), and that depends on a prior normative moral theory. The same holds of giving blankets with the intention of later infecting them to harm the Indians. Again the act is the same as the virtuous agent's under some descriptions (e.g., "giving the freezing people some blankets") but not under others (e.g., "giving the freezing Indians blankets in order to help them" as against "giving them blankets to hurt them"). If we have to say that an agent does the right thing when she gives the freezing people either preinfected blankets or blankets-to-be-infected-later, this seems to me to show only the moral insignificance of doing the right thing (*pace* filmmaker Spike Lee), at least, in that narrowly physical sense. I think, instead, that we do better to focus on acting (morally) rightly, that is, acting as and in the way that the morally virtuous agent acts, where we purposely require that "the way" in the relevant sense (use?) has to include those aspects of the action's motivation pertinent and crucial to its virtue or vice.

Roughly, what is most important for moral assessment is not so much the match between *what the actual and (targeted) virtuous agents do* as that between *how they both act.* If the actual agent acts viciously, then she does not therein act rightly. In the more important sense/use, also, I think she does not do the right thing because she does not do what (i.e., does not act as) the virtuous agent would, though there is an extended, misleading, and comparatively insignificant sense/use in which she both does what the virtuous agent would do and also therein does the right thing. In this latter sense/use, we also say that she makes a smart investment, and does the fiscally prudent thing, when she foolishly follows her astrological chart to buy a high-performing stock. Still, what is more important is that she therein acts imprudently, foolishly, in doing what it would be prudent to do. That is because making this investment is prudent *only* insofar as it is properly informed by prudence. It is a hypothetical—indeed, counterfactual—use in respect to this case of what we can call intellectually virtuous and vicious investments. I think the same holds for morally virtuous and vicious conduct. In fact, in the very concept of "conduct" we regard an action as a matter of our leading ourselves in a certain direction, that is, toward adopted ends, through chosen means, and thus from a process of reasoning. All that is on the action's input side. That, I maintain, is where the moral action is too. (At least, I think it is where the phenomena lie that determines the more important facets of an action's moral status.)

We should also observe, contrary to what Hursthouse and some others suggest, that making duty/right action logically dependent on character does not suffice to distinguish VE from utilitarian or neo-Kantian accounts. For a utilitarian may allow that a right act is one that a virtuous agent would perform, taking a virtuous agent to be one who consistently maximizes the good as a matter of character. The neo-Kantian might say the same, taking a virtuous agent to be one who always acts in accord with the Categorical Imperative. On my view of morality as virtues-based, however, these approaches are ruled out, because each utilizes a conception of virtue that itself depends on an axiological or deontic concept that is at least equally fundamental with virtue.[22]

Linda Zagzebski's version of VE takes a different approach to morally right and wrong action. She thinks that a right action is one that an agent characterized by virtuous motivation would perform. She understands "a moral duty [a]s what a person who is virtuously motivated, and who has the understanding of the particular situation that a virtuous person would have, would do in like circumstances."[23] She distinguishes that

22. A problem: What if the utilitarian defines virtue in terms of maximizing pleasure or happiness rather than "the good," and the neo-Kantian defines it in terms of universalizable maxims rather than an imperative? Won't using these seemingly neutral notions pass? I think not. The distinction is artificial, pretextual, and forced, since there is no way of justifying the importance of pleasure (etc.) or of maxims except by reference to their axiological or deontic significance. My claim is that on the best analysis those notions rely on more fundamental virtues concepts and judgments.

23. Linda Zagzebski, *Virtues of Mind* (Cambridge: Cambridge University Press, 1996), 135.

from a person's being "praiseworthy for doing an act" by claiming that the latter requires, in addition to meeting the conditions for doing one's duty as defined, the further requirement that the agent be "motivated by virtuous motives."[24] The condition that the model agent—that is, the one we emulate when we do our duty—be not merely a virtuous person (i.e., one with a virtuous character), but virtuously motivated in the situation, enables Zagzebski to avoid one difficulty: sometimes there is no one thing every virtuous agent would do because even a virtuous agent could, and even sometimes would, do something morally indifferent or vicious. However, problems remain for Zagzebski. Her explicit contrast of praiseworthy actions with doing one's duty makes it clear that, for her, someone can do her duty by performing an act that is not virtuously motivated. That is problematic because such actions bear only an external, observable resemblance to actions fulfilling moral requirement (in the sense of actions needed to avoid behaving viciously).

Gelfand himself endorses reliance on a hypothetical agent, siding with Hursthouse against some of Slote's claims. Gelfand also defines someone's moral duty (in circumstance *C*) as what a (every?) virtuous person would (always) do (in *C*).[25] The problems that arise from those claims move me closer to Slote's view. First, a virtuous person will do many things that are not moral duties (breathe, etc.) because they are trivial. More important, she might in a given instance of circumstance of type *C* do something vicious, and therein what we can call contrary to duty. So there may be nothing of the right sort that a virtuous person—that is, someone of moderate, imperfect virtue—would (always) do. Moreover, being such that a virtuous person would do it seems to be the wrong sort of feature to be right-*making.* What matters is not *who* would perform an act of this type, but *why* the agent whose action is to be judged would be doing it: What would be the reason for any token/instance of the type that *she* (not someone else) produces? Yet this factor will also make the action one that is virtuous or vicious in some way. So appeal to the virtuous agent as distinct from virtuous response seems unnecessary. I think this is the element of truth in the objection, noted above, that rightness must depend on features of the *actual* situation. It

24. Zagzebski, *Virtues,* 235, 236.

25. Scott Gelfand, "Hypothetical Agent-Based Virtue Ethics," *Southwest Philosophical Review* 17 (2000): 85–94.

derives from features of the actual agent (i.e., the one who is to be judged, and whose action is to be judged) and her motives, not from the features of some merely imagined agent. Moreover, without further specification, this position leaves it unclear whether to fulfill someone's duty her act must resemble the virtuous agent's in being virtuously motivated, or merely resemble it in its effects or its physical structure. That is important because it is counterintuitive to maintain, for example, that my doing what I promised fulfills my moral duty in cases where I did it, for example: (1) having forgotten the promise, or (2) in spite of the fact that I promised (having rejected promising as an impertinent effort to restrict the will of myself, whom I regard as *uebermensch*), or (3) only as a device for winning others' trust the better to bilk them later. Finally, this view cannot analyze well such "ought" judgments as those about what a *partially vicious agent* should do. To see this, suppose that a (fully) virtuous agent would immediately congratulate the player who just beat him at squash, but it is not the case that I, my short-tempered self, should do that, for I cannot: if I go near her now, I'll certainly just lose control and strike her.[26]

Finally, Christine Swanton proposes that "an action is right if and only if it is overall virtuous," where overall virtue is distinguished from its being virtuous in this or that respect—benevolent, courageous, or some such. Being virtuous in a certain respect, she defines, as "hit[ting] the target of [the] virtue," which she sees as equivalent to "realizing the [virtue's] end."[27] However, Swanton makes it clear that, like Zagzebski's, her position involves a success component inherent in virtuous—and thus in right—action. I think this problematic because, to the extent a moral theory allows an action's rightness or wrongness to hinge on its effects, it therein (1) holds moral wrongness hostage to result-luck; (2) divorces it from the centrality of agency, which resides in the agent's preferences, choices, expectations, commitments, and so on; (3) severs it from the bases of the moral admiration and blame that action assessments normally justify; and (4) dehumanizes human actions and agents by viewing them as mere mechanisms for the production of valued re-

26. I take this example and argument from Michael Smith, "From Metaethics to Normative Ethics," a talk to the Rutgers University Philosophy Department, New Brunswick, February 1999.

27. Swanton, "A Virtue Ethical Account of Right Action," *Ethics* 112 (2001): 34.

sults. Zagzebski's and Swanton's views do not go that far, allowing only general effects to count in a motivation's being virtuous, not its effects to make an action wrong. And it is reassuring that Zagzebski says that, for her, "the motivational component is more basic than the success component." Nevertheless, even this type of moderate or mixed view is unacceptable insofar as it allows success, and thus effects, such a role in determining right and wrong action that it undermines what we may call the morality of action's (and, ultimately, all morality's) "input drive." For, precisely because of that, it cannot do justice to the way in which people's motivations, feelings, and desires (for us) are important to us, and thus matter within morality, as such and for their own sakes, independently of their circumstantial or usual results. What matters to us and thus to her moral status (and that of her choices and actions) is how a moral subject feels about some person; it is her inner life, not her condition as a possible cause of external advantages or setbacks. That inner life matters to us, and therefore in morality, in its own right, not in a way that is merely contingent on its usual outcomes. This is a fundamental part of a needed "psychological realism" (and, I might add, psychological idealism), which some philosophers have urged on moral theorizing.[28]

In contrast, Zagzebski roots her claim that general success is a condition on any disposition to act's being a virtue in a deeper vision of the moral life as an institution rooted in a concern for "making the world . . . a better place."[29] I find this sort of talk very dubious in content, application, and significance, and I think it ill accords with a properly conceived virtue-based approach. First, we have little idea how to evaluate worlds as wholes and in general, though we can say that this sort of situation is good for farmers and their goals and a different situation good for picnickers and theirs. Second, it is hard to know what sort of function or purpose is supposed to lie behind functional evaluation of a world, as the adjunctive use of "better" in such phrases as "better world" suggests: *at what* is it that a better world is better, we want to ask, and what makes it true that *that* is what worlds are somehow for?[30] Third, if the better-

28. See Owen Flanagan, *Varieties of Moral Personality* (Cambridge, Mass.: Harvard University Press, 1991), ch. 2.

29. Zagzebski, *Virtues*, 137.

30. Or is it that a good world is one in which it is good to *do* this or that? But, if so, what? And why is doing that so important rather than doing something else?

ness of a world or its being a better place is to be understood as its having impersonal value, being more valuable, then a virtues-based account of such value judgments will need us to specify in what way we are being more virtuous when we want, value, or otherwise favor it. How does our wanting such a better world make us better, as virtue always does? In what way, especially, in which capacity or role? Fourth, we should be leery that Zagezbski introduces this concern with world betterment by calling it one of the "aims of the moral project."[31] I know of little reason to believe there is or ought to be such a "project," nor what it is supposed to be. Fifth, I fear that making much of the vague abstraction of bettering the world is a bad idea imported from early utilitarians' misunderstanding of benevolence, now forced into a better moral view into which it does not fit. World improvement seems to me not just a dubious and ethically insignificant project but a distraction from the morally serious business of loving and respecting each person, seeking her welfare, which constitutes the proper focus of our moral concern both as deliberating agents and evaluating critics. We might say that this forest, if it really exists, is a distraction from the trees, that is, real, needy, living persons. Classical utilitarianism misunderstood the nature and focus of the individually focused and input-constituted neighborly love that it inherited from Christianity and, as a result, it squandered that inheritance. Today's consequentialisms, utilitarianism's intellectual children, do not improve on this decisive and original fault. Virtues-based ethical theory presents moral philosophy with an opportunity to recapture what it then lost. It would be a pity if that chance were dissipated by following utilitarianism's lead in the probably futile and certainly dangerous pursuit of a goal of dubious reality and no genuine value.

3. VIRTUE, INTENTIONS, MOTIVES, AND ACTION: SOME OBJECTIONS TO THIS CONCEPTION OF VE AND ITS RELIANCE ON ACTUAL MOTIVATION

Judith Thomson insists on what she terms the "objectivity" of an action's being virtuous or vicious:

31. Zagzebski, *Virtues*, 137.

> [T]he question whether a person's act is unjust does not turn on what the person's beliefs or intentions are. What fixes whether the person's act is unjust is not the person's subjective state of mind, but instead the objective fact that something [*sic*] else does or does not have a nonoverridden right against him. . . . Suppose Alfred doesn't believe that anything has a nonoverridden right that he send Bertha a check for fifty dollars. But suppose that is because he has simply forgotten that he promised . . . Then his failing to send the check would be unjust. . . . The question whether a person's act is unjust is objective—just as . . . whether a person ought to do a thing is objective. . . . [T]his is true of justice too.

Extending this same point to the other pair of a moral virtue and vice that she thinks most important, she writes: "Whether a person's act is miserly [or generous] does not turn on his beliefs or intentions: rather it turns on what he (objectively) does."[32] To illustrate, she imagines a "muddled miser" who transfers money inadvertently. Even when he protests, against what Thomson imagines to be our characterization of the act as generous, "'But I didn't mean to be generous,'" we can properly respond, she tells us, "'All the same, you were.'"[33]

However, this position is highly counterintuitive because, as the Kantians have stressed, we recognize acts of injustice as unjust because they are disrespectful. Yet as the etymology indicates, whether we are respectful or disrespectful in our actions depends on how we see and respond to people. These can only count as "subjective" matters, in Thomson's sense. Of course, one could maintain that justice consists in observing rules that the citizens are (or would be) motivated by respect to establish, maintain, and enforce. Then it would not matter to the justice or injustice of her conduct whether the agent herself was respectful. However, this position is hard to credit, for it would seem that any argument that moves from respect to our having certain protective rules of conduct seems to go through the claim that we would be disrespectful and therefore unjust in failing thus to protect people. And that also gives us reason to criticize the actions themselves as unjust simply in that they express a certain attitude of the agents.

Beyond that, Thomson fails to attend to important and revealing

32. Judith Thomson, *Goodness and Advice* (Princeton, N.J.: Princeton University Press, 2001), 60–61, 64–65.

33. Thomson, *Goodness and Advice,* 65.

clues within the very language she uses. She has her imaginary muddled miser protest the characterization of his act as generous by saying, "But I didn't mean to be generous." This indicates that he thinks an action counts as generous only if the agent intends it to be generous. We can agree that this is too strong. My own generosity, and more generally my own virtue, need not be in my mind when I perform a generous, or otherwise virtuous, action. Still, this does not entail that no intentions matter to its proper classification; it shows only that it is other intentions that must be crucial. What matters is whether, for instance, I meant to help, did so for its sake rather than as part of some trick, and so on. More important, on another matter her miser seems less muddled than Thomson herself. For he sees that his action's generosity depends on whether *he* was himself being generous in performing it. Thomson's "objective" view of these virtues leaves no place for the way in which someone's acting *V*-ly and, what may be different, performing a *V* action are intimately connected to her being *V* in doing it. There is a serious cost in theoretical unity and cohesion in a position that, like Thomson's, so radically disconnects a person's acting *V*-ly from her being *V* in acting and from, what is also closely related, its being *V of* her to act as she does. Of course, that an agent is virtuous in some way in doing this or that shows only that she acted from a certain motivational input in that situation and on that occasion, not that she does so regularly, as a matter of character. So she can be generous (or in some other way virtuous) in doing this action without her being a *V* person. Still more, the virtue of generosity and the opposed vice that Thomson calls "miserliness" plainly relate to the inescapably mind-dependent concepts of kindness and unkindness. Finally, as Thomson sometimes seems aware, her position radically separates virtuous and vicious action from virtuous and vicious persons, allowing the former but not the latter to be "subjective" in the sense she counterposes to her "objective" one. That is surely both counterintuitive and theoretically overcomplicated.

Thomson also complains that intentions cannot be part of what makes some actions permissible or impermissible, on the grounds that consideration of the intentions with which one will act cannot be helpful in deliberation, and cannot adequately guide action. However, even if it were *useless* to tell someone who asks for advice that what she ought to do depends on what she would intend in doing it, that would not suffice to show that it is *false* that permissibility depends upon the agent's intentions. Moreover, there is no reason to believe that an agent cannot or should not consider *how* she would be acting, what she would be acting *from,* and thus whether her act would constitute an appropriate (i.e., virtuous) response to the involved person within the morally relevant relationship that links them.

One often-repeated charge against the relevance of virtuous intentions (and other virtuous mental states) to the permissibility of action says it is "strange" to think that two similarly situated agents (e.g., two physicians), who perform the same motions to the same effect, might nevertheless act differently morally (one rightly, one wrongly) "only because they have different motives."[34] Maybe so, but the claim is formally the same as saying that it is strange for act-utilitarians to think that two similarly situated physicians, who perform the same motions from the same motives, might nevertheless act differently morally solely because of their differing results. Or strange for the Kantian to maintain that two similarly situated physicians, who perform the same motions with the same results, might nevertheless act differently morally solely because of their differing maxims. The theses that effects (actual effects, at that) must matter to rightness, and motives must not, are merely assumed in these discussions. But they should not be. Reasons need to be given.[35]

4. ON THE MORAL VIRTUES AND "OUGHT" JUDGMENTS

I will not elaborate an account of the moral virtues, but should attempt to clarify what I mean and help situate my view among some others. In

34. See my discussion in J. L. A. Garcia, "Intention-Sensitive Ethics," *Public Affairs Quarterly* 9 (1995): 201–13.

35. Perhaps we should also comment on the recent charge that VE presupposes an inaccurate moral psychology, because recent studies in empirical psychology have shown that people generally don't manifest stable character traits and thus may not have virtues. Against this, there are several rebuttals to register, though I cannot here expand on any of them. First, appeal to virtuous attitudinal responses need not presuppose that virtuous traits are actual, let alone frequent. We ascribe bad character when people lack good traits—when they are inconsistent, unpredictable—as well as when they have bad ones. Virtuous traits may be something to which VE tells us to aspire, not something it assumes to be widespread. (Virtue ethics is not chiefly concerned with explanation, as Kamtechar notes against John Doris and some others. See Rachana Kamtekar, "Situationism and Virtue Ethics on the Content of Our Character," *Ethics* 114 [2004]: 458–91.) Likewise, once we understand the

general, I follow Aristotle's most general account, according to which a virtue in a kind of thing is a feature on account of whose possession both a thing of that type and its operation are good. The kind of virtue that interests me here, then, makes a person good morally by tending to make her good in one or more of certain role relationships—such as friend, fellow, spouse, citizen, or partner—which we can call morally determinative. Aristotle's account of moral virtue, more specifically, is that such a virtue (1) is a (character) disposition to act or be moved, that (2) is acquired by habituation, (3) consists in a mean between vicious extremes of excess and defect, and (4) is determined in accord with excellent (or, at least, correct) practical reason.

A few comments should help clarify my view relative to this classic position. (1) While I accept that the moral virtues are character dispositions, I am more interested here in responding virtuously (in a person's likes, preferences, and choices, with her actual resultant behavior less important) on the occasion (action) than in being deeply disposed so to do. (2) On the acquisition of virtues, it suffices for my purposes that a genuine virtue cannot be merely mechanical and that its promptings must be resistible. If I become an unfailingly kind or truthful person, for example, simply because you gave me a certain pill, bombarded me with a special ray, waved your magic wand, or some such, then this does not make me in any way virtuous, because that is not the sort of kindness or truthfulness that would count toward my being a good friend, or fellow,

virtues, we shouldn't expect virtues or vices simply consistently to show up in performed actions. Signs of virtue may be found (1) in the agent's attitudinal response to failing to act virtuously—guilt, shame, regret; or (2) in her later behavioral responses—apologies, efforts to compensate, trying to perform the omitted virtuous action later on; or (3) in a not-acted-on inclination so to act; or (4) in an acted-against compunction about behaving in certain ways. (Not every disposition or inclination or tendency to act or react is a mere statistical trend. It may instead consist in a psychological impetus or resistance, whether or not one of which the agent herself is aware at the time.) Moreover, even when the agent often fails to act in a certain virtuous way, it may be that another virtuous trait or a vicious trait, or a vicious lack of consistent disposition, serves as an obstacle. If so, then again, frequent failure to manifest a particular virtue in observed conduct underdetermines the question of whether the agent nevertheless has the virtuous disposition. Virtue is a more complicated and subtle matter than the cited experiments can well test. Doris concedes that people have "narrow" traits of character, such as a tendency to cheat on exams; see John Doris, *Lack of Character* (Cambridge: Cambridge University Press, 2002). What he denies are broader traits such as dishonesty, a general tendency to cheat in one's favor. However, as Kamtechar also remarks, oftentimes a person needs moral education and reflection to see that and how a narrow trait is morally linked to others so as to become a broad trait.

or citizen, or the like. Good friends are not automata, and the same goes *mutatis mutandis* for the other morally determinative roles, and their various virtues. (3) As for the famous but elusive Aristotelian doctrine that virtue is a mean between vices of excess and defect, I have nothing much to say, though it is important that my account allows in quite a different way for two types of vicious departures from the forms of goodwill that constitute most (or all) of the central moral virtues. For I can fall unacceptably short (i.e., fall short in a way that, if habitual, would tend to make me bad in my relationships to you) in generosity, trustworthiness, fidelity, or some other form of good either by being insufficiently devoted to achieving or maintaining the relevant good or, more egregiously, by being fixed on destroying or preventing it. The latter type of departure from goodwill is more vicious because more bad-making. (It counts toward my being worse in relation to you and, what seems different, it may also count more strongly toward my being a bad *R* to you.) (4) Finally, as to practical reason's role in the moral virtues, what is important is that reason both (a) operate, in the instance, in a way that normally fulfills its function, and (b) itself be virtuous by helping the orientations of the agent's will tend to make her good (in one of her morally determinative roles). This will have to suffice to situate my view of the virtues with regard to the chief classical account.[36]

Our narrower interest here is not so much on the virtues and vices, on those traits of character, but on virtuous and vicious actions (and omissions, though I'll say nothing about the special issues these latter raise). In general, I take immoral behavior, wrong actions, or omissions to be instances of vicious conduct, behavior whose motivational input is so far removed from the virtuous as to be vicious. That is, an action is wrong when it comes from such a motivational input as would, if habitual and deep (i.e., a trait of character), count toward the agent's being morally bad. (Again, that last, on the sort of role-centered version of VBMT that I accept, consists in her being a bad *R*, where *R* is one of those special

36. In his main account of virtue, Aquinas explicitly follows Peter Lombard in regarding virtue as "a good quality of mind, by which one lives rightly and which no one uses badly, that God works within us without us" (*ST,* I-II, q. 58 a. 1; q. 59, aa. 1, 2). However, Aquinas himself says this really applies mainly to the infused (theological) virtues, not to the habituation-acquired moral virtues. I judge him implicitly Aristotelian about the most important moral virtues, which are the kind of virtue that interest here.

role relationships that I call morally determinative.) Our talk of actions or omissions violating the moral law I construe as normally a way of saying that they are vicious, though a way that can be problematic in several ways and is less lucid than virtue discourse.

When, then, we (correctly) say that *S1*'s doing *V* would be against the moral law (immoral, wrong, forbidden, etc.), I claim that what we are getting at (and what makes it true) is that *S1*'s *V*-ing would be vicious in some respect, that is, it would be against honesty, veracity, fidelity, kindness, for example. And, according to me, that is to say that a disposition to perform such action would tend to make *S1* a bad *R* (count toward *S1*'s being a bad *R*) in some morally determinative role, *R*. Moreover, the principal interpersonal moral virtues are forms of goodwill (benevolence) because they consist in willing someone such a good as true belief, or a specific benefit or satisfied preference, or obedience, or the like. So there are at least two forms of deviation and departure from virtue: viciously failing to will the good and viciously willing the absence of the good. The latter, *counter*officious willing (and conduct) is the graver, more egregious departure from virtue and thus is presumptively more objectionable.

One salient advantage of construing immorality and moral wrongdoing, and with it our discourse of moral duty and law, as behaving viciously is that viciousness is plainly a scalar and comparative concept (one that admits of degrees and of more and less), while unanalyzed talk of the moral law and its violation seems to leave no clear place for this important aspect of immorality, since what is illegal cannot be more or less illegal than something else, nor illegal to just this extent. Of course, we could still talk of what is or is not egregiously, or blatantly, or flagrantly, or manifestly illegal; but these are epistemic matters (how plain its illegality is) not matters of the extent or degree to which it is illegal (how illegal). In contrast, we intuitively think that some immoral actions are very wrong (or only slightly wrong) and some more wrong than others.

Another advantage to this virtues-based way of understanding the immorality of actions and construing talk of breaking and obeying the moral law, as noted above, is that vice-talk contains or immediately calls for greater specificity than does unanalyzed talk of immorality and the moral law. What is vicious is always characterized by this or that vice—it is, say, unkind, cruel, or dishonest—where such specificity has the theoretical advantages both of lending our moral characterizations greater "thickness" and of rendering them more "transparent" by indicating not just *that something* is the matter with these actions but *what* is wrong with them (i.e., how they are wrong).

VBMT has resources to escape some of the objections leveled against other efforts to account for wrongdoing within VE. Various cases where her now acting rightly requires a certain agent's (1) apologizing, or (2) making restitution, or (3) counteracting (or aborting) some of her previous undertakings, or (4) acquiring virtues, or (5) avoiding what are morally risk-laden opportunities for good action, or (6) deferring to another's guidance, or (7) doing what the virtuous do not characteristically do, have all been presented as counterexamples to the claim of some proponents of VE that acting rightly consists in doing that which a virtuous agent would do. The idea behind them is that a fully virtuous agent would never be in a situation wherein she had to apologize or make restitution for (let alone, try to undo) her previous wrongdoing, nor would she have to acquire virtues (since she would already have them), or defer to the wiser and more virtuous, or fear that she will succumb to the temptations to do evil afforded by some opportunities to do good.

All these cases of contrary-to-virtue past conduct (or current traits), however, are directed against what, following Gelfand, we have called "hypothetical agent VE"; that is, they define right actions as those that a hypothetical (fully or very) virtuous agent would (characteristically) do (or approve or recommend), and then point out that such an agent wouldn't find herself, and might not know how to act, in such unfamiliar situations. My VBMT, in contrast, defines wrong action as action that in the situation is vicious (in enough of its motivation). There may still be vicious and nonvicious conduct by an agent, even in cases where she has already acted viciously and now has to apologize, or make amends, or counteract her earlier behavior; or where she risks losing one or more of her virtues; or where she needs to cultivate more virtues, or to gain another person's guidance, or to perform actions more common among the vicious. On my account, it is the psychological input to the actual agent's behavior on this occasion that shapes the morality of her conduct, not an imagined perfect agent. So there is no problem in our affirming that sometimes a particular agent can act rightly, in the sense of avoiding wrongdoing, only by doing something a fully virtuous agent would not do.

I will also try to show that and how some other complaints against VE lack merit against the account here given, whatever their success or failure against some other recent forms of VE. I recently heard one speaker complain that virtue talk can add nothing to discussion of negligence and risk-management policies, insisting that we would still need "principles of due care."[37] However, we should note against this that care of the relevant level and type is morally "due" only in that, beneath a certain level, someone's caring for another is vicious and actions or omissions informed by this viciousness manifest callousness, coldheartedness, heartlessness, or worse (as in the instrumental malevolence of manipulatively using someone as a means, or the worse malice of treating his or her loss of important goods as an end or means). Caring is important, and it needs to meet a minimum that we can call "due care," but all this is important morally in ways best articulated without reliance on the rhetoric or idea of "principles" (or rules or laws) of (due) care.

Other thinkers do or would object to such a VBMT's account of moral wrongdoing because they insist that the immorality of someone's action or omission cannot hinge on the psychological attitudes with and from which she behaves. They believe that in a certain type of case, for example, we can say that a jailer morally ought, and has a moral duty, to incarcerate those convicted and sentenced to prison, and that this implies that a particular jailer, call her Jane, ought and has a duty to imprison convict Connie in situation *S1,* even if Jane cannot jail Connie without therein acting with vicious resentment toward her for some past incident, relishing the loss of freedom that the justified imprisonment brings Connie. These thinkers worry that in making avoiding wrongdoing depend on acting without vicious motivation input we will be unable correctly to advise Jane that she ought and has a duty to jail Connie, because Jane will act viciously in imprisoning her.[38] They insist that *whether* a person *P1* ought, and is duty-bound, to do *A* has to be independent of *why* and *how P1* would be acting in doing so. Against this, I think we should say that the question "*What* ought she to do morally?" makes

37. Barbara Fried, in discussion following her talk to the Harvard University Center for Ethics, Kennedy School of Government, "Is There a Coherent Alternative to Cost-Benefit Analysis?" December 2007.

38. I interpreted Judith Thomson as advancing such a position in conversation with me at MIT's Department of Linguistics and Philosophy, spring 2007.

sense only where the context permits it to be read as "*How* morally ought she to act?" meaning from which choices and motives, with which intentions, in pursuit of what objectives, despite what considerations, she should act. So, in that sense, the question should be rejected as senseless when the context excludes that reading. Instead, what we should say of the agent bent on performing an act of a good (presumptively or normally virtuous) type for vicious reasons (or with a vicious intent) is not that she morally ought to perform these physical actions (or that she morally ought to perform any acts with those effects), since none of that has independent moral weight, but that she ought to change her mind. (What if she cannot? Then she cannot act well and there is nothing she morally ought to do, though there are some actions that are worse than others.)[39]

5. ON THE CONCEPTS OF LAW AND NATURE IN THE IDEA OF NATURAL LAW AS THE MORAL VIRTUES' PRACTICAL REGULATION

Even if VBMT offers an appealing way of thinking about immoral conduct, however, it remains to be shown that it can accommodate not only what we mean in our ordinary talk about moral duty and law but, more specifically, the theological and philosophical tradition of the natural law. I will try to anticipate and address a few relevant concerns about this. Law, according to Aquinas's most celebrated discussion, requires in its focal forms: (1) codification and formulation, as well as (2) this formal cause's principle: reason; (3) a special means, that is, public prom-

39. We can also agree with a point Slote makes: there is no obstacle to the proponent of VBMT (or, for Slote, of what he calls "agent-based virtue ethics") agreeing with common sense that his imagined Phyllis *ought not to continue* the futile and unjustifiably burdensome treatment *T*. We can say both that (1) Phyllis ought not to continue treatment *T* for Pat in that her doing so would be irresponsible and in(sufficiently) considerate, and that (2) Phyllis ought not to act resentfully or maliciously toward Pat in terminating it. Either way, Phyllis acts wrongly in that she wrongs Pat, by treating her viciously. Here she morally ought not in the strong sense that she morally *must* not. This sense is related to Aristotle's observation that one thing we can mean in calling something necessary is that without it an evil cannot be avoided. Here, the evil is the evil conduct itself. (For this reason, it seems to me unhelpful to follow Thomson in trying to fit all talk of what we morally ought to do and what action is morally required as "advice," and misleading to agree with her (Thomson, "Reply to Commentators [Schneewind]," in *Goodness and Advice*, 147–80) that talk of what we morally "must" do is just an especially emphatic way of employing the (supposedly) advisory "ought.")

ulgation, and agent, that is, one with care of and responsibility for the community; and (4) directedness to the common good. It is also characteristic of law, whether or not strictly a necessary condition, that it be (5) linked to penalties for infractions.[40] The most fundamental type of law, on this account, is what Aquinas calls the "eternal law" of God's providence over Creation, though this law can be said to be codified and enforced only in an attenuated sense, and the natural law is human "participation" in this, that is, its application to human beings. Thus, the natural law is natural insofar as God's plan is a plan for beings with our nature as humans. Moreover, human nature is normative in a special way, helping provide a standard for assessing as virtuous or vicious various human physical, cognitive, and emotional states, behaviors, responses, and so on. This is usually construed as simply assessing a person as fulfilling or bringing to realization, to a greater or lesser extent, the dynamic potential for development rooted in this nature. Is she in this or that respect a good (more developed) or bad (poorly developed) human being? However, this last need not be seen as the final and most lucid level of analysis. We can in principle press further by seeing human nature as fulfilled only in a variety of fairly specific modes of relationship to various persons—human, angelic, and divine. Moreover, within the human, we are morally assessed in relation to persons more or less closely connected to the subject of moral assessment, ranging from strangers remote in time and space (at one extreme of distance) to (in the limit case of intimacy) one's own self. Moral assessment, then, measures a person in the extent to which she is living up to these roles in the ways she responds to life's opportunities and challenges and conducts herself in relation to persons. Aquinas might be read as suggesting something along these lines in his discussions of various orders of the love that is humanity's highest achievement.[41] Being immoral, on this view, can be said to consist in being deficient in humanity, but only because being thus deficient itself consists in falling short in certain role relationships we naturally want and benefit from having fulfilled in our lives. In any case, however one reads Aquinas, that is the proposal of a role-centered VBMT.

40. Aquinas, *ST,* I-II, qq. 90–108.

41. Aquinas, esp., *Disputed Questions on Virtue* a. 9: "Whether there is some ordering within charity," and, especially, "Replies to Objections"; in Aquinas, *Disputed Questions on the Virtues,* trans. E. M. Atkins (Cambridge: Cambridge University Press, 2005), 159–66.

Human beings, by our nature, want to be, need to be, and profit from being connected to various persons in certain ways: as friends, parents, offspring, fellow citizens, confidantes, partners in joint undertakings, promisers, and so on. Anyone's moral life is a matter of how well she fulfills these role relationships, where the key to such fulfillment is the content of her will, preferences, likes, dislikes, and associated dispositions. So there is no problem for VBMT in acknowledging human nature as an ultimate source of moral virtue, vice, and derivative standards, though VBMT presents a more complicated picture of how this works than in standard interpretations of Aristotle and Aquinas. A naturalist approach need not conceive moral assessment as appraising people according to how well they fulfill natural human potencies, as if being human were itself a function or assignment that morality measures. However, human nature does establish certain forms of person-to-person relationship as ones in which our practical and emotional attitudes make us good or bad, make us morally virtuous or vicious. Such an understanding of morality, deriving moral virtues that serve as standards for judging conduct from interests and needs rooted in and shaped by human nature, can surely be counted a natural law theory, adapting the image of law and using the term in an extended and derivative sense. John Finnis correctly conceded that natural law is law only in an extended sense, and I think departing from the focal sense of "law" frees the moral theorist from having to offer detailed accounts of, and having to accommodate within morality and moral theory, the codification, promulgation, appeal to the common good, and background penalties that are characteristic of law in the strict, narrow, and focal sense of the term.[42] Let me close this section, however, with some comments on human nature itself and what morality needs from it.

Some kinds of responses are intrinsically ones that human beings, by their own human nature, tend to want, prefer, be averse to, benefit from, or suffer because of. That is common sense, and controversial only because some have a metaphysical stance against the very idea that humans have (for some, that anything has) a distinctive nature. It should be noted, however, that quite a weak concept of what humans by nature want, and so on, would suffice to secure many of the familiar forms of

42. John Finnis, *Natural Law and Natural Rights* (Oxford: Oxford University Press, 1980), 280.

virtue and vice and, what is somewhat different, of virtuous and vicious conduct within a role-centered VBMT. Humans tend naturally to want and benefit from having friends, spouses, offspring, community, partners in various collective enterprises, and other associates, and, beyond that, they want and benefit from having not just any kind of friend but ones who are devoted and loyal, not just any kind of spouse but a spouse who is loving and kind, and so on through such relationships that not only are natural but also determine our moral virtue, vices, and derivative moral features.

John Stuart Mill famously insisted that "nature cannot be a proper model for us to imitate. Either it is right that we should kill because nature kills, torture because nature tortures, ruin and devastate because nature does the like, or we ought not to consider what nature does, but what it is good to do."[43] Yet this last conclusion of Mill's is stronger than his original claim and does not follow from the reasoning he offers. For that we ought not slavishly ape whatever events we come across in nature, does not mean we ought not to "consider" what, by our nature as humans, works to thwart, benefit, threaten, sicken, cure, preserve, or kill us in figuring out not only what it is good for us to do, but also what is good for us to happen, or to have, want, like, choose, wish for, become, or just be. A sophisticated ethical naturalism, including a natural law approach, does not simplistically enjoin us to imitate nature.

A century later, Bernard Williams offers a much more modest conception of "naturalism" in ethical theory, defining it as "the attempt to lay down certain fundamental aspects of a good human life on the basis of considerations of human nature." While acknowledging that such "naturalism" can "offer some prospect of being both well-founded and contentful," however, Williams doubts such a project can succeed, claiming that "[t]he right sort of truths about human nature do not exist." That is because Darwinian evolution offers our best account of human nature, and it both "suggests human beings are to some degree a mess," so that "no form of life is likely to prove entirely satisfactory, either individually or socially" and also teaches as its "first and hardest lesson . . . that there is no such teleology at all, and that there is no orchestral score provided from anywhere according to which human beings have a special part to

43. J. S. Mill, "Nature," in *Nature, the Utility of Religion, and Theism* (Whitefish, Mont.: Kessinger, 2004), 31.

play."[44] Again, however, the critique overreaches. It is plainly asking too much of a properly naturalistic ethical theory to demand that it identify some "form of life" (whatever that is) as "entirely satisfactory," and it plainly goes far beyond the scope of Darwin's theories about the development of one species from another by so-called natural selection to claim humans neither have a *telos* distinctive to them nor participate in any larger, transcendent "score." What in the fossil record entails that, one wonders.

In any case, the human nature that underlies morality could be understood as weak in both epistemological and ontological respects without undermining much of ordinary common sense about the moral virtues and vices.[45] It can be weak ontologically in that what is natural in us (what it is natural for us to want, prefer, do, think, etc.) (1) may have developed over time, (2) might have been partially shaped by evolutionary forces, and, most radically, (3) could again change under these evolutionary (and/or other) pressures. At least, none of these possibilities is excluded by the combination of a role-centered VBMT and much common sense about of the moral virtues and vices. It could also be weak epistemologically. That the familiar moral virtues and vices take their status ultimately from human nature is compatible with the possibility that we justify our knowledge of human nature (what is natural in us) from a combination of sources, including introspection, what philosophers used to call "knowledge without observation," and common sense, but also (or instead), from quantitative (or ethnographic) social science, speculative extrapolation from other species, and human biology (evolutionary, molecular genetic, or other).

We should also note, on the other hand, that while nothing in the more general moral theory precludes such empirical backing, neither does it demand that we know what is natural for humans only by means of empirical science. Divine revelation and theological reasoning may also be sources of anthropological insight.[46] We should not be reluctant

44. Bernard Williams, "Evolution, Ethics and the Representation Problem," in *Making Sense of Humanity* (Cambridge: Cambridge University Press, 1995), 101, 109–10.

45. For summaries and rebuttals of antirealism and skepticism about human nature, see David Oderberg, *Real Essentialism* (New York: Routledge, 2007), esp. chs. 1, 8–10.

46. I think the Christocentric anthropology suggested in many writings of Pope John Paul II proposes a theological personalism that marks a promising and impressive recent addition to these inquiries.

to acknowledge that our knowledge of ourselves, of our nature as humans, can come from a rich variety of sources, both internal and external, some more and some less scientific.[47] It is but epistemological ideology, whose rebuttal is beyond my scope here, that collapses and restricts this richness. Also, for all that is required to ground many familiar virtues and vices in human nature, it could be that much, even most, of our knowledge of human nature from these sources may be fallible, and some of what we think we know of human nature may be quite wrong.

So far as I can see, then, using a weaker or stronger conception of human nature and a broad, extended, and nonfocal sense of "law," a theoretical understanding of our moral life and features that is generally role-centered and virtues-based is open to expression within the language of natural law and could even be considered one kind of extension of that tradition.

6. CONFLICTS IN VIRTUES-BASED MORAL THEORY, INTENTION-SENSITIVITY, AND EFFECTS-INDEPENDENCE

Even those who find something appealing in what has so far been asserted may think a deep problem lurks, which has not been acknowledged. Don't moral virtues conflict? Even if not in themselves, as Nietzsche perhaps thought they did, do they not at least sometimes clash in their practical demands on an agent?[48] And, if so, then mustn't we, both as agents and as critics, appeal to something beyond and deeper than the virtues themselves to determine how morality directs us to act? How, then, can virtues really be at the basis of morality for the theorist?

A strategy is needed for dealing with conflicts that at least appear to arise. It does not follow from this, however, that this strategy must assign virtues weights on some external basis, as the objection presupposes, so as

47. While some of what passes today as "empirical ethics" is of slight merit, there is no reason to deny the obvious truth that the methods of the empirical sciences can illuminate the study of humanity. As Appiah notes, however, the evaluation, interpretation, and implications of findings remain a task for philosophical scrutiny. See Anthony Appiah, *Experiments in Ethics* (Cambridge, Mass.: Harvard University Press, 2008) and "Experimental Philosophy," Presidential Address, Eastern Division Meeting, American Philosophical Association, Baltimore, December 2007.

48. On Nietzsche, see Philippa Foot, *Virtues and Vices* (Oxford: Oxford University Press, 1978), ch. 6.

to show that virtues are not truly "basic." In work already mentioned, Henry Richardson has insisted (against David Ross, among others) that apparent moral conflicts among moral features ought not to be approached through the misleading metaphor of "balancing." That rhetoric is speciously quantitative, tends either to be inarticulate and opaque or to degenerate into an implausible value, serves to mask bias and other irrationality, and obscures the interpretive nature of the reasoning needed. Richardson proposes an alternative method of conflict resolution that he calls "norm-specification." The general idea is that one needs to get clearer just what one or more of the apparently conflicting norms is and requires, and why, in order to see whether in fact it really does stand in conflict with the other norm in the agent's situation.

Adapting that suggestion for our purposes, the way to proceed in the face of apparent conflicts is to see just what virtues are involved, in what relationships to which moral patients, and determine how the agent's alternative courses of action stand in relation to the forms of response that constitute the role virtues. It is important to remember that, as here conceived, moral wrongdoing, behaving in a way that violates the moral law (i.e., the natural moral law), is acting (or omitting a type of action) from motivational input that, if a trait of character, would tend to make someone bad in one of the roles that determine our moral features. Oftentimes, an action or omission is only virtuous *in certain respects* or *to some extent,* especially, in its ultimate intentions, when other factors serve to make it vicious on the whole. Consider, for example, the cliché case of my robbing Peter to pay Paul. Here we are wont to say, somewhat misleadingly, that I am well intentioned toward Paul. However, I do not act virtuously, not even toward Paul, since my action is on the whole vicious, made so by the disrespect and (at least, instrumental) malice toward Peter, the viciousness to him, that inhabits my motivational input and infects the action in which it issues.

In fact, several strategies for dealing with apparent conflicts are needed, perhaps tied to a taxonomy of conflicts, and not all of them subordinate virtues to some externally determined weighting. Here is a start to the process of distinguishing different theoretical levels at which conflicts can be resolved. The point is to deny that some prior and independent overriding moral principle is needed to rank virtues or their importance.

Level 1. Some agent *S*'s taking act-option *A1* more deeply offends against (is more distant from, is more averse to) virtue *V1* (within morally constitutive role relationship *R1*) than would her taking act-option *A2* offend against *V2* (in any *R2*). Moreover, in a choice situation of the relevant sort, this comparative judgment grounds the further judgments that *S* ought to choose *A2* and ought to reject *A1*. (This holds, e.g., in cases where *A1* is a "counterofficious" act or omission, in a technical sense of being contrary, in its motivation, to that underlying virtuous conduct in the context, and *A2* is "inofficious," where this latter means the action is, in its motivation, at some distance from that behind fully virtuous behavior in the situation.)

Level 2. Virtue *V1*, against which *S*'s taking act-option *A1* offends within role *R1*, is more significant within *R1* than is virtue *V2*, against which her taking *A2* offends (within some *R2*). Moreover, in a choice situation of the relevant sort, this comparative judgment grounds the further judgments that *S* ought to choose and take *A1* and ought to reject *A2*. (This holds, e.g., in cases where *V1* is a "constitutive" virtue, in our technical sense of being a way of having the will so directed as would count toward the agent's being good in one or more of her morally determinative roles, and *V2* is merely "contributive," in the sense that it makes a causal contribution to her developing or maintaining such an orientation of will in the face of fears or other temptations.)

We should also allow in principle for a third possibility:

Level 3. Morally constitutive role relationship *R1*, against one or more of whose virtues *S*'s taking act-option *A1* offends, holds precedence over role *R2* in that *S*'s fulfilling *R1* in the life of someone *S1* counts more toward *S1*'s leading a flourishing life than does *S*'s fulfilling *R2* so count in the life of anyone *S2*. Moreover, in a choice situation of the relevant sort, this comparative judgment grounds the further judgments that *S* ought to choose and take *A1* and ought to reject *A2*. (This holds, e.g., in cases where *R1* is a central form of human sociality and *R2* is comparatively peripheral.)

The closest analogue to Richardson's "norm specification" occurs at Level 1, where we tease out the implications for action of various role virtues. Still, at Level 2 there is also a more distant analogue, as we uncover and understand the significance and place of various virtues within a role. However, I am skeptical about Level 3 conflicts. *S*'s having a flourishing human life involves her having a variety of forms of relationships filled and fulfilled in her life. The issue should be whether *S*'s having a bad friend would *count* against her life being a fulfilled one, not whether this person (*S1*'s) being a bad friend to *S* would, in light of *S*'s many other good friendships, *cause* a substantial diminution in the quality of *S*'s life. It is a *way/respect* in which *S1*'s life goes badly, not *itself* the *degree* or *extent* to which her life goes badly, and it may not even make sense to ask *how badly* it then goes. If that doesn't make sense, then the possibility of Level 3 conflicts and their resolution may be undermined.

If many of the principal virtues are forms of goodwill, and if vice is a matter of opposition to and attitudinal distance from some virtue, then one way of resolving an apparent conflict is to say that one action would express a motivational stance that is more distant from the relevant virtue than would the alternative course of action. What matters is that an agent would fail somebody more grievously in the morally determinative roles one plays in her life by performing one action than she would fail anyone in any role by performing the other. An act of intentionally harming Alicia, say, is more distant from the virtue of goodwill toward her—the stance that makes one a good friend, or partner, or simply fellow human being to her—than is an act of foreseeably (but without intention) failing to secure her or another some good. That will normally hold, except when intending her harm is not vicious making (and therein wrong making) because of some moral offense by Alicia that has lowered the standards of response to her in such a way that punitively willing her this evil need not make one bad in any of one's morally determinative role relationships to her. This provides support for the moral importance of the difference between instrumental and incidental agency, thereby securing a key claim behind the controversial form of moral reasoning called "double effect."

Fuller explication and defense of this much-derided, but I think essential, form of moral reasoning is a topic for another time. What is important for our purposes here is that adapting an analogue of Richardson's model of norm specification to our virtues-based account permits us to avoid the charge that virtues will conflict in ways requiring us to appeal to some intrinsic value, deeper than virtue, in order to assign the various vices and virtues (or, better, vicious and virtuous responses) comparative weights. Doing that would show that virtues are not basic in comparison with value and duty. However, I have tried to indicate that there is an attractive alternative procedure.

Consider this case of apparent conflict: my business partner, Jacob Marley, wants me to join him in exploiting our employee, Bob Cratchit. Must I then choose between being a bad (uncooperative) business partner to Marley and being a bad (exploitive) employer to Cratchit?[49] Obviously not, for we are bound (by the factors that would make us good occupants of the relevant role) not to serve the role respondent's actual preferences but, rather, to seek her genuine welfare, as best we can discern it. Thus, there is a limit to my departure from Thomson's so-called objective accounts of acting generously, justly, and in ways characterized by opposed forms of viciousness. That is because in order for my seeking the good for someone *S1* to be virtuous, I must seek genuine goods for her, at least ultimately, even if I mislocate them. Moreover, the kinds of respectful goodwill that constitute various moral virtues must acknowledge the other's view of her welfare as privileged, entitled to substantial, limited deference (though not as absolutely controlling, nor infallible). This also means there is a limit to how far I depart from the cognition-stressing conceptions of virtue offered by Lawrence Blum and John McDowell, among others. The moral subject responding to some person's situation with the virtue of benevolence must have some substantial understanding of what a person is and what, as a person, she needs or benefits from.

Among the advantages of this approach, then, is that the virtues-based account of wrongdoing makes the justification of claims that some action or omission is immoral to be more explicit, accessible. It also links duty to value without the problems that attend consequentialism. Additionally, it retains James Urmson's insight that wrongness may be scalar/gradient even if obligation is nonscalar.[50] (Or indirectly scalar—how distant from vicious is *S*'s *V*-ing?) Thus, when such a view is combined with patient focus, as I have urged, it enables the moral theorist to sidestep Kant's stark choice between the Scylla of hypothetical imperatives (contrast the difficulties of some of Foot's early writings) and the Charybdis of categorical imperatives, with the austere, formalistic, legalistic, ratio-

49. This type of problem was suggested to me by Roman Garcia, when I presented some of this material at Fordham University.

50. J. O. Urmson, *Emotive Theory of Ethics* (Oxford: Oxford University Press, 1969).

nalistic theory they bring.[51] Properly employed within VBMT, virtues can assess persons and reactions on a scale, as well as actions, while permitting verdictive, nonscalar classifications, and do so all on the basis of an action's motivational input. This avoids several familiar absurdities of consequentialism while retaining its commonsense insight that the right must derive from the good. Here, right (permissible, nonvicious) action connects to what is good by expressing attitudinal responses that tend to be good-making, as Aristotle said of the virtues.

In virtues-based theory, moral virtues can capture the crucial relational aspect of morality, especially when elaborated within a role-centered moral theory. Charles Larmore claims that the basic moral "situation" and "relationship" is not that of agent and spectator (which view he attributes to Adam Smith), but that of conversants each viewing the other and wanting to be so viewed by her.[52] However, this emphasis on discourse indicates too local, rarified, and recent a conception. Surely, it is deeper and more accurate to see such roles as those of friend, confidant, and the like as basic. What matters, then, is not the opinion that some hypothetical spectator has of our actions, not even her feeling of sympathy, but what a normal, properly reared, and socialized person would want *as* connected to us as friend, confidant, or whatever the relationship is that is pertinent in the situation. That is not merely epistemically useful in finding out what is right or wrong (as is Smith's hypothetical ideal spectator) but as justification, in making the act right/wrong, constituting its moral status and generating the application of moral predicates to it. *Pace* Larmore, "morality" is not "invented" by us in this account. Rather, the approach is naturalistic, identifying as a kind of natural law certain familiar person-to-person role relationships because they are ones it is human nature for a person to want, need, and benefit from having someone to fill in her life; and certain modes of psychological response as ones that, when

51. David Gallagher ("Person and Love in Aquinas," *Acta Philosophica* 4 [1995]: 51–71) says Thomas's account of natural moral obligation of a person *S* to love others as she loves herself (*ST* I-II, q. 26, a. 4; I, q. 60, a. 3) cannot be grounded in S's desire for happiness because what Scripture enjoins is a form of "friendship-love," love of others "*bona simpliciter*" (for their own sake), rather than a form of "desire-love." We friendship-love a person by loving some other thing (their happiness) for the person's sake, whereas we desire-love other goods relatively, "*bona secundum quid.*"

52. Charles Larmore, "Visible Hand," review of *Adam Smith and the Virtues of Enlightenment* by Charles Griswold, *New Republic* 221, no. 16 (October 18, 1999): 42.

developed into traits of character, tend to count toward the one filling (occupying) the role being good in it, including being disposed to act well in it. Since "morality," whatever that is, is not our invention in this account, it also allows us to avoid Larmore's talk of what morality's "point" or "purpose" is. (What is the point of color?) Of course, we can say that the reason we care so much about *these* predicates, making a big deal of our social practice of moral evaluation, virtue development, and so on, is that we naturally want these forms of relationships and so care about how others (and we ourselves) acquit themselves (ourselves) in them. Finally, as we saw, against Korsgaard, value facts can now be seen as commonplace, a subset of the world's facts.

7. INPUT-DRIVE: SEEING VIRTUES AS INTERNAL TO THE MORAL LAW OF NATURE

Central to the sort of VBMT here articulated and defended is the claim that an action's being morally right or wrong, permitted or obligatory or forbidden, its being consonant with or violative of the natural moral law, depends on the virtuous or vicious states of the agent's mind that input her conduct. We can call this an "input-driven" account of the moral status of behavior. Even if I am correct to think that such an account can overcome the problem, briefly raised in the previous section, of conflicts among the virtues and vices and across actions, the theorist may nonetheless ask why she should endorse such an approach to and understanding of actions' moral status. I will conclude by briefly indicating some of the theoretical advantages of a VBMT that incorporates input-drive and role-centering.

We can profit from contrasting the sort of virtues-based (and role-centered, patient-focused, and input-driven) account of the natural moral law defended here with some influential alternatives. As the moral law is here understood, it can properly be said to be a natural law in that it is natural human needs, interests, and welfare that shape and determine the morally constitutive role-relationships, their virtues, and their interaction, and therefrom the moral status, including the deontic status, of the actions and omissions that they inform.

My discussion of recent alternatives draws on a helpful summary, interpretation, and critique offered in the work of Fr. Arthur Madigan,

S.J.[53] Madigan expresses concern that John Wild, in *Plato's Modern Enemies,* and Mortimer Adler, in *The Time of Our Lives,* do little to justify their claims that natural law teleology grounds not only prudential advice but categorical duties and human rights. Moreover, he worries that Thomas Higgins, in *Man as Man,* and Austin Fagothey, in *Right and Reason* (2nd ed.), achieve moral laws only by construing them as a natural law that participates in the eternal law that is discerned through natural and philosophical theology. Finally, Madigan seems uneasy because Finnis, Germain Grisez, and their collaborators in what has been called the "New Natural Law" theory explicitly invoke additional freestanding principles of practical reason and of morality to make the crucial move from the goods that fulfill an individual in her nature to moral obligations.[54] My approach improves on all three of these camps of twentieth-century Aristotelians by interpreting (1) an action's wrongness (violation of law and duty) as its being vicious *(virtues-basing),* (2) its viciousness as its being such as to make the agent somehow bad when settled as a fixed disposition, (3) its being relevantly bad-making as within roles (role-relativity, indeed, *role-centering*), and (4) the morally constitutive roles as personal (especially, but not exclusively, *inter*personal) and as *patient-focused.* (Interestingly, Madigan ascribes to Fagothey an articulation of natural law in terms of the agent's "three principal relations: relations to material things, to other human beings, and of course to God," where "the living out of these three relations is the matter or content of the ethical life.")[55]

We should also consider a wider context. Robert Audi reminds us that C. D. Broad, in his influential *Five Types of Ethical Theory,* holds an action's rightness to be a function of its *fittingness* (to the agent's situation) and its *utility.*[56] Broad treated its fittingness as the tendency of a type of action to be wrong where an action may fit a situation in some

53. Arthur Madigan, S.J., "What Happens to Aristotelian Teleology in the 20th Century?" text distributed for Fall 2005 talk to Boston Colloquium in Medieval Philosophy.

54. We should note that Fr. Madigan explicitly allows that there are other camps of neo-Aristotelians, including that of the later Alasdair MacIntyre and that of Martha Nussbaum. His discussion is not meant to be exhaustive.

55. Madigan, "What Happens to Aristotelian Teleology, " 3, quoting Fagothey, 133–40.

56. Robert Audi, *The Good in the Right* (Princeton, N.J.: Princeton University Press, 2001), ch. 1.

ways (on account of some features) but not in others. He also held that there was no way to commensurate the different types of fittingness with each other, nor one for calculating its fittingness against considerations of utility. It is worth noting that my VBMT improves on this in several ways. First, by conceiving fittingness in terms of "good"-talk and this "good"-talk as a virtue ascription, it reduces fittingness to a moral concept with which we have more familiarity and of which we have better accounts. My lying to you "misfits," as we might say, the situation of your request for information in that the intent (to deceive?) with which it is made contributes to making me bad in certain role relationships I occupy in your life. Second, Broad's notion of a "tendency" to wrongness is also now supplanted by that of the viciousness of the action and therein with that of a contribution (causal or, more important, constitutive) to making someone into a vicious/bad *R*, where this variable stands for one of the morally determinative role relationships. Third, it therein also replaces fittingness with a concept that comprehends the moral agent more broadly as a full moral subject, a person, in relationships with (herself and other) persons. Fourth, it unifies fittingness with utility because, within VBMT, even utility takes on moral significance only as the virtue of benevolence within the agent, that is, on the input side of the (contemplated or completed) action, not on its output side.

Relatedly, Robert Goodin approvingly quotes Broad to the effect that any reasonable moral theory must accord an action's effects some moral importance. I deny that, agreeing with Abelard's insight that some intentions are "right in themselves" (i.e., in virtue of their content in their context), while any action is (called) "right" only because/in that it (relevantly) stems from good intentions.[57]

Among the reasons for treating wrongdoing as acting viciously, we have already mentioned Richardson's insistence on the desirability of transparency in norms, Williams's stress on the importance of thicker (more descriptively rich) moral terms, Thomson's arguments that there is no such thing as simply being good or bad but only a variety of ways of each, and my own suggestion that we adapt Thomson's value-theoretic point to model a variety of ways in which an action or omission can be

57. Robert Goodin, *Protecting the Vulnerable* (Chicago: University of Chicago Press, 1985).

wrong.[58] Each of these, in its own way, provides a reason to understand all moral wrongdoing, every violation of the natural law, as an instance of conduct that is vicious in being too far removed from and opposed to behaving virtuously. Such an account provides the most familiar, most natural, and richest way of meeting Richardson's demand that our normative discourse make manifest not just *that* but *why* a course of conduct is immoral, of accommodating Williams's well-motivated preference for moral language rich in descriptive information, and of adapting to the moral status of action the insight of Thomson's: as nothing is simply bad, so neither is anything merely wrong but only morally wrong, in that it is dishonest, cruel, disrespectful, deceitful, or in some other respect vicious.

Further, if it is true, as some of us have argued, that assertions often theorized as committed to intrinsic value (and disvalue) are properly construed instead as claims about what it is virtuous or (vicious) to want and otherwise favor, then the input-driven account of morally permissible, obligatory, and forbidden conduct lends important theoretical unity to the moral realm.[59] In such a theory, the central types of moral claim would be unified because (1) claims about what it is that ought and is required to be done, the so-called *Tunsollen,* would join (2) claims about what it is (the existence of) which is valuable, what has been called the *Seinsollen,* as grounded in and analyzable in terms of claims about what attitudinal features enhance a person, are the ones that make her good and that she should have, what we can call the *Soseinsollen.*

Construing wrongdoing as behaving viciously also avoids the problem of allowing consequence-luck a substantial role in determining whether a course of conduct was right or wrong. Thus, it evades a principal objection not only to classical aggregative, maximizing consequentialism but to any theory that permits what merely happens to occur as a result of one's action a role in making it permissible or impermissible.

Treating immorality as vicious conduct maintains and establishes the centrality of agency—the desires, valuings, likes, and volitions with or from which we act—in shaping the moral status of actions and omissions, therein preserving an insight of the Kantians. Moreover, by cen-

58. See Richardson, "Specifying Norms"; Williams, "Evolution"; Thomson, *Goodness and Advice.*

59. Again, see Zimmerman, "Nature of Intrinsic Value"; Hurka, "Vice."

tering on certain critical roles that a person plays in some person's life and, within those roles, concentrating attention on the psychological attitudes through which the moral subject regards persons, this approach captures the intuition, only recently noticed and discussed by ethical theorists, that establishes personal and interpersonal relations as the focus and heart of morality.[60]

Finally, this input-driven and virtues-based understanding of moral life accommodates insights from the history of modern moral philosophy. First, it captures and reveals the truth in Hume's claim that actions matter morally merely as signs of the agent's character, while avoiding the exaggeration in it. That is, it shows how Hume was right to think that a morally admirable or reprehensible action comes from an instance of admirable or reprehensible motivation, without the implausible implication in his view that this motivation must always already be established as one of the agent's character traits.

Second, it shows an insight behind Ross's terminology for his prima facie duties, one that Ross himself gleaned but resisted because of his commitment to a supposedly "deontological" school. Ross divided what he claimed to be irreducible prima facie duties into duties of fidelity, gratitude, justice, self-improvement, beneficence, and nonmaleficence. It is striking that the first three are plainly traditional virtues of will and the fourth can also be seen as pointing to the virtue of concern to improve one's own virtues and talents.[61] Indeed, even the duties he classifies as those of beneficence and nonmaleficence are plainly renamed versions of what the classical utilitarians and their theological forebears called "benevolence," which is also easily recognizable as a moral virtue. Because Ross was convinced (for reasons I have rebutted elsewhere and will not here review) that an agent's intentions and motives were no part of her duty, and because he was sure that moral virtue derives from prior duty, he wanted to be careful to select nonpsychological names for the major types of duty. It is thus especially significant that he found himself unable to distinguish the different types without repeated recourse to virtue terms. Where he did manage some success, in his terminology of

60. See Samuel Scheffler, *Boundaries and Allegiances* (Oxford: Oxford University Press, 2003), esp. ch. 6, and, more directly on this, his "Morality and Reasonable Partiality," talk to MIT Department of Linguistics and Philosophy, spring 2007.

61. Ross, *Right and the Good,* ch. 2.

"beneficence" and "nonmaleficence," it is noteworthy that the language seems strained, artificially constrained by dubious and independent theoretical convictions, and, worse, he exposes his theory to one of the same problems in the utilitarianism he rightly rejected; that is, he leaves himself open to making an action's moral status hinge on mere luck in how the course of events flows after the agent has stopped.

Here I quit this sketch and commend its further development to colleagues, especially those interested in extending and revising the moral tradition of natural law and uncovering its foundation in the virtues.

Jean De Groot

6 Teleology and Evidence

Reasoning about Human Nature

Appealing to natural law as a basis for moral judgments presupposes that human beings have a nature. In living things, a nature is something organic. That is, parts of the body have functions that serve ends. These ends harmonize to benefit the living thing as a whole.[1] Some ends are constitutive of the way of life distinctive to a kind of living thing—for example, the human being's rationality. The organic character of functions and ends applies not only to the involuntary—for example, the function of the liver—but also to what is within one's power to do or not do—for example, the way one satisfies desires for food, sex, or friendship. Human beings make choices in these areas, and our choices are guided by the happiness we seek. It is up to us to make choices consonant with the sort of natural goods—the harmonizing or constitutive ends—that belong to the embodied rational and mortal beings we are.

This is a teleological picture of the human being.[2] It presumes that

I am grateful to Msgr. Robert Sokolowski, Michael Gorman, Angela McKay, and Sophia Aguirre for comments on earlier versions of this essay and for references to the social science literature and to modern functionalist treatments of teleology.

1. For this meaning of organic *(organikos)*, see Aristotle *De Anima* II.412a28–b9.

2. John M. Cooper says that Aristotle's ethics is not teleological, as has always been assumed, because Aristotle does not make what is right follow what is good, right being intended to maximize the good. As Cooper points out, this is teleology "in a modern sense" and is a position defined in opposition to deontology. For Aristotle, *eudaimonia*, the ultimate good for human life, is not "specified independently" of the virtues that contribute to it. Happiness is "identical with a lifetime of morally virtuous action." See *Reason and Human Good in Aristotle* (Cambridge, Mass.: Harvard University Press, 1975), 88 (hereafter

we by nature act on desires and that these desires have particular ends proper to them. One may develop an approach to natural law based almost exclusively on the rational pursuit of human goods, but as teleology this is narrow. The teleological view is most plausible in a setting where the human is a distinctive kind of animal among other animals that also pursue natural ends. For if natural law involves claims extending to our physical and psychological nature, then it would be odd, given our kinship to other living things, if we were the only creatures whose physical and psychological nature involved natural goods. The scientific immaturity of Aristotle's astronomy and chemistry has made some classical philosophers conclude that they should also drop Aristotle's teleology of living things as the larger context for human goods. In doing this, they lose a rich background for understanding the teleology of the human being and society. For it was within consideration of the organic connectedness of natural ends in other living things that Aristotle developed his view of human life.[3]

In what follows, I will show how teleological thinking of an Aristotelian sort may be taken as a template for analyzing natural goods in contemporary human life. The achievements of modern biology are often taken as a stumbling block to natural law claims, which treat the human being in a way that combines his biological and rational natures. I will begin by addressing why claims that there are natural goods seem to fall short of scientific cogency (section 1). Next, I will present a rationale by which teleological thinking is not incompatible with evolutionist interpretations of human origins (section 2). I will address the nature of the necessity found in natural systems that are teleological (section 3). Finally, I will show that knowledge about natural goods in human life is gained by reasoning that follows this natural necessity (section 4). Throughout this endeavor, a central issue will be recognizing the way empirical facts figure as evidence within natural patterns that are teleological. My assumption is that teleology cannot be proven in a way that

cited as *Reason*). Cooper makes an important distinction, but it does not affect the sense of teleology used here. Cooper confirms the grounding of the moral life in human nature and practical experience. Aristotle treats *eudaimonia* as "the fulfillment of the natural capacities of the human species" (*Reason*, 89 n1).

3. On Aristotle's methodological commitment to considering animal nature in relation to man's, see Étienne Gilson, *From Aristotle to Darwin and Back Again*, trans. John Lyon (South Bend, Ind.: University of Notre Dame Press, 1984), 4.

would satisfy a skeptic or a Cartesian rationalist, but that it is the most plausible interpretation of a constellation of facts about human life that can be established with the degree of accuracy possible for social science. To see its plausibility, however, requires looking at facts in the way they actually relate to one another in teleological systems. Although there is little in contemporary philosophy of science to foster this view of facts, this way of thinking is present in contemporary efforts to capture the organic character of human life in society (section 5).

1.

In popular discussion and in day-to-day conversations, to say that there are distinctive goal-directed activities defining human happiness is a view regarded, even by those who believe it, as needing proof. This is because broad directives touching on intimate details of human life are read off the teleological view of human nature—things concerning sexual behavior; marriage; procreation; care of the sick, young, elderly, and unborn—and these directives meet stiff opposition in a secular society organized around utility, pleasure, and personal freedom.[4] It is thought that either very strong empirical evidence or a strong reason needs to be offered to convince others that happiness depends in some way on taking bodily powers, like the procreative, or deep-seated sentiments, like traditional filial piety, as indices of good choices and action. Much evidence has been brought forward by social scientists that, for instance,

—children in divorced families do not expect their own marriages to last;[5]

—cohabitation is less stable than marriage, and marriages undertaken after cohabitation are less stable than marriages without prior cohabitation;[6]

4. Widespread contemporary skepticism about moral foundations militates against acceptance of any moral claims as more than mere opinion. See Edward T. Oakes on the "emotivist" school of ethics in "The Achievement of Alasdair MacIntyre," *First Things* 65 (1996): 22–26, and John Rist, *Real Ethics* (Cambridge: Cambridge University Press, 2002), 1–9.

5. See, e.g., Jay D. Teachman, "The Childhood Living Arrangement of Children and the Characteristics of Their Marriages," *Journal of Family Issues* 25, no. 1 (January 2004): 86–111.

6. For a review of research, see David Popenoe and Barbara Dafoe Whitehead, *Should We Live Together? What Young Adults Need to Know about Cohabitation before Marriage,*

—abortion is associated with depression and anxiety in women choosing abortion;[7]

—a legal sanction for physician-assisted suicide in the case of terminal illness leads to assisted suicide for grief or depression.[8]

Taken by itself, however, evidence of this sort constitutes fragmentary consequentialist arguments. These are bad outcomes, most agree, but the ethical framework in which they are meaningful still needs to be determined. A utilitarian could say these consequences indicate only that adjustments are needed in how divorce, abortion, or euthanasia is administered by the parties involved or by the state so that the inevitable human self-concern, that is, avoidance of pain, is taken into account. The social scientist who is sensitive to natural law may reply to the utilitarian that a well-designed research model can rule out other causes—and hence other views of human nature—demonstrating a very strong connection between, for instance, a lifelong commitment to marriage, on the one hand, and success and happiness in other aspects of life. This is an important point in the context of the methodology of verification and falsification. Hypotheses consistent with natural law claims generate results that best fit the facts. From a logical standpoint, however, no explanatory hypothesis is ever proven true by accumulation of evidence, however well the theory fits the facts. In human affairs, the factors at work are notoriously diverse and complex, and this is an additional reason to discount even strong evidence in favor of the hypothesis of a fixed human nature that figures significantly in achieving human happiness. Thus, whatever the source of popular skepticism about natural law, both the logic of making claims in modern science and the complex and cluttered nature of the subject matter, human life, are taken to reinforce that skepticism.

If rejecting natural law claims can be rationalized on the basis of the logical structure of science, is there anything in the structure of science

---

National Marriage Project, Rutgers University, 2000, available online at *http://marriage.rutgers.edu*.

7. J. M. Thorp Jr., K. F. Hartmann, and Elizabeth Shadigian, "Long-Term Physical and Psychological Health Consequences of Induced Abortion: Review of the Evidence," *Obstetrical and Gynecological Survey* 58, no. 1 (January 2003): 67–79.

8. Herbert Hendin and Gerald Klerman, "Physician-Assisted Suicide: The Dangers of Legalization," *American Journal of Psychiatry* 150, no. 1 (January 1993): 143–45; H. Hendin, "Assisted Suicide, Euthanasia and Suicide Prevention: The Implications of the Dutch Experience," *Suicide and Life-Threatening Behavior* 25, no. 1 (Spring 1995): 193–203.

or its subject matter in nature that supports those claims? I contend that the sort of social science evidence cited above, drawn as it is from examination of actual human flourishings and dysfunctions, does legitimately serve as verification of a natural law approach to human goods, but that its evidential force works differently than verification within the hypothetico-deductive model of science. There are two ways this difference is manifest. First and most important, the logical structure of teleological relations does not readily conform to the model of geometrical deduction. The type of necessity structuring relations within a teleological system is different from the logical necessity of a modern axiomatic system. This difference brings with it that, secondly, evidence has a different import in reasoning about teleological relations.[9] Facts and states of affairs look backward and forward, so to speak. This is because, in the teleological patterns of animal and then human life, the empirical is present in a system of interdependent ends. The evidential force of any fact is not separate from the conditions that contribute to it nor from the ends or obstructions of ends to which it contributes. Accordingly, when we turn to reasoning about facts concerning human nature, there must be a distinction made between deductive reasoning incorporating teleological elements and the more familiar deduction based on the model of geometry. Though the hypothetico-deductive style of reasoning is what we always bring to analysis of facts, it is not the kind of reasoning appropriate to teleological connections presently or habitually holding.

The main burden of my essay, then, is showing how natural teleology works in general in order to make clear how facts are situated within it. I believe this project aids social science research supportive of natural law by placing these studies in a philosophical context that is teleological. The point is not that the ordinary scientific model of verification is somehow wrongheaded. This mode of reasoning fits the materials and methods of modern science. In order to be convincing because of its truthfulness and fidelity to the facts, however, any evidence must finally be

9. The conventional notion of evidence presupposes empirical facts or sensible data simple enough to be matched to conclusions or predictions in a structure of deductive proof, verification, or falsification. Facts constitute evidence, when brought to bear as verification for a theory. I will use roughly this sense of evidence in discussing teleology but will understand evidence as confirmatory in a different way. Facts and states of affairs of the ordinary sort are meaningful in teleological patterns, however. We do not need a different conception of a fact.

placed in the explanatory framework that fits the structure and interrelation of the facts themselves. If teleology is part of nature, then evaluating teleological claims empirically must take account of how empirical facts signify within teleological patterns. Correspondingly, teleological claims about particular aspects of human nature will not be convincing in the context of reasoning incapable of accommodating the sort of necessity at work in teleology. Accordingly, we must be able to identify the type of necessity involved in teleology and the reasoning suited to it.

2.

My exposition of the place of the empirical within teleology begins with an examination of Aristotle's most basic texts on goal-directed action: *Nicomachean Ethics* I, *Physics* II, *Parts of Animals* I, and *Movement of Animals* 4–7.[10] Two issues are crucial: (1) production *(poiêsis),* which is action bringing something about, and (2) the form of necessity attendant upon production, hypothetical necessity. Both natural generation and human action bring something about, and so production is strategic for understanding the way human action is related to natural ends. By hypothetical necessity, an existing end entails materials or processes on which that end depends in order to exist. A child, for instance, must have a minimum healthy diet to develop strong limbs or to be attentive enough to learn in school. The opposite number to production—what necessarily will be—is not subject to this dependence on antecedents. Apart from the divine, it is mathematical truths that most readily spring to mind as necessary in this way. The strong possibility that human goods will fail to be achieved, though aimed for, follows from this difference between the eternal and the produced. Only what must be brought into being can fail to be perfected.[11]

10. References to Aristotle use Bekker numbers in the Oxford Greek editions of these works. Abbreviations of titles, where used, are as follows: *Nicomachean Ethics (NE), Parts of Animals (Parts An), Eudemian Ethics (EE), Generation of Animals (Gen An), Movement of Animals (MA).* The edition of *Movement of Animals* is by Martha Nussbaum, *Aristotle's* De Motu Animalium: *Text with Translation, Commentary, and Interpretive Essays* (Princeton, N.J.: Princeton University Press, 1978). The edition of *Parts of Animals* is the Berlin and Oxford edition revised by A. L. Peck in *Aristotle,* vol. 23 (Cambridge, Mass.: Loeb Classical Library, 1968).

11. On this point, see Oliva Blanchette, *The Perfection of the Universe According to Aquinas* (University Park: Pennsylvania State University Press, 1992), 42–48, and Alasdair

That human goods are contingent—they must be brought about by our efforts—is important for understanding natural law. Broadly speaking, there are two ways that natural goods in human life may be contingent: (1) as natural ends fail to determine their matter, and (2) as voluntary action is taken contrary to the goals implicit in natural ends.[12] A child lacking a healthy diet is an example of the first. An adult ruining his health with drunkenness is an example of the second. Evidence for what constitutes a better way of life for a person or society is always brought to bear on a human situation in which either type of failure is possible. So, even if various human experiences, whether positive or negative, are evidence for some way of life being perennially better—for example, it is better not to live in a way that ruins one's health—still natural law does not either determine the better to happen or prevent its opposite. This seems obvious, but it is a point not drawn upon enough in discussions of natural law.

More than once in *Nicomachean Ethics,* Aristotle points out that people think there is not anything good by nature because they expect the naturally good to prevent choice of its opposite.[13] A natural good should show itself in the way fire burns, as necessary and always the same. On the contrary, he says, everything human is changeable or inconstant in effect *(kinēton).* Even good things sometimes bring harm in their wake.

MacIntyre, *Three Rival Versions of Moral Enquiry* (South Bend, Ind.: University of Notre Dame Press, 1990), 60–66.

12. Within this division, there is a range of ways ends may be contingent. A distinction may be made between action performed in accordance with or because of form, on the one hand, and the best action in accordance with form, on the other. In other words, there may be functional activity expressing form without the *telos* given by form being reached. Additionally, physical disability can prevent the realization of good and fulfilling ends ardently desired. It can also be the circumstance in which someone denies natural ends are truly natural and prior. For an interpretation of disability in relation to human ends, see Alasdair MacIntyre, *Dependent Rational Animals* (Chicago: Open Court, 1999), chs. 8–9. Another source of contingency appears when genuine fulfillment of the human good is sought but without the habitual disposition or strength of mind to achieve it. Finally, human goods can be known but deliberately thwarted because of boredom, recklessness, or malice. There is an important structural difference in types of human action that should be noted. Some actions are pursued for their own sake. In this case, when the end is present in the action itself, action is not a means to an end in the way typical of production. This is the distinction between *poiēsis* (production) and *praxis* (action). Virtuous action is *praxis* but involves productive analysis in the selection of actions to achieve an end that has been identified as desirable by the virtuous agent.

13. See *NE* I.3.1094b14–19 and V.7.1134b24–35a5.

Some people are harmed by possessing wealth, for instance (1094b19). This changeability is due to the need to bring goods into being in a human environment of many actors and many differing circumstances. It does not mean that the natural goods may themselves change. What should be clear, however, is that to understand how natural goods are involved with inclination and choice, we must grasp the sense of natural necessity that is consistent with the contingency of production. Evidence of natural goods appears in this context of the natural and voluntary interleafed.[14]

Aristotle's original presentation, in *Physics* II, of teleology in nature is relevant to this task of clarifying the relation of the natural and the contingent in human life. Form, in *Physics* II, is a cause that is determinative in some senses—that is, it regularly delimits the essence and character of natural things and defines an environment of what would be good for those things. At the same time, it does not narrowly determine natural outcomes with respect to that good. In the case of the human being, for instance, nature sets what a healthy body looks like for a seven-year-old child, but it does not determine how any child will get the range of nutrition that makes a healthy body. Similarly, human rationality determines that an educated person makes the best contributor to society, but it does not rule out that children will be poorly educated or perversely exploited. Apart from failures of execution, form also allows for adjustment to differing circumstances so that the *telos* of the living thing is expressed in different ways. Diets rich in fat, or low in fat but high in carbohydrates, can both produce healthy human beings. So also, human rationality permits different assessments by different people of what is the best form of society. Thus, some variations in production are impediments to actualization of *telos,* but others are simply variations within the range of form. What we seek to understand in the case of the human being is how an inborn natural disposition defines a situation so far as to affect what humans bring about for themselves, when they act without compulsion and for their own good. We are interested in making clear the *telos* expres-

14. I use the term "interleaf" to indicate separate stories, or rational accounts of action, consistent with one another and applying together. Where the necessary by nature does not rule out the voluntary in human action, the necessary and voluntary do not *mix* so that they are indistinguishable, nor do they compound to form a new whole different from either. Rather, each remains what it is.

sive of human form. An account by form does not rule out, however, that rational creatures sometimes choose actions inconsistent with the environment of their own good or falling short of their *telos*. Form allows for the underdetermination of outcomes by ends that is so typical of human behavior.

To understand how teleology works, then, we must consider form in the context of production. The sense of natural necessity appropriate to form will reside in the relation of materials and actions to the ends they serve or constitute. If naturally occurring teleological patterns define human life, then some cases of antecedents serving ends are exemplary of how the human *telos* is achieved. To pursue this question, it is helpful to distinguish levels of claims for the relation of an end to what produces it. Becoming thirsty on a hike, one can drink from a brook along the trail, but the brook is not made for thirsty hikers. A spider's web, on the other hand, seems made for catching food for the spider. But is the spider like the skilled carpenter? In making a cabinet, the furniture maker takes actions in succession with the specific aim of each contributing to the next stage of production. I will investigate differences in cases like these in terms of a lower and higher threshold of meaning for one thing being for the sake of another. The lower threshold is like the relation of the brook to slaking thirst. The higher threshold is the deliberate, intelligent utilization of materials by the furniture maker. The point will be to explicate the middle case, the natural orienting of means and subordinate ends to a natural *telos*.

In *Physics* II, Aristotle says that it is clear for most natural processes that parts of an activity or process are for the sake of the end. From his reasoning and examples, it seems that Aristotle has in mind the fact that there are intelligible, functional culminations of certain processes. Think of embryological developments, the activity of honeybees, and the growth of fat and fur in the polar bear at a particular time of year. Each of these is a process intelligible in relation to what I shall call a "macroend." A *macroend* is a natural goal that other subordinate goals serve in a natural context forming some sort of unit. The honeybee may be oriented at a particular moment only to obtaining nectar, but this does not prevent the macroend of its activity being discernible as honey making. For Aristotle as for us, local macroends like honey making are not in dispute. "Local" here refers to the encounter, by means of individual living things, with natural kinds occupying a particular slice of space and time. We distinguish honeybees and bumblebees, and it can only enrich our understanding to learn that what we call honeybees includes some species that are not honeybees at all.[15] Our understanding of the life history of individual honeybees stays roughly the same. They gather nectar to make honey. What we know about them in a local way can be fairly detailed. It constitutes useful knowledge for beekeepers and for anyone wishing to avoid small wasps that look like honeybees.

The idea of a local macroend includes recognition of natural kinds as well as acknowledgment of the hierarchy of ends involved in the life of individuals of the kind. The natural kind is here conceived as the actuality of being a honeybee. The actuality is defined by a range of activities and relations of ends—gathering nectar, making the comb, evaporating the nectar, capping the cells, tending larvae—and these activities are done by individual bees who may not accomplish them all equally well each time. Local macroends are commonplace knowledge for the layperson but are also both the beginning and the end of biological investigation of anatomy, function, and adaptive significance. Aristotle's term "for-the-sake-of-which" (*to hou heneka,* hereafter *heneka tou,* "for the sake of something") refers to some specific relation between process and macroends, a relation in which the process contributes to bringing about the end. Let us consider the meaning of this term in some detail.

Heneka tou involves but is not limited to conditional necessity.[16] Something is necessary conditionally if it must be or have a certain relation just because something else is so. The being or relation involves priority in some sense. Sometimes, this is only a priority of succession. If Y comes before Z, and X comes before Y, then X comes before Z.[17] While Aristotle does not address conditional necessity by name, he treats hypothetical necessity as a conditionality of existing. What contributes to the end must be present if the end does exist. The "if" clause gives the necessitating condition. The difference between conditional and hypothetical

15. True honeybees are *Apis mellifera.* I draw on the activity of the worker bees, not drones or queen. Honeybees also gather pollen. The pollen and honey together feed the larvae, drones, and queen.

16. On conditional necessity and hypothetical necessity, see John Cooper, "Hypothetical Necessity and Natural Teleology," in *Philosophical Issues in Aristotle's Biology,* ed. Allan Gotthelf and James Lennox (Cambridge: Cambridge University Press, 1987), 243–44.

17. Cooper uses the example of cities progressively "north of" one another.

necessity comes from the latter's involvement with production. In production, without materials and actions contributing to the end, the goal is not realized. Nevertheless, they clearly are not enough to produce the end. This dual aspect of hypothetical necessity—ends, when they exist, necessitate their contributing causes, but materials are necessary for ends to be realized—is important for reasoning about teleological connections. In the series of three above, if Z depends on X and Y for its existence, then if one is to produce Z starting from X, one must pass through Y.

At its lower threshold of meaning, *heneka tou* adds to conditional necessity merely that passing through Y serves arriving at Z. Motion, because it has direction, is *heneka tou* in this minimal sense. The difference between the simple case of covering a distance, on the one hand, and the progression of stages in producing honey, for instance, is that priorities, in the latter case, originate internal to the living thing and its community. The priorities are expressed in actions inseparable from the body and bodily parts that make the actions possible. The lower threshold of "for-the-sake-of-which" means that the spider's web really does serve the spider's health and longevity. This is expressed in the scholarly literature by saying the web is "good for" catching food. Here, a solid, though limited, aspect of valuation arising from a physical context comes into focus.

It is another step, however, to say that the spider builds the web in order to trap food. To make this claim is to say the connection of web and trapping food does not just turn up in a particular instance because the materials at hand and behavioral propensities of the spider are so disposed as to fall together to this result. This would be like the thirsty hiker happening upon the brook. Rather, each step of the building was laid down in order to accomplish the next step and the destination is the final step.[18] This is the higher threshold of the meaning of "for-the-sake-of-which"—the prior is not just needed for the next but was done to bring into being the next. The prior would not have been done or would not have existed without the next that it serves. It is often said that establishing this stronger sense of "for-the-sake-of-which" in natural things is simply beyond

18. This ordering applies even when a final step is not absolutely final. Making honey is hardly final from the standpoint of the worker bee. We can liken the relation of subordinate ends and final ends to musical phrasing. The intelligibility of a set of ends identifies an end as final with respect to some other ends. G. E. M. Anscombe treats this issue in relation to human action in *Intention* (Cambridge, Mass.: Harvard University Press, 2000), ¶ 23.

reach, by Aristotle or any other philosopher, because "in order to accomplish" is identified and defined by intelligence, and we can imagine no case in which such a high standard of relation between prior and next is present without intelligence.[19] "For the sake of" activity is intrinsically minded activity. It is important to note, however, that Aristotle explicitly denies this at the end of *Physics* II.8, where he says that it is a mistake to think that there can be action for the sake of an end only where there is deliberation. So, if intelligence means planning or forethought, then not every case of *heneka tou* activity must have an intelligent cause. Nature acts for an end without deliberation, he says, citing an analogy to craft.[20]

Although the focus of scholarly interpretation of final causality in Aristotle has been the difference between *heneka tou* action based on conditional necessity and the kind originating in mind, I suggest that the difference between them is less important than has been supposed, both for understanding Aristotle and for understanding natural ends. It is more important to understand the sort of relation of means and ends that actually holds for natural things. On this point, there is an area of overlap between an Aristotelian approach and modern biology, particularly in the areas of function and generation.

To say that gathering nectar is for making honey acknowledges that, regardless of how it came into being as bee activity, gathering nectar persists as the actuality of bee qua bee, because it serves the making of honey. Ruth Millikan is noted for making this connection clear in contemporary functionalist discussion.[21] In an evolutionary story about bees,

19. For a lucid treatment of this question from a contemporary standpoint combined with a survey of the philosophical literature, see Mark Bedau, "Where's the Good in Teleology?" *Philosophy and Phenomenological Research* 2, no. 4 (December 1992): 781–806.

20. Beyond the craft analogy, Aristotle explicates the nondeliberateness of nature in two related ways: (1) he speaks of the unfolding of a complicated goal-directed process without continuous contact with the initial mover (*Gen An* II, *MA* 7), developing a notion of *dunamis* as power residing in an array of underlying materials and conditions, and (2) he describes this unfolding as involving no projection of a plan or preparation for its execution by the agent of the action (*Physics* II, *Parts An* I.1). He connects these two approaches by refining the *dunamis* notion to connote a state, either developed naturally or inculcated by habit, that is already achieved and ready to be activated (*De An* II.5). The important point is that, whether he uses the craft analogy or draws on his more sophisticated theoretical notions, Aristotle believes that there are intermediate cases between the weaker and stronger meanings of the term *heneka tou*, between conditional necessity and intelligent planning, and that natural production, like craft activity, falls in the intermediate range.

21. Ruth Garrett Millikan, *Language, Thought, and Other Biological Categories* (Cam-

we would say that the nectar gathering remained as part of bee behavior because it duplicates a function it first performed, perhaps accidentally, on a prior occasion. The focus is on the connection between gathering nectar and honey making as the reason the bees' fieldwork is repeated. Being retained because of its functionality, henceforth nectar gathering takes place because of being good for honey making and the hive in general. Put in Aristotelian terms, the repetition of the behavior is a clue that there is more than the lower threshold meaning of *heneka tou* in the connection between the end and the very predictable activity that contributes to it. Larry Wright, using conceptual analysis, gives an account of function as cause without reference to an evolutionary history.[22] Both Millikan and Wright distinguish cases of antecedent materials and actions being merely good for an end from cases of their being present because of serving the end. Both understand function to be specific enough to entail being a cause of what serves the function. To this extent, functional accounts precede accounts by selection.[23]

The contemporary idea of function as causal does not include an Aristotelian notion of cause as inborn. Nevertheless, in his arguments in *Physics* II.8, Aristotle draws similarly on a combination of (1) the repetition of actions and (2) their functionality or serving the good of the organism, in order to argue for the end as a cause of these actions. He criticizes Empedocles, not for saying that organisms survive because of the functionality of their parts—indeed, Aristotle would endorse this part of Empedocles' account—but because Empedocles cannot explain the regularity of appearance and the specificity of these functional parts in the same type of animal.[24] Since the coincidental cannot produce such regularity, there must be another cause (199a3–5). Aristotle notes as signifi-

---

bridge, Mass.: MIT Press, 1984), ch. 1, and "In Defense of Proper Functions," *Philosophy of Science* 56, no. 2 (1989): 288–302. See also her "Biosemantics," *Journal of Philosophy* 86, no. 6 (1989): 281–97. Millikan's view presupposes biological evolution and understands function as cause without reference to innateness of the cause.

22. Larry Wright, "Functions," *Philosophical Review* 82, no. 2 (April 1973): 139–68, hereafter cited as "Functions," and *Teleological Explanation* (Berkeley and Los Angeles: University of California Press, 1976). See also Christopher Boorse, "Wright on Functions," *Philosophical Review* 85, no. 1 (January 1976): 70–86.

23. Wright argues for this point in "Functions," 162–65.

24. Terence Irwin points out that Empedocles' account itself shows why resort to function is a reasonable explanation of why some feature is present. See his *Aristotle's First Principles* (Oxford: Clarendon Press, 1990), 107.

cant that a particular order of actions leads up to and serves the end and asserts that these actions and their ordering would be the same, whether the end were produced by nature or by craft (199a8–20). This indicates to him that, in the case of the spider and its web, for instance, the materials are present and actions are taken in the particular way they are, each for the sake of the web coming into being. Aristotle recognizes this to be a stronger connection than these stages being simply good for a certain outcome.[25]

Comparing the accounts of the modern functionalists and Aristotle, it seems clear that both recognize a sense of *heneka tou* that is stronger than the relation of the thirsty hiker to the brook while yet not being the furniture maker's deliberateness in relation to his materials. To recognize this stronger but not strongest sense of *heneka tou,* one must only allow (1) that there are local macroends that we recognize on a regular basis, (2) that these macroends are regularly supported by the same antecedents, and (3) that the antecedents contribute to the end in ways that are rationally ascertainable. In such a context, there can be ordering of each step in order to attain an end, as long as there is a principle sufficient to overarch in its effectiveness an entire developmental process. In fact, we are quite familiar with such a principle on the material level, the genetic code or the DNA/RNA complex. We have no difficulty concluding that nectar gathering is for honey making in any event. But because of the genetic code, it is also clear that locally (i.e., for species occupying a definite slice of space and time) and in individual cases, embryological development is for the sake of the individual of the species that culminates that development. Aristotle would insist, however, that any material thing to which one can point, for example, the genetic material, is only the analogue of the true principle, form.

The purpose of my explication of lower and higher threshold meanings of *heneka tou* in relation to the notion of local macroends is simply this: that Aristotle's designation of natural form as a for-the-sake-of-which cause does not claim for form what can only belong to intelligence. Rather, it involves what is from a modern standpoint a lesser claim, namely, that ends reappear in a cyclical way because forms are causes

25. For an analysis of Aristotle's reasoning for final causality based on orderliness of action, see the author's "Form and Succession in Aristotle's *Physics,*" *Proceedings of the Boston Area Colloquium in Ancient Philosophy* 10 (1994): 1–23.

and because means are determined by ends having those forms. This is important for the rhetorical force of natural law claims in a public forum where debate continues about the biological origin of human life. If there are recognizable macroends in nature, then given their relation to the instrumental causes of generation, there are natural forms in a sense strong enough to ground claims for the locally nonaccidental in the life-forms of animals and humans.[26] Accordingly, all that is required to make a plausible claim for paying attention to the natural teleologies of the human being are macroends related to subordinate ends and to various goal-directed actions and other means in such a way as to constitute a naturally occurring network of the goods of human flourishing.[27] Form, taken as a principle of production, really is prior in such a network, and this priority can be the basis for acknowledging the natural contours of human flourishing in custom and law, without our having to agree beforehand on the source of inborn natures or their eternality.

26. There is an interesting confluence of views on this point between a Thomist, like William A. Wallace, who holds to a strong sense of immaterial substantial form for natural entities, and an evolutionary reductionist like William D. Casebeer, who denies immaterial realities. Both point to the stability of species over hundreds of thousands of years to argue for an Aristotelian understanding of definition (Wallace) or proper function (Casebeer) for biological entities. See Wallace's *Modeling of Nature* (Washington, D.C.: The Catholic University of America Press, 1996), 289, and Casebeer's *Natural Ethical Facts* (Cambridge, Mass.: MIT Press, 2003), 50–51.

27. This point could be seen as grounding natural law in an immanent teleology. I do not regard this grounding as absolute, but as serving understanding of how reasoning and evidence support natural law. It is *gnōrimōteron hēmin,* closer to us in the order of knowing. Where immanent teleology is concerned, some distinctions are in order. Larry Arnhart, in *Darwinian Natural Right* (Albany: State University of New York Press, 1998) and "Defending Darwinian Natural Right," *Interpretation* 27, no. 3 (Spring 2000), says that an immanent Aristotelian teleology is consistent with Darwinian evolution because emergent differences in kind are part of a comprehensive science of living forms ("Defending," 264). This seems correct as far as it goes. The way Arnhart argues for this point is less supportable. He says emergent differences include goal-directed action, like social rules for mating and against incest, all of which are explainable in terms of reproductive success ("Defending," 272). In answer, Richard Hassing suspects that the sort of Darwinian account Arnhart embraces in fact tolerates no explanation beyond the reductionist, because reproductive success is not species-specific. Evolutionary emergence as such does not stand over against reductionism; see "Reply to Arnhart," *Interpretation* 28, no. 1 (Fall 2000): 36. Selection of features would have to reflect what is good for the animal because of its own specific nature. In general, to be any support for natural law, hierarchies of reasons—for instance, *why* incest is wrong—must be more than nominal. This calls for a strong sense of natural form for local macroends.

3.

One thing being for the sake of another is the basic structure of actions and ends in an organism. A similar but less unifying interdependence applies to the network living things form among themselves. A network of naturally occurring ends, like the interdependence of all the honeybee activities, has a certain solidity. It is not easily disrupted as a whole, but disruptions that do occur have wide ramifications. The network commands attention on this account and provokes investigation of the reasons why it works as it does. This is important because those versed in natural law tend not to undertake this investigation in the case of human life but instead move quickly toward the divinely ordained reasons for the constitution of human flourishing. Although this grounding is vital, it moves discussion away from the human context harboring unexplored proximate causes of the network and also tends to cast in a theoretical mode what is more accessible in practical terms.[28] "Zipping up the chain of causes" toward the divine is due in part to a poverty of logical resources in modern philosophy for addressing natural production. Intermediate goals or functions are not taken as genuine determiners of what contributes to them in the natural realm, and so a causal account, to claim any sort of necessity, must originate in the sort of principles that ground deduction in an axiomatic system. While for the natural law philosopher, this means the first as divine, for the reductionist, it means the first as material elements or building blocks. This move to first principles dispenses with the contingency characteristic of natural production. This loss carries over into a tendency to treat practical decisions, which are concerned with bringing ends into existence, as if they should be determined by theoretical considerations, that is, deducing consequences from elements or principles. The practical situation is not allowed to "speak its wisdom," its wisdom being the details of interconnections and mutual influence. Let us consider another part of *Physics* II that assists understanding of systems of interconnections in teleological patterns

28. Cooper (*Reason*, 60–61) criticizes Jaeger's recourse to a natural theology for grounding Aristotle's ideas about the good in moral life. He regards this as substituting purely theoretical reasoning for practical reasoning. Kevin Flannery argues, in contrast, that the first principles of practical reason for Aristotle are investigated by metaphysics, and are hence linked to the divine. See his *Acts Amid Precepts* (Washington, D.C.: The Catholic University of America Press, 2001), 21–22.

and so offers a logical template for reasoning about production of ends in human flourishing.

In his discussion of hypothetical necessity in *Physics* II.9, Aristotle lays out the way to give more fine-grained accounts of one thing being for the sake of another.[29] Whatever is a necessary condition for a given end to exist must also be present if the end is present. For example, if there is a saw that cuts, it is made out of some hard material, like iron. Aristotle insists that this is a particular kind of necessity, distinct from the mathematical necessity of consequences following from prior simple principles. On the mathematical model, given what a straight line is, a three-sided closed figure formed from straight lines has angles equal to two right angles (200a16–18). This is the sense of prior and later found in deductive geometrical proof.[30] In natural generation, he says, the direction of necessitation is reversed. For a naturally produced entity, "If the end shall be or is, then what comes before also shall be or is" (200a20). The end, when it exists, necessitates the presence of what is for the sake of the end.

In this initial account, the contrast of mathematical and hypothetical necessity seems to involve no particular difference in the type of necessity involved. It is just that the causal account flows in opposite directions between constituent parts and constituted entity. There is one aspect of reasoning, however, that Aristotle attributes to the crafted and naturally produced entity but not to the triangle. For a natural generation, he says, if there is not what comes before, there is no end or for-the-sake-of-which. Without hard metal, there is no saw at all. It seems, at first, that this rule ought to apply to both the mathematical case and the case of production. That is, without hard metal, there is no saw. But also without straight line, there is no three-sided figure with angles equal to two right angles.

That Aristotle nevertheless contrasts mathematical reasoning and

29. See also the account in *Parts An* I.1.639b12–640a9. Discussions of hypothetical necessity in Aristotle have focused on whether Aristotle meant for it to reflect simply the dependence of ends on prior conditions, or whether he understood the end actually to be responsible for its antecedents being present so as to contribute to the end. On this topic, see Cooper, "Hypothetical Necessity," in particular 262–69, and David Charles, "Aristotle on Hypothetical Necessity and Irreducibility," *Pacific Philosophical Quarterly* 69 (1988): 1–53, in particular sections 5 and 6. I focus here on the fact that hypothetical necessity adds intelligible content to our understanding of particular ends.

30. For Aristotle, the priority of three straight lines is causal *(dia tauta)*, whereas for us, straight line and triangle might be considered a biconditional.

reasoning about hypothetical necessity using this "negation of the antecedent" rule shows that he takes the natural end as necessitating what precedes it in a way that goes beyond this commonality with mathematical constructions. The difference has to do with a natural or crafted object being produced. Produced objects are not simply arranged. That the end necessitates certain materials indicates that the end depends on the materials to the extent of somehow incorporating them into the end. For an eye to see, Aristotle believed, the liquid it contains must be transparent. Indeed, the physics of transmission of light was related to the physiology of vision for him. Modern examples of a similar kind might take note of the specialization of tissues to subordinate ends in living things. For example, the properties belonging to cartilage, as opposed to bone, or heart muscle, as opposed to muscles in the limbs, are essential to higher functions served by each. This difference between organic parts and straight lines is reflected in the fact that crafted and natural objects are produced through a series of steps. The materials must become part of the final end progressively by means of actions especially suited to forward this incorporation at a particular stage of the process. The eye or the heart develops gradually. The relation of straight line and triangle is, in contrast, without stages. The method of geometrical construction helps us to see the deductive priority of straight line. It is only by a weak analogy to production, however, that we would say the distinctive traits of triangle appear immediately upon the straight lines being configured to close the figure. The analogy depends on a construction in time that does not apply to the mathematical figure. In addition, a triangle is not a *telos,* an end, but a deduced result.

Because antecedents are integral to ends in natural production, the constituent, for example, transparent liquid, is not just prior to the end. It is inseparable from its functional *telos,* for example, vision. By his contrast of types of necessity, Aristotle is saying that our mode of reasoning needs to reflect this inseparability of materials and end. Ends causally bind certain subordinate ends and contributing causes. This is not plain deduction, then, but is deduction understood as reasoning lifted from a context and incorporating as an assumption the hylomorphic structure of the context.

Although both relations are called necessary, mathematical reasoning and reasoning about natural things accomplish very different things.

Mathematical reasoning uncovers connections that ramify by sheer logical inference. Hypothetical necessity, on the other hand, is a fundamentally binary relation. The character of this binary relation should affect how we reason about both materials and ends.

In *Parts An* I.1, Aristotle addresses how this connection of antecedents and end affects the sort of account one gives in the case of a produced object. The carpenter will explain his craftsmanship by mentioning which tool is appropriate for striking the blow that produces a particular effect (641a9–15). The craftsman thus takes his reason from the end but focuses mainly on the details of means. For the physiologist approaching man, the best account is to say that, because of what it is to be a human being, man could not exist *(endexetai einai)* without these parts (640a33–35). This focus on parts and subordinate actions means too that materials and means are informative about ends when we do not yet grasp ends fully. Let us consider this aspect of reasoning in accordance with hypothetical necessity.

Even without observing crustaceans in action, the matter in their shells would tell us something about their manner of life and their predators. We know the shell protects the soft body. The weight of the shell, its shape, and configuration with respect to other parts of the body would be informative about how they move. We would then inquire as to the function served by their movement—is it migration to maintain habitat or darting to avoid predators. Our investigation would then be enlarged to consider the larger ocean or wetland habitat of the animals, but we would know a great deal about them simply from inspection of materials and structure.

Craft too relies on the way materials are informative about their ends. The first rational men must have noticed how certain friable hard stone break in coming to the idea of using these stones as tools. They first noticed how the stone shattered because the sharp edges present from the breaking were so useful. Once the early toolmaker decided to reproduce these sharp edges, they became, for him, an end constitutive of a tool for hunting or cutting. This example from primitive craft shows how closely intertwined end and materials are in our understanding. Like Aristotle's craftsman in *Parts An* I, we concentrate on how materials may achieve an end. Similarly, when we reason about natural connections, our reflection could as easily start with materials as with ends.

Aristotle's treatment of hypothetical necessity provides a basis from which to see how one is obliged to reason about teleological connections. Materials inevitably participate in the intelligibility of the end although they do not determine that intelligibility. This shows that what we call teleology is always spread over a context. Accordingly, teleological patterns may be entered into by a reasoner at several different "nodes." We look for macroends and what contributes to them, but we can begin anywhere in a web of connected smaller ends and orderly actions. In this general approach, we can recognize actions as ordered to an end—that is, know the actions have ends—and inspect the character of the action for the clues it holds to ends. Because the intelligibility of natural teleological connections is systematically diffused, we have a recipe for giving an account as fine-grained as one would wish for any case of one thing being for the sake of another in natural generation or animal behavior.

It should be possible to see by now how the empirical functions in reasoning about teleological patterns. Any empirical element in the intelligibility of a teleological pattern does not stand alone nor does it provide a posteriori premises of deduction cast in the theoretical mode. Facts look both ways, toward a subordinate end or simpler materials, on the one hand, and toward other ends for which the fact under consideration is itself a contributing cause or constitutive part. Accordingly, this portrayal of the architecture of natural ends has implications for how we reason about human goods in everyday life. Before giving examples of this reasoning, however, it would be well to display Aristotle's model for generalizing the relation of materials, subordinate ends, and higher ends to the complete life of a human being. Let us consider this model of production in relation to body and soul.

4.

The way ends direct the operations of a living thing is an important part of Aristotle's hylomorphism. Aristotle discusses the different powers of the soul in *De Anima* II.2 and says that these powers are present in an ordered series. Nutrition belongs to all living things, and sensation and locomotion to some. Reason, as the soul function last in the order, belongs only to human beings. If reason is present, this means the powers of nutrition, sensation, and locomotion are also present. Conversely, the presence of nutrition or sensation does not necessarily implicate intellect. The presence of soul in an ordered series means there is no common form or common definition of soul. In this context, he names the soul in each living thing by the highest power it possesses in the order and says, furthermore, that the soul must be in a body suited for the actuality of which it is capable. Aristotle criticizes his predecessors, who he said simply fitted soul into body without adding specifications about the kind of body, as if any chance body would do (414a23–24).

A consequence of this interdependence of soul functions and the body is that the highest operation present in a living thing penetrates all the operations of soul, by ordering lower operations to the highest power possessed.[31] Aquinas develops the theme eloquently, when he explains how the human body is suited to the rationality of the human being.[32] So even though the explanation for the parts or capabilities of the human being is found by looking to form, the parts themselves show us something of the ends of man by the character of their contribution to rationality. For Aristotle, the passions may contribute to rationality too, through the ethical virtues, which are states, or habitual dispositions *(hexeis),* of soul. Reasoning from contributing parts and actions to higher functions was the method of reasoning recommended in *Parts An* I. In *De Anima* II.1–2, Aristotle applies this doctrine to the relation of the human soul to body. The potential separability of rational soul does not liberate soul from the hypothetical necessity of a particular body. So long as human beings are mortal, we cannot do without the operations of the body, which serve our own human flourishing.

This nesting of material means within rational aims is what distinguishes the human being from animals, and it applies to all the mate-

31. In *Eudemian Ethics* II.1.1219b38–40 Aristotle says that there is no distinctly human excellence of aspects of the soul that have to do solely with nutrition and growth, for they do not incorporate the rational principle. But there is human excellence of whatever involves desire and the passions *(orexis, pathēmata;* 1220a3). Later, in *EE* VII.15, he says that to the noble and good man, what is naturally good becomes also noble, because good things become noble when chosen for the sake of the noble (1249a6). On the definition of soul by its highest function, see St. Thomas, *in De anima* II, lectio 2, §242, and 4, §270.

32. See *Summa Theologiae* I, q. 76, a. 1–5, in particular article 5 where St. Thomas treats the human body as the power of sense for the intellect. See also q. 91, a. 3, and *Quaestiones De anima* q. 8. I am indebted to Kevin White's unpublished paper "*Corpus tale:* The Development in St. Thoms Aquinas' Account of the Human Body's Specific Character" for an understanding of the relation among these passages.

rial aspects of human life—to eating but also to sexuality and to the creation of a material environment by artifice.[33] Indeed, what Aristotle says, at the beginning of *Nicomachean Ethics* I, about all art, method, action, and choice, he could also say for action in the natural realm: it aims at *(ephietai)* some good, some end, either an action *(energeia)* or an accomplished deed *(ergon),* a product (1094a1–4). In *Nicomachean Ethics* I.1, Aristotle says that many arts will fall under a single capacity or power *(hupo mian dunamin),* and for these, each end serves the next in a progression toward an architectonic or governing art that is higher and is that for the sake of which *(charin)* the others are pursued. This is the pattern we have just seen described in the ordering of functions of soul.

This Aristotelian understanding of rational soul and its relation to body provide the framework for understanding the interleafing of necessary and contingent in human action. By nature, it is inevitable that humans pursue some good in accordance with rational aims. It is also the case that by nature certain things are better choices of the good to pursue. One way in which these better choices are available to knowledge is by analysis of the relation of soul to body. What is necessary in the use of bodily nature for the realization of human good reveals itself in the details of natural production, giving particular attention to the regular and recurrent in nature. This is so even for the human being, because rational aims cannot help but have their effect in bodily activities of the human being. Within this inevitable framework of action, human beings pursue what appears good to them, and for a variety of reasons, apparent goods may fall short of what is best for the human being. Accordingly, the pursuit of the good, which is necessary for the human being, involves the contingency of possibly acting contrary to one's own best interest. The necessary and the contingent in human action exist alongside one another, one or the other asserting itself more prominently at different times, depending on the personal experience of individuals and the life history of societies.

Let us apply this pattern of the relation of subordinate ends to rational life to concrete cases, focusing on reasoning about this relation, since

33. On eating, see Leon Kass, *The Hungry Soul: Eating and the Perfection of Our Nature* (Chicago: University of Chicago Press, 1999). For development of the theme of hylomorphism in relation to human sexuality and marriage, see St. Thomas, *Summa Contra Gentiles* 3.2.122–25.

this is our main concern. On a mundane level, being sensitive to how teleological patterns work is a guide to how it is fitting to think in a habitual way about human goods in practical life. Anyone should be confident in reasoning that the disposition of the parts of the male and female bodies points to the priority of heterosexuality as defining the human good in sexual matters. In a similar way, the normal connection between intercourse and procreation provides the point of departure for personal judgment about what relations between husband and wife will foster friendship in marriage and generosity within the family in general. In both these cases, it is important that the biological does not itself determine what constitutes the good. This would be casting interconnections of actions and ends in a linear, deductive way. Rather, because sexuality is a material subordinate end within larger patterns of human life, matters of sexuality are related by hypothetical necessity to ends of a rational and spiritual character. Accordingly, reasoning about the meaning of sexual behavior and the fitting expression of the human sexual drive appropriately has reference to material parts. The best fulfillment of rational life for an embodied creature is judged in part by the nature of the body. This "taking guidance" from material life extends to broader aspects of the material culture of the human being.

Leon Kass, for instance, unfolds arguments against human cloning based on the human wisdom held in common across cultures. Kass shows how biological features of sexual reproduction are taken up in intimate details of human rational expression.[34] "By nature, each child has two complementary biological progenitors. Each child stems from and unites exactly two lineages."[35] Because of this complementarity, each person's hereditary makeup is a combination of nature and chance. Neither nature nor chance figure in this way in cloning. Nature, that is, sexual reproduction, is circumvented, and chance as a contributor to individual biological traits is excluded. Especially because of the role of chance in sexual reproduction, each person is unique, a feature evident physically in the signatures of our fingerprints and immune systems. It follows that each of us, while different from one another, is equal in humanity. We are also dependent on a familial nexus to develop our biological heritage.

34. Leon Kass and James Q. Wilson, *The Ethics of Human Cloning* (Washington, D.C.: AEI Press, 1998), part 1.

35. Ibid., 24.

Kass says, "Human societies virtually everywhere have structured child-rearing responsibilities and systems of identity and relationship on the bases of those deep natural facts of begetting."[36]

The complementarity of sexual reproduction and the features of individual human uniqueness are amplified in human relationship. The most obvious instance of the integration of sexual reproduction in rational human forms is filial piety, "love of one's own." Kass points to its role in ensuring that children are well cared for and have a sense of belonging. Kinship has a natural grounding and brings with it an obligation based on the love that has generated the child and the family history into which the child has been born. The fragility characteristic of the development of a unique human being has a counterpart in the protectiveness of moral education within the family and community. These ramifications from materials and functions of bodily parts into universal features of familial society are there, I contend, because of the hypothetical necessity present in natural systems that are goal-directed. A social system is not rational in a human sense without these relationships, because sexual reproduction is an aspect of the matter, or substratum, for human society.[37]

To contend that the teleological connections between human material nature and human rational expression can be changed without deleterious consequences is a crude sort of idealism. It is the view that mind and its constructions are the real so that material nature is malleable and can be made to fit these constructions. The reciprocity of materials and ends typical of hypothetical necessity is not dispelled, however, when healthy natural networks are disrupted. These disruptions ramify in their effects, laterally and in the direction of higher ends served. Kass displays some of these disruptions, in developing the consequences of introducing asexual reproduction for human beings.[38] In this context, he points out that asexual reproduction is, in its essence, self-preservation, while sexual reproduction serves an end—the production of a different unique individual—that is potentially at odds with the self-serving character of biological self-preservation. In human society, this aspect of sexual reproduction is echoed in the rearing of children, where parents, by

36. Ibid., 24–25.

37. Ibid., 28. Kass contends that it is impossible for there to have been human life without sexual reproduction.

38. Ibid., 26–42.

acting generously and in self-denial, are given the opportunity for transcendence and self-forgetfulness.[39] Kass's analysis is remarkable for the clarity and detail with which he captures the integration of material aspects of the human body into social forms. Displaying this integration, he reasons from materials to the ends that best fulfill human nature, but in a way that reveals the priority of ends.

The difference between reasoning geometrically about human nature and reasoning in accordance with hypothetical necessity is relevant also to developments that have taken place in economic research on the subject of social capital. Population control policies in the mid-twentieth century were based on a Malthusian deduction of scarce resources exhausted by a burgeoning population.[40] More recently, it has become clear that resources include human and social capital and furthermore that these other resources foster the creativity and productivity that overcome scarcity. These other resources work by means of education, trust, order, and communication (to mention only a few features of social capital). Once these factors were taken into consideration, the Malthusian deduction seemed not to hold decisively, giving way in economic research to an assessment of the interrelated factors that foster human capital.[41]

This change in economic analysis signals, I would claim, a partial recognition of the teleological structure of human life, because the researcher begins to move back and forth between material culture and the optimal ways it is utilized in society. A key feature of this new type of reasoning is the identification of forms of human flourishing, for example, generosity, cooperation, self-confidence, and desire to learn, as inte-

39. Ibid., 30.

40. The social science literature on this topic is very extensive. For a comprehensive statement of the supposed danger of population growth, see Paul and Anne Ehrlich, *Population, Resources, Environment: Issues in Human Ecology* (San Francisco: W. H. Freeman, 1970), and their more recent *The Population Explosion* (New York: Simon & Schuster, 1990). Julian Simon counters the claim in *The Ultimate Resource* (Princeton, N.J.: Princeton University Press, 1981) and *The Ultimate Resource 2* (Princeton, N.J.: Princeton University Press, 1996).

41. On the history of the term "social capital" and its meaning, see Francis Fukuyama, *The Great Disruption* (New York: Free Press, 1999), 12–20, and James Coleman, *Foundations of Social Theory* (Cambridge, Mass.: Belknap Press at Harvard University, 1990), 300–313. For an example of the notion applied, see Robert D. Putnam, *Making Democracy Work: Civic Tradition in Modern Italy* (Princeton, N.J.: Princeton University Press, 1993), and Putnam's "Tuning In, Tuning Out: The Strange Disappearance of Social Capital in America," *PS: Political Science and Politics* 28, no. 4 (December 1995): 664–83.

gral to economic growth and as themselves needing more basic cultural foundations in order to exist at all. This is the classic dependency relation of hypothetical necessity. The existence of the end necessitates the presence of certain elements or constituents. Coleman defines social capital in just these terms: "Social capital is defined by its function. It is not a single entity, but a variety of different entities having two characteristics in common: They all consist of some aspect of social structure, and they facilitate certain actions of individuals who are within the structure. Like other forms of capital, social capital is productive, making possible the achievement of certain ends that would not be attainable in its absence."[42] This definition highlights several aspects of social capital that also figure in natural relations of hypothetical necessity:

—social capital concerns a relation characteristic of production, that is, bringing something into existence,
—it involves elements serving some function,
—the functions served are necessary for an end to be brought into being at all.

As we would expect from Aristotle's analysis of subordinate ends in *Nicomachean Ethics* I.1., an adequate treatment of social capital seems to involve reference to a hierarchy of ends. Certain social forms foster the virtues that, in turn, serve economic prosperity.

For some researchers, the family came to occupy a central place in assessing how social capital is fostered.[43] From this standpoint, the quality of the activities of obtaining and consuming depends on the human capital fostered in the family. A vivid example of this is the role of household economy in the use and distribution of food. From 1958–1961, there was a famine in rural provinces of China, despite the fact that there was enough grain to prevent it. Chang and Wen,[44] drawing on newly avail-

42. Coleman, *Foundations*, 302.

43. For a review of the literature on this topic, see Maria Sophia Aguirre, "The Family and Economic Development: Socioeconomic Relevance and Policy Design," in *The Family in the New Millenium*, vol. 1, ed. Scott Love and Thomas Holman (London: Praeger Perspectives, 2006), 54–93. Aguirre develops the role of the family as the "first form" of economic life. "[T]he family is the first and most fundamental place where production and spending acquire their meaning" (55).

44. Gene Hsin Chang and Guanzhong James Wen, "Communal Dining and the Chinese Famine of 1958–1961," *Economic Development and Cultural Change* 46, no. 1 (1997): 1–34.

able data and considering a range of contributing causes, were able to rule out weather conditions, availability of food, and even distribution as causes of the famine. They trace the famine to "consumption irrationality" due to government collectivization of communal eating. Families no longer prepared meals in their own kitchens, but everyone had to eat in collectivized dining facilities. They write: "The communes collectivized all means of production, including not only land and draft animals but also small private plots of land and orchards that had been retained by individual members under the preceding cooperative system. Many communes even collectivized members' personal property, such as kitchenware and furniture."[45]

The initial response of some of those collectivized was euphoria and a belief that communism would provide all necessary goods. Others, who had horded food of their own, quickly consumed it to avoid its being confiscated and no longer had any reserves. In the collectivized dining facilities, there was overconsumption and waste during the first six months of the radical collectivization. Within a year, there was famine in ten or more provinces. Declining food production after the onset of famine brought about even more deaths, but low production did not prevent an end of the famine, once collectivized dining was reversed. The point is that having enough to eat depended upon the economy of small households, families who, by a host of hidden conserving and resourceful practices, aimed at the well-being of their own families and thereby contributed to the prosperity of the society as a whole.[46] This case provides an example of one kind of social capital that is necessitated hypothetically for the achievement of a human good. The prudence of a natural social group, the family, was the hidden condition of having enough to eat. Aguirre places this Chinese experience in the context of other studies about the connection among family dinners, a healthy social fabric, and economic growth.[47]

45. Ibid., 3–4.

46. Ibid., 28. Chang and Wen give the sources of economic irrationality in this case as (1) denial of the fundamental scarcity of economic goods as a condition of economic activity, and (2) denial of an individual's right to control his food subsistence.

47. Maria Sophia Aguirre, "The Economy Begins in the Kitchen," *MercatorNet* (June 14, 2006); Maria Sophia Aguirre, "Comidas Familiares, Dietas, y Distribución de Alimentos: Plantando las Semillas del Crecimiento Económico," *Dirección en la Industria de la Hospitalidad* 11, no. 1 (2007).

It is interesting that studies of the deleterious effects of the absence of social capital are the most revealing of the mutual dependency of social capital and ends. Fukuyama comments on this fact in discussing the difficulty of measuring social capital. He notes that indicators of social dysfunction are more abundant than data on healthy social forms. He says, "The presumption is that since social capital reflects the existence of cooperative norms, social deviance ipso facto reflects a lack of social capital."[48]

What this heuristic strategy shows is that the dependence of ends on particular means does not disappear when social relations are rearranged. The reliance on contributing conditions just shows up differently, in patterns of self-destructive action. This is because, in teleological patterns involving the material culture of human life, norms that are entirely conventional or artificial cannot take the place of natural norms without negative effects that ramify throughout the system of mutual connections. Natural goods are often most evident as goods when they assert themselves as a "cancellation" of what is proposed as good by convention.[49] In systems of natural and human production, weakening the underlying structures that are necessitated hypothetically disrupts the functional end.

5.

This essay has ranged widely over Aristotelian philosophy, biological functionalism, and social science research on virtue and the family. These areas are connected by how they all contribute to disclosing natural goods in human life. I have maintained that discovering natural goods needs a form of reasoning suited to their structure, which is teleological.

In ethics, the pursuit of goods is treated almost entirely as a matter of practical reason. The mode of reasoning for ethics is deliberation, and excellence in deliberation is *phronēsis,* prudence. Aristotle makes clear

48. Fukuyama, *Disruption,* 23.

49. Robert Sokolowski uses the term "cancellation" to describe the way natural goods appear in criticism of the conventional, when established rules do not function as proposed. He draws a parallel to materials asserting themselves when the instrumental breaks down. See "Knowing Natural Law," in *Pictures, Quotations, and Distinctions* (South Bend, Ind.: University of Notre Dame Press, 1992), 280.

in *Nicomachean Ethics* I.9, however, that since happiness is not gotten by chance, we should seek to discover the stable goals productive of happiness. In *Nicomachean Ethics* I.13, he says that anyone who wishes to deliberate well or bring about good character in others (parents or rulers) must make a study of human nature (1102a13–25). It is no trivial matter that we should be able to reason about human action in a different way than we decide upon actions. The latter is deliberation, the former something more like science. The structure of science is usually taken to be deductive, like geometry. I have sought to show that most of the reasoning revelatory of human goods is not deduction from first principles but is rather reasoning from materials necessitated hypothetically to the ends served by these materials. This too can be the science of human nature.

Reasoning on the basis of hypothetical necessity came into focus, in my discussion, by considering the features of production. Teleology is inseparable from production, because production always aims at an end. Ethical action is located at the intersection of two kinds of end-directed action. Bringing about any apparent good has a teleological structure, regardless of whether the apparent good is wisely chosen. At the same time, the goods and virtues that bring about happiness are ends in the order of human nature. I have argued that bringing these natural goods into being depends upon identifying them in their relation to the material culture of human life.

Reasoning that follows the structure of teleological relations is not something new, inaccessible, or arcane. It is regularly practiced in the decisions of an ordinary life even moderately well lived. It takes a reckless person to disregard completely the sort of connections I have delineated. Once we are sensitive to this style of reasoning, it can be discerned also in discussions in practical ethics and social science.

Mary M. Keys

7 Politics Pointing beyond the *Polis* and the *Politeia*

Aquinas on Natural Law and the Common Good

This essay is a précis of sorts of my book *Aquinas, Aristotle, and the Promise of the Common Good.*[1] This book began with an interest in Aquinas's way of relating the personal good of individual human beings with the common good of their societies, and with a conviction that in Aquinas's theory moral virtue formed the chief nexus between the two. While almost from the project's outset I considered the role of human or civil law in the task of education in virtue, civic and also moral, it was only later, when reflecting on the differences between Aquinas's and Aristotle's accounts of the virtue of magnanimity, that I was brought back around, so

I am most grateful to Dean Kurt Pritzl, O.P., Professor V. Bradley Lewis, and all in the School of Philosophy at the Catholic University of America for the opportunity to participate in the 2005 fall lecture series on "Natural Moral Law and Contemporary Society." For their generous support of the work over the years that made possible both my lecture and its revision for publication in the present volume, I would like to thank the College of Arts and Letters of the University of Notre Dame, the Earhart Foundation, the Erasmus Institute at the University of Notre Dame, the Institute for Scholarship in the Liberal Arts of the University of Notre Dame, the Jacques Maritain Center of the University of Notre Dame, the Martin Marty Center for the Advanced Study of Religion at the University of Chicago, the National Association of Scholars, the Olin Foundation, the Program on Constitutional Government in the Department of Government at Harvard University, and the Strake Foundation, as well as the many colleagues, friends, and student assistants who have contributed in so many ways to whatever is valuable in this essay.

1. Mary M. Keys, *Aquinas, Aristotle, and the Promise of the Common Good* (Cambridge: Cambridge University Press, 2006).

to speak, to appreciate the full foundational import and implications of Aquinas's theory of natural law as it relates to both ethics and politics. And so there is a close fit, I think, between the intention of my book and the essays in the present volume. Let me explain more.

As my work on the book progressed, a strong undercurrent developed in its narrative and argument: that regardless of their religious beliefs political theorists today ought to take Aquinas and his theories of virtue and natural law seriously and consider the prospect that they may indeed contain much that is true. And here there are serious obstacles to be overcome, first and most fundamentally the widely held conviction among political theorists that faith and reason are at loggerheads; that instead of *fides et ratio* we can have only faith versus reason, and so one must choose between a life of piety and faith and a life of full-fledged philosophic inquiry. Natural law, or at least Aquinas's formulation of it, is in consequence rejected as an illegitimate attempt to bridge the unbridgeable gap between faith and philosophy. In the second place is a corollary opinion, that at least specifically Christian thinkers in medieval times are philosophically inferior to their ancient mentors and perhaps also to their modern counterparts. Finally and more narrowly, there is the monolithic and I will argue inadequate understanding of the medieval "commentary" genre as an exclusively interpretive enterprise, attempting to get at the "original intent" and only the original intent of the writers such as Aristotle whose works are commented upon. This in turn yields a widely shared impression that Aquinas and his confreres took a doctrinaire approach to Aristotle, revered as "The Philosopher"—a sort of *ipse dixit* attitude that kills dialectical inquiry and deadens the life of the mind.

In my book, as more briefly here, I argue that Aquinas's works are important for political theorists today to engage on the closely interrelated topics of virtue, law, and the common good; that it will not do to read only Aristotle, Aquinas's chief philosophic mentor, on these questions and themes. I contend that Aquinas's thought and not least his account of natural law are valuable for us in view of needs in current national and international affairs as well as in contemporary academia and political philosophy. Aquinas's work is especially significant for its openness to discovering and living out truth via both faith and reason, and to the cosmopolitan, transcendent, and religious, as well as the political dimensions of human life. Aquinas offers a robust theory of the foundations of political life that at the same points beyond the *polis* and the *politeia,* beyond the singular political community and its form of government or "regime." I want to challenge the oversimplified and, I am convinced, misguided conclusions that Aquinas merely repeats and unconditionally accepts Aristotle's judgments in practical philosophy and in all matters knowable through the natural inquiry of human reason; or alternatively that Aquinas is original in places but only by muddling or oversimplifying Aristotle's pristine philosophic reason, and this chiefly by inappropriate importations from Divine Revelation. These, it seems to me, have individually or in combination constituted the reigning positions in political theory in America, when it has considered Thomas Aquinas's thought at all, at least since the publication of *Thomism and Aristotelianism* by Harry V. Jaffa in 1952[2] and Leo Strauss's *Natural Right and History* in 1953.[3]

The thesis of this essay, a synopsis of two parts of *Aquinas, Aristotle, and the Promise of the Common Good,* is twofold: first, that Aquinas knowingly develops and in some respects deviates from Aristotle's theories of natural right and ethical virtue, and that he sees natural law as revealing important truths about political action and political virtue, not least that the common goods that they seek point beyond the *polis* and the *politeia;* and second, that Aquinas's accounts of certain ethical virtues are in consequence more capacious and indeed more fully human than Aristotle's corresponding accounts. The argument I will present has three parts, the first treating Aquinas's commentary on Aristotle's account of natural right in the *Nicomachean Ethics;* the second on Aquinas's response by way of natural law to problems in Aristotle's regime-relative political science and account of political virtue as developed especially in book 3 of the *Politics;* and the third, an illustration of the first two parts of the argument with an explication of Aquinas's revision of Aristotle's virtue of magnanimity, by paradoxically positing humility as its "twin virtue" *(duplex virtus)* rooted in natural law and conducing to both personal and common goods.

2. Harry V. Jaffa, *Thomism and Aristotelianism: A Study of the "Commentary" by Thomas Aquinas on the "Nicomachean Ethics"* (Chicago: University of Chicago Press, 1952).

3. Leo Strauss, *Natural Right and History* (Chicago: University of Chicago Press, 1953).

1. NATURAL RIGHT AND NATURAL LAW: AQUINAS'S "TENDENTIOUS GLOSSES" ON *NICOMACHEAN ETHICS* 5.7

In *Thomism and Aristotelianism* Harry Jaffa argues a position contrary to the argument I am making here.[4] On Jaffa's reading Aquinas clearly imputes to Aristotle his own understanding of the inclination to moral goodness or virtue and his corresponding account of indemonstrable first principles of practical reason and precepts of natural law. Aquinas does this, moreover, simply because he gets the chapter of *Nicomachean Ethics* on natural right wrong; he reads Aristotle in patristic terms. Jaffa's assessment of Aquinas recalls Rousseau's famous critique of earlier Enlightenment thinkers, who thought they had depicted natural man but had painted civil man instead.[5] Like Hobbes, Locke, and others who according to Rousseau did not go far enough to reach a true account of nature and the natural man that they were seeking—who were too conditioned by social conventions and insufficiently radical in their thought for the task at hand—so Aquinas wanted to uncover purely rational philosophy in the original meaning of Aristotle's texts, but in the end read them through a distorting lens fashioned by his Christian faith and the late classical and patristic traditions.[6] Aquinas sought natural or pagan ethics, but painted Christian ethics instead. And Christian ethics, Jaffa rightly stresses, is in crucial respects quite different. As Jean-Pierre Torrell expresses it, to identify Thomistic and Aristotelian ethics "is to forget that between their two moralities lies the entire difference added by the Gospel."[7]

I cannot address here all the nuanced points of interpretation and critique made by Jaffa in his concluding chapter on "Natural Right and Natural Law." Instead, I will summarize three of Jaffa's most important

4. Jaffa, *Thomism and Aristotelianism,* 167–88. The phrase "tendentious glosses" in the heading is borrowed from John I. Jenkins, C.S.C., "Expositions of the Text: Aquinas's Aristotelian Commentaries," *Medieval Philosophy and Theology* 5 (1996): 39–62.

5. Jean-Jacques Rousseau, *The First and Second Discourses,* ed. Roger D. Masters, trans. Roger D. and Judith Masters (New York: St. Martin's Press, 1964), 102.

6. See also Strauss, *Natural Right,* 157–58.

7. Jean-Pierre Torrell, *Saint Thomas Aquinas: The Person and His Work* (Washington, D.C.: The Catholic University of America Press, 1996), 228; cf. Servais Pinckaers, O.P., *Sources of Christian Ethics,* trans. Sr. Mary Thomas Noble, O.P. (Washington, D.C.: The Catholic University of America Press, 1995), 188–89.

arguments concerning Aquinas's commentary on *Nicomachean Ethics* 5.7, the famous and notoriously difficult chapter on the natural and the legal right or just, as two distinct parts of political justice. I will then offer three objections to Jaffa's conclusions in support of my contention that in developing his theory of natural law Aquinas is consciously laying new, deeper, and broader foundations for ethics and political science.

Jaffa begins his chapter by summarizing Aquinas's account of natural law in the *Summa Theologiae (ST),* and then goes on to argue that in the *Commentary on the Nicomachean Ethics (Comm. NE)* Aquinas writes this same natural law teaching into his interpretation of Aristotle's quite different account of natural right. On account of Aquinas's glossing Aristotle's natural right theory with shades of natural law and also because of Aquinas's failure to criticize Aristotle explicitly concerning what philosophic reason can know about human actions and ethics, Jaffa concludes that "it is only reasonable to assume that Thomas understands his own natural law doctrine to be identical, in principle, with the moral doctrine of Aristotle."[8] Jaffa points out several passages in *Comm. NE* where Aquinas offers what John I. Jenkins, C.S.C., aptly terms "tendentious glosses" on Aristotle's text.[9] The first group of these remarks, Jaffa argues, wrongly imputes to Aristotle's natural right teaching Aquinas's own theory of a natural inclination to moral virtue, hence to practically reasonable action in accord with a law written by nature on the mind. By contrast, Aristotle's natural right regards objective states of affairs or moral facts, not moral psychology or moral agency.[10] A second salient objection that Jaffa makes is to Aquinas's explicit mention in his exposition of natural right of the naturally known, indemonstrable principles of practical reason which Aquinas also elaborates in the *ST* as the foundation of natural law. Jaffa concludes from this anomaly that "Thomas apparently takes Aristotle's statement, to the effect that what is naturally right or just does not depend on opinion, as an outright endorsement of his own doctrine that there is a natural habit of the understanding [synderesis], by which *we know* what is, in principle, right and wrong according to nature."[11] Third and last for our discussion here, Jaffa writes that Aquinas with-

8. Jaffa, *Thomism and Aristotelianism,* 168.
9. Jenkins, "Expositions of the Text: Aquinas's Aristotelian Commentaries," 39–62.
10. See Jaffa, *Thomism and Aristotelianism,* 169–71, 174.
11. Ibid., 175 (emphasis in original).

out foundation in Aristotle's text qualifies the Philosopher's unequivocal statements that natural right is entirely changeable—as malleable (or in Aquinas's Latin text of the *Politics*, "similarly malleable") as legal or positive right. Again, Aquinas does so along the lines of his own natural law teaching: there are first principles of natural right that are unchangeable, because the essence of our human nature is unchangeable. While these hold always and everywhere, there are also secondary principles or more specific conclusions from the first principles that fail to hold in a few cases, due to the mutability of concrete human actions and circumstances. Again, Jaffa claims, this is a clear misreading of Aristotle's text, attributable ultimately to Aquinas's faith in Divine Revelation and his Catholic theological presuppositions.[12]

Jaffa is right to find important elements of Aquinas's account of natural law in the *Comm. NE* 5.7, on natural and legal right. He is further correct to note that we readers of the *Comm. NE* can take away an erroneous understanding of key aspects of Aristotle's ethical thought, if we read all of Aquinas's glosses as endeavoring to clarify precisely what Aristotle meant, and only what Aristotle meant, and if we further assume that Aquinas, as such an influential and careful commentator, always (or virtually always) got Aristotle right. Jaffa's point of departure is the keen concern that many mid-twentieth-century readers of Aquinas's works—some of the only scholars who at that time took the contemporary relevance of classical political philosophy seriously—did in fact hold all these assumptions. He wishes in *Thomism and Aristotelianism* to complicate the picture especially with regard to the second premise, that Aquinas's commentaries are wholly accurate or at least the best available accounts of Aristotle's literal, intentional meaning. He thereby seeks to clear a path to a fresh examination of Aristotle's texts and alternative commentary traditions in the hopes of reinvigorating a genuinely Aristotelian ethics and social science for our times.[13]

There are, however, problems with Jaffa's overall reading of Aquinas's texts and his appraisal of our theologian's intention. Jaffa's approach is too one-dimensional, perhaps inspired by a generous desire to give Aquinas the benefit of the doubt in this regard: so devoted a student of the Philoso-

12. See Jaffa, *Thomism and Aristotelianism*, 179–93.

13. Ibid., 4–7.

pher could not have intentionally distorted Aristotle's teaching, virtually the embodiment of natural reason regarding ethics, in his *Comm. NE.* It would therefore seem most probable that Aquinas did so unconsciously, so immersed in his task as a theologian that he could not help understanding Aristotle's words in a deeply Christian sense.[14] Contrary to this assumption, however, there are clear textual indicators that in the *Comm. NE* Aquinas consciously goes beyond Aristotle's intentional meaning in his explication of natural right, and that he is fully aware that his account of natural law differs from Aristotle's foundational understanding of natural right in important respects.

First, Jaffa describes the question on natural law in the *ST* (I-II q. 94) without noting that Aristotle's *Nicomachean Ethics* is nowhere cited where it should be—indeed it is almost not cited at all—if it were a major source of Aquinas's account of the naturally known first practical principles and the accompanying inclinations to moral virtue and religion. Likewise neither Aristotle nor the *Nicomachean Ethics* is mentioned by Aquinas in the earlier article *ST* I-II q. 91 a. 2, where Aquinas first inquires into the existence and nature of "natural law." This is odd, given that Aquinas in his article on the precepts of natural law explicitly cites Aristotle's *Metaphysics* on the existence of indemonstrable first principles of speculative reason.[15] Why would Aquinas not also call our attention to the *Nicomachean Ethics* with equal directness on the matter of first practical principles, especially given that this article is a key part of the section of the *ST* on the moral life and the virtues? It is even odder since, as Jaffa rightly observes, these crucial elements of Aquinas's argument in *ST* I-II q. 94 a. 2 are also part of the elaboration of Aristotle's natural right in Aquinas's *Comm. NE* 5.7. These are all, it seems to me, salient facts for ascertaining Aquinas's intention and appraisal of his own theory in relation to Aristotle's.

In his summation of Aquinas's *ST,* Jaffa fails to call our attention to the one citation of the *Nicomachean Ethics* in the question on natural law. In a subsequent article of question 94,[16] Aquinas does explicitly refer to Aristotle's text on "the naturally just" and incorporate it in to his dialectical inquiry regarding natural law. He does so, however, primarily

14. Ibid., 168, 188.

15. See *ST* I-II q. 94 a. 2.

16. *ST* I-II q. 94 a. 4.

in the context of an "objection." This *argumentum* and Aquinas's reply merit our attention, and will also help us note some important features of Aquinas's *Comm. NE* that Jaffa does not discuss. Aquinas's question is "Whether the Natural Law Is the Same in All Human Beings?" The second objection he raises to affirming this proposition runs as follows: "Further, 'Things which are according to the law are said to be just,' as stated in *Nicomachean Ethics* 5. But it is also stated in the same book that nothing is so universally just as not to be subject to change in regard to some men. Therefore even the natural law is not the same in all men." To this Aquinas replies: "This saying of the Philosopher is to be understood of things that are naturally just, not as general principles, but as conclusions drawn from them, having rectitude in the majority of cases, but failing in a few."[17]

Two features of these passages seem especially important: First, in formulating this objection *(argumentum),* Aquinas as it were "cuts and pastes" together two different comments from the *Nicomachean Ethics,* on the legal just and the natural just, respectively. But in his *Comm. NE* 5.7, Aquinas consistently and faithfully reflects Aristotle's own separation of *nomos* from *physis,* of law or convention from nature. Even when he incorporates elements of his understanding of natural law into his *Commentary* here, Aquinas never once uses the precise term "natural law." In my view this is another strong indicator that Aquinas is aware of and indirectly acknowledges the absence of a full-fledged natural law theory in Aristotle's *Nicomachean Ethics,* as indeed in classical Greek thought generally.

Second, it is critical to note how Aquinas introduces his reply to Aristotle's trenchant "objection" based on the mutability of natural right. He does not say, "What the Philosopher means is" or "The correct literal interpretation of Aristotle's words is. . . ." Rather, in a deliberately ambiguous and open way, Aquinas says "[t]he saying of the Philosopher is to be *understood* . . ." (emphasis added). He does not here, as he often does, point to any other passage of the *Nicomachean Ethics* or another work where Aristotle actually says what Aquinas will say in elaboration or clarification. We can paraphrase Aquinas's reply thus: "The words of the Philosopher are true if understood in this way, and so we should un-

17. *ST* I-II q. 94, a. 4, obj. 2 and ad 2.

derstand them thus."[18] Turning to the text of the *Comm. NE,* we find Aquinas almost always using similar formulae when he goes beyond Aristotle's express statements or likely literal meaning, glossing passages in terms of his own understanding of the deepest truth, of the fuller reality they signify in his own estimation. He does not try to pass off his theory as Aristotle's, but neither is he only expounding the Philosopher's express understanding with every elaboration in the *Commentary.* Here are some examples of Aquinas's introductory clues, from some of the passages Jaffa finds most objectionable: "Est autem considerandum, quod iustum naturale est ad quod hominem natura inclinat" (It is to be considered, however, that the natural just is that to which nature inclines man) according to a "twofold nature": material and sensible, in common with the other animals and specifically rational.[19] "Est tamen attendendum quod quia rationes etiam mutabilium sunt imutabiles . . ." (It is nevertheless to be noted that, since the essences of mutable things are immutable), the primary principles of natural justice are likewise unalterable.[20] "Est autem hic considerandum, quod iustum legale sive positivum oritur semper a naturali, ut Tullius dicit in sua rhetorica" (However, it is to be considered here that the legal or positive just is always derived from the natural [just], as Cicero says in his *Rhetoric).*[21] Even when Aquinas follows a direct paraphrase of Aristotle with a specifically Thomistic gloss and no similar preface, he almost always refrains from saying what he often says elsewhere: "Aristotle manifests"; "Aristotle proves"; "Aristotle shows us his intention"; "here the Philosopher raises (or resolves) a doubt."[22]

18. Cf. Jenkins, "Expositions of the Text: Aquinas's Aristotelian Commentaries," 39–62.

19. *Comm. NE* 5.12 n. 1019; cf. *ST* I-II q. 94 a. 2.

20. *Comm. NE* 5.12 n. 1029; cf. *ST* I-II q. 94 a. 4–5.

21. *Comm. NE* 5.12 n. 1023; cf. *ST* I-II q. 91 a. 3 and q. 95 a. 2.

22. While revising this lecture for publication, and after my book's publication, I noticed one subsequent formulation of Aquinas on Aristotle's *NE* that in this context is more problematic for my argument: in *ST* I-II q. 95, a. 2, where Aquinas is inquiring "whether every human law is derived from natural law." Three "objections" to this derivation come from Aristotle's *Ethics* 5.7 while the *sed contra* arguing in its favor is taken instead from Cicero, as we might have expected along the lines of my argument and the texts cited above. In response to objection 1, however, Aquinas replies to Aristotle's statement that "the legal just is that which originally was a matter of indifference" (which the natural law most definitely is not) as follows: "the Philosopher is speaking [*philosophus loquitur*] of those enactments which are by way of determination or specification of the precepts of the natural law" (*ST* I-II q. 95 a. 2 ad 1). Due to constraints of time I can for now only note the existence of this

In my judgment, then, this evidence indicates that Aquinas's *Commentaries* are intended not only to clarify the Philosopher's literal meaning and reveal the richness of his thought, but also at times to correct, supplement, or point beyond Aristotle's exact account. In Aristotle's own spirit, Aquinas attempts to "save the appearances" whenever possible and credit all he considers true in the Philosopher's sayings—as he does regularly with his other interlocutors as well—even while showing what more he thinks needs to be said or what should be differently understood. In this instance, Aquinas takes the truth of natural right to comprise also and especially its interrelation with natural law. Parts of Aristotle's account must be jettisoned or reinterpreted in order to incorporate this insight; Aquinas indicates some of them in the *Commentary,* while reserving the full account he has to offer and even the un-Aristotelian term "natural law" for his *ST.* The fact that Aquinas rarely openly takes issue with Aristotle does not indicate that Aristotle's authority always in his view holds, even on the terrain of natural or philosophic reason. Aquinas's commentaries are living works of dialectical inquiry, not simply historical studies.[23]

2. NATURAL LAW AND THE PROBLEM OF REGIME-RELATIVE POLITICAL VIRTUE

In his *Commentary on the "Politics,"* Aquinas follows with care Aristotle's investigation in the opening chapters of *Politics* 3 into the meaning of "citizen" and the excellence proper to citizens. Across the most varied regimes, that person is a citizen who shares in or is eligible to share in deliberation and decision making in the city. The citizen is thus one who either has or can have an active role in running the regime, admin-

---

complication, which I think can be resolved along the lines of Jenkins's argument ("Expositions of the Text: Aquinas's Aristotelian Commentaries") and my interpretative argument here, but which also is more difficult thus to reconcile than the other relevant passages quoted and discussed in my original lecture and its revised text above.

23. For a fuller discussion of Aquinas's relation to Aristotle in matters philosophical, see my *Aquinas, Aristotle, and the Promise of the Common Good,* especially 70–74. This section of my lecture is in general much indebted to Jenkins, "Expositions of the Text: Aquinas's Aristotelian Commentaries," which helped me to assess more comprehensively some perplexing features I had noted and begun to explain in Aquinas's *Commentaries* on Aristotle's *Ethics* and *Politics.*

istering its justice, and helping to guide policy with a view to its welfare. Aquinas repeatedly stresses that according to Aristotle, political or citizen virtue is properly defined relative to the regime. Just as a ship's diverse crew members all act well by contributing to its preservation and safe voyage to port, so a city's diverse citizens all contribute to the regime's persistence and well-being, though in different ways and according to various functions. Their common excellence or virtue as citizens is always a function of the regime governing their *polis,* just as the decision as to who is or is not offered citizenship in a city depends on the nature of its current regime. A person qualifying in democratic Athens, for instance, might well fail to meet Sparta's property qualification for citizen sharing in the regime.

Aquinas's comments further highlight the regime's role as the "form" of the city, in a sense analogous to Aristotle's and Aquinas's teaching on the soul as the form of the human body (the example is mine, not Aquinas's). The regime crafts the city's specific identity and holds it together: it is its principle of both unity and common action, the glue, as it were, that holds the association of citizens together in common life. When the regime changes the city is in the most significant sense "other" than it was, despite the fact that the city's territory and population may be virtually the same as they had been previously.[24]

One strength of Aquinas's *Commentary* is the way it elucidates the tension latent in the first five chapters of Aristotle's *Politics* 3 between citizenship as defined by law or *nomos* (civic status issued by and exercised with a view to the regime in power—de facto or realist citizenship, we might call it), and citizenship as it should be by nature or *physis,* according to the chief needs of any city and with a view to achieving its fullest common good (natural or *de jure* citizenship, we might call it, in the sense of *jus naturale* or natural right). Both definitions are in some sense a product of what polities all have in common.[25] In the first case, each city has some regime in place, the right to participate in the activity and administration of which captures the core meaning of citizenship.

24. See *Commentary on the "Politics"* 3.2 n. 364 [8].

25. See Ralph McInerny, "What Do Communities Have in Common?" in *What Right Does Ethics Have? Public Philosophy in a Pluralistic Culture,* ed. Sander Griffioen (Amsterdam: VU University Press, 1990), 47–59, for reflections in contemporary context on natural law and "what [political] communities have in common."

In the second case, all political societies are in need of governance from persons possessing *phronesis* or *prudentia,* practical wisdom with a view to the preservation of the common life and the community's flourishing amid changing and often difficult circumstances. On the first count, citizenship is defined by the regime's permission to participate, normally expressed in a general legislative code concerning citizenship requirements and regulating the filling and administration of offices. On the second count, the citizen is defined pointedly by Aristotle as one who knows,[26] the person who possesses the political wisdom required both to carry out well the many tasks involved in public office and to be ruled well in turn. It is a strong perennial possibility, to say the very least, that the persons in these two "groups"—the citizens according to nature and the citizens according to law—may not be the same.

Part of the subtle irony inherent in Aristotle's account of citizenship is conveyed in the *Commentary on the "Politics"* through Aquinas's glosses on the rightful, as it were natural, claims to citizenship versus the claims defined by positive law. Most people think "natural" or simply just citizenship is defined primarily by birth: birth on this city's soil; birth to citizen parents; birth into a family of this socioeconomic class. Aquinas follows Aristotle in appearing at first to cater to these parochial or even prejudiced views of who counts as a "good citizen," a "real" or "genuine citizen," even while challenging their foundational premises on a deeper level. Birth-based definitions cannot in any way apply to a city's founder or founders, or to its first generation of citizens; yet these people more than any ought to be considered full-fledged citizens for instituting their city and establishing and launching its regime. The most serious truth underlying the often comical common opinion on citizenship concerns the natural social and civic need for prudence and the other virtues; the need in other words not just for politically or legally rightful participation as defined by the regime, but also and especially for wise participation in governance and judging based on the very nature of political society and its normative *telos,* the common good.[27] In this deeper

26. See *Politics* 3.4; *Commentary on the "Politics"* 3.3 n. 375, 12.

27. Another important truth embedded or implicit in such opinions about citizenship and birth is that good statesmen must have genuine affection or love for their people and polity and that cities need friendship above all else. Birth is one way of improving likelihood of "familiarity" which often—but clearly not always—"breeds affection" in citizens,

sense the best model of citizenship and civic virtue is not any ordinary citizen, however respectable or even conscientious and honorable he or she may be; as Aquinas's helpful gloss on Aristotle's text reveals, the citizen par excellence is rather the outstanding statesman.[28]

With regard to the chief question of *Politics* 3.4, whether the virtue of the good citizen and the good human being are the same or not, or whether the good citizen is ipso facto a good person, and vice versa, there thus comes to the fore the distinction between ruling and being ruled, between statesmen and ordinary citizens. In regimes that do not promote full ethical virtue or seek the common good of all citizens (such as democracy as defined by Aristotle, oligarchy, and of course tyranny), there is never a direct correlation between human and civic virtue. Among other regimes it still seems that only the best regime, a perfect aristocracy, can unite civic virtue and complete human virtue in those citizens who have the prudence or practical wisdom it takes to rule and be ruled well. Writes Aquinas, ". . . in a certain city, namely that of the best, in which the ruling offices are granted according to the virtue which is that of the good man, the good man and the good citizen are identical, while in other cities . . . the good citizen is not the same as the good man. Furthermore, the one who is identical to the good man is not any citizen whatever but the ruler [actual or potential] of the city. . . ."[29]

Yet it is striking that neither Aristotle in his *Politics* nor Aquinas in his *Commentary* provides an extant example of a truly aristocratic regime. In virtually all political communities, the majority of the citizens together with their rulers find themselves in this undesirable shared situation: the end that they and their city seek in common, to live well, is defined differently by the city and regime, on the one hand, and by human nature and philosophy (to say nothing of Aquinas's Christian theology), on the other. The regime recognizes and reflects a part, but only a part,

---

both among themselves and for their city as a whole and its officials, and in rulers for the people. Knowledge without love will not secure the common good or even motivate its attempt, especially in the face of difficulty and danger. Aristotle has emphasized this already in *Politics* 2.5; Aquinas also does so in *ST* I-II q. 105 a. 3, referring the reader back to *Politics* 3. Hence, for example, Aquinas as well as Aristotle would appreciate the basic rationale behind the constitutional proviso that only a native-born citizen can become president of the United States. The language of "naturalization" of immigrants and its implications merits reflection in this context.

28. *Commentary on the "Politics"* 3.4 n. 383, 7.

29. *Commentary on the "Politics"* 3.4 n. 383, 7.

of the requirements of justice and happiness, easily mistaking that part for the whole. How, then, can citizens rightly devote themselves to action for the common good, if in so doing they act for an end the regime establishes and enforces, yet which cannot simply or completely perfect them as human beings? The problem seems especially acute for those citizens who are subjects or ruled by others: if their prudence is merely "true opinion," as Aristotle on his part opines, crafted by the practical wisdom of their rulers and the laws and decrees, how can it even be true opinion, when the vision of justice and the public good those rulers impart is itself partial, hence partially defective and false?[30] And if the rulers and future rulers themselves have no time (and perhaps no inclination) to study philosophy, even political philosophy, busied as they are by the practical necessities of civic life such as training for war, how will even they be able to rise above received opinion or, at best, partial knowledge of the good for humans?[31]

One way around this dilemma would be to redefine civic virtue as in its essence other than regime-relative. Sensitive to regime volatility and the dangers of instability and anarchy, one might still argue that to be a virtuous citizen is to promote the common good as fully and effectively as possible, unimpeded by the regime's truncated and perhaps positively warped version of the social and civic end. Thus to be a good citizen in the antebellum United States, for instance, would often entail work against or at least outside of and in a wholly different spirit than the legal structures and policies of the time, to benefit those persons deprived of citizenship through slavery. Likewise, on this model the best citizen of the former Soviet Union (USSR) would paradoxically have to refuse first-class citizenship by not joining the Communist Party and by fostering free and truthful (if clandestine) speech, thereby promoting the true human dignity and social trust demolished by the regime. But on second thought, such persons would seem excellent not as members of the

30. See also *Pol.* 3.4.1277b25–29; *Commentary on the "Politics"* 3.3 n. 375, 12.

31. It is one of Aquinas's glosses on Aristotle (who is in turn quoting Euripides) that underscores this ordinary absence of philosophy from the education of rulers, as commonly conceived and practiced in the real world. Aristotle does not mention philosophy explicitly in this passage—indeed he very rarely does in the *Politics*—yet Aquinas's remark seems right on target and illuminating of Aristotle's intention. Cf. *Pol.* 3.4.1277a16–21 with *Commentary on the "Politics"* 3.3 n. 370, 6.

USSR but rather as members of a society in many ways oppressed by the regime that defined the USSR, as a political society. It is no accident that as soon as its Marxist-Leninist regime was no more the USSR received a new name—or rather new names, as its empire fragmented and its citizens became citizens of Russia, Ukraine, or one of a dozen other nations.

Following a similar line of reasoning, for Aristotle and for Aquinas as his commentator, the regime remains central to a correct notion of citizenship and civic virtue. And for at least this reason, the tension between good humanity and good citizenship must remain. There are many regimes in which to be an excellent citizen is to be a bad human being, and even in decent polities one must rise above the imperfect civic standard and see farther than the regime if one is not to stunt one's full growth as a human being and as a member of society. Neither Aristotle nor Aquinas would deny that this critical distance can be quite difficult, even painful, for public-spirited citizens to achieve. On Aristotle's account, moreover, it is difficult to understand how a citizen who does not possess at least those capabilities required of an excellent ruler in the best regime could ever achieve such regime-transcendence.

In his *ST,* in contrast to the *Commentary on the "Politics,"* Aquinas does appear to privilege the generically social character of human nature over the regime-relative political in several key respects.[32] One may even say that while retaining an awareness of the importance of regimes and the virtues and vices they require to perdure and tend to promote, Aquinas redefines the political or civic character of human nature as more fundamentally in function of human sociality and its ethical requirements.[33] In doing so Aquinas offers readers some probing new possibilities for harmonizing human and civic excellence. And, by arguing for the naturalness of humanity's religious character and quest, taking this dimension of humanity more seriously in ethical context than Aristotle appears to have done, Aquinas opens up space for transcendence on the part of ordinary, nonphilosopher citizens who are aware (however vaguely) of their citizenship in a universal community under God, and

32. John O. Riedl, "Thomas Aquinas on Citizenship," *Proceedings of the American Catholic Philosophical Association* 37 (1963): 159–66, 160–61; Kevin White, "The Virtues of Man the Social Animal: Affabilitas and Veritas in Aquinas," *Thomist* 57 (1993): 641–53, 641; cf. Brian J. Shanley, O.P., "Aquinas on Pagan Virtue," *Thomist* 63 (1999): 553–77.

33. See, e.g., *ST* I-II q. 113 a. 1.

perhaps through grace are cognizant as well of being members of God's own household.[34]

According to Aquinas's foundational natural law theory, by virtue of aiming at the common good and the human good in which moral virtue is central, politics presupposes and foreshadows a human *telos* more common than any particular political regime can provide for or reflect and which should serve as the North Star for the compass of political theory. Aquinas's *Commentary on the "Politics"* nudges the reader toward recognizing the need for a quest for a social and civic standard at once guiding and transcending the horizon of this-worldly regimes. The problem of political virtue and regime particularity impels Aquinas to seek a political foundation that respects the legitimate, unavoidable requirements of real regimes yet that also assists all humans, not just philosophers, in some way to see beyond and transcend them. That foundation is to be found in the first place in Aquinas's account of natural law, and ultimately in the divine Giver of that law; the edifice is "cosmopolis," the universal polity on the order of nature, elevated and perfected to become the City of God in the order of grace and glory. Ernest Fortin expresses the Thomistic difference this way:

> [I]n taking over Aristotle's concept of the political nature of man and of human living, Aquinas has modified it profoundly under the influence of Christianity and Stoicism and . . . the notion of God as a lawgiver in both of these traditions. Civil society . . . is itself judged by a higher standard to which human actions must conform universally. It becomes part of a broader whole, embracing all men and all cities and is by that very fact deprived of its privileged status as the sole horizon limiting the scope of man's moral activity, setting the goals to which he may aspire, and determining the basic order of his priorities.[35]

I would add that at least in part, this Thomistic modification of the Aristotelian ethical-political paradigm is a profoundly human and philosophic response to problems of regime-relative political virtue and political science internal to Aristotle's *Politics.*

34. Cf. *ST* I-II 94, 2; Ernest L. Fortin, *Collected Essays, Vol. 2: Classical Christianity and the Political Order,* ed. J. Brian Benestad (Lanham, Md.: Rowman & Littlefield, 1996), 2.160–61.

35. Fortin, *Collected Essays,* 2.160–61; cf. 169.

3. NATURAL LAW, MAGNANIMITY CUM HUMILITY, AND CONTEMPORARY POLITICS

In *Thomism and Aristotelianism* Jaffa also notes an important dissonance between Aristotle's and Aquinas's respective accounts of a paramount ethical and political virtue, magnanimity or greatness of soul (Greek *megalopsychia;* Latin *magnanimitas*).[36] The difference can be expressed succinctly in this way: Aristotle's magnanimity (see *NE* 4.3) seems incompatible with deeply felt gratitude and especially with humility, whereas Aquinas's magnanimity cannot exist as a true virtue without the support and, as it were, collaboration of either of these two qualities. In the case of humility, Aquinas goes so far as to posit it as magnanimity's "twin virtue" *(duplex virtus).* Yet as Aquinas himself also observes, it is far from clear how humility in particular can be compatible with magnanimity, a virtue conducing to outstanding statesmanship: "humility is apparently opposed to the virtue of magnanimity, which aims at great things, whereas humility shuns them."[37]

Jaffa further and rightly refers us to Christian (or, as he stresses, "revealed") theology as an important source of Aquinas's divergence from Aristotle. Radical doctrines such as creation *ex nihilo* as a free expression of divine goodness, certainty concerning divine "particular" providence as extending to each and every being and in particular to rational or human beings, and a vision of each human person as *imago Dei* and invited to friendship with God cannot help but influence the Christian thinker's understanding of moral conduct and ethical excellence. In his postscript Jaffa quotes with approval this pithy summary of the distinction between Thomistic and Aristotelian ethics that can well be applied to their specific understandings of magnanimity: ". . . Aristotle did not look upon God as Creator nor as exercising conscious government and providence, but regarded Him as the final Cause alone. . . . The virtuous man of Aristotle is, in a sense, the most independent man, whereas the virtuous

36. Section 3 of this essay is excerpted from Mary M. Keys, "Aquinas and the Challenge of Aristotelian Magnanimity" (*History of Political Thought* 24, no. 1 [Spring 2003]: 37–65), which was included as chapter 6 of my book, *Aquinas, Aristotle, and the Promise of the Common Good,* by kind permission of the journal *History of Political Thought* and its publisher, Imprint Academic.

37. *ST* II-II q. 161 a. 1 obj. 3.

man of St. Thomas is, in a sense, the most dependent man, that is, the man who realizes truly and freely expresses his relation of dependence on God [i.e., a personal God who governs human affairs]."[38]

It still remains to be inquired, however, whether the foundations of a magnanimity humbly conscious of its dependence on God, as well as happily cognizant of its need to look to other human beings and acknowledge their support with enduring gratitude, are wholly and exclusively supernatural. Jaffa implies as much throughout *Thomism and Aristotelianism,* where he alleges that Thomas's revisionist ethic flies in the face of common sense and threatens the very possibility of human or social science. Aquinas, I believe, would maintain that they are not, and he is certainly able to offer plausible reasons for so maintaining based on his foundational theory of natural law. In this discussion I cannot attempt a thorough explication of these arguments, much less anything approaching a demonstration of their validity. My aim is simply to say enough to make the reader aware of some core Thomistic claims and their sources in Aquinas's texts, and to suggest that in some instances at least similar arguments should resonate well with us today at the dawn of the third millennium.

Aquinas's natural theology, the high point of his metaphysics, teaches that unassisted human reason is in principle capable of knowing the existence of God and certain of his attributes.[39] Aquinas judges that finite and contingent being must be created being, and that reason can attain to this truth; what he judges unknowable in the absence of divine revelation is whether the world was created "in time" or from all eternity.[40] Someone thus aware that his or her existence is in this way utterly dependent upon a good, wise, benevolent, powerful, and provident God, and sensitive to the dimension of mystery inherent in a created universe and each of its

38. Frederick Copleston, S.J., *A History of Philosophy,* vol. 2, *Medieval Philosophy from Augustine to Duns Scotus* (New York: Image Books, [1950] 1993), 410–11, quoted in Jaffa, *Thomism and Aristotelianism,* 191–92; see also John O'Callaghan, "Creation, Human Dignity, and the Virtues of Acknowledged Dependence," *Nova et Vetera* 1 (2003): 109–40; Alasdair MacIntyre, *Dependent Rational Animals: Why Human Beings Need the Virtues* (Chicago: Open Court, 1999).

39. *ST* I q. 2; I q. 12 a. 12; Aquinas, *Summa Contra Gentiles* [SCG] 1.10–102); cf. Etienne Gilson, *History of Christian Philosophy in the Middle Ages* (New York: Random House, [1922] 1955), 365–75; Ralph McInerny, *Characters in Search of Their Author: The Gifford Lectures, 1999–2000* (South Bend, Ind.: University of Notre Dame Press, 2001).

40. *ST* I qq. 44–46.

beings, has the foundation for an attitude of profound philosophic reverence.[41] Such a natural modesty or humility is thus in truth a human or ethical virtue, even for "the princes of this world," be they statesmen or, as Aquinas judges, in the highest instance "philosophers."[42]

A difficulty here, however, as Aquinas himself is quick to note, is the trouble that unassisted reason has in reaching metaphysical truths about the world and its ultimate cause. Left to their own devices, only a tiny minority of human beings would have discovered them, after years and perhaps decades of effort; and even then their conclusions would often contain much error admixed with truth. Only the most fortunate of humans, those blessed with quick, penetrating intellects and dogged self-discipline, living in peaceful lands and privileged to enjoy much leisure and learning, would ever have achieved philosophic knowledge of many of the truths that are essential for leading a good life and achieving happiness—or so Aquinas argues. Hence God in his mercy reveals what the reason of so many would necessarily have failed to grasp, and the reason of none perfectly comprehended.[43]

Against those who fear that Aquinas's emphasis on God's will as the

41. Cf. Paul Woodruff's (*Reverence: Renewing a Forgotten Virtue* [Oxford: Oxford University Press, 2001]) thoughtful and timely recovery of *reverence* as a human virtue. While I very much agree with the book's central tenet that certain forms of reverence are good and even indispensable for our social and political lives to be well ordered and to flourish, Woodruff seems to me to argue wrongly when he maintains that "[r]everence has more to do with politics than with religion" (4).

42. Cf. *ST* I q. 12 a. 13 s.c. with q. 32 a. 1 ad 1. Thus Aquinas would contest Pierre Manent's claim (in *The City of Man*, trans. Marc A. LePain [Princeton, N.J.: Princeton University Press, 1998], 200) that "[b]y nature—at least if one isn't telling himself stories—the man who is truly superior necessarily and legitimately disdains the man who is truly his inferior." See also *ST* I q. 27 a. 1 ad 3, where Aquinas notes that the "very nature" of creatures "entails dependence on God." See also Aquinas's treatment of the virtue of religion *(religio)*, a moral virtue and a "part" of justice, which inclines its possessor "to show reverence to the one God under one aspect, namely as the first principle of the creation and government of things" (*ST* II-II q. 81 a. 3 c.), thus following "a dictate of natural reason" (*ST* II-II q. 81a. 2 ad 3). Douglas Kries ("Thomas Aquinas and the Politics of Moses," *Review of Politics* 52 [1990]: 102; cf. also 98–101) makes a related religious and political observation, concluding that Aquinas considers the best regime of Aristotle's *Politics* to be *rationally* inferior to the polity established by the Mosaic law, insofar as the former fails "properly [to] take into consideration that aspect of [natural] justice which orders human beings to God in regulating that aspect of justice which orders human beings to each other." For an analogous but not identical argument in contemporary context, see Václav Havel, *Open Letters: Selected Writings, 1964–1990*, discussed below (pp. 192–94).

43. Cf. *SCG* 1.4; *ST* I q. 1 a. 1; I-II q. 99 a. 2 ad 2.

foundation of both creation and revelation undermines the possibility of science, both natural and especially ethical and political science,[44] Aquinas in effect maintains that if the risks of a lapse into an antirational fideism are avoided, then the practice of science and the quest for wisdom stand rather to gain and be strengthened.[45] Presumptuous pride—according to Aquinas, one of the vices principally opposed to the virtue of magnanimity[46]—is a great threat to genuine knowledge. It focuses the thinker on an exaggerated image of his or her own excellence, obscuring accurate perception and disposing one to overconfidence and rash judgment. Those reasoners theoretical and practical who, through believing in things unseen yet attested to by divine authority, accustom themselves to self-doubt and humility, are more capable of wonder at the otherness of beings; more apt to proceed with due caution and care in their study; and more cognizant of the possibilities for error in their conclusions and unethical misuse of their results.[47] Faith likewise nourishes the difficult, never completed quest for truth and justice and sustains it in hope. Faith thus provides grounds for a noble magnanimity in scholarly as well as civic life.[48]

Yet what of those many readers who do not accept some or all of Aquinas's philosophy of being and his natural theology, to say nothing of his revealed theology? Are they bound to prefer the magnanimity of the *Nicomachean Ethics* to that of the *ST*? Jaffa suggests that this is the likely outcome of a comparison of the two theories.[49] Aristotle keeps the ethical and political sphere of human life properly separate from the speculative or theoretical domain, and hence his account of magnanimity and other virtues does not depend on his metaphysics in the same way Aquinas's does. Aristotle's conclusions are therefore in themselves

44. Cf. Larry Arnhart, "Statesmanship as Magnanimity: Classical, Christian, and Modern," *Polity* 16 (1983): 274–76.

45. See, e.g., *ST* I q. 19 aa. 4–5.

46. See *ST* II-II q. 130 a. 2.

47. Cf. *SCG* I.5.4; *ST* II-II q. 130 a. 2 ad 3; q. 133 a. 1 ad 4.

48. Cf. inter alia *SCG* I.2.2; *ST* I-II q. 40 and II-II q. 17; *ST* II-II q. 129 a. 6. For a political theorist's recent reflections on the meaning and import of hope, see Glenn Tinder, *The Fabric of Hope: An Essay* (Atlanta: Scholars Press, 1999); those of a contemporary analytic philosopher, Peter Geach, *Truth and Hope* (South Bend, Ind.: University of Notre Dame Press, 2001); and for an important twentieth-century Thomist's, Josef Pieper, *On Hope*, trans. Sister Mary Frances McCarthy, S.N.D. (San Francisco: Ignatius Press, [1949] 1986).

49. See Jaffa, *Thomism and Aristotelianism.*

both more accessible and more persuasive to us and our multicultural, multiethnic contemporaries. The heroic *megalopsychia* that the classical statesman evinces is much needed in modern times, Jaffa holds, and it is the great vice of Thomistic Aristotelianism that it obscures such important aspects of the Philosopher's ethical wisdom from needy enquirers in search of a realistic yet ennobling social science.

Yet it is important to note that metaphysics is not the first or foremost teacher of ethics according to Aquinas. There is also the ground-up moral phenomenology beginning from natural law and rooted in what Aquinas terms *synderesis* and *conscientia.*[50] The ethical experience of each human person, Aquinas maintains, evolves in the context of an inborn inclination toward good and an aversion to evil.[51] Natural knowledge of the first and very general precepts of natural law enjoins personal, rational reflection on human relationships, social norms, the example and advice given by others, and one's concrete lived experiences, to deepen one's understanding of the requirements of virtue and upright conduct and the connection of these with *beatitudo,* with happiness or flourishing.[52]

Reflecting on the problem of a person's moral responsibility in a political society or culture that (perhaps inevitably) propagates some defective views of human fulfillment and ethical conduct, MacIntyre considers Aquinas to hold that the universal experience of friendship in its myriad instantiations offers unique possibilities for ethical growth.[53] Insofar as one is genuinely committed to a friend's welfare, one gradually learns how virtue develops in various kinds of conduct, and by contrast,

50. For Aquinas's understanding and explication of *synderesis,* the "natural habit" of the first principles of practical reason, and *conscience,* the application of moral knowledge to the judgment of a particular act, see *ST* I q. 79 aa. 12 and 13; I-II q. 19 aa. 5 and 6; 94 q. 1 aa. 4 and 6.

51. "All the inclinations of any parts whatsoever of human nature, e.g., of the concupiscible and irascible parts, in so far as they are ruled by reason, belong to the natural law, and are reduced [from the Latin *reducere,* to be led or brought back] to one first precept [namely, 'good is to be done and pursued, and evil is to be avoided'], as stated above: so that the precepts of the natural law are many in themselves, but are based on one common foundation" (*ST* I-II q. 94 a. 2 ad 2). Aquinas thus argues later in the *ST,* for example, for the viciousness of magnanimity's chief foil pusillanimity because it runs contrary to the natural law, that is, to the natural inclination to attempt to accomplish the good that is within one's power, "refusing to do that which is commensurate thereto" (*ST* II-II a. 133 q. 1, c.).

52. *ST* I-II q. 94 a. 2; cf. q. 94 aa. 4 and 6.

53. Alasdair MacIntyre, *Whose Justice? Which Rationality?* (South Bend, Ind.: University of Notre Dame Press, 1988), 179–81, 198–200.

which actions and attitudes impede concern for and esteem of another's good. In so doing, one comes to an ever-deepening understanding of the requirements of one's own good as a human being.

So, we might consider Aristotle's magnanimous man who is naturally disinclined to rejoice in the good turns others have done him or to acknowledge them after those favors have been returned with interest. Aristotle implies that the *megalopsychos* nonetheless does have friends and is even willing to "adjust" his life to spend time in their company and to meet their needs.[54] Insofar as he comes to esteem his most virtuous companions, his soul-mates, as other selves, he might reflect that just as he appreciates hearing the good he has done recounted and remembered, so his friends likewise appreciate and even deserve to hear their own noble deeds recalled. More than that, he may come to realize that the genuine love and affection he has for his friends should make his being their moral debtor more often than not a pleasant reality. Friendship of the noblest kind issues in a kind of individual self-transcendence that propels towards mutual self-fulfillment. It may be that Aristotle himself hoped that readers who matched the description of the *megalopsychos* (the magnanimous man) in book four of the *Nicomachean Ethics* might be brought to reconsider their excessive concern with superiority and consequent ingratitude, by the time they had studied the lessons on *philia* or friendship in the eighth and ninth books.[55] Such at least is one possible implication of Jaffa's interpretation of the structure of the *Ethics* as one of ethical ascent from common attitudes and appearances to deeper truths about the human condition,[56] although we should note as

54. Cf. *NE* 1125a1.

55. Indeed, an invitation to this sort of ethical ascent could be read in two of the chapters following almost immediately on the treatment of *megalopsychia* in the *NE:* that on friendliness or affability (*NE* 4.6), and that on truthfulness, defined as the disposition willingly to reveal the reality of oneself and one's character in attitude, word, and deed (*NE* 4.7). For a recent analysis of ethical growth by way of *philia* and its role in Aristotle's political science and theory of the common good, see Thomas W. Smith, "Aristotle on the Conditions for and Limits of the Common Good," *American Political Science Review* 93 (1999): 628–31. For a parallel discussion of *amicitia* in Aquinas's political thought, see John Finnis, *Aquinas: Moral, Political, and Legal Theory* (New York: Oxford University Press, 1998), 111–17, on "Egoism, Self-Fulfillment, and the Common Good." On this theme generally, cf. Lorraine Smith Pangle, *Aristotle and the Philosophy of Friendship* (Cambridge: Cambridge University Press, 2002), and James V. Schall, "Friendship and Political Philosophy," *Review of Metaphysics* 50 (1996): 121–41.

56. Jaffa, *Thomism and Aristotelianism,* 64–66.

well that Jaffa doubts anyone other than a true philosopher could experience the fullness of friendship as described in those passages.[57]

If the experience of friendship can be posited as in some sense universal, transcending the historical or cultural particularities in which it is embodied and by which it is informed, Aquinas's natural law teaching also implies that different sociopolitical contexts tend to obscure some content of the natural law, and hence of human virtue, even while illuminating other aspects of it. In our times, the moral sensibility shown by dissenters in the former Soviet Union and its satellites offers strong experiential support—generally from outside Thomist circles and at times from non-Christians—for the humanity of humility, and its role in forming the character of the truly magnanimous person. In a 1984 essay entitled "Politics and Conscience,"[58] to give one powerful example, Václav Havel urges jaded modern men and women to recover their primordial awareness of their "life-world" or "the natural world," together with the sense of ethical responsibility this dimension of humanness enjoins. This task entails recovering the simplicity and capacity for wonder manifested by small children.

> They are still rooted in a world which knows the dividing line between all that is intimately familiar and appropriately a subject of our concern, and that which lies beyond its horizon, that before which we should bow down humbly because of the mystery about it. . . . [This "natural world"] is the realm of our inimitable, inalienable, and nontransferable joy and pain, a world in which, through which, and for which we are somehow answerable, a world of personal responsibility. . . . At the basis of this world are values which are simply there, perennially, before we ever speak of them, before we reflect upon them and inquire about them. It owes its internal coherence to something like a "pre-speculative" assumption that the world functions and is generally possible at all only be-

57. It is also important to note that the constrained nature of friendship based on a common love of noble deeds, some of which can only be performed by one person or another, is reflected to the end of the *NE*: "[O]ne will wish the greatest good for his friend as a human being. But perhaps not all the greatest goods, for each man wishes for his own good most of all" (*NE* 8.7.1159a11–13; cf. 9.8.1169a18–1169b2). Aquinas might well argue that the divine friendship of *caritas* (see *ST* II-II qq. 23–33, especially q. 23 aa. 1 and 3) finally frees all virtuous human friendships to be themselves, so to speak, by loosing the tension created by the all-too-human concern of each friend for his or her own superiority.

58. Havel wrote this as a speech to be delivered on the occasion of his receipt of an honorary doctorate from the University of Toulouse in May 1984, but at that time he was prohibited from traveling abroad and so could not deliver his speech in person (Václav Havel, *Open Letters: Selected Writings, 1964–1990* [New York: Knopf, 1991], 249).

cause there is something beyond its horizon, something beyond or above our grasp, but, for just that reason, firmly grounds this world, bestows upon it its order and measure, and is the hidden source of all the rules, customs, commandments, prohibitions, and norms that hold within it. The natural world, in virtue of its very being, bears within it the presupposition of the absolute which grounds, delimits, animates, and directs it, without which it would be unthinkable, absurd, and superfluous, and which we can only quietly respect. Any attempt to spurn it, master it, or replace it with something else, appears, within the framework of the natural world, as an expression of hubris for which humans must pay a heavy price, as did Don Juan and Faust.[59]

In the conclusion of this essay, Havel alludes to the surprising impact of the "antipolitical politics"[60] practiced by dissidents as diverse as physicist Andrei Sakarov, novelist Aleksandr Solzhenitsyn, philosopher Jan Patočka, and Solidarity trade union leader Lech Walesa, whom Havel could then describe as a "simple electrician with his heart in the right place, honoring something that transcends him and free from fear."[61] The writings and even more so the lives of these heroes of Central and Eastern Europe have much to teach us Westerners, Havel suggests:

I am convinced that what is called "dissent" in the Soviet bloc is a specific modern experience, the experience of life at the very ramparts of dehumanized power. As such, that "dissent" has the opportunity and even the duty to reflect on this experience, to testify to it and to pass it on to those fortunate enough not to have to undergo it. Thus we too have a certain opportunity to help in some ways those who help us, to help them in our deeply shared interest, in the interest of mankind.[62]

One of the "essential and universal truths" in the dissidents' experiences is the personal, social, and political importance of a courageous, magnanimous humility:

59. Ibid., 250–51.

60. Havel loosely defines this concept as "politics as one of the ways of seeking and achieving meaningful lives, of protecting them and serving them . . . politics as practical morality, as service to the truth, as essentially human and humanly measured care for our fellow humans" (Ibid., 269).

61. Ibid., 270–71. Or better, in Walesa's case as also in Solzhenitsyn's, and in Aquinas's, honoring *Someone* who transcends yet also creates and grounds and governs one's person and indeed the entire universe.

62. Ibid., 269–70; cf. Thomas L. Pangle, *The Ennobling of Democracy* (Baltimore: Johns Hopkins University Press, 1992), 84–90.

We must draw our standards from our natural world, heedless of ridicule, and reaffirm its validity. We must honor with the humility of the wise the limits of that natural world and the mystery which lies beyond them, admitting that there is something in the order of being which evidently exceeds all our competence. We must relate to the absolute horizon of our existence which, if we but will, we shall constantly rediscover and experience.[63]

From this evidence I would conclude that Aquinas's natural law-based ethic of humility cum magnanimity is not one with which, humanly and philosophically speaking, "the facts [of our moral experience] soon clash" (*NE* 1145b and ff.).[64] Indeed, at the dawn of a new millennium our many memories of the past "century of sorrows"[65] suggest that humility constitutes a more central social and political virtue than even Thomas Aquinas may have recognized.[66] And this alone should give us pause and lend credence to the thesis of our lecture series, that recognition of and reflection on the natural moral law are urgently needed in our contemporary society as well as in the study of ethics and politics.

63. Havel, *Open Letters*, 267, emphasis added; cf. Aviezer Tucker, *The Philosophy and Politics of Czech Dissidence from Patočka to Havel* (Pittsburgh: University of Pittsburgh Press, 2000), 155–61.

64. Jaffa, *Thomism and Aristotelianism*, 22, 27–29.

65. The phrase is from another former Soviet-bloc dissident, Karol Wojtiła, as Pope John Paul II in his Address to the Fiftieth General Assembly of the United Nations Organization, October 5, 1995, § 16–17: "In order to recover our hope and our trust at the end of this century of sorrows, we must regain sight of that transcendent horizon of possibility to which the soul of man aspires.... *We can and we must do so!* And in so doing, we shall see that the tears of this century have prepared the ground for a new springtime of the human spirit" (emphasis in original) (available online at http://www.vatican.va/holy_father/john_paul_ii/speeches/1996/documents/hf_jp-ii_spe_05101995_address-to-uno_en.html [October 5, 1995]).

66. Cf. *ST* II-II q. 161 a. 1, ad 5.

V. Bradley Lewis

8 Natural Right and the Problem of Public Reason

The dominant line of thought in Western political philosophy for most of its history has understood and evaluated political realities in light of the naturally right or just. Philosophy itself emerges out of the distinction between the natural and the conventional in the search for a common and universal explanatory principle of the whole. The natural is a name for that principle and its application to political life was the central task of political philosophy from the pre-Socratics until the end of the eighteenth century. Already in the early modern period a much reduced understanding of the natural had begun to transform political inquiry; the discovery of history as a powerful rival to nature began a second assault on the classical understanding.[1]

While natural right has never been completely effaced from the conversation of political philosophy (that it can never be effaced from political practice is an important theoretical claim of natural right), it has been confined to a somewhat marginal position in the debates of the last two centuries or so. This situation has changed in the last three decades, with a variety of efforts at retrieval of various elements of the classical tradition in moral and political thought. The rise of neo-Aristotelian virtue ethics and the renewed interest in especially Thomistic natural law theory exemplify this development. These retrievals, however, have run

1. In general my understanding of this narrative is informed by Leo Strauss's *Natural Right and History* (Chicago: University of Chicago Press, 1953), but there are other versions of the same basic narrative, differing largely in emphasis and detail.

head-on into another development in political philosophy, the rise of what could most broadly be called justificatory liberalism.

While what has achieved the status of a kind of canonical narrative of contemporary political philosophy centers around Peter Laslett's judgment that, as of 1956, political philosophy was "dead" and John Rawls's (again, initially certified by Laslett, and subsequently established by *consensus gentium*) miraculous revival of it in 1971, the book that accomplished this feat, *A Theory of Justice*, could perhaps better be seen as social contract theory's end.[2] *A Theory of Justice* began what might be called the last fling of the old dispensation in its aim "to generalize and carry to a higher order of abstraction the traditional theory of the social contract as represented by Locke, Rousseau, and Kant," thus to develop the theory "so that it is no longer open to the more obvious objections often thought fatal to it."[3] There is a sense in which Rawls ushered this age to a close. The debate provoked by *A Theory of Justice* sparked the last great controversy of that age, one that often, albeit, ultimately incompletely and unsuccessfully, appealed in some cases to the claims of history, but in others to the premodern claims of natural right, the so-called liberal-communitarian debate.

It is then appropriate that Rawls himself made the next and transformative move with the series of essays modifying and recontextualizing his theory and which ultimately became his 1993 book, *Political Liberalism*. That work aims to answer the question: "How is it possible that there may exist over time a stable and just society of free and equal citizens profoundly divided by reasonable though incompatible religious, philosophical, and moral doctrines?"[4] Rawls's answer to this question is that it is possible to work out the appropriate principles of a freestanding political conception of justice that can be the focus of what he calls an "overlapping consensus" of reasonable comprehensive doctrines. One

2. See Peter Laslett, introduction to *Philosophy, Politics and Society, First Series* (New York: Macmillan, 1956), 1; John Rawls, *A Theory of Justice* (Cambridge, Mass.: Harvard University Press, 1971); and Peter Laslett and James Fishkin, introduction to *Philosophy, Politics and Society, Fifth Series* (New Haven, Conn.: Yale University Press, 1979), 1.

3. Rawls, *A Theory of Justice*, viii.

4. John Rawls, *Political Liberalism*, 3rd ed. (New York: Columbia University Press, 2003), xviii. *Political Liberalism* has now gone through three editions: the first as published in 1993; a second paperback edition, which included some new material, was published in 1996; now a third "expanded edition" includes even more material, although the pagination of the material from the first edition remains the same.

aspect of that overlapping consensus being maintained is that citizens honor the demands of what Rawls calls "public reason." This means that when considering constitutional essentials and matters of basic justice the citizens of a constitutional democratic regime should only deploy arguments the grounds of which are such as all citizens may reasonably be expected to endorse. Citizens who hold one or another comprehensive doctrine, whether religious or secular in nature, must recognize that the whole truth cannot be embodied in politics and thus voluntarily restrain the extent of their claims.

This is the beginning of justificatory liberalism. The scope of political philosophy in this new dispensation contracts even more than in classical social contract theory. The main question is not the premodern question, "What is the best regime?" Nor is it the modern question, "What principles explain and vindicate supreme political authority?" Now the question is "What sorts of arguments should citizens use in deliberating about the most important political matters?" or "How should important laws and policies be justified in pluralistic democratic societies?" The question of what we should do must wait on an answer to the question of how we should discuss it. Since Rawls began writing about these questions, around 1980, the debate has increasingly gravitated toward them, and now it seems to be the principle focus of mental energy in Anglo-American academic political philosophy. Rawls's own initial questions and proposals have led to many amendments and counterproposals as well as to the development of complete alternate theories so that the field is now populated not only by "political liberals," but also by "deliberative democrats" and "justificatory liberals," each coming in several varieties.

It is this new movement that collides, as I suggested above, with the various efforts of retrieval appealing to the premodern tradition of natural right. My specific concern in what follows is the relationship of this now pervasive approach to political philosophy with what was the dominant approach to political things for most of the history of Western philosophy, natural right, within which we find the tradition of inquiry into the natural moral law.[5] The natural law has usually been thought to pro-

5. For present purposes I take natural law theory (as exemplified by medieval thinkers like Aquinas, modern thinkers by Grotius and Locke, and more recent thinkers like Jacques Maritain, Yves Simon, and John Finnis) to be part of a larger family of political and moral theories rooted in the notion of natural right, a family that his its beginning in the thought

vide a basis for dialogue among those who hold different religious commitments and among different cultures. The natural law is also thought to be the stable basis of social arrangements that in their particulars differ from time to time and place to place. Given this important aspect of natural law, it may seem obvious that natural law might continue to play a role in public deliberation under a regime of public reason among those who differ over much else. Many have seen precisely this as the great advantage of the natural law tradition. On this view the natural law is the very basis of public reason. Yet the question of whether and to what extent the natural law can be a basis of political judgments under public reason is a matter of great controversy, with a number of thinkers committed to the justificatory project rejecting the applicability of natural law theory or restricting the scope of its possible relevance in public debates. So my basic question is this: Is natural law theory at odds with the justificatory project and its notion of public reason? How should we understand this debate from the perspective of the tradition of classical natural right? My discussion falls into three parts. First, I describe in more detail Rawls's theory of public reason and raise some initial questions about it. Second, I discuss three representative views of the relationship of the natural law to public reason: those of Stephen Macedo, Kent Greenawalt, and John Finnis, noting some initial problems or questions about their respective accounts. Third, I assess these views from the perspective of a reading of the natural right tradition in terms of the character of natural law theory itself, the extent to which political practice can embody the truth, and the context of modern democratic politics. I conclude that the tradition of natural right is not only compatible with the most defensible elements of public reason, but its resources provide a helpful explanation of it, one less restrictive and more flexible than that of Rawls and some others and one more in line with our hopes for (realistic) political practice.

---

of Plato and Aristotle, who did not yet use the phrase "natural *law*," and still other recent thinkers like Leo Strauss, who, while not hostile to natural *law*, prefer the Platonic-Aristotelian formulation for substantive reasons. The family quarrel here is not of concern to me in this essay, while what the members of the family have in common is. That there is a quarrel I acknowledge, but ignore in this essay, using the phrases "natural law" and "natural right" interchangeably. The dispute between the premodern and modern natural law theories is of concern in the way indicated above, and I do have more to say about just how "natural law" and "natural law theory" should be understood below in section 3.

1. RAWLS AND PUBLIC REASON

Public reason, for Rawls, names a kind of ideal. It represents the way that democratic citizens would deliberate among themselves over laws that concern the most fundamental aspects of a political system shared by persons who otherwise differ greatly in their most basic religious and moral commitments. It describes the character of political debate under the conditions of pluralism and grows out of an attempt to remedy what Rawls took to be a serious deficiency in his earlier *Theory of Justice.* There Rawls proposed and defended a set of principles of justice that should inform the basic structure of society. The principles were arrived at by means of an idealized model decision procedure called by Rawls the "original position," in which persons shorn of their particular identities and armed only with reason and general knowledge about human psychology and the natural world choose principles of justice that will inform the society in which they live in their real lives.[6]

Rawls later came to the conclusion that part of his account in *Theory of Justice* was inadequate, specifically, the discussion of stability in the book's third part. That account unrealistically assumed that citizens of a "well-ordered society" would accept the principles of justice on the basis of a comprehensive version of liberalism (not utilitarianism, but a version of social contract theory closest in many respects to Kant). The notion of "comprehensive doctrines" was not present in *Theory of Justice,* but Rawls came to see it as crucial in the context of contemporary pluralism: "A modern democratic society is characterized not simply by a pluralism of comprehensive religious, philosophical, and moral doctrines but by a pluralism of incompatible yet reasonable comprehensive doctrines. No one of these doctrines is affirmed by citizens generally."[7]

A comprehensive doctrine is a more or less systematic and comprehensive worldview including theoretical and practical elements that are relatively stable over time.[8] Citizens are reasonable when they are willing to govern their conduct by principles that others accept. Reasonableness also reflects a willingness to accept what Rawls calls the "burdens of judgment," which explain difficulties in arriving at agreement on ques-

6. *Theory of Justice,* 17–22; 118–92; *Political Liberalism,* 22–28.

7. *Political Liberalism,* xvi.

8. Ibid., 59.

tions of religion and morality; they include things like conflicts over admissible types of evidence and their weights, indeterminacy among all our concepts, the way evidence is assessed in light of people's overall life experience, and the presence of different types of normative considerations on both sides of issues.[9] The burdens of judgment and the presence of many conflicting comprehensive doctrines mean that no ultimate agreement is possible, nor is the complete victory of any one comprehensive doctrine over rivals. Nevertheless, agreement on detached, purely political matters is possible between these competing doctrines provided that they are reasonable, that is, willing to admit the burdens of judgment and thus unwilling to attempt to repress other reasonable comprehensive doctrines. Unreasonable comprehensive doctrines are another matter.[10]

Political Liberalism, then, represents a recasting of Rawls's theory of justice in light of the existence in society of a plurality of reasonable comprehensive doctrines. The aim of the revised theory is "to uncover the conditions of the possibility of a reasonable public basis of justification on fundamental political questions. It should, if possible, set forth the content of such a basis and why it is acceptable. In doing this, it has to distinguish the public point of view from the many nonpublic (not private) points of view." Political liberalism aims to establish a freestanding political conception of justice not rooted in any particular comprehensive doctrine but impartial among them.[11] It is important for Rawls that the condition of reasonable pluralism is not something to be regretted. It is rather "the natural outcome of the activities of human reason under enduring free institutions."[12] It does mean that political institutions in constitutional democracies cannot be rooted in any particular comprehensive doctrine. Principles of justice are understood as freestanding and capable of being endorsed by all reasonable comprehensive doctrines.

In the first stage of political liberalism, principles of justice that can inform the basic structure of society are worked out through the device of the original position. The idea of public reason is a key feature of the second stage, which concerns the stability of such a society over time. A stable and just political society is possible when the principles of jus-

9. Ibid., 54–58.

10. See ibid., xvi, lv, 32–33, 39, 126.

11. Ibid., xix.

12. Ibid., xxiv, 4, 36–37, 135, 144.

tice arrived at in the first stage can become the focus of an overlapping consensus among reasonable comprehensive doctrines. In a reasonably well-ordered constitutional regime questions about constitutional essentials and matters of basic justice are as far as possible settled by appeal to political values alone, and those values are understood normally to have sufficient weight to override all other values that may come into conflict with them.[13] In an overlapping consensus, then, conflicting comprehensive doctrines come to agreement not on the most basic or important matters of religion, metaphysics, or morals, but on freestanding political principles. They agree to disagree about the deepest matters out of a recognition of the very great value of membership in a just and stable political society, and they refrain from using political power in ways not acceptable to all citizens with their differing comprehensive doctrines.

An overlapping consensus, however, is not morally neutral. Rawls stresses that the consensus is not a mere modus vivendi, a peace treaty in which the various parties agree to terms that serve their mutual interests until such time as they may acquire the upper hand, after which all bets are off. The overlapping consensus is affirmed on moral grounds ultimately supplied internally by the comprehensive doctrines. In this way the principles of justice are rooted in comprehensive doctrines (which, together, Rawls refers to as the "background culture"), albeit differently in each case: a utilitarian would justify the principles according to the "greatest happiness principle," a Kantian according to the *Allgemeine Rechtsprinzip*, and a Thomist perhaps on the basis of the *bonum commune*. All would endorse a regime of toleration and political values that support it. There is no possibility of a resolution to such conflict among comprehensive doctrines on Rawls's view: it is assumed to be a permanent feature of free societies, and, as I said above, not an evil.[14] Among the most important elements of an enduring overlapping consensus is the idea of public reason.

Public reason names an ideal of democratic citizenship by which citizens agree how coercive political power will and will not be used when fundamental questions are at stake: "[O]ur exercise of political power is proper and hence justifiable only when it is exercised in accordance with

13. Ibid., 137–38.
14. See above, note 12.

a constitution the essentials of which all citizens may reasonably be expected to endorse in the light of principles and ideals acceptable to them as reasonable and rational."[15] In public reason, then, citizens recognize limits to the kind of justifications they can give for policies that affect their fellow citizens who may not share their comprehensive doctrines. Accordingly such arguments are made on the basis of ideas that can be shared:

> [O]n matters of constitutional essentials and matters of basic justice, the basic structure and its public policies are to be justified to all citizens, as the principle of political legitimacy requires. We add to this that in making these justifications we are to appeal only to presently accepted general beliefs and forms of reasoning found in common sense, and the methods and conclusions of science when these are not controversial. . . .
>
> . . . [W]e are not to appeal to comprehensive religious and philosophical doctrines—to what we as individuals or members of associations see as the whole truth—nor to elaborate economic theories of general equilibrium, say, if these are in dispute. As far as possible, the knowledge and ways of reasoning that ground our affirming the principles of justice and their application to constitutional essentials and basic justice are to rest on plain truths now widely accepted, or available, to citizens generally. Otherwise, the political conception would not provide a public basis of justification.[16]

Put another way, "the zeal to embody the whole truth in politics is incompatible with an idea of public reason that belongs with democratic citizenship."[17]

It is important that public reason represents an ideal: it is a moral duty, but not a legal one, as this would illegitimately restrict free speech.[18] Similarly public reason applies mainly to judges in making their decisions, the discourse of other elected and appointed public officials, and that of candidates for office. It does not strictly apply to individual citizens. Also, public reason does not apply to all political questions, but only to those that concern "constitutional essentials and matters of basic

15. *Political Liberalism,* 217.

16. Ibid., 224–25.

17. "The Idea of Public Reason Revisited," in ibid., 442. This essay was originally published in the *University of Chicago Law Review* 64 (1997): 765–807, and is reprinted in the (3rd) expanded edition of *Political Liberalism,* from which I quote.

18. *Political Liberalism,* 213, 217; "Public Reason Revisited," 445.

justice."[19] In many other matters Rawls concedes that citizens may licitly justify their views by reference to comprehensive doctrines. It is also important that commitment to public reason like commitment to the political conception of justice that is the focus of the overlapping consensus is not a modus vivendi, but a genuinely moral commitment. If it were not, the problem of stability would remain unresolved. Finally, it is important that the opposite of public reason is not "private reason" (of which there is no such thing), but "nonpublic reason," the reasoning grounded in comprehensive doctrines. One should also note that Rawls does not see public reason as an all-or-nothing proposition: there are degrees of public reason corresponding to the type of constitutional democratic society one actually has. In a perfectly well-ordered society all political debate about the specified types of issues would take place in perfectly public reason. The less well-ordered a society is, the less true this would be. This is how Rawls explains what seem to represent important counterexamples from American history, for example, the abolitionists' invocation of religious values, Lincoln's political rhetoric (especially the Second Inaugural Address), and the language of the civil rights movement, especially that of Martin Luther King Jr. In these cases nonpublic reasons were deployed; however, they were deployed in a considerably less well-ordered society in the attempt to make it more well-ordered by establishing and extending important principles of justice now constitutive of the regime and thus bases of public reason.[20]

If one stands back and looks at this account, I think one can interpret it almost as a kind of transcendental argument. We have a constitutional democratic regime and we have pluralism about religion, philosophy, morality. And in these conditions of pluralism the constitutional democratic regime has endured. Now imagine it even better than it is: "well-ordered" and stable, to use Rawls's terms: How is all this possible? What must be the case for such a phenomenon to exist and continue ex-

19. *Political Liberalism,* 10, 214, 224; "Public Reason Revisited," 442–43, 446.

20. *Political Liberalism,* 247–54. In addition to this, in "Public Reason Revisited," 462, Rawls introduces an exception he calls "the *Proviso,*" which states that "reasonable comprehensive doctrines, religious or nonreligious, may be introduced in public political discussion at any time, provided that in due course proper political reasons—and not reasons given solely by comprehensive doctrines—are presented that are sufficient to support whatever the comprehensive doctrines introduced are said to support." This notion makes the theory somewhat more flexible, but does not materially change it.

isting? What conditions would be required? Rawls's answer is that the regime must be based on principles of justice that can become the focus of an overlapping consensus among reasonable comprehensive doctrines (and note well: there cannot be too many unreasonable comprehensive doctrines around): people must be able to agree on some restricted matters of justice, the most important, even though they disagree on their ultimate grounds. Moreover, political debate and deliberation about the most important matters in such a society must take place by means of a kind of self-restraint in which citizens appeal to widely shared ideas that other citizens who hold reasonable comprehensive doctrines could be expected to endorse.

Two other points about public reason: first, it should again be emphasized that the principle is aimed at recognizing that in a constitutional democratic regime public reason is a recognition that "[t]he zeal to embody the whole truth in politics is incompatible with an idea of public reason that belongs with democratic citizenship."[21] Public reason is a kind of self-restraint whereby citizens refrain from appealing to what they take to be the whole truth when laying down laws that affect everyone and instead appeal to widely shared notions that all could be reasonably be expected to endorse.

The second point concerns examples that Rawls gives of how this might work. In describing the content of public reason in his 1997 essay "The Idea of Public Reason Revisited," Rawls emphasizes that there are a variety of liberalisms, by which he means possible sets of principles appropriate to government in a free and democratic society, not just his own favored idea, "justice as fairness," proposed in *Theory of Justice.* He mentions specifically Habermas's discourse conception of legitimacy "as well as Catholic views of the common good and solidarity when they are expressed in terms of political values." In a footnote attached to this sentence Rawls especially cites books by John Finnis and Jacques Maritain as examples of how this may be done.[22]

In the earlier *Political Liberalism* Rawls gave a quite different sort of example, one that has since become notorious. Having specified that citizens must explain their votes and positions under public reason in terms

21. "Public Reason Revisited," 442, 447.
22. Ibid., 451–52, with note 29.

of "a reasonable balance of political values," Rawls, in a footnote, asks the reader to consider the case of abortion. Rawls proposes that for purposes of the example abortion be considered in terms of "three important political values: the due respect for human life, the ordered reproduction of political society over time, including the family in some form, and finally the equality of women as equal citizens." He goes on to write:

> Now I believe any reasonable balance of these three values will give a woman a duly qualified right to decide whether or not to end her pregnancy during the first trimester. The reason for this is that at this early stage of pregnancy the political value of equality of women is overriding, and this right is required to give it substance and force. Other political values, if tallied in, would not, I think, affect this conclusion.

A few lines later he adds that

> any comprehensive doctrine that leads to a balance of political values excluding that duly qualified right in the first trimester is to that extent unreasonable; and depending on details of its formulation, it may also be cruel and oppressive; for example, if it denied the right altogether except in the case of rape and incest.[23]

In the 1997 article, as a result of criticism of the footnote, Rawls returned to it. There he wrote that he intended the abortion example only as an illustration of a point made later in the note: "The only comprehensive doctrines that run afoul of public reason are those that cannot support a reasonable balance [or ordering] of political values [on the issue]." This would be true in the case of abortion, Rawls went on to say, if the sort of justification he had suggested works under public reason, but no comparable case can be made (again, using a balance of public values) against allowing abortion in the first trimester.[24]

These two examples are instructive. The first involving Habermasian discourse ethics and the Catholic view of the common good and solidarity show how comprehensive doctrines can communicate associated political values in terms of public reason. It seems relevant that Rawls chose to identify the Catholic perspective on politics with the common good and solidarity. Certainly those two notions are important in Cath-

23. *Political Liberalism*, 243–44, with note 32.
24. "Public Reason Revisited," 479n80.

olic social thought,[25] although, interestingly, in the footnote mentioning them Rawls writes that they derive from Aristotle and St. Thomas but then writes that one should see works by Finnis and Maritain, adding "Finnis is especially clear, while Aquinas is occasionally ambiguous." The work cited by Finnis is *Natural Law and Natural Rights.* When identifying the Catholic perspective on politics, especially if one takes those authors to be representative, I think most people would mention natural law along with (if not before) the notion of the common good.[26] Rawls does not. So far as I can tell, the only references to natural law in *Political Liberalism* are two references to H. L. A. Hart's notion of the minimum content of the natural law,[27] and one early reference to the "dictates of what some regard as natural law" about which there is no agreement among citizens.[28] That Rawls never discusses natural law in any real detail could suggest that he did not think it an appropriate part of public reason, which brings me back to the second example.

It would be difficult to overstate the gratuitous character of the abortion footnote. For one thing, Rawls could have picked any number of examples to make his point. For another, the choice of political values to balance seems almost entirely arbitrary, as does the specific balance he strikes. Why, for example, is the value of equality of women overriding during the first trimester of pregnancy? And why is the right to abort "required" to give women's equality "substance and force"? And how, given the lack of explanation for what has just been said can one simply assert that any comprehensive doctrine that arrives at the opposite conclusion is thereby exposed as unreasonable (at least on that issue)? My point is not simply that Rawls was in error here (although I think he certainly was), but that if this is his model of how public reason might work in practice, his sense of the possibilities seems much narrower than one had

25. See, e.g., *Catechism of the Catholic Church,* secs. 1905–1912 (on the common good) and 1939–1942 (on solidarity).

26. The two are mentioned together in the "Doctrinal Note on Some Questions Regarding the Participation of Catholics in Political Life," nos. 2–4, issued by the Congregation for the Doctrine of the Faith on 24 November 2002, and signed by then Cardinal Joseph Ratzinger. See also *Catechism of the Catholic Church,* secs. 1954–1960 (on the natural moral law), and Ratzinger, *Values in a Time of Upheaval,* trans. Brian McNeil (New York: Crossroad / San Francisco: Ignatius Press, 2006), 24, 27, 39, 51, 54, and his (as Benedict XVI) Encyclical Letter *Deus Caritas Est* (25 December 2005), nos. 28–29; and *Caritas in Veritate* (29 June 2009), nos. 45, 59, 68, 75.

27. *Political Liberalism,* 109n15, 161.

28. Ibid., 97.

been led to believe. With respect to abortion, it is true that its most vocal opponents are closely associated with certain (usually religious) comprehensive doctrines, but this is not universally so: among opponents of abortion are others, for example, Nat Hentoff and Christopher Hitchens, both of whom profess to be atheists. Consider that Nat Hentoff, Christopher Hitchens, and the Catholic bishops of the United States all oppose abortion and do so from the perspective of what would seem quite different comprehensive doctrines. Is it so difficult to imagine the sort of arguments that Hitchens or Hentoff (leave aside the bishops) might mount as so outside the bounds of readily available political values intelligibly balanced as to render them unreasonable?

The two examples would seem to lay down a stiff challenge to the natural law tradition, even though that tradition has often been seen as providing a kind of common ground, a basis for dialogue among different faith traditions and cultures. Rawls's relative silence on natural law seems, as I have suggested, intentional. However, other scholars who are committed to Rawls's notion or something close to it have discussed its relationship to the natural law.

2. PUBLIC REASON AND NATURAL LAW: THREE RIVAL VERSIONS

Rawls never explicitly discusses natural law in *Political Liberalism* or, so far as I can tell, anywhere else. The relationship between the tradition of natural law and public reason, however, has been addressed by Rawls's allies, interlocutors, and critics. In this section I consider a representative example of each as a way of discussing the status of the question. I begin with Stephen Macedo, a self-identified ally of Rawls, indeed, an ally who goes a good bit further than Rawls himself in his cultural expectations for public reason. Next I consider Kent Greenawalt, who has produced a large body of his own work on the question of public reason, including several essays that consider natural law. Finally I look at John Finnis's explicit response to *Political Liberalism.*

Macedo's Virtues

Stephen Macedo's 1990 book *Liberal Virtues* was actually published three years before *Political Liberalism,* but he made thorough use of the articles Rawls published between 1980 and 1989 which were the basis of that book, as well as of the work of Charles Larmore and Thomas Nagel, and has extended his arguments in subsequent papers.[29] Macedo, however, sought to go further than Rawls, insisting that liberalism should not be conceived as merely political or in any sense neutral.[30] Liberalism does encourage some ways of life and discourage others and should be seen to do so openly. Nevertheless, Macedo argues that political argument in liberal democracies should appeal to widely shared premises and that the "liberal ideals of citizenship, virtue, and community can be located in an ideal of liberal constitutionalism sustained by a basic political commitment to public reasonableness."[31] At the center of Macedo's liberalism is the practice of political justification.

> Public justification is a liberal attempt to establish practices of critical reasonableness among people whose capacity for reason is limited. And so, liberals typically seek justifications that are widely acceptable to reasonable people with a broad range of moral and philosophical commitments and interests. The aim is reasonable agreement: to be both reasonable and agreeable in a widely pluralistic society.[32]

In explaining more about the content of "public justification," Macedo explains that it is not equivalent to philosophy: public justification is a kind of fusion of politics and philosophy "shaping and moderating the aims of both."[33] Public justification cannot simply be philosophy because it must be accessible to citizens: it moderates the aims of philosophy "so as to insure the wide accessibility of the relevant forms of reasoning and evidence: these should be not too difficult and (if possible) not too deep-

29. Stephen Macedo, *Liberal Virtues* (Oxford: Clarendon Press, 1990), 45–50. Cf. Macedo's "Against the Old Sexual Morality of the New Natural Law," in *Natural Law, Liberalism, and Morality,* ed. Robert P. George (Oxford: Clarendon Press, 1996), 43–44; "In Defense of Liberal Public Reason: Are Slavery and Abortion Hard Cases?" in *Natural Law and Public Reason,* ed. Robert P. George and Christopher Wolfe (Washington, D.C.: Georgetown University Press, 2000), 14–18, 21–24.

30. *Liberal Virtues,* 50–64; "In Defense of Liberal Public Reason," 23; and cf. Macedo's "Liberal Civic Education and Religious Fundamentalism: The Case of God v. John Rawls?" *Ethics* 105 (1995): 468–96.

31. *Liberal Virtues,* 38.

32. Ibid., 44; in the immediate sequel Macedo cites Rawls's paper, "The Priority of Right and Ideas of the Good," *Philosophy and Public Affairs* 17 (1988), which is the basis of lecture 5 of *Political Liberalism.*

33. *Liberal Virtues,* 45.

ly at odds with firmly held and not unreasonable views."[34] Moreover, it "does not aim to identify what are simply the best reasons, where best is a function of only the quality of the reasons as reasons leaving aside the constraints of wide accessibility."[35] Public justification, then, is a sort of halfway house between politics and philosophy: it is more than politics, but less than philosophy.

This for Macedo is the problem with natural law. Macedo considers natural law in the course of discussing plausible theoretical alternatives to liberalism (I leave that claim aside for now, but will return to it). The case against natural law consists of two counts: first, natural law consists in a theory about how human beings flourish by participating in various forms of good. Those forms are drawn from the seven identified by Finnis in his 1980 book, *Natural Law and Natural Rights:* life, knowledge, play, friendship, and practical reason (Macedo omits aesthetic experience and religion). "The problem," Macedo writes, "is that these categories are extremely abstract and a long way from yielding publicly justifiable solutions to specific practical controversies."[36] Macedo's example concerns Finnis's argument that "only sexual relations in heterosexual marriages for the purpose of procreation integrate and express full participation in human goods." Macedo argues that nonpromiscuous homosexual relationships can participate in those same goods and that none of Finnis's arguments convincingly precludes this.[37] He continues:

> However, there is a deeper problem with natural law arguments: in many of its versions, natural law is incompatible with the political morality of public justification. Because there is such a large gap between the first principles of natural law and actual moral norms (such as those found in the Ten Commandments) much work needs to be done by a process of inference. And Finnis acknowledges that in many cases the moral inference will require a wisdom or reasonableness "not found in everyone or even in most people." Natural law may be incompatible with the equality of respect that liberalism attempts to embody in its canons of public justification. As a public, political matter, inferences beyond the capacity of "most people" are not proper grounds for law. Natural law might try to save itself from elitism by licensing not public reasons but popular prejudices about how human beings should behave. Natural law would, then, deflect

34. Ibid., 49. Rawls is again cited liberally in an appended note.

35. Ibid., 50.

36. Ibid., 211.

37. Ibid.

the charge of elitism only to fall into an unreasoned populism of the kind deployed by Lord Devlin and Robert Bork.[38]

The charge is that natural law is either too vague or that it is too complex and thus that it either collapses into an undemocratic elitism or an illiberal populism.

Robert George and Christopher Wolfe have responded to Macedo by pointing out the odd "catch-22" quality of the argument: natural law arguments are based on principles that are too distant from ordinary practice to really support them. However, when a rigorous and sophisticated argument is presented to bridge the gap that argument is ruled out of court as too complex.[39] When such principles are held by citizens via something like habituation absent rigorous justification, they are simply prejudice and similarly unacceptable as public justification.

In the long quotation above Macedo compares natural law arguments based on this sort of prejudice to the argument for the legal enforcement of morality now (infamously) associated with Lord Patrick Devlin. While Macedo's invocation of Lord Devlin is doubtless intended to frighten his already white-knuckled readers, there is a certain inherent logic in it. Devlin held that society had a right to defend its morality every bit as much as it had a right to defend its physical integrity. Immorality, he held, was analogous to treason in that it undermined that morality and thus society itself.[40] In his famous reply to Devlin, H. L. A. Hart argued that it was not personal immorality that eroded traditional mores, but free public discussion, suggesting in particular that the findings of contemporary social science, notably psychology and anthropology, showed that there was wide variation in sexual practices and that the repression of individual sexual impulses was cruel and ultimately unhealthy.[41] While Hart cited no actual scientific literature, there is little doubt (given the time) that he had in mind the work of Margaret Mead and Alfred Kinsey.

It seems likely that Macedo's argument has a similar forensic func-

38. Ibid., 211–12.

39. "Natural Law and Public Reason," in *Natural Law and Public Reason,* 65–67.

40. Patrick Devlin, *The Enforcement of Morals* (Oxford: Oxford University Press, 1960), 12–14.

41. H. L. A. Hart, *Law, Liberty and Morality* (Stanford, Calif.: Stanford University Press, 1963), 66–69.

tion: the practice of liberal public justification is neither politics nor philosophy, so it avoids naked appeals to force or prejudice on the one hand, while avoiding rigorous philosophical argument on the other: its substance is drawn from the nostrums of the dominant public culture and insulated from both traditional mores and the sort of moral argument associated with the tradition. Confining public political argument within the dominant public culture, a culture that still grants both Mead and Kinsey iconic status despite the fact that both have been largely discredited,[42] accomplishes what Macedo later reveals to be the goal of public justification: the psychological internalization of pluralism and diversity.[43]

Citizens of tolerant liberal regimes are likely to be shaped deeply by diversity: social pluralism penetrates to the core of the liberal personality, provoking the inner experience of value conflict and stimulating reflection. At the most obvious level, living in a pluralistic society widens the options that people typically have available to them, persons living in such societies must choose more often and are encouraged to reflect more deeply than those living in societies with few real alternatives.[44]

The liberal personality thrives not on a harmonious inner life, but on both "internal" and "external" value plurality, and a consequent unease or dissatisfaction. The internalization of diversity and conflict allows the reflective self to maintain some distance from any single end, or the values of any particular community with which we happen to identify: each of our ends and the whole set of our ends can be seen as less than absolute, and not simply fixed or given. We cannot put aside all our ends and act from pure will or rationality. We can recognize, however, that we are not unreflectively, necessarily, or irrevocably tied to any particular end. For liberals, the capacity to choose is more basic then what is chosen.[45]

42. See Derek Freeman, *Margaret Mead and Samoa: The Making and Unmaking of an Anthropological Myth* (Cambridge, Mass.: Harvard University Press, 1983); and Judith A. Reisman and Edward W. Eichel, *Kinsey, Sex and Fraud: The Indoctrination of a People*, ed. John H. Court and J. Gordon Muir (Lafayette, La.: Huntington House, 1990), with the note affirming elements of Reisman and Eichel's criticisms, "Really, Dr. Kinsey?" *The Lancet* 337 (2 March 1991): 547; and Robert E. Rodes Jr., *On Law and Chastity* (Durham, N.C.: Carolina Academic Press, 2006), 3–4 (citing Robert T. Michael et al., *Sex in America* [Boston: Little Brown, 1994], 15–21, with a critique of Kinsey's methodology).

43. Macedo, *Liberal Virtues*, 237–40.

44. Ibid., 237–38.

45. Ibid., 239.

There would seem to be two problems here: first, Macedo's account, although its ideal of public justification is drawn from Rawls's work, effectively abandons Rawls's ambition to present simply a freestanding political view and collapses into a form of comprehensive liberalism. Macedo denies that this is the case, but the outcome is surely closer to a comprehensive liberalism (as evidenced by the quote above) than mere political liberalism. It is "not metaphysical" to invoke Rawls's famous formulation, but that is in part because liberalism in general eschews metaphysical speculation out of what are ultimately epistemological and then metaphysical principles, that is, the political liberalism of the early modern philosophers was itself a product of philosophy in the full sense: Locke's *Second Treatise* can be read independently, but its substance and force derives from the hard labor of the *Essay*. The whole force of Macedo's argument would seem to undermine Rawls's ambition to explain the stability of genuinely pluralistic societies. This is related to a second point.

It is difficult to see how the point about internalizing pluralism does not get Macedo into something of a bind with respect to questions of self-reference: once everyone has internalized pluralism and diversity, what counts as pluralistic and diverse? The ultimate destiny of those living in liberal societies would seem to be that they all become liberal, that is, internally pluralistic and detached from any permanent ends or commitments. But that is no longer pluralism. Macedo's invocation of Isaiah Berlin on this point is telling, for it is precisely the seeming conflict between the ideals of negative liberty and pluralism that has always most troubled even friendly critics of Berlin's own political thought.[46] Macedo's criticism of natural law, then is deeper than it first appears. Natural law is not simply problematic because of what it requires in terms of knowledge (or what it lacks), but because of its attachment to the thesis that there are determinate answers to moral questions that carry with them the compelling force of reason. Natural law seems crucially at odds with the centrality of individual choice.

46. See John Gray, *Isaiah Berlin* (Princeton, N.J.: Princeton University Press, 1996), and cf. his more general *Two Faces of Liberalism* (New York: New Press, 2000). The issues surrounding this conflict are also a leitmotif of the very interesting correspondence between Berlin and Beata Polanowska-Sygulska in *Unfinished Dialogue* (New York: Prometheus Books, 2006).

Greenawalt's Questions

Kent Greenawalt is broadly supportive of the public reason project, holding that political judgments, especially authoritative judgments about the use of coercion, should generally be justified by reference to publicly accessible reasons and that this entails a kind of self-restraint in advocacy by officials, but also to some extent by citizens.[47] His position on just what this means, however, is considerably more nuanced and flexible than those already considered. Much of his writing has focused on the specific role of religious ideas in public debate and legal reasoning. In his 1988 book *Religious Convictions and Political Choice* Greenawalt argues that the basic notion of liberal democracy and the model of citizenship appropriate to it suggest that legislation should be justified in terms of largely secular objectives, but that in some circumstances, when such argument persistently fails to issue in a resolution, citizens can appeal to their religious ideas.[48] In this respect Greenawalt's general view is more permissive than that of Rawls, although some of Greenawalt's concerns are quite similar: "[T]hough liberal democracy involves a limited commitment to publicly accessible reasons for decision, it does not entail for the political realm either exclusive reliance on such reasons or an unqualified acceptance of a narrow form of rationalism."[49]

Among the other important nuances that Greenawalt has proposed is a sensitivity to the context of argument under consideration. He advocates a kind of continuum requiring comparatively less self-restraint for citizens in their advocacy of policies, more for legislators, and the most for judges.[50] He also distinguishes between reasons for decision and reasons used in advocacy and calls for self-restraint mostly with respect to the latter.[51] Finally, Greenawalt concludes, on the basis of his discussion of many hypothetical and actual cases, that one rarely finds in politi-

47. Kent Greenawalt, *Religious Convictions and Political Choice* (New York: Oxford University Press, 1988), 12, 24, 25; *Private Consciences and Public Reasons* (New York: Oxford University Press, 1995), 6–7; "What Are Public Reasons?" *Journal of Law, Philosophy and Culture* 1 (2007): 81–82.

48. *Religious Convictions and Political Choice,* 12 (et passim).

49. Ibid., 25.

50. *Private Consciences and Public Reasons,* 7 and chs. 13–14; cf. "What Are Public Reasons?" 79.

51. *Private Consciences and Public Reasons,* 134.

cal and legal argument a clear distinction between public and nonpublic reasons, but rather reasons that are more or less public.[52] This makes outright exclusions difficult and has the advantage (true of Greenawalt's account generally) that the norms he proposes about advocacy based on publicly accessible reasons are relatively close to actual practice in the United States.[53] That suggests that history and custom play a role in the analysis and would be somewhat different in other times and places, but this simply makes his account more realistic.

It is in this spirit and context that Greenawalt has addressed the question of the extent to which natural law arguments should be acceptable as arguments in public reason. His consideration of natural law leads Greenwalt to conclude that some aspects of natural law argument would be permissible while others would not, but also that the very exercise of thinking through the question supports his judgment that the line between public reason and nonpublic reason is not a clear one. He concludes that one should rather speak of "degrees of publicness."[54]

Greenawalt's way to this conclusion traverses a range of what he takes to be key features of natural law theory, drawing on the thought of a number of contemporary natural law theorists.[55] Given the sort of general position Greenawalt spells out, his procedure with respect to natural law is not to render a decisive judgment as to acceptance or exclusion, but to explore just how public natural law reasoning can be. He thus mainly poses questions. Does natural law argument necessarily entail religious beliefs? If so, it ordinarily and to that extent could fall outside the bounds of public reason. Does natural law reasoning in particular cases require an overall theory with metaphysical, teleological, and cosmological elements? If so, that too falls outside the bounds of public reason to the extent that it entails extensive elements of a comprehensive doctrine. More specifically, does natural law depend on teleological arguments (as more traditional versions seem to suggest) or is it based on self-

52. "What Are Public Reasons?," 103–5.

53. *Private Consciences and Public Reasons*, 6–7, 134.

54. "Natural Law and Public Reasons," *Villanova Law Review* 47 (2002): 531–52, 549, 552.

55. John Finnis's work is prominent: see ibid., and Greenawalt, "How Persuasive Is Natural Law Theory?" *Notre Dame Law Review* 75 (2000): 1647–79, 1647–48; note also Greenawalt's earlier review of Finnis's *Natural Law and Natural Rights, Political Theory* 10 (1982): 133–36. However, he also draws on the work of Yves Simon, John Courtney Murray, Jean Porter, and Mark Murphy. See also "What Are Public Reasons?" 92–94.

evident purely practical precepts (as with Finnis)? Does natural law rest on purely rational deductions or can it be based on the fruits of "lived experience"? Relying on experience, especially that provided by the social sciences, is, Greenawalt argues, more in keeping with the demands of public reason (and this is one of his main points against Finnis). Is natural law dependent on ideas of the good? Public reason eschews such controversial notions, but then some natural law arguments do not seem to concern propositions about the good life as such. Greenawalt suggests that the controversy over the morality of research on human embryonic stem cells is like this, and yet it is still controversial. Is natural law really accessible to all or are important parts grasped only by some, the wise, as Aquinas suggests? The latter may be a prima facie problem from the perspective of public reason unless the wise can be (1) recognized by all and (2) explain their conclusions to all. Science may work like this in many cases, but, Greenawalt argues, who counts as an expert in morals is much more controversial than in science and successful popular explanation of scientific arguments seems more likely and more common than in the case of morals. It seems to me that the debate over global climate change may be a counterexample here, but how troubling it would be to Greenawalt I cannot say. Finally, Greenawalt asks, is natural law argument and understanding independent of time and place or does it vary? The more it is admitted to change, he suggests, the more acceptable it may be to public reason, but the less helpful it may be in providing explicit and specific conclusions.[56]

Greenawalt concludes that this survey precisely illustrates the complexity of the relationship between natural law and public reason. Given any particular issue or argument one could give different answers to each of these questions and thus a menu of important reasons may well manifest an exceedingly complicated range of acceptability at the bar of public reason depending on where the argument falls on any one of these dimensions. "As difficult as it may be to say whether any particular argument is 'in' or 'out' of the domain of public reasons, generalizing across the wide

56. This list of questions is taken from "Natural Law and Public Reasons," 539–49; similar albeit not identical sets of questions are posed in "How Persuasive Is Natural Law?" 1655–78, and in "Questions about the Place of Natural Law," in *Natural Law and Contemporary Public Policy,* ed. David F. Forte (Washington, D.C.: Georgetown University Press, 1998), 363–79.

range of natural law arguments is virtually impossible." Moreover, if this is true of natural law arguments, it may be true of arguments from other moral perspectives as well. Thus, Greenawalt concludes, "we might find that many reasons and arguments seem to be more or less 'public' rather than public or not."[57] Indeed, Greenawalt entertains the possibility that the upshot of all this is simply that public reason "founders completely on the impossibility of specifying just what reasons are public," but rejects skepticism on the basis of the example of the law. Greenawalt thinks that law is generally a realm governed by public reason.[58]

Greenawalt, then, does not simply exclude natural law arguments as does Macedo; indeed, he doesn't completely exclude even religious views, although he favors a general commitment to secular public reason, meaning appeals to notions that are widely shared. His concerns about natural law are, at bottom, connected to internal ambiguities within the contemporary natural law camp as well as in the history of natural law argument. Indeed, while acknowledging in a number of essays the influence of John Finnis on his understanding of natural law, in the catalogue of questions about natural law discussed above Greenawalt cites, at various times, works by Robert George, John Courtney Murray, Yves Simon, Jean Porter, Lloyd Weinreb, Russell Hittinger, and Mark Murphy. The very breadth of contemporary natural law seems an obstacle to establishing with precision whether natural law is acceptable to public reason. In all fairness, I think one should point out that if one considered, say, consequentialism, deontology, or virtue ethics as a candidate for inclusion of public reason, one would encounter much the same range of different views. However, it is not uncommon for critics of natural law theory to cite the untidy variety of natural law views on offer as an objection to its claim to constitute a uniquely decisive approach to moral and political questions. This is a question I return to in section 3.

Finnis and Reason

Given the importance of John Finnis's views to both Macedo and Greenawalt, it is appropriate to ascertain Finnis's own views on the issue of public reason. Finnis's most important book, *Natural Law and Natural*

57. "Natural Law and Public Reasons," 549.

58. Ibid., 551; and "What Are Public Reasons?" 103–5.

Rights, was published before the public reason conversation really got going, but the theory of natural law contained in it has played an important role in the debate, especially Finnis's claim that an adequate theory of natural law is comprised of three elements: (1) an account of self-evident basic forms of good that are premoral and thus serve as premises in any train of practical reasoning; (2) a set of basic methodological requirements of practical reason that lead to awareness of what acts are reasonable or unreasonable; and (3) a set of general moral standards.[59]

It is worth recalling that Finnis presents his account as the best theoretical account of natural law, but also bases important elements of it on an interpretation of Aquinas that he has subsequently defended on its own.[60] Among the signature features of Finnis's account are his defense of natural law theory against the charge that it fallaciously derives evaluative moral conclusions from merely factual premises, thus violating "Hume's Law."[61] This feature also has the effect of keeping natural law reasoning distinct from deeper and more foundational metaphysical claims about human nature and the good often seen as stumbling blocks particularly with respect to *public* reason. Connected closely to this is the theory's claim to be one about specifically *practical* reason.[62]

Finnis's theory is therefore a natural law theory based on a model of reasonableness. Moreover, just as in Rawls, Macedo, and Greenawalt, Finnis reserves a special place for the value of reciprocity as descriptive of the relationship among citizens in his political theory.[63] However, already in *Natural Law and Natural Rights,* Finnis rejects the notion that the state should be neutral with respect to its public claims about human

59. John Finnis, *Natural Law and Natural Rights* (Oxford: Clarendon Press, 1980), 23.

60. John Finnis, *Aquinas: Moral, Political, and Legal Theory* (Oxford: Oxford University Press, 1998).

61. See Finnis, *Natural Law and Natural Rights,* 17, 19, 33, 66, 81, 85; *Aquinas,* 86–90; and see the discussion in Robert P. George, *In Defense of Natural Law* (Oxford: Clarendon Press, 1999), chs. 1–3.

62. While my concern here is with Finnis's theory, it should not go unremarked that a number of other recent important contributions to natural law theory emphasize natural law's character as an account of practical reason in a way that is distinct from older accounts of natural law. See, e.g., Mark C. Murphy, *Natural Law and Practical Rationality* (Cambridge: Cambridge University Press, 2001); and Martin Rhonheimer, *Natural Law and Practical Reason: A Thomist View of Moral Autonomy,* trans. Gerald Malsbary (New York: Fordham University Press, 2000).

63. *Natural Law and Natural Rights,* 83, 152, 272–74, 277, 292.

flourishing and the good life. Claims to neutrality, he argues, are self-refuting, since they inevitably trade on a rejection of conceptions of the good life at odds with the neutrality claim essential to liberalism, itself a claim about (aspects of) the good life.[64]

Finnis has since addressed himself specifically to public reason, especially Rawls's formulation of it. In general Finnis approves of "public reason" insofar as he thinks it exemplifies aspects of Aquinas's own political thought, most importantly (1) the limited competence of the state; (2) that the state should promote the public good by way of "only those practical principles which are acceptable to all people whatever their religious beliefs or cultural practices," which principles are called "natural" just insofar as they are "rational"; (3) government as most centrally the rule of free people through law; and (4) in public argument one should "above all use authorities acceptable to those with whom you are disputing. . . . And if you are disputing with people who accept no authority, you must resort to natural reasons."[65]

Finnis, however, finds a number of faults with Rawls's formulation of the requirements of public reason. He holds first that Rawls's central requirement that arguments in public reason should be based on principles and ideals that all citizens "may reasonably be expected to endorse" "bafflingly ambiguous" in that it is unclear whether Rawls means this to be a predictive statement or one that is normative. If it is predictive, it would seem to empower majorities and even minorities to veto lots of proposals with little explanation; if it is normative and internal, it would seem to require specific critiques of specific sorts of arguments, which it manifestly does not provide. Second, Finnis argues that if the principles of justice provided in the first part of *Political Liberalism* (and in a somewhat different form in *A Theory of Justice*) stand or fall with the ideal decision model that is the "original position," and since that is based on contestable assumptions about human psychology, the model fails to produce the right principles and the principles it produces thus fail. Finally, Finnis contests the exclusion of "nonpublic" truths and reasons from important political deliberations.

64. Ibid., 221–23.

65. Finnis, "Abortion, Natural Law, and Public Reason," in George and Wolfe, *Natural Law and Public Reason*, 77–78; cf. "Is Natural Law Theory Compatible with Limited Government?" in *Natural Law, Liberalism, and Morality*, 10–11; and *Aquinas*, ch. 7.

No doubt a defense is intended in the remarks about "reasonable pluralism," the "ideal of democratic citizenship," and "civility." But all these simply assume what needs to be shown, that it is uncivil and undemocratic to propose to one's fellow citizens theses (on matters of fundamental justice) that one regards as true and established by evidence or reasons available to any reasonable person willing to consider them in an open-minded way.[66]

It is the exclusions of public reason that Finnis objects to most strenuously: "Rawls's legitimacy principle is a distorted and unwarranted analogue of a genuine principle of public reason, namely, that fundamental political, constitutional, and legal questions ought to be settled according to natural right, i.e., to principles and norms that are reasonable, using criteria of evidence and judgment that are accessible to all."[67]

Rawls's most serious error is his conception of liberalism as fundamentally opposed to the premodern tradition of moral argument, which was, on Finnis's view, precisely a tradition of rationalism and not of any kind of authoritarianism, religious or secular. The great divide between the tradition and Rawls, Finnis argues, concerns what Rawls calls "the fact of reasonable pluralism" or disagreement. Recall that for Rawls such disagreement is the natural result of the free operation of human reason in a democratic society and largely explained by the "burdens of judgment." Not only is no one to blame for such disagreement, but there is nothing to lament about it either since that would suggest some flaw with freedom itself. To think otherwise is either to devalue free institutions or to accuse those with whom one disagrees of ignorance, perversity, interest, or greed. The tradition, Finnis holds, distinguishes between disagreements in which there is no correct opinion (even if there are many incorrect ones) and other disagreements:

But in relation to some matters, including at least some matters of basic rights, there are correct moral beliefs, accessible to all. In relation to such matters, differing opinions can only be rooted in ignorance or some subrational influence, and it is impossible to say that there is more than one "fully reasonable" or "perfectly reasonable" belief. If by *"perfectly reasonable though erroneous belief"* Rawls means a belief that is held without subjective moral fault in respect of the forming of it, I would say that that is an important category of *de facto* beliefs

66. Ibid., 81.
67. Ibid., 82–83.

but one that would better be called, not "perfectly reasonable"—which it quite clearly is not—but "inculpably erroneous" or, in one traditional idiom, "invincibly ignorant." Public reasoning should be directed to overcoming the relevant mistakes, and public deliberations should be directed to avoiding them in practice, not preemptively surrendering to them.[68]

Finnis, then, would lift any restriction on rational moral argument aimed at truth. Public deliberation about the public good, especially as regards basic institutions and justice, must seek correct answers. Finnis never mentions the Rawlsian notion of comprehensive doctrines, implicitly arguing that there is one mode of rational argument and it is the one recognized by most educated persons. Such persons are perfectly capable of weighing arguments and evidence and arriving at rationally supported conclusions. This leads to an ambiguity that I shall consider in the next section.

It should be noted in addition that Finnis, while rejecting the strictures of public reason as proposed by Rawls, is in general opposed to the kind of paternalism sometimes associated with natural law theory. The state on his view should not generally seek to regulate private acts between consenting adults that do not cause harm. The state is free, however, to use its policies and public voice to discourage what its citizens regard as immoral or disgraceful conduct in other noncoercive ways, that is to endorse and promote views of right conduct and the good life.[69]

3. NATURAL RIGHT, TRUTH, AND THE POLITICAL

Having looked at Rawls's own account and at three representative philosophical perspectives on the role of natural law in public reason and offered some initial critical remarks, I now want to pull together some elements of the criticisms in light of the tradition of natural right. I will do this in three parts: first I want to ask how we should understand "natural law" and its role in political debate; next, I want to challenge an implicit assumption behind Rawls's repeated statements that political liberalism against natural right eschews any zeal to embody the whole truth in poli-

68. Ibid., 83–84.

69. Finnis, "Law, Morality, and Sexual Orientation," *Notre Dame Journal of Law, Ethics, and Public Policy* 9 (1995): 11–39; and cf. "Is Natural Law Theory Compatible with Limited Government?" and *Aquinas*, ch. 7.

tics; finally, and in light of this, I want to say something about how these questions relate to the character of the modern state as a political form. In all three points I appeal to the tradition of natural right as exemplified in the moral and political thought mainly of Plato, Aristotle, and Aquinas.

What Is Natural Law?

First, I have throughout taken for granted the notion that "natural law" names a distinct type of moral theory or, to use Rawls's term, a comprehensive doctrine. I have done this because that is the way it is treated by Rawls, Macedo, and Greenawalt (although not by Finnis).[70] But this characterization is not unproblematic. By "natural law" one could mean at least three things. In its original and most basic meaning the natural law simply *is* morality. Indeed, it was thought of this way right into the early nineteenth century. Aquinas did not think he was contributing to the natural law school of moral philosophy, but rather simply explaining morality, which meant, in part, explaining the natural law, understood to be an extrinsic principle of human actions sharing central features of other such principles called law, but also distinct from the others, mainly in its mode of promulgation, which is reason itself (as distinct from positive human enactment or divine revelation). Later moral theories are thus rival accounts of *the* natural law, which is to say, of morality. To take this meaning as decisive is to ask whether moral argument is acceptable under public reason, and the answer must be, for the most part, yes. The doctrine of public reason cannot simply eliminate moral discourse from political discourse and have much left to talk about. That it aims to eliminate some is clear, but how much? That's how much of the natural law is eliminated.

The second common meaning of natural law is much closer to what the writers discussed above have in mind. According to the second meaning natural law names a meta-ethical theory. Here one would contrast natural law to utilitarianism, social contract theory, intuitionism, (the various versions of) noncognitivism, and the like. All are rival theories of the foundations of ethics with connections to other and deeper aspects of philosophy (or religion), for example, metaphysics (or revela-

70. See Finnis, *Natural Law and Natural Rights*, 23–25.

tion). Moreover, there are, of course, alternative and rival versions of natural law theory itself. Here natural law theory looks more like a Rawlsian comprehensive doctrine (with the caveat that different versions of natural law theory can be different enough as to constitute perhaps distinct comprehensive doctrines). There is nothing like the notion of a comprehensive doctrine until relatively recent times. One can note in this context that Alasdair MacIntyre's conception of traditions is somewhat similar, albeit considerably more worked out.[71] MacIntyre, however, seems thoroughly skeptical about the possibility of anything like an overlapping consensus.[72] To stick with Rawlsian terminology, one would have to say that the furthest one could hope to get for MacIntyre is to a kind of modus vivendi, and it is precisely this situation that causes MacIntyre to vastly reduce the moral possibilities of the modern state, even to doubt that its claims to authority can be rationally sustained.[73]

Finally, by natural law, one can mean a rather specific doctrine in philosophical jurisprudence: most broadly the notion that there is some constitutive connection between law and morality. The nature of the connection is much disputed and is one of the nucleus issues in contemporary debate within a wide spectrum of natural law views.[74] Moreover, the issue is primarily one of methodology and interpretation largely confined to legal theorists.

When critics of natural law theory reject it in the name of public reason they do so on the assumption that natural law names a meta-ethical theory of a very specific type, one that seems necessarily connected to a Rawlsian comprehensive doctrine and to that extent an inappropriate source of public arguments. But to what extent do the public arguments based on natural law require more extended speculative content or have it?

71. Alasdair MacIntyre, *Whose Justice? Which Rationality?* (Notre Dame, Ind.: University of Notre Dame Press, 1988), chs. 18–19.

72. See MacIntyre, *After Virtue,* 2d ed. (Notre Dame, Ind.: University of Notre Dame Press, 1984), 252–53; cf. "Toleration and the Goods of Conflict," in *Ethics and Politics: Selected Essays,* vol. 2 (Cambridge: Cambridge University Press, 2006), 205–23.

73. Alasdair MacIntyre, "Politics, Philosophy and the Common Good," in *The MacIntyre Reader,* ed. Kelvin Knight (Notre Dame, Ind.: University of Notre Dame Press, 1998), 235–52. That a modus vivendi is the most one could reasonably hope for has also been argued by John Haldane, "Public Reason, Truth, and Human Fellowship: Going beyond Rawls," *Journal of Law, Philosophy, and Culture* 1 (2007): 175–90.

74. For a recent authoritative survey, see John Finnis, "Natural Law Theories," *The Stanford Encyclopedia of Philosophy (Spring 2007 Edition),* Edward N. Zalta (ed.), available online at http://plato.stanford.edu/archives/spr2007/entries/natural-law-theories/.

More specifically, Macedo and Greenawalt worry about the extent to which natural law arguments may be grounded in complicated metaphysical speculation. This is not an uncommon charge against natural law and one that goes back at least to Rousseau.[75] It seems at one level to be a real problem: if natural law argument requires one to engage in metaphysical speculation and argument, how can it be known by the vast majority of ordinary persons to whom notions like *actus essendi* are as foreign as the details of string theory? Here one needs to make a distinction between knowing natural law practically and knowing it as a theoretical matter. Surely any *complete* philosophical account of morality must open onto metaphysics since morality concerns the actions of human beings who are *beings* of a particular sort and who live in a cosmos that *is*, and so on. Nevertheless, making correct moral and political distinctions requires, at best, implicit metaphysical presuppositions of a pretty basic character and these are rarely stated or even thought by agents in deliberation about their own actions or those concerning the common good. Even though practical principles are rooted in metaphysics, practical deliberation begins with practical principles.

These two observations lead to a larger point, one that both supports something like the notion of public reason, but also, I think, casts doubt on Rawls's version of it (and, I think, although I cannot go into it here, all the other versions that are currently on offer). If public reason describes the language of *political* deliberation, it is hard to see why it doesn't just *equal* natural law deliberation about the content of related but distinct human positive law. After all, the basic precepts of the natural law, as traditionally understood, name norms without which no form of complex cooperative relationships among persons can be sustained over time. They are the most basic precepts of morality precisely because such precepts are *conditiones sine qua non* for human beings to live together in such a way as to achieve their distinctive sort of flourishing. No society is possible without their general efficacy, much less an overlapping consensus of reasonable comprehensive doctrines.[76] This is something that becomes obscure on Rawls's account because of his way of accounting

75. *Discours sur l'Origine et les fondements de l'inégalité parmi les hommes*, preface (sixth paragraph); and cf. *Du Contrat social*, bk. 2, ch. 6 (third paragraph).

76. For an extensive treatment of this issue, see Martin Rhonheimer, "The Political Ethos of Constitutional Democracy and the Place of Natural Law in Public Reason: Rawls's *Political Liberalism* Revisited," *American Journal of Jurisprudence* 50 (2005): 1–70.

for pluralism. Rawls holds that the rise of pluralism is a consequence of the religious and cultural developments of early modernity and his most pressing concern in explaining how free societies in pluralistic cultures can sustain themselves is the fell possibility of something like the wars of religion of the seventeenth century. But those wars were not fought over the natural law—they were not fought over moral questions at all, but over explicitly religious issues (i.e., when such issues were not simply cover for more conventional motivations like dynastic claims, greed, or the lust for power). There is something very peculiar in moral ideas that survived the most violent religious disputes now becoming matter for contention, as they have really only in the last five decades or so.

As noted above, the most basic precepts of the natural law are necessary conditions for the sort of human cooperative association that is both a means to and constitutive of human flourishing. As we saw in both the arguments of Macedo and Greenawalt, the very notion of human flourishing is controversial here. The natural law seems to require such a notion and if it is ruled out of court it is difficult to see how the natural law could make a go of it.[77] But why should we think that many people do not implicitly if not explicitly continue to operate with such a notion or at least important fragments of it, fragments which, along with most if not all of the basic natural law precepts (the most persistent controversies do tend to concern somewhat more remote conclusions from the basic premises) could perhaps still provide starting points for the kind of dialectical engagement practiced by Socrates, Plato, and Aristotle?

The obvious Rawlsian objection here would be, I think, that important aspects of such a notion of flourishing require for their full articulation some kind of metaphysical premises that are outmoded or at least controversial given the discoveries of modern science. Recall that in public reason one can appeal to the "methods and conclusions of science when these are not controversial."[78] They can also appeal to "presently accepted general beliefs and forms of reasoning found in common sense."[79] Natural law certainly claims that its basic precepts are matters

77. See Alasdair MacIntyre, "Theories of Natural Law in the Culture of Advanced Modernity," in *Common Truths: New Perspectives on Natural Law,* ed. Edward B. McLean (Wilmington, Del.: ISI Books, 2000), 91–115.

78. *Political Liberalism,* 224.

79. Ibid.

of common sense, even if more remote conclusions and inferences are not, although in this natural law is no different from any other type of moral argument. The only reason to rule out important aspects of the natural law, it seems to me, is by way of an argument showing that these ideas have been refuted by modern science. In its most complete form such an argument would entail a reduction of moral phenomena to some nonrational and nonhuman material substrate. Now there are arguments propounded by both scientists and philosophers that attempt to do just this, however, they are not commonly accepted by most people and they are, therefore, emphatically "controversial." Indeed, much of the modern scientific project grows out of a desire to expose common sense as frequently mistaken, putting two elements of public reason at odds with one another in a way that, at a minimum, is left unresolved, and unremarked, by Rawls.

Truth and Politics

Rawls repeatedly notes that political liberalism eschews any zeal to embody the "whole truth" in politics.[80] He also repeatedly invokes the value of "reciprocity" as a standard for the relationship of citizens.[81] No important thinker in the central tradition of natural right held that politics should or could embody the "whole truth" and all affirm the necessity of reciprocity in the relationship of citizens to one another. The first point could (pace Macedo, in particular)[82] be said to constitute the principal teaching of Plato's *Republic*. Plato there conducts a kind of thought experiment of imagining a politics that attempted to embody the whole truth by the establishment of a regime ruled over by a rotating committee of communist polygamous philosophers, who exercise their power through the concoction of ridiculous lies, and founded among a group of (evidently kidnapped) children, ultimately to be bred like chickens or horses so as to maximize the city's precise functional division of labor. Plato meant this tale to show precisely that such a thing couldn't be done

80. See *Political Liberalism*, 42–43, 216–19, 225, 243; "The Idea of Public Reason Revisited," 442, 447.

81. *Political Liberalism*, 16, 49–50; "Idea of Public Reason Revisited," 442–50, 455–56, 478–79.

82. Macedo, "In Defense of Liberal Public Reason: Are Slavery and Abortion Hard Cases?" 18.

(and shouldn't be attempted). In one of the dialogue's most important passages Plato's young and spirited interlocutor, Glaukon, asks how it is possible for this ideal city to come into being. Socrates reminds him that the whole point of discussing the city was to illuminate the nature of the soul as a way of getting at knowledge of the nature of pure justice and that the whole discussion is a "pattern in speech" *(paradeigma logō)* and distinguishes the goodness of the pattern from its possible realization, concluding that it is "the nature of acting [*praxis*] to attain to less truth than speaking [*lexis*]."[83]

This view is represented even more starkly in the *Republic*'s most famous image, that of the cave at the start of its seventh book. The image of the cave is said to illustrate "our nature in its education and lack of education."[84] But it illustrates more than this since man's nature is social or political, that is, it illustrates the tensions between education and lack of education in human affairs, in the human context, which, for Plato, is the city. The cave is an image of the city: it is repeatedly referred to as a "home" or "dwelling" *(oikēsis)*.[85] The inhabitants there are chained (a durable image of political association) and view the world only as reflected images, the famous shadows on the wall, and they pass their time discussing what they "hold" those images to be. The word translated as "hold" is *nomizo*, which also can be rendered as "believe."[86] It is closely related to *nomos*, "law" or "custom." Laws, Plato elsewhere writes, are the "authoritative opinions of the city."[87] Insofar as the city is constructed out of laws, then, the city is constructed out of opinions. The prisoners' discourse is one of opinion between truth and falsehood, as also suggested in the famous discussion of truth and opinion at the end of the fifth book. There Socrates contrasts the stable truth of philosophy with the "many beliefs [*nomima*] of the many."[88] The law is opinion, Socrates says in the *Minos*, that "wishes to be the discovery of what is."[89] That very formulation suggests the gap between the wish (truth) and the reality (opin-

83. *Republic* 472b–473a. I cite the edition of S. R. Slings (Oxford: Clarendon Press, 2003). For other Platonic works I cite the edition of John Burnet, 5 vols. (Oxford: Clarendon, 1900–1907). Unless otherwise noted, translations are mine.

84. *Republic* 514a.

85. *Republic* 514a3, 516c4, 517b2.

86. *Republic* 515c2.

87. *Minos* 314c; cf. *Laws* 644d.

88. *Republic* 479d.

89. *Minos* 315a1–3. For discussion, see V. B. Lewis, "Plato's *Minos:* The Political and Philosophical Context of the Problem of Natural Right," *Review of Metaphysics* 60 (2006): 17–53.

ion). The story of the cave concludes with the fate of the man released from his bonds and having seen the truth of the world outside the cave: it is the story of Socrates. The fate of Socrates is for Plato the ultimate symbol of the tension between truth and politics.

The *Republic* considers an ideal city, one in which the tensions between truth and politics could be resolved, and its practical impossibility suggests an alternative, a "second-best" city,[90] a city that is in crucial respects a self-conscious compromise between the ideal and the all-too-common. The second-best city, one which, while still perhaps too ideal, is closer to the cave. It is the subject of Plato's *Laws*. The theme of compromise is stated in its first book in a way that links it to something very like reciprocity. The discussion begins with an anonymous Athenian asking his companions, a Kretan called Kleinias and a Spartan called Megillos, who is held responsible for the Kretan and Spartan laws, a god or some human being. They answer that it is in each case a god: Zeus in the case of Krete and Apollo in the case of Sparta. The Athenian then asks what the purpose is for the Kretan laws concerning barracks meals, gymnastic training, and weapons and tactics used in war. Kleinias replies that the purpose of these institutions and practices is the same as that of all the Kretan laws, victory in war. Minos saw the central truth of politics as a truth about war. He "condemned the mindlessness of the many, who do not realize that for everyone throughout the whole of life an endless war exists against all cities."[91] He saw rather that "what most humans call peace . . . [is] only a name; in fact, for everyone there always exists by nature [*kata phusin*] an undeclared war among all cities."[92] The Kretan lawgiver always legislated according to this principle because he saw that without victory in war all of the good things are lost to one's enemies. What one might call the "Kretan thesis," however, goes even beyond this. The Athenian asks if it is also the case that the perpetual war also existed within cities, that is, between neighborhoods, between households, between individuals, and even within individuals. Kleinias affirms this with enthusiasm, saying that the Athenian has correctly seen that "all are enemies of all in public, and in private each is an enemy of himself,"

90. *Laws* 739a, 807b.

91. *Laws* 625e. Translation is that of Thomas L. Peogle (with some modifications), *The Laws of Plato* (New York: Basic Books, 1980).

92. *Laws* 626a.

so that the first and greatest victory is victory over oneself.[93] The thesis certainly had its contemporary analogues: within the Platonic corpus we can recognize elements in it articulated by Kallikles in the *Gorgias* and Thrasymachos in *Republic* I.[94] Something very like it is articulated by the representatives of different cities in Thucydides's *History of the Peloponnesian War.*[95]

It is a principle that the Athenian stranger immediately challenges. He does this by initially asking what it could mean to describe one as superior or inferior to himself. This is difficult to answer about an individual but perhaps in the case of cities it reflects whether better or worse men rule. He proposes an analogy as a means of thinking about this: imagine a large family with many brothers. More, the Athenian suggests, would be unjust than just. But now he dismisses the question of when we should call such a family superior or inferior to itself as a matter of mere words, of interest only to the many. The present inquiry should rather concern laws and the three elderly men should seek "whatever in them constitutes correctness and faultiness *according to nature* [*phusei*]."[96] He then asks who an appropriate judge for the brothers would be and proposes three options: first, a judge who would destroy the unjust brothers and set the just up to rule themselves; second, a judge who would destroy no one, but would get the unjust to agree to be ruled by the just; and third, a judge who would neither destroy nor establish a permanent ruling class, but who would "reconcile [*dialassō*] them by laying down laws for them for the rest of time and thus securing their friendship for one another."[97]

One recognizes these three proposals as possible solutions to the political problem as such. The first is a purge that attempts to eliminate injustice by eliminating the unjust and starting fresh. In a certain respect, this first solution aims to "embody the whole truth" in politics. It has the advantage of literally eliminating injustice, but the disadvantage of removing the majority of the population and so rendering the city physi-

93. *Laws* 626c–e.

94. *Gorgias* 483a–e; *Republic* 338c–339a.

95. See, e.g., Thucydides 1.76.2, 4.61.5, 5.105.2; and cf. 5.89.

96. *Laws* 627d. On Plato's broader understanding of natural right, see Lewis, "Reason Striving to Become Law: Nature and Law in Plato's *Laws*," *American Journal of Jurisprudence* 54 (2009): 67–91.

97. *Laws* 627e.

cally weaker than it might be. The second is a kind of aristocracy and thus has the advantage accrued to that form of government in which the virtuous rule. It has the disadvantage of creating a permanent division in the city which could also weaken it by division. The third solution, the one chosen, has the advantage of avoiding the first two problems, but also has two characteristic disadvantages: in accepting the permanent presence of the unjust it dilutes the influence of virtue in the city by accepting a kind of moral alloy, and it is subject to the disadvantages of the rule of law, that is, that the law is static and general in the face of the almost infinite variety and complexity of human affairs. This is the solution embraced by the Athenian stranger's interlocutors, and it is the one that informs the long discussion to follow, a discussion that includes proposals for a complete legislative code for a city.

The classics understood that man's nature, which Aristotle described as both rational and political, can lead to tensions that manifest themselves in political life and which they seem to have attempted to mitigate. In his more realistic account of politics, the Athenian stranger urges a reconciliation among the brothers in the example quoted above, but also later among different claims to rule: freedom, friendship, and prudence. The resulting "second-best" regime is less perfect than one grounded in the superior claim of prudence, but it is also more likely to be established and maintained, more stable, if you will. It nevertheless requires the maintenance and enforcement of a basic morality grounded in natural right, as all political association does. A similar compromise is suggested by Aristotle in the *Politics,* when he argues that the practically best regime is a kind of compromise between quite similar elements: freedom, wealth, and virtue.[98] Indeed, Aristotle's political philosophy is predicated on a quite sophisticated sense of realism. He reminds one frequently that the best political institutions require preconditions that are fundamentally beyond one's control ("according to prayer").[99] One must accept the conditions one finds and attempt to tailor institutions to get the best result that can be realistically achieved: as he suggests at the beginning of the forth book of the *Politics,* one must understand the best regime, the second-best regime, a regime that is best for a particular peo-

98. *Politics* 1283a14–22.

99. *Politics* 1260b29, 1265a17–18, 1288b21–27, 1295a25–29, 1325b35–39, 1327a3–4, 1330a25–26, 1331b18–23, 1332a28–31.

ple, one that could work almost anywhere, and the various versions of all the common regime types.[100] The best regimes simply, versions of monarchy or aristocracy where rule is entrusted to the simply and universally acknowledged best man or in some group of rulers manifestly distinguished by their excellence, are rare. Understanding them is necessary for one to understand what is by nature the best, but political practice inevitably aims lower.

Both of these examples illustrate the realism and concern for stability present in the classical tradition and at the root of natural law, as does the later work of Aquinas, whose ambition for law and politics is perhaps even more realistic still. "Human law," Aquinas wrote, "does not prescribe all the acts of every virtue, but only those capable of being ordered to the common good"; and "human law does not prohibit everything that is prohibited by the natural law"; and finally,

> human laws do not prohibit all the vices from which virtuous men abstain, but only the more grievous ones, from which it is possible for the greater part of the community to abstain; and especially those which do harm to others, without the prohibition of which human society could not be maintained. Thus human law forbids homicide, theft and things of that kind.[101]

The question whether a type of conduct is morally dubious is, of course, entirely separate from the question whether it also ought to be legally prohibited. Arguments about whether or not such conduct should be legally prohibited must be made in the context of political societies in which considerations about and by what Thomas calls "the greater part of the community" are relevant, even central. To ignore "the greater part of the community" is to invite contempt and disorder.

My point then is that the most important thinkers in the tradition of natural right were well aware of the perils of attempting to embody the "whole truth" in politics and never imagined such a thing. All were aware of the limitations of politics as a means of promoting human excellence while at the same time affirming that the only adequate starting point for inquiry into politics was rational inquiry about the good life

100. *Politics* 1288b21–1289a7.

101. *Summa Theologiae*, I-II, q. 96 a. 2 c. and ad 3, a. 3 c, trans. Fathers of the English Dominican Province (New York: Benzinger, 1947). See generally on this point John Finnis, *Aquinas*, ch. 7.

and the rational standards of personal conduct. The zeal to embody the "whole truth" in politics seems to me to be much more a modern than an ancient problem: the ideological mass movements of the twentieth century, fascism and Marxist-Leninism, and the violent and repressive Salafist political movements of the present day seem to present much more serious challenges in this respect than the political thought of the classics, which provide explicit arguments for political moderation.[102]

Natural Right and the Modern Democratic State

I want to conclude with a note about the political context of Rawls's conception of public reason and the controversy surrounding it in light of the proponents of classical natural right. Rawls quite openly holds that his account is not one proposed sub specie aeternitatis, but that it grows from particular soil, that is, out of the public culture of modern liberal democracy.[103] I have already noted that modern democracy itself has roots that go back to the premodern tradition of natural right and are thus the basis of a still available and salutary resource for a partly immanent constructive critique of the shortcomings of liberal democracy.[104] The classics, particularly Aristotle, already appreciated salient characteristics of both democracy and of conditions that are particular to the modern nation-state and that bear on the issue of public reason.

On the first point, it is well to recall that for Aristotle the defining mark of democracy was a particular twofold understanding of freedom. In one sense, freedom meant "to rule and be ruled in turn, for popular justice is numerical equality and not equality according to merit."[105] In another sense freedom means "to live as one wishes."[106] The first sense of democracy is that all participate equally in citizenship; the second is that this equality entails personal freedom. Aristotle's observation anticipates

102. The similarities between the ideological movements of the twentieth century and the present challenge of Salafism are canvassed in Paul Berman's theoretically underdeveloped, but still valuable book, *Terror and Liberalism* (New York: Norton, 2003).

103. *Political Liberalism,* 3 (and in many other places).

104. The thought of Tocqueville provides what is perhaps still the preeminent example of the possibilities of such an enterprise. See Pierre Manent, *Tocqueville et la nature de la démocratie* (Paris: Fayard, 1993), but one can see Finnis's work in this light as well as that of an earlier Thomist political philosopher, Yves Simon, in his still undervalued book, *The Philosophy of Democratic Government* (Chicago: University of Chicago Press, 1951).

105. *Politics* 1317b2–4.

106. *Politics* 1317b11–12.

two of the animating tensions of modern democratic theory: that between liberty and equality and that between what is usually called positive and negative liberty. These remain animating tensions in Rawlsian political thought and form part of the background to his understanding of the necessity for something like an overlapping consensus whereby important debates are carried out in terms of public reason.

On the second point, in describing the necessary and sufficient features of a true *polis* in the third book of the *Politics,* the book that explains the central Aristotelian theoretical concept of the regime *(politeia),* Aristotle contrasts it with what he calls an alliance *(summachia).* A mere alliance is concerned with preventing mutual harm among the members, their defense against external threats, and their mutually beneficial participation in commercial transactions. A true city includes these things, but also requires offices in common and, most importantly, a concern manifested in its laws and policies with the character of the citizens: "the true and not just nominal city must make virtue its care."[107] The alliance is concerned with mere life; the true city with the good life. The model of the alliance is the contract; that of the true city friendship.[108] The modern state is closer to being an Aristotelian alliance than a true city, although it continues to share in some of the features of a city.[109] One recognizes in Aristotle's account of the alliance important aspects of modern political philosophy, especially the concept of the social contract. This along with other distinctively modern claims made by the state and its officials has led some thinkers to identify the modern state as essentially intelligible by reference to considerations of utility and material advantage, that is, by reference to an entirely reductive conception of the common good. But most citizens, I think, consider the state more than this, if still less than the true city.[110]

An important connection between these two ideas is found in anoth-

107. *Politics* 1280a34–b8.

108. *Politics* 1280b10–11, b36–39.

109. See Peter L. Phillips Simpson, "Making the Citizens Good: Aristotle's City and Its Contemporary Relevance," *Philosophical Forum* 22 (1990): 149–66.

110. Here I differ with MacIntyre, who takes the state to be explicable only in terms of the reductive view. See his "Politics, Philosophy, and the Common Good," and my "The Common Good against the Modern State? On MacIntyre's Political Philosophy," *Josephinum Journal of Theology* 16 (2009, forthcoming).

er set of observations by Aristotle related to the size of political communities. In his discussion of the best regime simply, a kind of aristocracy, Aristotle argues that the population of the city must not be too large. Too large a city cannot be well governed because deliberation among citizens becomes impossible as does a knowledge of the citizens' characters, essential to the law's concern to inculcate the virtues.[111] The city, Aristotle stipulated in the first book of the *Politics,* is the human community that is final because it aims at self-sufficiency with a view to the good life.[112] There is nothing to prevent a city from growing larger, even to the point of assuming what would be a new political form, like the nation *(ethnos),* which Aristotle knew (in the forms of Macedonia and Persia), or the modern national state, which he did not know. The city has the advantage of being large enough to achieve self-sufficiency, but not so large as to be ungovernable with a view to human flourishing *(eudaimonia).* The larger communities possess obvious advantages with respect to natural resources, physical power, and the kind of internal differentiation and labor force that enable the construction and development of modern economies. But the increase in size entails a contraction in aim with respect to the good life. The substance of the community becomes necessarily thinner and the relations between citizens (their friendship) accordingly attenuated. These are inevitable consequences of the change in scale. Aristotle also suggests that the larger a city gets, the more likely it is to be democratic in character. This is because the many are likely to so vastly outnumber the relatively fewer virtuous and/or wealthy citizens that they will insist on sharing rule.[113]

Large modern states are by no means destined to be governed democratically. The means provided by modern technology have enabled and created modern forms of tyranny just as they have modern forms of democracy. Nevertheless, it seems inevitable (and entirely intelligible from Aristotle's perspective) that large modern societies, internally differentiated and characterized by pluralism of many sorts, will be characterized by a distinctive kind of political discourse, one that appeals to the widest set of shared presuppositions and preferences consistent with (modern)

111. *Politics* 1326a25–b24.
112. *Politics* 1252b27–1253a1.
113. *Politics* 1286b8–22.

democratic politics. This is an empirical observation, although not in conflict with any of the substance of natural right, which, as understood by the classical authors, provides both the necessary theoretical context for an adequate description of social reality and a basis for evaluative conclusions and criticisms,[114] which is to say, of public reason.

114. See Finnis, *Natural Law and Natural Rights,* ch. 1.

Francis Slade

9 Two Versions of Political Philosophy

Teleology and the Conceptual Genesis of the Modern State

INTRODUCTION

"[T]he substitution of a natural claim or right in place of a natural law, the substitution of will for law, as the starting point of a political philosophy . . . [c]ontrasted with the 'classical and theological tradition' . . . is certainly new." To this observation Michael Oakeshott adds the following: "And the modern concept of sovereignty which sprang from this new starting point involves perhaps the greatest revolution that has been in Western European political philosophy."[1] My remarks comment on this new starting point and the concept of sovereignty that sprang from it. Their theme is the conceptual genesis of the state. From this perspective they could bear the title "Machiavelli's New Form." The connection between sovereignty/state, and the theme of this lecture series, "Natural Law," is the term end/*telos*. Natural law presupposes the ontological priority of ends, teleology in the proper sense of the term, and it is the repudiation of end in the sense of *telos*, foundational for all modern philosophy, that makes possible the conception of state/sovereign. The versions of political philosophy to which the title refers are the version that thinks about political life in the light of the ontological priority of ends and the version which does not, the political philosophy of natural right, or the

1. Michael Oakeshott, "Dr. Leo Strauss on Hobbes," in *Hobbes on Civil Association* (Indianapolis, Ind.: Liberty Fund, 1975), 156–57.

rights of man, modern political philosophy. Different as these versions are they share a common characteristic of great importance for political philosophy. They, each of them, possess political specificity.

The rejection of teleology is usually discussed in terms of the origins of modern natural science. It is said that "[t]he problem of the origin of mathematical physics is the crucial problem of modern history and modern thought,"[2] that "[t]he core of modernity is mathematical physics. . . . Therefore the origin of modernity is primarily a question of the origin of mathematical physics."[3] Now mathematical physics dispenses with ends and constructs form. But dispensing with ends and construction of form also defines modern political philosophy, which does not depend upon mathematical physics. If the core of modernity is mathematical physics, then the core of that core is the rejection of ends and the construction of form.[4] Hence it seems better to say that the core of modernity *simpliciter* is the rejection of ends and the construction of form.

Since ends prescribe what have been called "the great directive purposes of our lives,"[5] it should be no cause for surprise that their systematic rejection—such as we find in the programmatic announcement of the fifteenth chapter of Machiavelli's *Prince*—occurs in what Aristotle calls the "philosophy of human things,"[6] in our terms moral and political philosophy, independently of what was to take place in natural philosophy. With respect to ends the principle, or law, of inertia, is the counterpart in natural philosophy to Machiavelli's dismissal of best possible regimes. Inertia, called by Descartes "law of nature," is the antithesis of nature as end. That nature is not an end is what is formalized in modern political philosophy's foundational notion, "state of nature." And, like the condition described by inertia, the state of nature is an imagined possibility constructed by the mind.

2. Jacob Klein, *Lectures and Essays* (Annapolis, Md.: St. John's College Press, 1985), 79.

3. Richard Kennington, review of *Lectures and Essays, Review of Metaphysics* 41 (1987): 145.

4. "The human understanding . . . of its own nature . . . gives a substance and reality to things which are fleeting. Matter rather than forms should be the object of our attention, its configurations and changes of configurations and simple action and law of action or motion; for forms are figments of the human mind, unless you will call those laws of action forms"; Francis Bacon, *Novum Organum,* bk. 1, Aphorisms, 51: [*Idols of the Tribe*].

5. Burton Rascoe, Review of T. S. Eliot's poem *The Waste Land,* "A Bookman's Daybook," *New York Tribune,* 5 November 1922, section 5, p. 8.

6. "Ta anthropeia philosophia"; *Nicomachean Ethics* 10.9.1081b15.

FORM AND SPECIFICITY

It is not sufficient for a philosopher to talk about political things to have political philosophy. What is said must have the formality of political philosophy. That formality consists in the presentation of political form. Political philosophy properly speaking manifests political form, setting it forth in its distinctness. Political philosophy possesses, or should possess, what I have referred to as political specificity. Lacking such specificity political philosophy itself is formless. Clarity about political form is the defining mark of political philosophy properly speaking. The importance of this consideration has been underlined by Pierre Manent:

> There is no such thing as an indefinite, undefined, political form. . . . That there are a determinate number of political forms is one of the most important "theoretical" propositions of political science. The human world insofar as it is political does not present an indefinite variability; it is articulated, it is ordered. . . . [F]rom the moment people live politically, they live in a political form, or in the transition from one form to another.[7]

There are at our disposal two versions of political philosophy possessing political specificity, the politics of sovereignty or the state, and the politics of the common good or the political community. The former is consubstantial with modern political philosophy, the latter with what came before the modern, call it simply premodern. Each sets forth political form with great clarity, the clarity appropriate to each form. Aristotle speaks about the *polis/civitas/*city, that is, the political community, Hobbes about the state or sovereign and civil society.

MODERN AND PREMODERN

A comment about the choice of the term "premodern" to designate what comes before the modern and the significance attributed to it. Premodern designates conceptual distance, rather than, as modern philosophy

7. My translation of *Cours familier de la philosophie politique* (Paris: Fayard, 2000), 75: "[I]l n'y a pas de forme politique indéfinie. . . . Il y a donc un nombre déterminé de formes politiques. C'est une des propositions 'théoriques' les plus importantes de la science politique. Le monde humain, en tant qu'il est politique, ne présente pas une variabilité indéfinie: il est articulé, il est ordonné. Dès lors qu'on vit politiquement, on vit dans une forme politique, ou alors dans la transition d'une forme à une autre."

would have us believe, historical distance, something whose being is to be absent. For before there was modern philosophy there was philosophy. Modern philosophy presented itself as a new beginning—"a path as yet untrodden by anybody" as Machiavelli puts it[8]—and understood itself in opposition to philosophy as it had hitherto been practiced. If there is "new philosophy," there must be "old philosophy." "Philosophy becomes ancient or old," Thomas Prufer has written, "only when there is a sense of newness which sets itself up in difference to what until then was simply philosophy, philosophy *tout court,* not ancient or old philosophy."[9] Philosophy as "ancient" and as "medieval" is the creation of "modern" philosophy. The new philosophy understands itself in the light of the rejection of what it calls "old," a rejection it constantly recalls and reenacts. This historicization of philosophy is essential to modern philosophy. It makes it seem as if the consideration of what came before modern philosophy cannot be present now as philosophy, and therefore does not endure as philosophically significant. Historicization is intended to divest philosophy as it had been practiced of philosophical significance except as something that has to be overcome and replaced. Modern philosophy is tied to philosophy in the form in which it came before it in order to show its own necessity. In this respect what are called "ancient" and "medieval" philosophy function as a "state of nature" for the modern version. But if in order to justify itself modern philosophy must always be returning to the situation from which it emerges, if it recognizes the constraint under which it is placed to argue its necessity against philosophy as it preceded it, it thereby acknowledges the presence of premodern philosophy beyond the historicization it attempts to impose upon it. It implicitly acknowledges the permanence of premodern philosophy. Historicization is a rhetorical posture, a tactic for winning an argument. Taken in the most formal sense philosophy has no past. To the extent that it might be said to have one, it is not philosophy. All philosophy insofar as it is philosophy is contemporary. And so with the issue between the two versions we are presently considering, the politics of the state and that of the common good.

8. Machiavelli, *Discourses on Livy,* trans. Harvey C. Mansfield and Nathan Tarcov (Chicago and London: University of Chicago Press, 1996), 5.

9. Thomas Prufer, "The Logic of Modernity," in *Recapitulations: Essays in Philosophy* (Washington, D.C.: The Catholic University of America Press, 1992), 66.

THE TWO VERSIONS

Although *polis*/*civitas*/city and state/civil society signify very different kinds of political entities, each signifies a determinate defined political form. There is at the present moment no other version of political philosophy that sets forth with such clarity and specificity any other account of political form.[10] The difference between the two versions is a difference about form. For the politics of the common good, the premodern version, form is something found, for the politics of sovereignty or the state, the modern version, form is created.

The premodern version begins with the givenness of the political community and of men ruling men according to the various arrangements of rule called "regimes," *politeia,* the well-known "constitutions": kingship, aristocracy, the republic, democracy, oligarchy, tyranny. In the regimes the rulers rule by virtue of what they obviously are: wealthy, or most numerous, or distinguished notables, for instance. The *politeuma* is the *politeia,* Aristotle says, those who rule are the regime.[11] Rule in the political community, the city/*civitas*/*polis,* is never separated from the human beings who exercise the rule. A regime is rule embodied in those who rule, which means rule is never representative. As rulers they are not separated from themselves as the human beings they are, a separation that representation requires. What is primary for the premodern version is the disclosure of the form of the city, the political community, a form it reflects upon by reflecting upon the city's own understanding of itself. Every city wishes to understand itself as "the best city," a claim easily disputed since every city contains within it those who consider themselves by virtue of the kind of men they are more suited to rule than to be ruled.[12] Premodern political philosophy turns from the consideration of men living in cities and their claims to rule to the consideration of the paradigmatic form of the city, the regime known as "the best city," in the light of which all regimes can best be understood. "It is in things whose condition is according to nature," Aristotle says, "that one ought partic-

10. As an instance of political formlessness attempting to supplant a well-defined political form, take the proposed (and rejected) European Union Constitution of October 2004. "To call this a constitution is to misuse the word"; Jeremy Rabkin, "Continental Drift," *Claremont Review of Books* 5, no. 4 (Fall 2005): 47.

11. *Politics* 3.6.1278b11.

12. Cf. Aristotle's *Politics* 3.

ularly to investigate what is by nature not in things that are defective."[13] The "best regime," to which Thomas More gave the name "Utopia," is the end/*telos* for the sake of which cities exist. The form of the best city, Socrates says, is "laid up in the heavens,"[14] meaning the end/*telos* constitutive of the city possesses ontological priority, or, as Aristotle says, "the city, or *civitas,* or *polis* exists by nature."

"But for an utmost end, in which the ancient philosophers have placed felicity, and have disputed much concerning the way thereto, there is no such thing in this world, nor way to it, more than to Utopia."[15] So Thomas Hobbes. This denial of end/*telos,* a denial first clearly pronounced in *Prince* 15, is where the modern version begins. The denial of the reality of ends makes it possible to postulate a condition called "the state of nature." Modern political philosophy turns from the consideration of men living in cities to the condition of men living in the "state of nature," a formless condition in which human beings are "clanless, lawless, hearthless,"[16] where no one rules anyone, a condition which is never given and

13. Aristotle *Politics* 1.5.1254a36–39. Aristotle adds the following: "Thus the human being to be studied is one whose state is best both in body and soul—in him this is clear." Clear because the end realized as form is present in its complete actuality. See *Politics* 3.13.1284b26–34: "In the case of the best regime there is considerable question as to what ought to be done if there happens to be someone who is outstanding . . . on the basis of virtue. . . . what seems the natural course is for everyone to obey such a person gladly, so that persons of this sort will be permanent kings in their cities." *Politics* 4.2.1289a39–b1: "Kingship must necessarily have the name alone without being such, or rest on the great superiority of the person ruling as king." *By nature* means by actualization of the end. The hereditary king, the king simply by birth, is not the "natural king." In the dedication of the *Discourses on Livy* (4), Machiavelli says: "writers praise Hiero the Syracusan when he was a private individual more than Perseus the Macedonian when he was king, for Hiero lacked nothing other than the principality to be a prince while the other had no part of a king other than the kingdom." This recalls Aristotle's sentence at 1289a39. Machiavelli's Hiero is not a "natural prince" in any sense, not by birth—for Machiavelli the *principe naturale* (7)—nor by actualization of the end/*telos*—for Aristotle the natural prince—but by what Machiavelli calls *virtù.* Machiavelli concludes *Prince* 6, "New Principalities That Are Acquired through One's Own Arms and Virtue," by speaking of Hiero of Syracuse, a "lesser example" added to the "high examples" of Moses, Theseus, Romulus, and Cyrus, "and I want it to suffice for all other similar cases," saying "he lacked nothing of being a king except a kingdom" (Niccoló Machiavelli, *The Prince,* trans. Harvey C. Mansfield Jr. [Chicago: University of Chicago Press, 1985], pp. 22, 25). Aristotle's real prince, not one in name only, is a prince by nature. Machiavelli's Hiero is a real prince, but not a natural one. Aristotle's natural prince is for Machiavelli an "imagined prince."

14. *Republic* 9.592b3.

15. *The Elements of Law Natural and Politic,* ed. Ferdinand Tönnies (Cambridge: Cambridge University Press, 1928), 26.

16. Aristotle *Politics* 1.2.1253a5, quoting Homer, *Iliad* 9, 63.

is accessible only in thought.[17] The classic form of the modern version is the unique political form created by modern political philosophy, sovereignty, or the state, something also not given, also something accessible only in thought. The conception of this unique political form, supplanting that of a best possible regime, becomes possible only by the denial of end/*telos*. For the modern version what is first is something postulated, the absence of form and therefore its generation. Form follows generation. "I took my beginning from the very matter of civil government [*civitatis*]," Hobbes says, "and thence proceeded to its generation and form."[18]

The state of nature, a condition of indetermination and formlessness, is a condition of pure *potentia*, one in which thought encounters itself as loosened from experience, unbound from the actual.[19] Thought defines itself as access to indefinite possibilities, thus to what it may be able to cause to be. In Hobbes's words, "imagining anything whatsoever, we seek all possible effects, that can by it be produced, that is to say, we imagine what we can do with it, when we have it. Of which I have not seen any sign, but in man only."[20] Understanding itself as freedom from the actual, that is, as not determined by ends, thought comes into view as power, the power to create forms, forms that have no actuality except as thoughts, and in that sense ideal forms. Such considerations supply a context for understanding what Machiavelli means when he speaks of himself as having "decided to take a path as yet untrodden by anyone."[21] The modern version of political philosophy abandons the perspective of actual political life, the contention about who should rule in the city, which is implicitly the question of the best city (*Prince* 15). It steps back from that, it steps back toward possibility, toward what takes its origin from within our minds, that is, toward *potentia*/power, toward what I

17. Hobbes makes an effort to argue the contrary in *Leviathan*, ch. 13.

18. *De Cive The English Version*, ed. Howard Warrender (Oxford: Clarendon Press, 1983), 32.

19. In contrast: "Potentiality is nothing but a capacity to act or be acted upon; it essentially involves a relation to actuality and can only be defined in such terms"; Thomas Aquinas, *Commentary on Aristotle's De Anima*, I2.6.304 (South Bend, Ind.: Dumb Ox Books, 1994), 97. "Power is said in reference to possible things"; Thomas Aquinas, *Summa Theologiae* I q.25 a.3.

20. Thomas Hobbes, *Leviathan*, ed. Richard Tuck (Cambridge: Cambridge University Press, 1992), 21.

21. *Discourses on Livy*, 5.

can bring about, that is, toward effectivity. This is the movement from end to ideal, or projected possibility, for the ideal is a projection of a form whose origin is within our own power to effect. The state is such an ideal. Detached from ends, ideal forms, forms that take their origin from thought, lack the end's "gravitational pull." Ideal forms "push," they do not "pull." Ideal forms, because they exist only as posited by thought, manifest thought's power to realize itself. From contemplation philosophy turns to action.

THE STATE: THE POLITICAL SUBJECT

Modern political philosophy created a unique new political form, the state, one unassimilable to any of the well-known regimes because the state is intended to replace them all. It is a form that supplanted, one might say dissolved, all previous political forms in the West and which has been exported throughout the world. As Hegel puts it, "The state is universal in form, a form whose essential principle is thought."[22] Modern political philosophy achieved this by constructing an understanding of government as such, something entirely different from the regimes, or forms of political rule, which had been the concern of premodern political philosophy, things like kingship, aristocracies, republics, tyrannies, oligarchies, and democracies. This point is made with great force by Hobbes when he says in *Leviathan:* "Because the name of Tyranny, signifieth nothing more, nor less, than the name of Sovereignty . . . toleration of a professed hatred of Tyranny, is a toleration of hatred to commonwealth in general."[23] Modern political philosophy reduces all regimes to government, for government is what every regime is.[24] Being treated as

22. *Philosophy of Right,* trans. T. M. Knox (Oxford: Clarendon Press, 1953), 172. See also *Elements of the Philosophy of Right,* ed. Allen W. Wood, trans. H. B. Nisbet (Cambridge: Cambridge University Press, 1991), 299–300. Hegel's German reads: "das Prinzip seiner Form als Allgemeines wesentlich der Gedanke ist."

23. *Leviathan,* Review and Conclusion, 486. *De Cive The Latin Version,* ed. Howard Warrender (Oxford: Clarendon Press, 1983), 83–84: *Omni tamen civitati, potestatem summam & æqualem tribuendum esse passim & expresse dico.* "I say everywhere explicitly that every commonwealth must be allowed supreme and equal power": *On the Citizen,* ed. and trans. Richard Tuck and Michael Silverthorne (Cambridge: Cambridge University Press, 1998), 14.

24. "There is no specifically 'democratic,' or republican, or monarchical apparatus of governing"; Michael Oakeshott, *On Human Conduct* (Oxford: Clarendon Press, 1975), 196.

government transforms all regimes into something different, "states." I am here calling government what Jean Bodin and Hobbes called sovereignty. But that is what sovereignty means, government as such. "I speak not of men, but in the abstract of the seat of power," Hobbes says in the dedication of *Leviathan*.[25] If the regime is to be understood as the embodiment of rule, sovereignty is its disembodiment. It is this understanding of political rule that makes the new political form, the state, possible.

The state as a political form is not visible, as the regimes are, in the obvious, the almost inevitable, the almost natural, articulations of a large society. The state does not "appear." We can see the city and the parties in the city that believe they have the right to rule the city and who put forward their claims: the notables or distinguished men, the *aristoi*; the "few" who are the wealthy; the "many" lacking both distinction and wealth; the "leader" who loves "the people" and who claims to be their voice. As the city comes into view so do the regimes; the regimes are inherent in those who make up the city. In *Federalist* 10 James Madison says, "[T]he latent causes of faction are sown in the nature of man; and we see them everywhere brought into different degrees of activity, according to the different circumstances of civil society." What we see, then, are the regimes, or, what Madison calls them, "the factions." The state is not visible to the eyes. It does not exist outside of thought, and therefore it does not exist until it is thought.[26] But being thought, and being a thought, it possesses brilliant clarity, an idea that can be "conceived very clearly and distinctly."[27] The state is something effected by thought, "a creation out of nothing by human wit," Hobbes says.[28] In these few words Hobbes has managed to set forth everything important in modern

---

"The three authorities in a state, which arise from the concept of a commonwealth as such *(res publica latius dicta)*, are only the three relations of the united will of the people, which is derived *apriori* from reason. They are the pure Idea of a head of state which has objective practical reality. But the head of state (the sovereign) is only a thought-entity [*nur ein Gedankending*] (to represent the entire people) as long as there is no physical person to represent the supreme authority in the state . . ."; Kant, *The Metaphysics of Morals*, trans. Mary Gregor (Cambridge: Cambridge University Press, 1991), 146.

25. *Leviathan*, 3.

26. Rousseau speaks of "la personne morale qui constitue l'État comme un être de raison parce que ce n'est pas un homme"; *Du contract social*, in *Oeuvres complètes*, vol. 3 (Paris: Éditions Gallimard, 1964), 363.

27. Descartes, *Discours de la méthode* (Paris: Vrin, 1970), 92.

28. *The Elements of Law Natural and Politic*, 84.

philosophy, a measure, it seems to me, of his stature as a thinker. Machiavelli was the first to understand political rule in this manner as something effected by thought. He deserves to be recognized not only as the first modern political philosopher, the founder of the modern version, the politics of the state, or sovereignty, which he often is, but he should also be reckoned the first modern philosopher, the founder of philosophical idealism, which he is not, the honor, of course, going to Descartes. In speaking of "the prince" Machiavelli is speaking of a new entity, government, government as such. Machiavelli employs the old, traditional, term "prince" to designate something quite new, the political entity effected by thought, which later writers will call "sovereignty." Machiavelli's term "prince" designates the political subject—an indispensable coinage I borrow from *Le travail de l'oeuvre Machiavel,* Claude Lefort's book on Machiavelli[29]—just as *cogito* designates the epistemological subject. Machiavelli's prince is the prince who effects himself as ruler, meaning that his being as ruler is not determined by an end that is ontologically prior. The political subject, the prince, or state, does not come forth as the actualization of an end. In this consists the newness of what Machiavelli calls prince. Government and the state emerge when rule is detached from any context defined by an end, from any teleological understanding of rule. The emergence of this new form, the state, whose essential principle is thought, can be directly—and perhaps most easily—encountered in chapter 9 of *The Prince* entitled "De principatu civili," "The Civil Principality." The politics of the state is the politics of what I will call decontextualized rule, rule detached from men and from the societies over which it is exercised. Government conceived in terms of this abstractive imagination, the sovereign of modern political philosophy, puts us in mind of the epistemological subject of modern philosophy, the *cogito.* Both are inventions of thought, ideal constructions effected by thought. Neither the state nor the epistemological subject is something thought finds in the sense that it comes upon them as things somehow "overlooked"; both are things effected by thought—thus their "newness"—and have no reality apart from that effectuation. We can express this in the language of Hegel, a language devised after all just to express such notions, by saying state and *cogito* determine themselves to be in their existence *(Da-*

29. Claude Lefort, *Le travail de l'oeuvre Machiavel* (Paris: Gallimard, 1972), 445.

sein)—that is, as standing over against themselves—what their concept is, in other words because the pure concept has the intuition of itself as its reality.[30] This is the sense of Rousseau's statement about the sovereign in *The Social Contract:* "The sovereign by the sole fact that it is, is always everything that it ought to be."[31] The "ought to be" does not stand over against the "is." The actuality of the sovereign, unlike that of the king, is complete as soon as it exists. Whereas a king is measured and limited by the form he aspires to embody in his kingdom, realizing that form in varying degrees, there being good, bad, and mediocre kings and kingdoms, the sovereign is never less than a sovereign. The sovereign has no need to look into a mirror for princes such as Thomas Aquinas's *De regno* to find out what he and his kingdom should be and is. Unlike the king the sovereign is not engaged in the activity of embodying a form.

In the *Critique of Pure Reason* Kant explicitly draws the parallel between *cogito* and state, or sovereign.

> The critique of pure reason can be regarded as the true tribunal for all disputes of pure reason; for it . . . is directed to the determining and estimating of the rights of reason in general, in accordance with the principles of their first institution.
>
> In the absence of this critique reason is, as it were, in the state of nature, and can establish and secure its assertions and claims only through war. The critique, on the other hand, arriving at all its decisions in the light of fundamental principles of its own institution, the authority of which no one can question, secures to us the peace of a legal order, in which our disputes have to be conducted solely by the recognized methods of legal action. . . . The endless disputes of a merely dogmatic reason thus finally constrain us to seek relief in some critique of reason itself, and in a legislation based upon such criticism. As Hobbes maintains, the state of nature is a state of injustice and violence, and we have no option save to abandon it and submit ourselves to the constraint of law.[32]

30. *Hegel, Lectures on Natural Right and Political Science,* trans. J. Michael Stewart and Peter C. Hodgson (Berkeley and Los Angeles: University of California Press, 1995), 55. This is a translation of Hegel's *Vorlesungen über Naturrecht und Staatswissenschaft,* Heidelberg 1817/1818.

31. "Le Souverain, par cela seul qu'il est, est toujours tout ce qu'il doit être"; *Du contract social,* in *Oeuvres complètes,* 3.363.

32. *Kant, Kritik der reinen Vernunft,* ed. Raymond Schmidt (Hamburg: Felix Meiner Verlag, 1952), 687–88, in *KrV.* English translations are from *Kant's Critique of Pure Reason,* trans. Norman Kemp Smith (London: Macmillan, 1950), 601–2.

A "critique of reason itself and . . . a legislation based upon such criticism" is the rule of the epistemological subject, sovereign reason. The philosopher, Kant says, "is not an artificer in the field of reason, but himself the lawgiver of human reason."[33] Thinking means ruling. The philosopher effects himself as the rule of reason,[34] the *imperium rationis* of Enlightenment. What this means is, as Robert Pippin expresses it, that "thought's self-legislation cannot be anchored in a 'beyond' . . . or 'pure form.'"[35] In short what is ruled out is any teleological understanding of thought. The *cogito,* like the sovereign, is "always everything that it ought to be."

The epistemological subject is reason as ruler and, just as is the case with the political subject, the sovereign, the prince, this subject can only be generated by means of the repudiation of objective teleology.[36] The parallelism of epistemological subject and political subject is striking. Right from the beginning modern philosophy consisted of two components, the epistemological and the political. "Epistemology" is mind effecting itself as knower, mind establishing its right to know. The parallelism manifests their underlying unity. Both epistemological subject, the *cogito,* and political subject, the state, show that thought is freedom, something essentially self-determining, for thought effects them beyond anything that is given, both are the creations of thought. Man is revealed to be self-determining subjectivity originating the forms that it realizes

33. *Kritik,* 753; *Critique,* 658.

34. *Kritik,* 549–60; *Critique,* 486; *Kritik,* 753–54; *Critique* 657–58. "[An] ideal of reason, which must serve . . . as a rule and archetype, alike in our actions and in our critical judgments"; *Kritik,* 550; *Critique,* 487.

35. Robert B. Pippin, *Idealism as Modernism* (New York: Cambridge University Press, 1997), 171.

36. What I mean by "objective teleology" is the ontological as opposed to the psychological priority of ends. Psychological priority means that ends are purposes. Hobbes's *Thomas White's De Mundo Examined,* trans. Harold Whitmore Jones (London: Bradford University Press in association with Crosby Lockwood Staples, 1976), 463, makes the psychological priority of ends evident: "First, it is clear that anyone's happiness consists in what he finds good: *no-one finds something good for which he has not appetite.* So he who has nothing to seek after enjoys no happiness; and, because everything we seek must be sought with an eye to the future, we must class happiness as 'the desire for good that is to come.'" Note here the rejection of happiness = fulfillment, completion, perfection. Happiness is not an end in the ontological sense, it is a purpose in the psychological sense. The italicized words make clear that for Hobbes it is appetite, desire, that creates the good. It is not the good that creates appetite and desire. This is why Hobbes can reduce final cause to efficient cause. It is appetite, desire (i.e., a force that pushes men), that moves men to seek what they seek.

in itself, which is to say man is *potentia*/power. There is nothing he is; he is formless prior to his own determination.[37] That act does not precede potency is what is meant by natural right. Man's freedom is the priority of potency to act. Heidegger speaks of "the basic concept of potency (Aristotle's δύναμις as "philosophy's ultimate concept, its concept of origin").[38] This has to mean that philosophy comes into being not as the fulfillment of man's perfectedness as a human being, but as the supreme expression of human freedom and power. The rejection of teleology bore the most profound implications for philosophy. Philosophy had been understood to be the fulfillment of "all men by nature desire to know" and the *eros* for the good of which Socrates speaks in the *Symposium.* It is wisdom as the good which creates in man that love for it which is called philosophy. The perfection and fulfillment of man is in the activity of understanding of being, the life of *theoria,* the contemplation of the intelligible realities. Modern philosophy rejects that. Philosophy is the creation of man, an expression of human freedom. Descartes gives us an account of how the mind actualizes itself apart from nature as philosophy, therefore independent of nature. This is the *cogito,* the "I think." Philosophy becomes the self-generation of the mind as something that is not given by nature. And this is exactly what the state as sovereignty is, the generation by thinking out of itself of something not given by nature.

COMMON GOOD AND STATE

The term "common good" comes to us from the premodern version of political philosophy. It designates the ontologically prior end which is the origin of the political community, the reason why it can be said to "exist by nature." The state, in contrast, is understood to be the creation of man's power, his freedom, or right. In his autobiography, *No One Could Have Known,* the Catholic philosopher Josef Pieper records a conversation that occurred in 1943 between himself and Carl Schmitt, the political theorist and legal scholar, a prominent figure in the intellectual life of

37. These points are made with force in Rousseau's *Second Discourse.*

38. In his course for the winter semester 1919–1920 at the University of Marburg; see T. Kisiel, *The Genesis of Heidegger's Being and Time* (Berkeley and Los Angeles: University of California Press, 1995), 131.

Weimar Germany who was to continue to be an influential one in political philosophy into the later twentieth century.

The opposition between the notions common good and state, and so between the two versions of political philosophy, appears in sharp relief in the exchange between the Thomist Pieper and Schmitt, who explicitly identified himself with those of whom he speaks as "the founders of my discipline, Bodin and Hobbes."[39] When Schmitt says, "my discipline," he means political philosophy founding the political form we call "the state." Referring to Schmitt's book, *The Concept of the Political*—a book that has been called "one of the very rare classic works of political theory in this century"[40]—Pieper says, "I asked him [Carl Schmitt] why, in his book on the concept of the political he had not written a syllable about the *bonum commune,* since the whole meaning of politics surely lay in the realization of the common good. He retorted sharply: 'Anyone who speaks of the *bonum commune* is intent on deception.'"[41]

A sentence from one of Schmitt's most famous books, the opusculum *Political Theology: Four Chapters on the Doctrine of Sovereignty,* makes the meaning of his reply to Pieper's question clear. "Everyone agrees," Schmitt writes, "that whenever antagonisms appear within a state, every party wants the general good—therein resides after all the bellum omnium contra omnes."[42] What the fundamental issue for modern political philosophy is, and how it is opposed to premodern political philosophy, could not be made clearer than Schmitt's response to Pieper makes it when taken together with the words that immediately follow the sentence just quoted from *Political Theology:* "But sovereignty (and thus the state itself)," Schmitt says, "resides in deciding this controversy." "This controversy" about the common good is what Schmitt terms the *bellum omnium contra omnes.* But the *bellum omnium contra omnes* is the state of nature.[43] Thus the concept of the state of nature is seen to be a formal-

39. *Schmitt at Nuremburg, Appendix III,* TELOS, no. 72 (Summer 1987): 128.

40. Pierre Manent, "Notre Destin Libéral," in Heinrich Meier, *Carl Schmitt, Leo Strauss et la notion de politique* (Paris: Commentaire/Julliard, 1990), 9.

41. Josef Pieper, *No One Could Have Known: An Autobiography: The Early Years,* trans. Graham Harrison (San Francisco: Ignatius Press, 1987), 175.

42. *Political Theology: Four Chapters on the Concept of Sovereignty,* trans. George Schwab (Cambridge, Mass.: MIT Press, 1985), 9.

43. Hobbes, *Leviathan,* in *Opera Latina,* ed. William Molesworth, vol. 3 (London: 1845; reprint, Aalen: Scientia, 1961), 99–100.

ization of the controversy about the common good, which naturally arises in the city as the question, who ought to rule in the city. Modern political philosophy translates the political community as it is understood in the premodern version into what it calls "the state of nature," "the war of all against all."[44] But that question "Who ought to rule in the city?" leads to the question—it is the Socratic discernment—"What is the end for man?" the question from which Aristotle begins political philosophy in the *Nicomachean Ethics.*

In his reply to Josef Pieper, taken together with the two statements that follow upon one another in *Political Theology,* Schmitt repeats the founding conceptual moment from which modern political philosophy emerges. It emerges by turning away from the foundational question for premodern political philosophy, by turning the question about ends into what Hobbes calls the *bellum omnium contra omnes.* The state cannot be thought in terms of ends.[45] "The state is in the decisive case the ultimate authority." Take note: the determination of the decisive case does not arise from consideration of the *bonum commune,* the common good, the end. The state, or sovereign, is undetermined by anything except its own will and to anything except by its own will. This indetermination, the absence of any determination outside its own act, is the state's power or right. Indeed this indetermination is why it is called "power," that is, *potentia.*

Sovereignty, or rule as it is understood in modern political philosophy, is independent of claims made concerning what the end is. The political form, the state, becomes possible only with the rejection of political community defined by end-*telos*-good, that is, actuality, determination, limit. What defines the political form of sovereignty is this power to effect. It is what Machiavelli calls *la verità effetuale.*[46] The political entity is precisely the effect of rule as sovereignty. Sovereignty is rule defined independently of the society over which it is exercised. What is ruled over

44. That the premodern form of political existence, the city/*civitas*/*polis,* is in effect a state of nature is evidenced in *Federalist* 9 (Hamilton): "It is impossible to read the history of the petty republics of Greece and Italy without feeling sensations of horror and disgust at the distractions with which they were continually agitated, and at the rapid succession of revolutions by which they were kept in a state of perpetual vibration between the extremes of tyranny and anarchy."

45. This, surely, is the ground for what is called "separation of Church and State" as a structural requirement of political existence in modern western societies.

46. Niccolò Macchiavelli, *Il Principe,* in *Il Principe e Discorsi,* ed. Sergio Bertelli (Milan: Editore Feltrinelli, 1960), 64–66.

by rule exercised as sovereignty cannot properly be spoken of as a "community." Hobbes, as usual, expresses clearly the opposition of sovereignty and communities constituted by a common good: "The . . . error is this [that] the members of every commonwealth, as of a natural body, depend upon one another. It is true they cohere together, but they depend only on the sovereign."[47] It is because they depend on the sovereign that they are able to cohere together in society. As Rousseau's variant of the version makes clear, end as constituting the political community is replaced by the general will. The general will is not something determined by an end-*telos* at all. It is undefined by anything outside itself for it "is always what it ought to be." The political entity, sovereignty, the state, is not constituted by "the common good," for then it would be a community and it would owe its existence to, as well as be measured and limited by, an end. It would not be something effected by thought, but uncovered and found by thought. Sovereignty, rule divorced from end, defines itself as power, and first of all, as power of self-generation, *causa sui.* Schmitt, Hobbes, Bodin, Rousseau—it is Machiavelli who stands behind them all.

MACHIAVELLI'S CIVIL PRINCIPALITY

Aristotle calls the city *koinē politikē,* "political community." Modern societies are not political communities. They are states and civil societies. State and civil society does not add up to political community. What is civil society? It is the web of associations formed by the interaction of individuals as they seek the fulfillment of the purposes peculiar to them as individuals pursuing their private happiness. Why is civil society called "civil society"? Calling it "civil society" indicates two things. It is not a natural form of society, for no societies, the modern version holds, are natural, not even the family; and it is society that comes into existence as the consequence of the creation of government. Civil society is possible only subsequent to the existence of the political entity, the state or sovereign.[48] Although the sovereign does not make civil society, the sovereign's rule makes it possible. But while civil society always presupposes

47. *Leviathan,* 397, 230. See also footnote 21 above.

48. Civil society "presupposes the state, which it must have before it as a self-sufficient entity in order to subsist itself. Besides, the creation of civil society belongs to the modern world"; Hegel, *Elements of the Philosophy of Right,* §182, Addition H.

government, in contrast to the regime, which is the focus of attention for the premodern version of political philosophy with its aim of discerning "the best possible regime," civil society is society from which what is political has been removed. Society becomes "civil" only insofar as it is nonpolitical, only insofar as it ceases to be political. It is precisely because it is depoliticized that it can be society. Depolititicized society and decontextualized rule are the great innovations effected by modern political philosophy. It is what originally was meant by liberalism. The West in its difference from the rest with respect to government and society testifies to the very large dimensions of the modern version's achievement. There may be a certain reluctance to admit it, but Niccolò Machiavelli must be reckoned among our political founding fathers.

The essence of the regime as the term is understood in premodern political philosophy is that it is rule by human beings over human beings. It is just Machiavelli's point to deny this proposition and to assert that rule in itself is not something that belongs to human beings in the givenness of their natural humanity, something that will be highly amplified in the notion of states of nature. What makes the ruler is not "those infinite good parts"[49] that are thought to make some worthy to be princes. Such is the "imagined prince."[50] The "real prince" is an invention outside and beyond men's natural givenness as human beings. Machiavelli indicates this in different ways. One of them is the many examples of, and references to, the inhumanness of some rulers, as, for instance, Agathocles, the tyrant of Syracuse, in *Prince* 8, who, if we consider his *virtù,* "one does not see why he has to be judged inferior to any most excellent captain," but whose "savage cruelty and inhumanity, together with his infinite crimes, do not allow him to be celebrated among the most excellent men."[51] Hannibal's "admirable actions . . . could not have arisen from anything other than his inhuman cruelty . . . together with his infinite virtues."[52] And "whoever examines minutely the actions" of the Roman emperor Septemius Severus "will find him a very fierce lion and a very astute fox."[53] They "show . . . how well he knew how

49. *Discourses on Livy,* 3.

50. *The Prince,* trans. Harvey C. Mansfield Jr. (Chicago: University of Chicago Press, 1985), 61. On the difference between imagined and real princes, see *Prince* 15–19.

51. Ibid., 35.

52. Ibid., 67.

53. Ibid., 79.

to use the persons of the fox and the lion whose natures . . . are necessary for a prince to imitate."[54] With such examples the distance between rule and human beings, between the real prince and the imagined prince, is indicated by qualities that are manifestations of the nonhuman. This conception of the nonhuman, nonnatural character of rule is conveyed in Machiavelli's treatment of those rulers whom the calls "the greatest examples," Moses, Cyrus, Romulus, and Theseus. Of them he says, "to such high examples I want to add a lesser one . . . and I want it to suffice for all other similar cases. . . Hiero of Syracuse."[55] In this manner Machiavelli equates what he has presented as "the most excellent" instances of rule with a more ordinary one, making the point that rule in itself is indifferent to the human qualities for which men are praised and blamed. These human qualities are not what constitutes rule. Rule is a construction beyond the humanly given. What men invent to carry them beyond their natural givenness is reason in its distinctly modern sense, mind as the effector of its own reality as reason, the power to originate what has never been given. In this sense reason is not a natural endowment, nor is then rule as reason's construct. With respect to rule one might say all men are created equal, but not by nature and not by God, but by their own invention. They invent their equality by inventing a superior that does not naturally exist.

The separation of rule from human beings, so prominent in Machiavelli's *The Prince,* begins modern political philosophy, for without the separation of rule from human beings in their natural givenness, sovereignty, the state, could not be thought. Sovereignty is that separation, and the separation cancels regimes as the outstanding fact about cities. Rule by human beings, the regime, is embodied form. The separation of rule from human beings is the separation of form from embodiment. The separation of form from embodiment in society, the decontextualization of rule, is the dissolution of political society, the condition for understanding rule or government as something separate from society. It is the condition for moving from "political society" to "civil society."[56] We

54. Ibid., 78.

55. Ibid., 22, 25.

56. It is just the point of these remarks that "civil society" and "political society" are two very different things, but it is not uncommon to find them used as if they were interchangeable.

think of this separation as representation, "the great principle which we owe to modern Europe," Madison calls it in *The Federalist*.[57] It is Thomas Jefferson's opinion that "the new principle of representation has rendered useless everything written before on the structure of government and in a great measure relieves our regret if the political writings of Aristotle or of any other ancient have been lost or are unfaithfully rendered or explained to us."[58]

The political subject, the sovereign, the state, an artificial person, is something that comes to be in thinking. The sovereign is a thought, for only in thought can something like a sovereign make an appearance and be seen. This thought, the thought that is the state, possesses great clarity. There is nothing obscure or indefinite about it as there can be in the case of the regimes of premodern political philosophy, which, since premodern political philosophy does not separate ruling from human beings, tend to blur around the edges and shade into one another exemplifying the realism of premodern political philosophy as over against the idealism of modern political philosophy[59] for which state, civil society, and the individuals who inhabit them are creatures that exist primarily in thought. The moderns say that the ancients, the premoderns, could not separate rule from the rulers because they could not think the thought, which separates them. They could not think the separation which we call "representation." Montesquieu notes that this is the reason "the ancients . . . could not achieve a correct idea of monarchy," which he distinguishes as "the monarchies we know."[60] He finds evidence for this incapacity in Aristotle's "confused," as he calls it, treatment of monarchy. Aristotle, he says, distinguished among monarchies "by accidental things like the virtues or vices of the prince." In other words, Aristotle finds the difference between king and tyrant in their difference as human beings ruling for or against the end that belongs to the city as a whole, the common good. "Kingship," Aristotle asserts, "must necessarily . . . rest upon the great

57. *The Federalist Papers,* ed. Clinton Rossiter (New York: New American Library, 1961), 100.

58. Letter to Isaac H. Tiffany, August 26, 1816, in *Selected Writings of Thomas Jefferson,* ed. Harvey C. Mansfield Jr. (Arlington Heights, Ill.: AHM Publishing Corp., 1979), 86.

59. This is precisely Machiavelli's criticism of the six regimes of premodern political philosophy; see *Discourses on Livy,* 1.2.2, 11. See Aristotle *Politics* 4.13.1297b30–31.

60. Montesquieu, *The Spirit of the Laws,* trans. and ed. Anne M. Cohler, Basia Carolyn Miller, and Harold Samuel Stone (Cambridge: Cambridge University Press, 1989), 168, 166.

superiority of the person ruling as king."[61] Montequieu's implies that Aristotle does not think the separation between rule and human beings.[62] Not knowing "the monarchies we know," he did not know that the institution of monarchy does not depend on the virtues and vices of the natural person of the ruler.[63]

In *Prince* 9, the chapter entitled "De principatu civili," "Of the Civil Principality," Machiavelli generates the distinction between state and civil society. The term itself, civil principality, is Machiavelli's invention.[64] A new name is required for a new thing. This new thing, civil principality, which is in effect state and civil society, is generated in thought, thought thinking through Aristotle's political science of regimes, and in so doing thinking into existence a new form, one intended to supersede the Aristotelian account of the city and its regimes. Machiavelli's account in *Prince* 9 closely follows Aristotle's *Politics* 5.10–11 (1310a39–1315b10), in which Aristotle addresses "monarchy and the things naturally apt to cause its destruction and its preservation,"[65] but whereas Aristotle's treatment of monarchy distinguishes between kingship and tyranny, Machiavelli's does not. What Machiavelli calls "principality," embracing both, is indifferent to the distinction. Machiavelli weaves together threads taken out of Aristotle's account into a new text *(textura).* The old text is unraveled and a new text is rewoven from the threads of the old.[66] *Prince* 9 thus makes visible the way Machiavelli takes apart the premodern city as it is understood in *The Politics,* replacing it with what will come to be known as the "state." Civil principality replaces all regimes of whatever kind, and cannot itself be understood as a regime, the subject matter of Aristotelian politics.

In contrast to Aristotelian rulers moved by ends, Machiavellian princes are differentiated in terms of how they produce their effects as distinguished from any differences about ends. That is, Machiavellian princes are not defined by what they rule, rather they define what they rule,

61. *Politics* 4.2.1289a41–b1.

62. *The Spirit of the Laws,* 167–68. See also Pierre Manent, *Les libéraux* (Paris: Gallimard, 2001), 219.

63. The moderns rest their case against the premoderns on the primacy of history.

64. Machiavelli says, "il quale si può chiamare principato civile," "this may be called a civil principality"; *Il Principe,* 45.

65. *Politics* 5.10.1310a39–40.

66. Machiavelli says "e andrò tessendo li orditi soprascritti"; *Il Principe* II, "De principatibus hereditariis," 16.

their success measured by the extent to which they are independent of and create what they rule, "shape it into the form they think fit."[67] Rule undefined by end is *potentia,* power, something protean, capable of assuming many forms. "The civil prince," Machiavelli says, by "una astuzia fortunata," a fortunate astuteness, "establishes himself with the support either of the people or the great [the nobles], for in every city these two diverse humors are found. The people desire neither to be commanded nor oppressed by the great and the great desire to command and oppress the people. From these two diverse appetites one of three effects [*effetti*] occurs in cities: principality or liberty or license,"[68] rule by the one, or the few, or the many. But whereas premodern political philosophy distinguishes between just and unjust forms of each, the six regimes, Machiavelli does not. These are not diverse understandings of what is just, of regimes, of ends, but effects, either effects of "diverse humors" or of *astuzia.* The rule of the great (the few) and the rule of the people (the many) are the effects of diverse appetites, of the desire to command and of the desire not to be oppressed. "In every city these two diverse humors are found."[69] Implicit in cities, they are what the city is, something in itself indeterminate. Principality, however, does not arise from appetite; it is not the effect of a "humor." It is the effect of *astuzia fortunata* in devising its opportunity out of what is presented by appetite. Rule of the great and rule of the people are the city as it is naturally given, the consequences of diverse wills rooted in natural appetites. Principality, the invention of *astuzia,* is beyond the city as it is naturally given. It is rule that has been disengaged from a naturally given context. *Astuzia,* "knowing how to get around men's brains,"[70] or "outsmarting," is what enables us to become *fortunata* and overcome nature. Civil principality is nature outsmarted.[71]

67. *Prince,* 23. Modern political science emphasizes the means by which political orders are effected, not the ends which constitute them. How political orders are effected takes the place of that for the sake of which they exist. For modern political science how political orders are effected is the measure of legitimacy.

68. Ibid., 39; *Disourses on Livy,* 1.2.2, 11: "[S]ome who have written on republics say that in them is one of three states—called by them principality, aristocrats, and popular."

69. Ibid., 39.

70. Ibid., 60. In Italian "e che hanno saputo con l'astuzia aggirare e' cervelli delli uomini"; *Il Principe e Discorsi,* ed. Bertelli (Milan: Feltrinelli, 1960), 72.

71. Ibid., 39: ". . . civil principality . . . neither all virtue nor all fortune is necessary to attain it, but rather a fortunate astuteness."

Demagogues are always dividing the city into two, Aristotle says, "and waging war against the well-off."[72] This is what Machiavelli, playing the demagogue, does here in *Prince* 9. He attacks those who pursue political life as the good, as the end or *telos* that constitutes completion, happiness in human life. Seeking the end they seek to rule. Machiavelli presents the desire for political distinction and greatness as the desire to oppress the people: "One cannot satisfy the great with decency and without injury to others, but one can satisfy the people; for the end of the people is more decent than that of the great, since the great want to oppress and the people want not to be oppressed."[73] Demagogues win the people's confidence, Aristotle notes, "by slandering the notables."[74] Treating the regimes as effects either of humors or of *astuzia,* and not as ends, allows Machiavelli to ignore the distinction between just and unjust regimes and, consequently, the political arguments for rule, the regime arguments, particularly those for the three just regimes. To ignore that distinction is to abandon the peculiarly human perspective on rule. But Machiavelli is considering things from a position outside that perspective. Playing the demagogue, Machiavelli favors the people, but favoring the people does not mean favoring the political arguments of the people, the arguments with which the people make their claim to rule over the city. Machiavelli does not give the people an argument that supports their claim that they should rule, for that would be the claim that it is just for the people to rule. Such a claim asserts a natural right to rule and Machiavelli denies a natural right to rule to both the people and the great. For a natural right to rule would derive from the end sought in exercising rule and ends are imaginary. Of the people's desire to rule Machiavelli says not that it is just, but that it is "more decent" than that of the great.

Instead of offering an argument on behalf of the people justifying their claim to rule, Machiavelli provides an explanation of why they seek to rule, just as he offers an explanation of why the great seek to rule: "The people desire neither to be commanded nor oppressed by the great and the great desire to command and oppress the people." Of course this is not what either the people or the great say in laying claim to rule, it is

72. *Politics* 5.9.1310a4–5.

73. *Prince* 9, p. 39.

74. *Politics* 5.10.1310b15.

what Machiavelli says explaining why they seek to rule. The people are moved, according to Machiavelli, to seek rule by fear, fear of oppression, not because they desire rule for its own sake, not as an end. Unlike the great, they do not want to rule for the sake of rule as something good in itself. Their desire for rule is out of necessity: "The people ask nothing but not to be oppressed." The people's fear of oppression explains why they seek to rule, it is not an argument that they should rule. Aristotle observes that if no one acted arrogantly toward them, nor sought to aggrandize themselves at their expense, the people would be content in a regime in which they had no share in the offices of rule.[75] In his treatment of the people Machiavelli imitates Aristotle's observation. His explanation of the people's desire to rule implies that the people do not want to rule. From the recognition that, although the people do not wish to be oppressed, they do not want to rule, is born the opportunity for the rule of the civil prince. The civil prince, who with "a kingly hand that with absolute and excessive power puts a check on the excessive ambition and corruption of the powerful,"[76] relieves the people of their necessity, of their need to rule. *Astuzia* recognizes that what the people fear and desire—their humor—are the means to the establishment of civil principality. Without the "humors" of the people, and of the great, there would be no opportunity for principality, but without *astuzia* there would be no recognition of it as opportunity, therefore no seizure, no exploitation, of it as the means to establish civil principality. The civil prince effects what the people want, for what the people want is not to rule, but to be free from oppression. Having taken the part of the people against the great, as ruler the civil prince takes the place of the people. Through his instrumentality the people achieve what they desire, not to be oppressed. In this sense Machiavelli's civil prince represents the people.

Machiavelli's treatment of the people can be formulated as a dictum: "The people do not want to rule." The sense of this dictum is that rule is not to be pursued in terms of ends, that the issue of who ought to rule in the city is not resolvable in such terms, and that to attempt to do so is to have recourse to "imagined principalities and republics." Which is what the great do, who pursue rule as the end of human life, and it is why one

75. *Politics* 4.13.1297b5–7.
76. *Discourses on Livy*, 112.

"who comes to the principality with the aid of the great maintains himself with more difficulty than one who becomes prince with the aid of the people."[77] Because the great believe that ruling is happiness, "one cannot satisfy the great."[78] As matter they are not disposed to the introduction of a new form. Machiavelli favors the people because the people, who don't want to be oppressed by the great and who don't want to rule, are receptive to the introduction of the new form, civil principality, which Machiavelli favors.[79] "For a prince it is always necessary to have the people friendly."[80] What Machiavelli calls the greater "decency" of the people consists just in this, they do not understand ruling as human fulfillment. "One can satisfy the people."[81]

With dispositions toward rule of the great and resistance to that rule, what the city is in itself is in Machiavelli's presentation indeterminate. The great and the people do not share anything common. A state of war obtains between them with rule over the city at stake. Aristotle says that "there is a single end for the city as a whole."[82] Machiavelli's account of the city is intended as the repudiation of that proposition. The city as it naturally exists—the great and the people—has no end; there is no common good. The *bonum commune* is, in Carl Schmitt's words, "a deception." It is the rule of Machiavelli's prince that effects political identity. Rather than rule originating in the end of the whole which is ruled, rule is that which effects the being of what is ruled. The civil prince shapes what is in itself indeterminate ("the matter") into "the form he thinks fit"[83] and that form requires favoring the people more than the great. Though he arrives at the principality with the aid of the people, the civil prince "finds himself alone there."[84] Machiavelli's civil prince can be identified with no one inside the city, for this civil prince, unlike the great and the people, does not occur naturally within the city. In this the civil prince is differentiated from the tyrant. The civil prince originates not in the city but in thought.

77. *Prince*, 39.

78. Ibid. The civil prince "can never feel safe with them." In the *Discourses on Livy* (55) Machiavelli recommends "the elimination of the gentlemen."

79. "Et, esaminando le azioni e vita loro, non si vede che quelli avessino altro dalla fortuna che la occasione, le quale dette loro material a potere introdurvi drento quella forma parse loro . . ."; *Il Principe*, 31.

80. *Prince*, 41.

81. *Prince*, 39.

82. *Politics* 8.1.1337a.

83. *Prince*, 23.

84. *Prince*, 39.

Separating rule from both the great and the people the civil prince effects what Machiavelli asserts the people actually want: to be left alone, not to be compelled to be concerned with ruling, free to pursue their various versions of happiness. Again Machiavelli imitates Aristotle. In *Politics* 5.8.1308b34–38 Aristotle says: "The many do not chafe as much at being kept away from ruling—they are even glad if someone leaves them leisure for their private affairs—as they do when they suppose that their rulers are stealing common [funds]; then it pains them both not to share in the prerogatives and not to share in the profits." Of Machiavelli's "people" it could be said that they "set themselves no other end than one which is domestic and private."[85] The program of modern political philosophy is summed up in the dictum "the people do not wish to rule, they wish only not to be oppressed." The people want the private, not the public, life; they want commerce, they want liberty, and what have been called "penumbral rights of privacy and repose."[86] Montaigne, one of the first distinctly modern minds, states their case when he says, "You can attach the whole of moral philosophy to a commonplace private life just as well as to one of richer stuff. Every man bears the whole form of the human condition."[87] Hegel was to identify this as the distinctly modern principle: "the right to the satisfaction of the particularity of the subject." Rule or government separated from the political context defined by end or *telos*, that is, decontextualized, comes to the rescue of "the people." The rule of the civil prince opens the space for private life, the space of "civil society." "The people loved quiet and therefore loved modest princes."[88] Rule has been removed from both the great and the people and belongs to the prince alone, but it belongs to the prince not as an end sought by a human being—a monarchical regime—but as the political subject effecting the political entity, the state. The people's fear provides the occasion for the exercise of Machiavelliian *astuzia* in the introduction of a form of rule in which government is separated from politics.

In *Prince* 9 Machiavelli cites one example of a civil prince, Nabis,

85. Montaigne, *Essais*, ed. Maurice Rat (Paris: Éditions Garnier Frères, 1953), 1.1. I have applied to Machiavelli's "people" what Montaigne says of himself: "[J]e ne m'y suis proposé aucune fin, que domestique et privée."

86. Justice Douglas's majority opinion in *Griswold v Connecticut (1956)*.

87. Michel de Montaigne, *On Repentance*, in *The Complete Essays*, trans. M. A. Screech (London: Penguin Press, 1991), 908.

88. *Prince*, 76.

prince of the Spartans. Nabis was a tyrant. Tyranny is not rule of the city as a whole for the common good, and the tyrant understands himself to be a ruler independently of any end shared with those whom he rules. Among the regimes it is tyranny that most closely approaches what I have called "decontextualized rule." Thus Aristotle characterizes it as "the farthest removed from being a regime."[89] And since regime means political society, it is the farthest removed from being political society, farthest removed from nature as end. Tyranny lends itself to Machiavellian transformation into civil principality, a ruler not embodied in the society which he rules and individuals pursuing private aims and purposes, that is, state and civil society. Principality means rule by one. If we are speaking of human beings as rulers, the term elides the difference between king and tyrant. Machiavelli's indifferent use of principality is an assertion that as rule there is no difference between them. Principality, rule of one, signifies the political entity as a single will, a will that originates in and is effected by thought *(astuzia)*. "A wise prince must think of a way by which his citizens always and in every quality of time, have need of the state and of himself."[90] Machiavelli's account of civil principality has for its context Aristotle's account of tyranny in the *Politics*, but his prince is not simply Aristotle's tyrant. Aristotle's tyrant is, as all Aristotlean rulers are, a human being; Machiavelli's prince or tyrant is a theoretically elaborated political subject or sovereign, "which is in fact thinking itself,"[91] something quite different from and more radically decontextualized than tyranny, for it is rule undefined by the human beings who exercise it. This is the reduction of the most personal of regimes to "that impersonal entity, government,"[92] the political subject. Machiavelli can effect this transformation, tyrant into prince or sovereign, because he does not understand the exercise of rule as constitutive of human fulfillment and perfection, as an end that completes a human being.

Prince 9, in contrast to Aristotle,[93] shows that the city does not exist for the sake of its own life as city. It shows that the city has no end. To

89. *Politics* 4.2.1289b2.

90. Ibid., 42. Note Hobbes's amplification of this point in *Leviathan*, 230–31.

91. Hegel, *Elements of the Philosophy of Right*, 257. Hegel's German reads: "zwar das Denken selbst ist."

92. The phrase is Margaret Thatcher's in a speech delivered at Hofstra University, April 2000.

93. *Politics* 3.9.1279b24–1281a10.

recognize that the city has no end transforms it into the state. What takes the place of the common good, what creates the commonness, and thus the public character, is not the end or *telos,* but the power that makes the common unity of them all and of the individuals a public which is not the same as all the individuals nor the same as civil society. The common will does not make the common good, the common will makes the political entity, the existence of which can be called the collective, or general, interest. Will replaces end or *telos.* The *polis/civitas/*city is understood to have its origin in nature, that is, in end or *telos,* the state in will, that is, in freedom, freedom understood as absence of determination by end or *telos.*

Machiavelli's new form defines the modern version. Noel Malcolm in his book *Aspects of Hobbes* says, "readers will search Hobbes' works in vain for anything like a depiction of the Machiavellian prince."[94] My thesis is this: Machiavelli's prince is understood as political subject or sovereign. My claim is that in *Prince* 9 a political form is set forth that will be elaborated in the subsequent significant variants of modern political philosophy from Bodin to Hegel. That Hobbes follows and imitates Machiavelli's presentation can be gathered from passages such as that found in *De Cive,* 1, 4, a passage matched by an even more celebrated one in *Leviathan* 13:

> All men in the state of nature have a desire and will to hurt, but not proceeding from the same cause, neither equally to be condemned. For one man, according to that natural equality which is among us, permits as much to others as he assumes to himself; which is the argument of a temperate man, and one that rightly values his power. Another, supposing himself to be above others, will have a license to do what he lists, and challenges respect and honor, as due to him before others; which is an argument of a fiery spirit [*ingenii ferocis*]. This man's will to hurt ariseth from vain glory, and the false esteem he hath of his own strength; the other's from the necessity of defending himself, his liberty, and his goods, against this man's violence.[95]

94. "Hobbes Theory of International Relation," in *Aspects of Hobbes* (Oxford: Clarendon Press, 2002), 440.

95. *De Cive The English Version,* 46. See also *Leviathan,* ch. 13, as well as *Elements of Law,* pt. 1, ch. 14, sect. 3. Since neither of the English translations of the *De Cive* are Hobbes's own English, I give here the Latin text which is his own. "Volunta laedendi omnibus quidem inest in statu naturae, sed non ab eadem causa, neque aeque culpanda. Alius enim

Hobbes's account of the "state of nature" argues the same points about the people and the great as those presented in *Prince* 9. Looked at in the light of *Prince* 9 it is clear that what is called "state of nature" recapitulates the contentions that define the condition which Machiavelli holds to be that of the city as such. For premodern political philosophy these contentions concern what is just with respect to who ought to rule. They are understood to constitute the political condition and are thought to point to the best regime, the measure of all regimes. For modern political philosophy they point toward the political subject, the prince/state/sovereign, and escape from the political condition. What Machiavelli calls *principato civile,* which I have called his new form, Hobbes will call "Leviathan, King of the Proud."[96] Astuteness combining shrewdness and perspicacity to the point of being artful or crafty and able to take advantage of what opportunity offers is exactly what we think of as "Machiavellian." The effecting of this new political form in thought and as thought shows us an instance of *una astuzia fortunata,* that of Machiavelli himself.

SUMMARY

In *Discourses on Livy* 1.55.3 Machiavelli gives the same advice to the founders of republics as that which Periander, the tyrant of Corinth, is said to have given to Thrasyboulus, tyrant of Miletus, concerning the preservation of a tyranny. That advice as related by Aristotle in *Politics* 5.10 (1311a20–22)[97] consisted of "the lopping off of the preeminent ears [of corn], the assumption being that it is necessary always to eliminate

secundum aequalitatem naturalem permittit caeteris eadem omnia, quae sibi (quod modesti hominis est, & vires suas recte aestimantis.) Alius superiorem se aliis existimans omnia licere sibi soli vult, & praecaeteris honorem sibi arrogat (Quod ingenii ferocis est.) huic igitur voluntas laedendi est ab inani gloria & falsa virium aestimatione; Illi ex necessitate res suas & libertatem contra hunc defendendi;" *De Cive The Latin Version,* caput 1, p. 93. In *Behemoth or The Long Parliament,* ed. Ferdinand Tönnies (London, 1889), 93, Hobbes says "the Lords . . . following the principles of warlike and savage natures envied his [the Earl of Strafford's] greatness." *Warlike and savage nature* suggests, given the context, an alternate rendering for *ferocis ingenii.* It has the advantage of being Hobbes's characterization of the nobility in his own vigorous English. The words quoted from Tönnies's edition of *Behemoth* do not appear in *English Works,* vol. 6, of the Molesworth edition. In the preface to his edition, p. ix, Tönnies explains why.

96. *Leviathan,* 221.

97. See also *Politics* 3.13.1284a25–30.

the prominent among the citizens." In *Discourses* 1.55.3, Machiavelli says: "he who wishes to found a republic where there are very many gentlemen cannot do it unless he first eliminates all of them." If the necessary measure for founding a republic is the same as the measure necessary to preserve a tyranny, the conclusion may be drawn that so far as rule is concerned there is no difference between republics and tyrannies. Qua government they are the same. Government as such is indifferent to form. That government qua government is the same whatever its form is sovereignty. Form does not define what government is, but only the mode of its exercise. The term "sovereignty" translates the Machiavellian decontextualization of rule. If rule is decontextualized, then there are no natural rulers. Rule is something constructed beyond nature. The Machiavellian decontextualization of rule points to the state of nature. Decontextualization of rule is exactly what state of nature means. There are no states of nature without the decontextualization of rule. Rule must have been removed as a natural relation between human beings for states of nature to appear. It is only when rule has been understood apart from the contexts in which it is naturally exercised that states of nature show themselves, that is, can be conceived. The understanding of rule independent of the contexts of rule precedes the state of nature. The understanding of rule independent of the context of rule is sovereignty. Independence of the context of rule means no end specifying rule. Sovereignty is rule understood nonteleologically, rule undefined by ends. Rule so understood is inaugurated by Machiavelli. He is the founder of the modern version.

Luke Gormally

10 ∽ The Good of Health and the Ends of Medicine

This essay will focus quite narrowly on the terms of the title—the good of health and the ends of medicine. It will therefore exclude discussion of the doctor-patient relationship, or any reflection on the virtues required of a good medical practitioner. These are indeed important subjects, but an adequate discussion of them can only follow upon some resolution of the issues addressed in this essay.

1. A POLARIZED DEBATE ON THE CONCEPT OF HEALTH

There has been much debate over the past thirty years or so about how to understand the notion of health. It is a commonplace to describe the debate as dominated by a polarization between an empirical, value-neutral concept of health, on the one hand, and a value-loaded concept, where evaluation is thought to be a function of preferences, individual or social. A brief account of this polarization is an instructive point at which to begin.

The most vigorous and intellectually tenacious exponent of an empirical, value-neutral understanding of health has been the philosopher

I am grateful to Professor The Rev. Kurt Pritzl, O.P., Dean of the School of Philosophy at the Catholic University of America, for the invitation to deliver the lecture from which this essay derives, and for the kind hospitality extended to me on the occasion of its delivery. In revising the text for publication I am particularly indebted to an important criticism of it I received from Professor The Rev. Stephen Brock.

Christopher Boorse. Boorse starts from the intuition that the normal is the natural, and that health is what, for a given species, is the normal functioning of an organism, by which he means disease-free functioning. He gives an expansive interpretation to the notion of disease to include injuries, poisonings, environmental traumas, growth disorders, functional impairments, and so on.

What is important for the value neutrality of the concept of health is the interpretation Boorse gives to the idea of the nature of a species. The nature of a species is "a functional design empirically shown typical of it."[1] Functional design certainly shows goal-directedness:

> . . . the structure of organisms shows a means-end hierarchy with goal directedness at every level. Individual cells are goal directed to manufacturing certain compounds; by doing so they contribute to higher-level goals like muscle contraction; these goals contribute to overt behaviour like web-spinning, nest-building, or prey catching; overt behaviour contributes to such goals as individual and species survival and reproduction . . . the function of any part or process . . . is its ultimate contribution to certain goals at the apex of the hierarchy.[2]

Function statements, Boorse emphasizes, are value-free "since what makes a contribution to a biological goal is certainly an empirical matter."[3] It is empirical in the sense that the picture of the functional design of a species has a statistical basis: it emerges from averaging over a sufficiently large sample of a population. Hence, normal functioning just means the performance by each internal part of an organism of all its statistically typical functions with at least statistically typical efficiency. Medical theory, for Boorse, has precisely this basis. Its history, he writes, "is nothing but a record of progressive investigation of normal functioning on the organismic, organic, histologic, cellular and biochemical levels of organization, and of the increasingly subtle kinds of pathology this investigation reveals."[4]

The notion of normal functioning in a species has to be qualified by reference both to sex and age. There are functions performed in the young—for example, skeleton enlargement—which are not performed in

1. Christopher Boorse, "Health as a Theoretical Concept," *Philosophy of Science* 44 (1977): 542–73.

2. Ibid., 555–56.

3. Ibid., 556.

4. Ibid., 560.

adults, and males produce sperm whereas females ovulate. So health is to be defined in terms of statistically normal functional abilities within a particular age group of the sex of a species. You are healthy providing that, as an organism, none of your relevant functional abilities are performing below statistically typical efficiency levels. If one or other functional ability is falling below a statistically typical efficiency level you have, in that sense, a disease. To be without a disease, in that sense of the term, is to be healthy.

One might simply note here the most obvious objection that Boorse's account of the concept of health invites, without at this point broaching more fundamental criticisms. Medicine speaks of the "universal diseases" of old age, such as atherosclerosis (arterial thickening). But if health is defined in terms of age-relative statistically normal functioning, universal disease conditions of ageing will not count as diseases.

The commonest counterposition to Boorse's position—a counterposition he has vigorously criticized[5]—is one for which an evaluative understanding of health, by which is meant an understanding of health as a human good, is a function of a preference, whether individual or social. The counterposition is well exemplified in the criticism that the late Professor Richard Hare made of Boorse's understanding of health.[6] The central criticism he made focused on Boorse's understanding of natural function as a species-typical contribution to survival and reproduction. Some natural functions do not contribute to those ends, Hare objected; for example, growing hair on our heads. And yet we regard baldness as a disease. Why? Contrast the growth of hair on our legs. If someone invented an organism that had no other consequence than that it inhibited the growth of hair on our legs, no one would call the resultant condition a "disease." On the contrary, many women would welcome the outcome. Why, then, think the condition of having a bald head involves disease? To which Hare's revealing answer was: "The reason why we call conditions [causing] baldness a disease is simply that people do not like being bald." A remarkable statement if one bears in mind that loss of scalp hair may be due to pituitary or thyroid conditions, to poisoning or to radiation injury. Common male pattern baldness is not so obviously patho-

5. Christopher Boorse, "A Rebuttal on Health," in *What Is Disease?* ed. J. M. Humber and R. F. Almeder (Totowa, N.J.: Humana Press, 1997), 1–134.

6. R. M. Hare, "Health," *Journal of Medical Ethics* 12 (1986): 174–81.

logical. But as Boorse points out, if head hair has an insulating function, then failure to grow it is a failure of function that one might reasonably call objectively pathological if not subjectively troublesome.

Hare's observations on the concepts of health and disease as having application in virtue of preference or one's attitude (pro or con) to whatever condition is in question, are, of course, completely consistent with his general position on evaluation. Those who have read Philippa Foot's book *Natural Goodness* may recall the following passage:

> Expressivist theories have the remarkable though seldom mentioned consequence of separating off the evaluation of human action not only from the evaluation of human sight, hearing and bodily health but also from all evaluation of the characteristics and operations of plants and animals. For it is obvious that no expressivist account will do in those other domains: we cannot think that the use of the word "good" is to express a "pro-attitude" in what we say about the roots of nettles or the fangs of ferocious beasts. Nowadays such evaluations are apt to be marginalized as if they were fanciful extensions of the "proper" evaluations that express our attitudes, practical decisions, or desires. But when I was told by a certain philosopher who wanted to explain "good" in terms of choices, that the good roots of trees were roots of the kind we "should choose if we were trees," this finally confirmed my suspicion of the kind of moral philosophy that was his.[7]

The "certain philosopher" who came out with that line to Philippa Foot was, unsurprisingly, Richard Hare.[8] Hare may not be thought to be a particularly influential contributor to the debate about the concept of health. But reference to him serves to bring out what underlies the position of an influential contributor like Professor Tristram Engelhardt. "[A] disease is a disease," Engelhard wrote, "because it is disvalued—in a particular way."[9] So the fact that unwanted pregnancy is a disvalued condition that doctors can deal with—by aborting babies—makes it to be the case that unwanted pregnancy can be said, according to Engelhardt,

7. Philippa Foot, *Natural Goodness* (Oxford: Clarendon Press, 2001), 25–26.

8. The "certain philosopher" remains unnamed in *Natural Goodness* but his identity was confirmed by Professor Foot in discussion at a meeting of the Royal Institute of Philosophy in 2002.

9. H. T. Engelhardt Jr., *The Foundations of Bioethics* (New York and Oxford: Oxford University Press, 1986), 174. The same statement is made at p. 206 of the second edition (New York and Oxford: Oxford University Press, 1996).

to count as a "disease."[10] It is characteristic of the kind of position Engelhardt expounds to hold that what counts as health or disease is socially relative because it depends upon the preferences and attitudes that prevail at a particular period of time. Engelhardt is emphatic in his denial that nature contains "ingredient goals and purposes by which dysfunctions, disfigurements and disabilities could be judged objectively."[11]

It is not the reality of health and disease which are determined by personal and social preferences and values, but rather the subjective experience of health and disease, which in the case of disease we call "illness." The sense of being unwell or of suffering from some remediable or chronic condition obtrudes into consciousness at least in part as a function of what one expects of oneself and of what one thinks one ought to be capable of. And clearly what people think they ought to be capable of is often determined by standard social expectations, which may vary from society to society.

What needs to be highlighted about the polarization of views in the debate about the concept of health (exemplified here by reference to Boorse on the one side and Hare on the other) is that it occurs at least in part because of a shared assumption that there is a gap between the empirical and the evaluative which has to be plugged by chosen preference; an assumption that there are no values which have a grounding in nature. Boorse represents those who think that medical practice needs an objective scientific basis free of subjective preference. Hare and Engelhardt represent those who think that you cannot eliminate subjective preference in determining what is to count as health and disease.

2. OVERCOMING THE CARTESIAN LEGACY IN THE UNDERSTANDING OF HEALTH

If we were to look for the roots of the polarization in relation to the concept of health we could hardly do better than to turn to the sixth of Descartes's *Meditations on First Philosophy*. He there wrote:

10. Engelhardt, *Foundations* (first edition), 175. The statement about unwanted pregnancy being a "disease or clinical problem" does not appear in the second edition of *The Foundations of Bioethics*, despite the fact that according to the preface to the second edition chapter 5 (in which the statement originally appeared) is the only chapter in the book not to be "significantly recast."

11. Engelhardt, *Foundations* (second edition), 197.

I may consider the human body as a machine fitted together and made up of bones, sinews, muscles, veins, blood and skin in such a way that, even if there were no mind in it, it would still carry out all the operations that, as things are, do not depend on the command of the will, nor, therefore, on the mind.

He makes a comparison between the human body so conceived and a clock. If the clock goes wrong it is obeying the laws of nature just as much as when it goes right.

Of course [he writes] if I consider my preconceived idea of the use of a clock I may say that when it does not show the right time it is departing from its "nature." Similarly, if I consider the machine of the human body in relation to its normal operations, I may think that it goes astray from its nature if its throat is dry at a time when drink does not help to sustain it. But . . . in this sense nature is a term depending on my own way of thinking [a *cogitatione mea*], on my comparison of a sick man, or an ill-made clock, to a conception of a healthy man or a well-made clock; it is something extrinsic to the object it is ascribed to. In the other sense, nature is something actually found in objects.[12]

This is a beautifully clear statement of the basic mechanistic doctrine of the body. It is like a machine, not merely in having functional parts, which anyone would admit the body to have, but in not having intrinsic to it any nature which tends to the good of the body; any nature which is gone against by disease. It is only because we impose our ideas of what a body ought to be like onto a body that we can speak of a diseased body falling short of its "nature."

Against the Cartesian picture of the body, and modern variants of it, one should oppose the following conception: a human or animal body has a way that it naturally tends to be; it develops and behaves in virtue of powers and tendencies proper to the nature which characterizes it as a whole.

To understand the human body by analogy with a machine is to say that we can explain the kind of thing it is exclusively by reference to the natural laws which govern the parts of the thing, considered not as parts but as entities with independent natures of their own. The art of making machines is the art of putting parts together in ways that take advantage

12. Descartes, *Meditations on First Philosophy: Sixth Meditation*, in *Descartes: Philosophical Writings: A Selection*, trans. and ed. Elizabeth Anscombe and Peter Thomas Geach (Edinburgh: Nelson, 1954), 120.

of the natural laws which govern those parts. By contrast, an organism, like all natural kinds, is characterizable in terms of natural tendencies—in terms of what it is about in doing whatever it does.

The phrase "what it is about in doing whatever it does" is a way of talking about final causes. The notion of cause is used here to refer to that which explains some phenomenon. We are most at home with the idea of final causes in relation to human action. The final cause of what a man deliberately does is his purpose in acting—what he is aiming at in doing what he does.

We fairly readily extend this notion to artifacts, since artifacts such as tools are produced with a specific purpose. And so the final cause of a knife is the object for which it was made, namely, cutting. Its being a tool apt for that purpose is explained by the fact that it was made to cut.

We do not have difficulty with the notion of final cause in relation to human actions and human artifacts. But there has been a long-standing rejection of the belief that final causes characterize either inanimate or living things. Nonetheless, it seems that final causes—in the sense of what substances are about in their observable activities—are indispensable to our identification and understanding of substances. Take the more difficult case of inanimate substances. We may not be able to make much of what scientists say about the composition of these things in terms of atomic and molecular structure, but we still may be able to distinguish samples as being of one kind or another by employing tests to detect distinctive activities.

To take an example developed by Stephen Makin:[13] suppose we associate the activity of donating protons with the kind of substances acids are. We do not mean in saying this that acids are in all circumstances donating protons. If I have acid in a suitably sealed container it may never donate protons because it will never react with any other stuff. The conditions have to be right for the distinctive activity to occur. For example, if an acid is in aqueous solution, and in contact with zinc, and the zinc is not rusted over, and there is no neutralizing alkali present, and the temperature is not such that the acid breaks down, then the acid will donate protons. A large number of conditions have to be met if acids are to do-

13. Stephen Makin, "Aquinas, Natural Tendencies and Natural Kinds," *New Scholasticism* 63 (1989): 253–74.

nate protons. When we say, therefore, that it is characteristic of acids to donate protons we mean that what distinguishes acids is their tendency to donate protons. But they can be prevented from doing this or they can fail to do it. To speak of prevention and failure is to imply that there is a proper end to activity; acids, for example, act so as to donate protons.

Natural kinds of substance, then, are to be characterized by natural tendencies or dynamic powers, and those tendencies give us what the substance is about in doing whatever it is doing.

The modern form of the denial that there are many different kinds of natural substance understands natural substances by analogy with artifacts. A bed is the kind of thing it is because of the nature of its parts and the arrangement in which the maker has placed them. It is characteristic of many people today to believe that visible things can be explained by reference to the nature of the parts of which they are made and the relations in which those parts are to be found.

Against this belief as it is applied to living substances we need to take account of the following facts:

First, we cannot explain the phenomenon of "being alive" by reference to some arrangement of preexisting parts, since at no level in the organization of a living organism can we identify preexisting parts such that all and only living organisms have that arrangement of parts.

Second, it is obvious that at a high level of organization at which the parts would be identified as organs and organ systems, our understanding of what they are about in doing what they do derives from our understanding of what the total organism is about in doing what it does. The activity of organs is, so to speak, shaped by the life of the organism as a whole.

Third, not merely is the activity of the organs shaped by the life of the organism as a whole, but the organism as a whole grows, in the course of its development, the organs that are needed by an organism of its nature.

Fourth, there is a natural law about living things that they act to reproduce their own kind. New members of a species do not come about by random assemblage of preexisting parts.[14]

It seems clear then that a living organism has natural powers. To un-

14. These four points are extremely compressed summaries of theses expounded at some length in Mary Geach's unpublished doctoral dissertation, *The Soul* (Cambridge University, 1981).

derstand what is going on in the life of an organism we have to think of the organism as a whole. What makes for its wholeness is what explains its development and the powers it possesses. The form, otherwise called the soul in the case of a living organism, is the activating principle of the life of a living thing. It is the soul that explains the wholeness of living organisms, their possession of a distinctive unified life with powers and tendencies characteristic of the organism as a whole.

Living human beings are evidently organisms—animal organisms. What is it that these organisms are about? The fundamental tendency is the tendency to *eudaimonia,* to our flourishing. The goods that are perfective of our nature are what fundamentally engage practical reason. Hence, as St. Thomas teaches, the first principle of the natural law is that good is to be done and pursued and evil is to be avoided.[15]

The life that gives unity to the human organism is the life of the human soul which is essentially rational life. All bodily activities are activities of the soul, but not all human activities are bodily activities. All bodily activities are activities of the soul because they are only adequately intelligible in terms of the role they play in that unified life which is caused by the rational soul. Thus, for example, you have an adequate understanding of the role of the eye in a human life only if you understand the role perception plays in our intellectual life.

The function of some organic activities is maintenance of what Claude Bernard called the "milieu intérieur"—a certain normal inner condition of the organism.[16] Some of the body's homeostatic systems are designed to keep its inner state normal in face of a constantly changing environment (including factors like temperature, light, and moisture). Other organic activities are designed to protect the primary homeostatic systems from stress and shock, from bacteria and viruses, and to help restore normal functioning. In general, organic activities are coordinated to maintain well-ordered functioning of the organism as a whole, in other words, a state of somatic health.

Yet other bodily activities are the exercise of powers of sensation, imagination, and memory, which provide the materials for our rational activities.

15. *Summa Theologiae* I-II q. 94 a.2.

16. Claude Bernard, *An Introduction to the Study of Experimental Medicine*, trans. H. C. Greene (New York: Dover Press, 1957).

Our rational activities as such—the grasp of meaning, the affirmation of the truth about what is the case, and the practical reasoning that leads to choice—are not bodily activities, though they are not possible for us without bodily activities.

So the malfunctioning or nonfunctioning of the organic systems of the human body can affect our life at every level internal to its unity. Nonetheless, if health is understood as the well-ordered organic functioning of the body, we will not characterize in terms of health—as "healthy" or "unhealthy"—the full range of dispositions and associated activities proper to human life. Virtues such as prudence, justice, and courage and their opposed vices, understanding and misunderstanding, knowledge and false belief, can be described only by remote analogy as states of health and disease, though there are misunderstandings and false beliefs which can certainly have damaging effects on organic functioning. And the vice of gluttony, it should be remarked, in part consists in organic malfunctioning exhibited in disorderly bodily appetites which dispose a person to continue to make bad choices in the matter of food and drink.

Beginning from the stalemate in the debate about the concept of health and from the proposal that the stalemate has its origins in Cartesian mechanism, I am suggesting that in order to overcome the stalemate we need to recover precisely what Descartes rejected, namely, the teaching about the rational soul as the unique substantial form of human bodily life and the teleological understanding of this life. Descartes replaced this teaching with an understanding of the human body as a machinelike substance which is conjoined to a distinct substance, the soul, which is the locus of consciousness. Naturalism and materialism have subsequently dispensed with the idea of the soul, and consciousness is construed as a mysteriously emergent property of brain development.

Machines and artifacts are apt to serve the human purposes for which they were designed, and in that sense "have" those purposes. But they have those purposes in virtue of the fact that we have so arranged matter to secure those purposes; there is nothing intrinsic to the matter of which artifacts are composed that would make of our human purposes ends intrinsic to the matter.

Cartesian mechanism about the body looks like an important source of the assimilation of human ends to human purposes, thus obliterating a distinction the importance of which has been emphasized of late by both Francis Slade and Robert Sokolowski.[17] Since a mechanism is not characterizable in terms of intrinsic teleological tendencies which belong to it as a unified whole, the body is no longer thought of as having a nature with natural ends that are constitutive ingredients of human flourishing. A mechanistic understanding of the body represents the essential intellectual move to regarding the body, no longer a locus of intrinsic value, as manipulable material, the vehicle for a whole range of human purposes.

3. PRACTICAL REASON AND THE GOOD OF HEALTH

A traditional natural law theory at the very least assumes a hylomorphic understanding of the basic human constitution along with a teleological orientation of the nature so constituted. St. Thomas identifies the human good by reference to a range of natural inclinations:

> Because however the good has the intelligibility of an end, evil the intelligibility of the contrary, thus it is that all those things for which man has a natural inclination reason naturally apprehends as good and thus as actively to be pursued, and their contraries as evil and to be avoided. Consequently, with respect to the order of natural inclinations, there is an order of the precepts of the law of nature. First of all, there is in man the inclination to good according to the nature that he shares with other substances—just as, that is, any substance desires the conservation of its own being in accordance with its nature. And in accordance with this inclination, those things by means of which the life of a man is conserved (and the contrary impeded) pertain to natural law.[18]

17. Francis Slade, "Ends and Purposes," in *Final Causality in Nature and Human Affairs,* ed. Richard F. Hassing (Washington, D.C.: The Catholic University of America Press, 1997), 83–85, and "On the Ontological Priority of Ends and Its Relevance to the Narrative Arts," in *Beauty, Art and Polis,* ed. Alice Ramos (Washington, D.C.: The Catholic University of America Press, 2000), 58–69; Robert Sokolowski, "What Is Natural Law? Human Purposes and Natural Ends," *The Thomist* 68 (2004): 507–29.

18. *Summa Theologiae* I-II q. 94, a. 2: "Quia vero bonum habet rationem finis, malum autem rationem contrarii, inde est quod omnia illa ad quae homo habet naturalem inclinationem, ratio naturaliter apprehendit ut bona, et per consequens ut opere prosequenda, et contraria eorum ut mala vitanda. Secundum igitur ordinem inclinationum naturalium, est ordo praeceptorum legis naturae. Inest enim primo inclinatio homini ad bonum secundum naturam in qua communicat cum omnibus substantiis: prout scilicet quaelibet substantia appetit conservationem sui esse secundum suam naturam. Et secundum hanc

Now for any living organism what is most fundamentally opposed to its preservation is death. Among the causes of death for a human being are those progressive functional failures at different levels of the organism which are numbered among what we call human diseases. Human diseases are types of prevention and failure of functional powers to achieve their proper ends in maintaining the organism in a healthy state. The research programs that underpin medical practice should be understood as confirming that the well functioning of the organism is the proper end of organic activity; it is given in the intelligibility of the functional parts of the organic whole. The intelligibility of the organism is a value-laden intelligibility.

Health belongs to the fullness of the good of being alive, being what St. Thomas calls "the natural good of the human body";[19] it consisted, as he thought, in "a certain balance of humours appropriate to an animal body."[20] What one should note is his evident view that when we are talking about health we are talking about a condition of the human body, its being in good order as an organism.

It helps to clarify what it is that establishes our practical interest in organic well functioning as a "natural good of the human body" to consider St. Thomas's statement, from the passage just quoted, that "because . . . the good has the intelligibility of an end . . . thus it is that all those things to which man has a natural inclination, reason naturally apprehends as good." This statement might be read as representing reason's grasp of human goods as itself based on natural inclination, and in the case of a human good such as bodily health the inclination or inclinations in question would be taken to be subrational. But such a construal of St. Thomas's thought does not obviously comport well with a general principle that he enunciates in considering the question of whether there is a natural love in angels:

> Now every nature, without exception, is the subject of some tendency or other, which is its natural appetition or love. But this differs in different natures ac-

inclinationem, pertinent ad legem naturalem ea per quae vita hominis conservatur, et contrarium impeditur." Translation in the text is by Kevin Flannery, S.J., in his *Acts Amid Precepts* (Edinburgh: T & T Clark, 2001), 233.

19. *Expositio super Dionysium De Divinis Nominibus* 4.21 n. 4 [551].

20. *Summa theologiae* I-II q. 73 a. 3c: "quaedam commensuratio humorum per convenientiam ad naturam animalis."

cording to the mode of each: where the nature is intellectual, the natural tendency takes the form of willing; where it is sentient, the tendency is sensuous desire; where it is devoid of all knowledge, the tendency is simply a natural orientation.[21]

We have to distinguish two different kinds of natural inclination in relation to the good of health. On the one hand, there is the subrational natural orientation of the organism to health exhibited by biological functions. On the other hand, there is the equally natural rational orientation to health, the starting point of which is the intellectual apprehension of the good of health as a good to be pursued. The practical intellectual apprehension is the way in which the foundation of the good of health in our subrational tendency to somatic health becomes practical and regulatory for human choice. Without the intellectual apprehension of a good to be pursued there is no start to practical reasoning about health and about the "preventions and failures," that is, the evils of disease, that are to be avoided.

Is the intellectual apprehension of the good of health an inference from the evidence for the subrational tendencies to well-ordered functioning of the human organism? Recognition that there are such tendencies would not as such constitute recognition that well-ordered functioning of the human organism is a basic human good. Practical reasoning's grasp of any human good assumes at least an implicit background understanding of the human being as possessing a nature teleologically ordered to a fulfillment or perfection (which constitutes *eudaimonia*). So the grasp of a human good is initially, as it were, the apprehension of something as perfective of our nature. Some goods are immediately apprehended as perfective of our nature, and health seems to be one such.[22]

21. *Summa Theologiae*, trans. Kenelm Foster, vol. 9 (New York: McGraw-Hill / London: Eyre & Spottiswoode, 1968), I q. 60 a. 1, p. 187. The significance of this statement for understanding what St. Thomas has to say about human tendencies to human goods was drawn to my attention by reading Professor Steven Brock's unpublished doctoral dissertation, *The Legal Character of Natural Law According to St. Thomas Aquinas* (University of Toronto, 1988), 161–62.

22. I do not believe that all basic goods are apprehended in this immediate fashion. The good of marriage, e.g., can be recognized as such only in virtue of argument. There is argument *to* first principles as well as argument *from* first principles. See Mary Geach, "Marriage: Arguing to a First Principle in Sexual Ethics," in *Moral Truth and Moral Tradition: Essays in Honour of Peter Geach and Elizabeth Anscombe*, ed. Luke Gormally (Dublin: Four Courts Press, 1994), 177–93.

The basis of the apprehension surely cannot be anything other than the obviousness of the truth that it is only in being alive that we can flourish and that to be successfully alive as an animal organism involves the well functioning of the organism. The apprehension of the good of bodily health precisely in virtue of it being an obviously perfective ingredient of *eudaimonia* is a nonderivative apprehension of what is *per se nota quoad nos.*[23] But, as Kevin Flannery has argued, "the things that are known *per se quoad nos* are things that are grasped by all in an indeterminate way—that is to say, without the knowers necessarily having a very scientific understanding of that which they have grasped in an initial way."[24]

The natural (rational) tendency to the good of health, in engaging practical reasoning's interest in organic well functioning, underpins our interest in theoretical, scientific knowledge of organic well functioning for practical reasoning about health and disease. For it is precisely a scientific understanding of the good of health which makes possible the kind of practical reasoning about health and disease that characterizes a medical practice that is effectively directed to the maintenance or restoration of health and the cure and alleviation of disease. But it is important to note that scientific understanding in turn needs to assume an ontological understanding of the human individual as a rational animal in which subordinate tendencies within the organism are thought of as serving the well functioning of an organism which is integral to a more than organic whole.

Diseases in their occurrence instantiate the phenomena of prevention and failure which, as noted earlier, are quite generally characteristic of teleologically ordered natural substances—in the case of disease, characteristic of organisms. Human diseases are specific preventions or failures at some level of the organism of functions the goal of which is the health of the organism. You do not understand the functions if you have not grasped the end they exist to serve. James Lennox[25] has pointed out that Boorse's understanding of the idea of health is guided by a distinct empiricist analysis of the notion of "function": to identify the function of

23. The apprehension of something as perfective of our nature is what apprehension of it being a human good consists in.

24. Kevin Flannery, S.J., *Acts Amid Precepts,* 35.

25. James Lennox, "Health as an Objective Value," *Journal of Medicine and Philosophy* 20 (1995): 499–511.

a biological structure or activity is to determine its efficient causal contribution to a biological goal. While the analysis preserves the distinction between contributors to goals and goals, "goals" are treated simply as a type of effect. In genuine teleological explanation it is the goal which is explanatory: you have to refer to what is being aimed at in order to explain why some part or subsystem is supposed to function in a certain way. It is because of Boorse's understanding of "function" that goals are identified as the statistically normal biological states of the members of a particular reference class (e.g., males within a certain age range). As noted earlier, the universal diseases of the elderly, for example, make implausible the construal of health in terms of statistically normal biological states. Medical research into health does not, despite its heavy reliance on population studies, assume a statistically determined concept of health. "Appropriate cholesterol levels," for example, are not defined in terms of what is statistically normal; rather "it is a matter of determining what level increases the probability of cardiovascular malfunctioning."[26] Lipoprotein levels above a certain range threaten the vital contribution cardiac function makes to the maintenance of life. So it is healthy functioning of the heart which in fact determines what is to count as healthy levels of cholesterol.

I have proposed that the well functioning of the human organism as a whole is what we can readily grasp as the good of health. Organic well functioning is a perfective end of the human being which is intrinsic to the organic constitution of human beings. It is not as such a function of preference, though our preferences may aid and abet health as well as leading to disease. But what remains fundamental to health are our organic powers in their natural teleological functioning. As St. Thomas observed:

> bodily healing is at times wholly from within, as when one is cured by the power of nature alone. But there are times when one is cured from within and from without simultaneously; for example, when the operation of nature is helped by the external benefit of medicine. But it never happens that one is cured entirely from without, for he still has within himself the principles of life, and from these the healing is somehow caused within him.[27]

26. Ibid., 508.

27. Thomas Aquinas, *Summa Contra Gentiles: Book Four: Salvation,* trans. Charles J.

We can now turn to a more detailed consideration of why and how we should think this good determines the ends of medicine.

4. THE ENDS OF MEDICINE

If health, understood as well-ordered organic functioning, is a proper end of the human rational animal, intrinsically perfective of his or her existence, then somatic health is a good intrinsic to human flourishing. But health in this sense is not only an intrinsic good, it is also an instrumental good: well-ordered organic functioning is a state of being that favorably disposes us to the pursuit of other human goods: play, skilled work, energetic pursuit of knowledge, and so on. Somatic health is a basic human need.

We can do much ourselves to favor its maintenance and development. We can eat prudently, in moderation. In the early history of medicine a large part of medical advice consisted in dietary recommendations. We can take physical exercise—if we have not already got to the point at which we no longer have the energy to do so. We can avoid toxic substances that disturb normal biochemistry.

Nearly all of us, however, sooner or later, and some quite frequently, suffer damage or impairment to functional abilities at some level of the organism which compromises organic functioning to a degree that begins to register in symptoms of the disorder. We become ill to the point at which we are beyond self-help and need the skilled help of others. This typically is the point at which the medical practitioner has a necessary role.

There are those who argue that the ends of medicine are identifiable as the ends which are internal to the practice of medicine. There is a problem, however—acute in our society—of determining what is to count as the practice of medicine. If we take an empirical view of the phenomena conventionally identified as medical practice, then we find it

---

O'Neill (South Bend, Ind., and London: University of Notre Dame Press, 1975), 4.72.2, p. 278: "Considerandum est autem quod corporalis sanatio quandoque quidem ab intrinseco totaliter est: sicut quando aliquis sola virtute naturae curatur. Quandoque autem ab intrinseco et extrinseco simul: ut puta quando naturae operatio iuvatur exteriori beneficio medicinae. Quod autem totaliter ab extrinseco curetur, non contingit: habet enim adhuc in seipso principia vitae, ex quibus sanitas quodammodo in ipso causatur."

is devoted to very disparate and ill-assorted purposes which do not relate to unifying ends. What do abortion, cosmetic surgery, and nontherapeutic sterilization have in common with antibiotic therapy for bacterial infections, chemotherapy for carcinoma of the bladder, and vaccination against measles, mumps, and rubella? We need some principle for determining what coheres as medical practice and what is at odds with what to count as medical practice, and empirical observation of medical practice does not uncontroversially yield the principle.

Our need for somatic health, both as intrinsic and instrumental good, does point us toward a coherent account of medical practice in terms of its proper ends. It is precisely insofar as medicine is dedicated to the restoration and maintenance of somatic health that it can be understood to be a profession. Professions exist precisely because there are some goods so necessary to human well-being, and which can be secured only by the exercise of skills which are informed by a complex body of knowledge, that we require a body of learned practitioners dedicated to securing those ends and to cultivating the necessary knowledge and skills. The human good of justice should be the good to which the practice of the law is directed. The human (albeit instrumental) good of a dwelling place suitable for domestic life is the good to which the practice of domestic architecture is directed. Our need for such professions places us in a position of dependence on the professional, and therefore in varying ways vulnerable. Which is why we require it to be the case that the professional on whom we are relying is genuinely dedicated to the human good we are seeking to have served in our lives.[28]

The dedication of the medical practitioner to the good of somatic health has to be twofold: to the science and to the art of medicine. A physician must be devoted to acquiring a knowledge of the teleologically ordered mechanisms that underlie well-ordered organic functioning, and the ways that functioning can fail, be damaged, be defective, be impaired. Second, a physician must be dedicated to acquiring the skills that will enable him to serve the good of health in the individual sick,

28. See Robert Sokolowski, "The Fiduciary Relationship and the Nature of Professions," in *Ethics, Trust and the Professions: Philosophical and Cultural Aspects,* ed. E. D. Pellegrino, R. M. Veatch, and J. P. Langan (Washington, D.C.: Georgetown University Press, 1991), 23–43; reprinted in Robert Sokolowski, *Christian Faith and Human Understanding* (Washington, D.C.: The Catholic University of America Press, 2006), 250–67.

damaged, or physically defective patient who presents himself for treatment. It is of critical importance that the acquisition and use of technique be informed by a sense of the good it is intended to serve. If it is not, and if the physician or surgeon regards himself as a mere technician—as numbers of them indeed do—then patients cannot be confident that they have placed themselves in the hands of someone who is dedicated to their good.

If medical practice is to be defined by its dedication to the good of somatic health in the lives of individual human beings, what ends are implicit in that commitment?

First, the maintenance of health, working for which can range from advice on regimens of diet and exercise to vaccination programs against infectious diseases.

Second, cure or healing—the restoration of health where possible in the patient who presents himself as suffering from an illness. This may be diagnosed as due to damage, or impairment or defect in some part of the organism, or to a systemic disease, such as a blood-borne infection that disrupts central homeostasis. Where there is a defect of functional ability, whether congenital or otherwise, that impairs well-ordered organic functioning, the science and art of medicine are properly directed to correcting that defect. It is not the proper task of doctors, in the absence of functional defects and impairments—in other words, when a person enjoys somatic health—to be seeking either to enhance functional abilities or to devote their technical resources to schemes of social control. The use of pharmaceutical agents, for example, to inhibit vicious or unruly behavior which is not caused by organic malfunction has doctors treating human beings as nonrational animals.

Third, where cure is not possible, it is a proper end of medicine to help patients approximate as far as possible to organic well functioning. This may take the form of supplying for functional defects, as when, for example, insulin is supplied to provide for defective insulin production by the pancreas in diabetes.

Fourth, where an approximation to organic well functioning is not possible, symptom control is a proper end of medicine, so that the symptoms of an organic disorder (e.g., the pain caused by certain cancers) are kept from unnecessarily obtruding on a person's capacity to enjoy some of the other goods of a human life.

The ends of approximating to organic well functioning and controlling the symptoms of organic malfunctioning are warranted ends of medicine just because health is an instrumental as well as an intrinsic good. So medicine's dedication to the good of health in patients encompasses a dedication to securing what organic well functioning is instrumental for, namely, the body's readiness for the pursuit of other human goods—a dedication that reasonably extends to mitigating a damaged or ailing body's unreadiness for the pursuit of other human goods. Hence palliative medicine is a proper part of the practice of medicine though it has no curative *telos*.

The ends here enumerated are the ends that are internal to the practice of medicine—the ends constitutive of the kind of practice it is. They can be recognized as such insofar as we recognize somatic health as a basic human good and a basic human need.

Of course it is intrinsic to the practice of medicine that if one undertakes to meet the varied forms of need for somatic health in the persons of the patients who come to one, many of whom will be extremely vulnerable, one may also (as in a hospital setting) have a responsibility to ensure provision for their basic care—of food, warmth, shelter, and hygiene. Furthermore, one is committed to treating one's patients in ways consistent with their dignity as human beings. But though these commitments are intrinsic to the practice of medicine they are not precisely what distinguish it as a profession.

The account given here of the profession of medicine in terms of the ends implicit in a learned and practical devotion to the good of somatic health doubtless invites many objections. One is that it represents too narrow a conception.

One form of this objection is that in confining the notion of health to "somatic health," and interpreting the correlative notion of ill-health in terms of organic disorder, disease, or defect, I am proposing an understanding of medicine that is inadequate to the reality of what patients expect from doctors. Patients come to doctors not necessarily with identifiable somatic disorders but with a range of "complaints" only some of which are diagnosable in terms of organic malfunction or defect. This certainly makes it necessary for doctors to be sensitive to the fact that something other than medical expertise may be needed by the patient. Suffering that is a consequence of loss of meaning or of injustice or of the inability to forgive, for example, is outside the province of medicine. In serving the good of somatic health in the lives of patients, doctors need to be conscious of the fact that they are contributing to the realization of just one ingredient good of human flourishing, and so should resist the expectation that there are medical solutions to problems that have no basis in organic disorder.

The complaint that somatic health represents too restrictive a notion of health is likely to be felt most acutely in relation to what are called mental illnesses. Here we need to distinguish between mental afflictions that are caused by organic disorders, and mental afflictions with no detectable organic component but which are related to factors ranging from unresolved conflicts of emotion to self-destructive vices.

The first group of mental afflictions seems to fall clearly within the ambit of medical practice devoted to somatic health. The remedies for the second group of afflictions could not be envisaged in terms of the restoration of somatic health or any approximation to somatic health. The absence both of the kind of knowledge base associated with somatic healing and of somatic health as the controlling end of therapy in the treatment of nonsomatically based mental afflictions suggests that it merely creates confusion in our understanding of medicine if we seek to include all forms of psychological treatment within its ambit.

It is not a passion for neat classification which motivates this observation. The utility of recognizing somatic health as the good which controls the ends of medical practice is threefold.

First, it allows for a coherent understanding of medicine as a profession. This is not some purely theoretical gain, since what is at issue is whether we are able to think of the practice of medicine as devoted to a specific human good and as therefore demanding in its practitioners dispositions appropriate to the realization of that good in the lives of patients. If we cannot defend such a conception of medical practice, then medicine is too readily thought of as mere expertise in the deployment of technical skills, which might be exercised either to secure whatever purposes patients want secured, or to secure the purposes for which the state can enlist the services of doctors.

The second reason for recognizing the usefulness of thinking of the good of somatic health as the controlling end of medical practice is that we are thereby provided with a rational basis for the allocation of healthcare resources. Much that passes for healthcare and as such commands resources is not healthcare at all.

Third, if the ends of medicine were clearly understood to be the ones adumbrated here, a much-needed clarity might be brought to decision making in medicolegal cases. For on the evidence of a series of cases over the past twenty years, it is clear that the judiciary badly needs to be able to distinguish between a judgment that medical treatment is no longer worthwhile—that is, when the ends proper to medicine are no longer achievable—and, on the other hand, the wholly unjustifiable judgment that a human life is no longer worthwhile. Well-grounded choices to end treatment should never be choices to end lives by ending the due basic care of patients.

Nelson Lund

11 Montesquieu, Judicial Degeneracy, and the U.S. Supreme Court

I. INTRODUCTION

In a 2003 case called *Lawrence v. Texas*, the Supreme Court invalidated a Texas statute that criminalized private acts of homosexual sodomy.[1] The Court found that the statute violated the Due Process Clause of the Fourteenth Amendment, and went on to hold that statutes criminalizing heterosexual sodomy are unconstitutional as well. John O. McGinnis and I have published a detailed critique of this case, and I want to stress that we believe the Texas statute was a pernicious law.[2] For obvious reasons, any enforcement of the statute was bound to be extremely rare, painfully capricious, and unlikely to accomplish any useful public purpose. But that does not necessarily imply that it was unconstitutional.

Rather than discuss the details of legal doctrine, I want to focus here on the nature of the Court's approach to its judicial task, in part because the first paragraph of Justice Anthony Kennedy's majority opinion may be the most self-consciously philosophic pronouncement the Court has ever issued. This opening paragraph comprises the following six sentences:

> [1] Liberty protects the person from unwarranted government intrusions into a dwelling or other private places. [2] In our tradition the State is not omnipresent in the home. [3] And there are other spheres of our lives and existence, out-

1. 539 U.S. 558 (2003).

2. Nelson Lund and John O. McGinnis, "*Lawrence v. Texas* and Judicial Hubris," *Michigan Law Review* 102 (June 2004): 1555–614. Much of my discussion of the *Lawrence* decision here is drawn from this article.

side the home, where the State should not be a dominant presence. [4] Freedom extends beyond spatial bounds. [5] Liberty presumes an autonomy of self that includes freedom of thought, belief, expression, and certain intimate conduct. [6] The instant case involves liberty of the person both in its spatial and more transcendent dimensions.[3]

While this passage is clearly meant to resonate with philosophic profundity, I believe that it is literally incomprehensible.

—Consider the first sentence: "Liberty protects the person from unwarranted government intrusions into a dwelling or other private places." Is liberty a divinity, like Nike or Eros? If not, the Court's reification or personification of liberty accomplishes nothing except to dodge the obligation to say what exactly it is that protects against unwarranted intrusions. Unspecified unwarranted intrusions, I might add.

—Sentence [2] is similarly high flown, and empty: "In our tradition the State is not omnipresent in the home." Does this mean that the State dwells in some rooms of the house but not others? What would that mean, exactly? And if that is not what the sentence means, what does it mean?

—Sentence [3] says: "And there are other spheres of our lives and existence, outside the home, where the State should not be a dominant presence." When you look at the previous sentence in light of this one, you might suspect that the author believes that "omnipresent" means "being a dominant presence." Of course that is not what the word means, and one cannot help wondering whether the author cares more about the sound of words than about their meaning. In any event, it is hard to be sure about much of anything here. Are our lives and our existence two different things, as this third sentence suggests? Who claims that the State should be a "dominant presence" in every sphere of our lives, and what is the point of denying such a far-fetched claim?

—Sentence [4] creates more mysteries when it declares: "Freedom extends beyond spatial bounds." How exactly does freedom extend beyond spatial bounds? By spreading through space despite

3. 539 U.S. at 562 (bracketed sentence numbers added).

some kind of physical obstacles? By spreading beyond space itself into some other dimension? What dimension would that be? Maybe the sentence just means that freedom can entail more than an absence of physical obstacles to physical movement. But who has ever denied such an obvious proposition?

—In sentence [5], we finally seem to get the main point of the paragraph: "Liberty presumes an autonomy of self that includes freedom of thought, belief, expression, and certain intimate conduct." The idea seems to be that there should be limits on governmental intrusions on "freedom of thought, belief, expression, and certain intimate conduct." But that is not what the sentence says. Instead, we have "liberty" presuming an "autonomy" that includes certain forms of "freedom." Does that mean that liberty and freedom are different things, and that both of them are different from autonomy? What would the differences be? As to "an autonomy of self," is this just a pointless redundancy, or are we meant to contrast autonomy of self with an autonomy of something other than self? What might such a thing be?

—In sentence [6], we are back to what looks like complete gibberish: "The instant case involves liberty of the person both in its spatial and more transcendent dimensions." "Transcendent dimensions" has a splendiferous ring to it, but the term has no obvious determinate meaning at all in this context. And that difficulty is aggravated by the author's assumption that there are degrees of transcendence among these transcendent dimensions.

When the U.S. Supreme Court opens a judicial opinion with a pronouncement whose meaning can only be guessed at, one may be tempted to pass on with a chuckle or an embarrassed sigh. But Justice Kennedy has made that hard to do, for *Lawrence* also repeats a similarly nonsensical flight of rhetoric from the opinion he coauthored in the 1992 *Casey* decision that reaffirmed the right to abortion. Here is the passage he quotes:

> These matters [namely, marriage, procreation, contraception, family relationships, child rearing, and education], involving the most intimate and personal choices a person may make in a lifetime, choices central to personal dignity and autonomy, are central to the liberty protected by the Fourteenth Amendment.

At the heart of liberty is the right to define one's own concept of existence, of meaning, of the universe, and of the mystery of human life. Beliefs about these matters could not define the attributes of personhood were they formed under compulsion of the State.[4]

The analytical problems here are similar to the problems with *Lawrence*'s opening passage. What exactly would be involved, for example, in defining one's own concept of existence, meaning, and so on? Americans surely have a right to define words however they wish, especially if they do not care to communicate with other people. But how would one define one's own "concept" of these things? Perhaps by adopting an opinion that others might not share? People do that all the time, without the Supreme Court's assistance.

In any event, whatever this "heart of liberty" might be, it is difficult to imagine what it has to do with the concluding sentence, which says: "Beliefs about these matters could not define the attributes of personhood were they formed under compulsion of the State." If the State could find a way to compel an individual to believe one thing or another about such matters as existence or the universe, we are told that such beliefs could not "define the attributes of personhood." Does this mean that the attributes would be determined in some other way? Or that personhood would then have no attributes? Or that the person would have no personhood? What is personhood, anyway, and how does it differ from its attributes?

There are three legal, rather than mystical, propositions that the Court might be groping for in this passage, and I agree with them all:

1. Supreme Court precedents protect the freedom to make certain choices about matters relating to sex;
2. people are legally free to think whatever they find themselves thinking about existence, meaning, the universe, and the mystery of human life; and
3. the First Amendment sharply limits the power of government to attempt to compel beliefs about these matters.

But what could propositions (2) and (3) possibly have to do with the legality of governmental restrictions on abortion or sodomy? Aborting a pregnancy is not a thought or a belief, nor is an act of sodomy.

4. Ibid., 574 (quoting *Planned Parenthood v. Casey*, 505 U.S. 833, 851 [1992]).

Perhaps the Court has ascended to one of those "more transcendent dimensions" referred to in *Lawrence*'s opening passage, and perhaps such elementary distinctions as that between beliefs and acts have been transcended in that dimension. Unfortunately, there are indications that something like this may well have occurred.

First, *Lawrence* relies on the doctrine of "substantive due process," which has no basis in the text of the Due Process Clauses, and which the Supreme Court has never even attempted to derive from that text. Second, the opinion in this case utterly demolishes all of the doctrinal restraints that previous Courts had adopted in an effort to cabin the reach of substantive due process. Third, Justice Kennedy puts forth a series of patently sophistical arguments, and fails to present even a single valid legal argument. Fourth, the case establishes no intelligible legal rule for the future. In *Lawrence*, the Court's jurisprudence is reduced to empty bombast and the naked will of Supreme Court majorities.

Rather than defend these propositions here,[5] I would like to explore the background of this appalling judicial performance, and offer some suggestions about its significance. Parts II and III briefly discuss the roots of judicial hubris in American constitutional law. Part IV looks for the deeper roots of judicial activism in the political philosophy of Montesquieu and in the practice of the English common law, where it has a defensible theory to support it and a long history of largely benign effects. Part V suggests that the hubristic activism on display in *Lawrence* comes at least in part from a mismatch between Montesquieu's politically moderating judiciary and the novel American device of judicial enforcement of a written constitution. I conclude that the U.S. Supreme Court is neither authorized nor qualified to correct written human law through appeals to higher laws, including the natural moral law.

II. ORIGINS OF SUBSTANTIVE DUE PROCESS

If one wanted to offer a completely noncontroversial example of something that violates the natural moral law, slavery would be a pretty good choice. Indeed, most of us today could say what Abraham Lincoln said:

5. All of these propositions are defended in detail in Lund and McGinnis, "*Lawrence v. Texas* and Judicial Hubris."

"I am naturally anti-slavery. If slavery is not wrong, nothing is wrong. I can not remember when I did not so think, and feel."[6] For contemporary Americans, indeed, it may come as some surprise to learn that slavery has until quite recently been a well-accepted practice in a great variety of human societies.[7] To take just one example, I am unaware of any record of moral objections to slavery by substantial numbers of people—slave or free—in the ancient Greek and Roman world from which our own civilization descends.

Alexis de Tocqueville offered the following explanation for this seemingly odd fact:

> All the great writers of antiquity were a part of the aristocracy of masters, or at least they saw that aristocracy established without dispute before their eyes; their minds, after expanding in several directions, were therefore found limited in this one, and it was necessary that Jesus Christ come to earth to make it understood that all members of the human species are naturally alike and equal.[8]

As Tocqueville was acutely aware, of course, slavery and slave trading were widely practiced in Christendom, and accepted by leading Christians, for many centuries after Jesus lived on earth. Certain Christians eventually did lead a determined effort to abolish slavery, but that effort faced tremendous opposition from non-Christian cultures throughout the world and from some thoroughly Christian polities as well, including several American states.

The obvious explanation for the establishment and persistence of slavery, at least in the United States, involves economic self-interest and the political forces generated by economic interests. Our independent federal judiciary is insulated from such forces by the life tenure given to its members. One might therefore not expect these judges to be directly influenced by the pressures to which elected politicians are always subjected. How, then, do we explain the behavior of the U.S. Supreme Court, which created special protections for slavery out of some exceedingly thin constitutional air?

6. Abraham Lincoln to A. G. Hodges, 4 April 1864, in *Collected Works of Abraham Lincoln* (New Brunswick, N.J.: Rutgers University Press, 1953), 7.282.

7. For a brief and useful summary, see Thomas Sowell, *Black Rednecks and White Liberals* (San Francisco: Encounter Books, 2005), 111–57.

8. Alexis de Tocqueville, *Democracy in America*, vol. 2, pt. 1, ch. 3, trans. Harvey C. Mansfield and Delba Winthrop (Chicago: University of Chicago Press, 2000), 413.

The 1857 *Dred Scott* decision held, without any basis in the constitutional text, that black slaves and their descendants could never become American citizens.[9] In addition, the Court held that an 1820 statute that outlawed slavery in the federal territories was unconstitutional.[10] This second conclusion was based on the Due Process Clause of the Fifth Amendment, which forbids the federal government to deprive any person "of life, liberty, or property, without due process of law." In other words, whenever the government takes away your life, liberty, or property, as it is often entitled to do, it has to give you due process of law first. *Dred Scott* was the first case in which the Supreme Court used the Due Process Clause to protect substantive rights, and Chief Justice Roger Taney's entire analysis was comprehended in the following expostulation:

> [A]n act of Congress which deprives a citizen of the United States of his liberty or property, merely because he came himself or brought his property into a particular Territory of the United States, and who had committed no offence against the laws, could hardly be dignified with the name of due process of law.[11]

In dissent, Justice Benjamin Curtis explained in considerable detail why Taney had to be wrong. The essence of Curtis's argument was that the right to hold human beings as property is founded entirely on positive law, having no basis in natural law, and that this property right must be lost when the owner voluntarily brings such men within a jurisdiction that does not recognize the right.[12] Taney himself acknowledged that Congress had the authority to legislate for the territories,[13] and the slave states themselves recognized their own right to forbid the importation of slaves, notwithstanding the due process clauses in their own state constitutions.[14] The Due Process Clause of the Fifth Amendment, whose lineage traced to Magna Charta and which had an analogue in the law of every American state, had never been thought to have any bearing on the right of legislatures to regulate or abolish slavery. Taney gave no reason for suddenly imputing any such substantive effect to the Clause,

9. *Scott v. Sandford,* 60 U.S. (10 How.) 393, 406 (1857).
10. Ibid., 452–53.
11. Ibid., 450.
12. Ibid., 624–26 (Curtis, J., dissenting).
13. Ibid., 446–49 (opinion of the Court).
14. Ibid., 627 (Curtis, J., dissenting).

which would among other things imply that the Fifth Amendment silently withdrew from Congress its unquestioned power to regulate or ban the slave trade.

Dred Scott proved to be a pretty good paradigm for the future development of what came to be called substantive due process. Offering no reason at all to explain how the due process provision of the Constitution could suddenly operate to invalidate a substantive law that was well established at the time the provision was enacted, Taney must simply have believed that his political and moral judgments were superior to those of the benighted legislature.

One might have expected substantive due process to be buried along with *Dred Scott* after the Civil War. And the nation might appear to have done exactly that when the Fourteenth Amendment overruled *Dred Scott*'s holding on the definition of citizenship in the Fourteenth Amendment, and adopted a new due process provision (applicable to the state governments) that used the very same terminology that Taney had misinterpreted. But the Supreme Court has not seen things that way. Instead, this doctrine from *Dred Scott* has popped up repeatedly over the years to create new constitutional rights under the Fifth and Fourteenth Amendments. There have been many dissents from these decisions, and there have even been periods when the doctrine had little effect on legal developments. But the doctrine has always come back to life.

The latest phase of rights creation began in 1965, when the Court created a right of married couples to possess contraceptives.[15] The Justices then created a number of other new rights connected with sexual freedom, the most important of which was the right to abortion in *Roe v. Wade*.[16] This series of decisions was something brand new in America. One might call it "liberation jurisprudence," or perhaps the constitutionalization of Hugh Hefner's Playboy Philosophy.[17]

Lawrence is the latest step in the development of that jurisprudence, and the opinion in *Lawrence* puts on full display the Court's supreme self-confidence in its own moral judgment and in its own intellectual

15. *Griswold v. Connecticut*, 381 U.S. 479 (1965).

16. 410 U.S. 113 (1973).

17. This "philosophy" was set out in an ambitious series of essays in Hefner's *Playboy* magazine in the 1960s. The essays have been collected online at http://www.playboy.com/worldofplayboy/hmh/philosophy/.

brilliance. Whether one sees in this performance the Wizard of Oz or Hans Christian Andersen's naked emperor, it is worth asking how we got here.

III. SELF-EVIDENT TRUTHS

The proximate cause of our contemporary Supreme Court's moral self-confidence is probably *Brown v. Board of Education,* in which the Justices unanimously overturned half a century of precedent and declared segregated schools unconstitutional.[18] This 1954 decision had two especially salient features. First, the Court's opinion contained no legal reasoning. It was based instead on pop psychology, of a kind that rather resembles the pop philosophy at the beginning of the *Lawrence* opinion.[19] Second, the Court's opinion was a tremendous political success insofar as it came to be seen as the first major step in the civil rights revolution that took place about a decade later.

The combination of these two features led to the view, especially prominent in the press and the academy, that the Supreme Court's most important function is to provide moral guidance to a morally retarded, or at least morally challenged, nation. This view makes sense only on the highly questionable premises that the Constitution as written permits Jim Crow segregation, and that the *Brown* Court had to look beyond the Constitution in order to reach what our generation now regards as the incontestably right result.

I doubt the validity of both premises. Furthermore, *Brown* may have had less practical effect than we usually attribute to it.[20] But the myth of the Supreme Court as the people's moral shepherd took hold nonetheless. The classic statement was offered a few years later by Alexander Bickel of the Yale Law School:

18. 347 U.S. 483 (1954).

19. For more detail, see Nelson Lund, "The Constitution, the Supreme Court, and Racial Politics," *Georgia State University Law Review* 12 (June 1996): 1129–50.

20. For an introduction to the debate over the nature and extent of *Brown*'s practical effects, cf. Gerald N. Rosenberg, *The Hollow Hope: Can Courts Bring about Social Change?* (Chicago: University of Chicago Press, 1991), 9–174, with Neal Devins, "Judicial Matters," *California Law Review* 80 (1992): 1027, 1039–46.

> The function of the Justices—and there is no question but what this accords with the great authoritative body of opinion on the subject—is to immerse themselves in the tradition of our society and of kindred societies that have gone before, in history and in the sediment of history which is law, and, as Judge Hand once suggested, in the thought and the vision of the philosophers and the poets. The Justices will then be fit to extract "fundamental presuppositions" from their deepest selves, but in fact from the evolving morality of our tradition. No doubt, as the late Zechariah Chafee Jr. wrote, "the man himself is a part of what he decides." But, as he concluded, "if law is the will of the Justices," it is "the will of the Justices trying to do that which is right."[21]

Leaving aside the obvious echoes of this passage in Justice Kennedy's laughably pompous pseudophilosophy, and leaving aside Bickel's unsubstantiated allusion to an authoritative body of opinion, I want to focus attention on Bickel's interesting suggestion that "fundamental presuppositions" can be extracted from a changing tradition, and that judges can find those "presuppositions" within themselves. The idea here seems to be that a certain type of liberal education will enable a lawyer to find unchanging truths within himself through some sort of intellectual intuition.

In another passage, Bickel approvingly quotes Justice Felix Frankfurter's claim that judges "must have something of the creative artist in them; they must have antennae registering feelings and judgment beyond logical, let alone quantitative, proof."[22] That would certainly be one way to describe Anthony Kennedy. But why in the world would one think that these lawyers have better moral antennae than anyone else? Can such antennae really be developed through the kind of studies that lawyers and judges specialize in (supplemented, of course, with a little philosophy and poetry)? The idea is sufficiently odd, but also sufficiently widespread, at least in legal circles, that I think it deserves serious attention.

The key, I suspect, lies in a notion of self-evident truths accessible only to "feelings and judgment beyond logical . . . proof."[23] This may be usefully compared with what I think is the closest thing we have in America to an official statement of a national political philosophy:

21. Alexander M. Bickel, *The Least Dangerous Branch* (Indianapolis, Ind.: Bobbs-Merrill, 1962), 236.

22. Ibid., 239.

23. Ibid.

> We hold these truths to be self-evident, that all men are created equal, that they are endowed by their Creator with certain unalienable Rights, that among these are Life, Liberty and the pursuit of Happiness.—That to secure these rights, Governments are instituted among Men, deriving their just powers from the consent of the governed,—that whenever any Form of Government becomes destructive of these ends, it is the Right of the People to alter or to abolish it, and to institute new Government, laying its foundation on such principles and organizing its powers in such Form, as to them shall seem most likely to effect their Safety and Happiness.[24]

This is all so familiar and so publicly respectable that Americans tend to regard these as self-evident truths indeed. These propositions, moreover, and especially the assertion about inherent and unalienable rights, seem to be the core of what is ordinarily taken for the natural moral law by our Supreme Court. Do these claims hold up to scrutiny?

Self-evident truths certainly do exist. Leaving aside abstract propositions—that the whole is greater than the part, for example—no one of ordinary experience should require a proof that all human beings are animals. But is it really self-evident that every human being is endowed by his Creator with rights to life, liberty, and the pursuit of happiness? Our most obviously inherent qualities are the ones we share with other animals, and few of us believe that other animals have such inherent rights. Think for a moment about the films most of us have seen of life among the animals of the Serengeti plain. When a leopard attacks a wildebeest, I do not suppose anybody objects that it has violated the victim's "right" to life and liberty. And when a pack of hyenas comes along and drives the leopard from its kill, I do not suppose that anyone would seriously maintain that the leopard has a "right" to the property it acquired by mixing its labor with the wildebeest's flesh.

The reason we do not say that beasts have "rights" that are good against other beasts is the same reason that we do not think any of them has a "right" to be safe from lightning strikes. Similarly, we do not think that human beings have a "right" to be spared by a hungry leopard, or by a lightning bolt. In ordinary usage, a right implies a correlative obligation to respect that right, and we do not believe that it makes any sense to impute such obligations to beasts or to thunderstorms.

24. The Declaration of Independence of 1776.

The rights that we actually see enforced—especially but not only legal rights—arise from human institutions. And countless cultures have existed for long periods without our notions of inherent rights and natural equality, as Tocqueville has reminded us. None of this disproves the substantive claims in the Declaration of Independence, but it surely suggests that their truth is a long way from being self-evident.

Rights could, of course, be inherent without necessarily being natural in the same sense that our bodies are natural, if they were given to us by God. We find this suggestion in the Declaration of Independence—which holds that we are self-evidently endowed by our Creator with unalienable rights—but that suggestion cannot resolve the difficulty. The language used in the Declaration could be another way of saying that such rights are natural, in which case the reference to the Creator adds nothing at all to the claim that the existence of natural rights is self-evident. Or, it could be a way of saying that the existence of a God who endows us with unalienable rights is self-evident. This is manifestly false, as one can easily recognize by considering the great difficulty that many people have in maintaining their belief in God even when they strongly desire to keep their faith.

Whether one views these unalienable rights as given by nature or by God—or by what the Declaration ambiguously calls "the Laws of Nature and of Nature's God"—their existence is hardly self-evident. And no matter how strongly one may wish it were otherwise, I think one must say the same about the Declaration's claims with respect to the purpose of governments and the provenance of their just powers.

The Declaration, of course, says that "we hold" these truths to be self-evident, which tacitly acknowledges, I think, that they are not self-evident, at least in the ordinary sense of the term: evident of itself without proof.[25] One might say: "I hold that man alone among the animals

25. There is a sense in which one might say that a proposition is self-evident if it is demonstrably true. Socrates' playful exhibition with Meno's slave boy could be taken as an illustration—or exploration—of this possibility. Alternatively, one might say, with St. Thomas, that a proposition about a certain kind of being will be self-evident to those who understand what that being is, so that, for example, one who knew that an angel is not a body would know that an angel is not circumscriptively in a place; see *Summa Theologica,* I–II, Q. 94, art. 2. Ultimately, of course, it may be that all true propositions are self-evident to one who possesses perfect knowledge, and that one who lacked perfect knowledge could therefore "hold" that a proposition is self-evidently true if he holds that it is true. Because this eliminates the distinction between truths and self-evident truths, however, I do not

has an immortal soul." But one would not ordinarily say: "I hold that men must eat in order to live." Perhaps the Declaration's paradoxical treatment of the propositions it asserts is merely a way of indicating that a political manifesto is not the place for efforts to prove the truth of fundamental political principles. The paradox, then, might be a sign of genuine philosophic sophistication in what is surely among the greatest of all revolutionary proclamations.

But in that case, we should be able to find the proofs elsewhere, and presumably in the seminal works of liberal political philosophy, such as Locke's *Second Treatise of Civil Government*. Unfortunately, I think that arguments establishing the truth of the Declaration's assertions cannot be found there either. Instead, what one finds are assertions (e.g., that men are "all the workmanship of one omnipotent and infinitely wise Maker"),[26] along with arguments in favor of the usefulness of treating such propositions as true, or even as self-evident truths.[27]

But if utility measures the value of these propositions—and I do not question the utility of proclaiming them in the Declaration of Independence—that opens the possibility that there may be circumstances in which they should not be treated as self-evident truths. And I claim that at least one such circumstance does exist: The U.S. Supreme Court should never rely on these propositions, or any other conception of the natural moral law, to declare any statute unconstitutional.[28]

My reasons for making this claim are twofold. First, I think that history demonstrates pretty conclusively—and contrary to Bickel's assertion—that Supreme Court Justices are ill-suited to the task of discovering and applying the natural moral law in opposition to the written law. Second, I think that our political system provides different and better

believe it makes a helpful contribution to understanding the Declaration of Independence or to understanding the place of natural moral law in our political tradition.

26. John Locke, *Second Treatise of Civil Government*, ch. 2, § 6.

27. See Nelson Lund, "Rousseau and Direct Democracy (with a Note on the Supreme Court's *Term Limits* Decision)," *Journal of Contemporary Legal Issues* 13 (2004): 459, 466–74. The discussion of self-evident truths above is adapted from this article.

28. As Philip Hamburger has shown with rich historical evidence, the revolutionary generation believed that natural law should guide the writing of constitutions and other laws, but that it could not imply the precise content of those laws; see Philip A. Hamburger, "Natural Rights, Natural Law, and American Constitutions," *Yale Law Journal* 102 (January 1993): 907–60. This should make us very chary of supposing that they expected judges to correct "mistakes" in the written law by appealing to natural law.

political mechanisms for pursuing this task. The inspired revolutionary spirit of the Declaration of Independence is apt to have sinister effects when indulged by judges charged with enforcing the existing law.

IV. MONTESQUIEU AND ENGLISH COMMON LAW

Although *Brown v. Board of Education* seems to have been the proximate cause of the modern Supreme Court's frequent moral preening, the problematic cause of that development must be sought at a deeper level. The place to begin, I believe, is with Montesquieu.

The Spirit of the Laws, first published in 1748, is the primary philosophic source of a proposition that we take for granted, namely, that an independent judiciary is an indispensable element of any free and well-functioning polity. The book from which this proposition emerges is very long, and extremely complex. In discussing it here, I will have to perform a hazardous act of distillation, which carries risks both of error and of oversimplification. That said, let me begin with two brief and striking quotations.

Toward the end of *The Spirit of the Laws*, Montesquieu makes the following announcement:

> I say it, and it seems to me that I have written this work only to prove it: the spirit of moderation should be that of the legislator; the political good, like the moral good, is always found between two limits.[29]

Although striking, this statement is quite uninformative. Unless you know what the two limits are, and where the appropriate midpoint between those limits lies, you have no way of identifying the political or the moral good. Helpfully, though, Montesquieu provides what he calls an example:

> The formalities of justice are necessary to liberty. But, their number could be so great that it would run counter to the end of the very laws establishing them: suits would be interminable; the ownership of goods would remain uncertain; one of the parties would be given the goods of the other without examination, or both would be ruined by the examination.

29. *The Spirit of the Laws*, bk. 29, ch. 1, ed. and trans. Anne M. Kohler, Basia C. Miller, and Harold S. Stone (Cambridge: Cambridge University Press, 1989), 602.

> Citizens would lose their liberty and their security; accusers would no longer have the means to convict nor the accused, a means to vindicate themselves.[30]

Montesquieu's illustration of the spirit of moderation is taken from the realm of judicial procedure, perhaps because legal formalities are quintessentially "moderating" devices: as the etymology of the word *moderation* suggests, they reduce conflicts by regulating and controlling them. But Montesquieu's point here is that you can have too much moderation: an excess of legal formalities can actually prevent conflicts from being resolved.

As I mentioned, this somewhat paradoxical passage comes near the end of *The Spirit of the Laws.* Near the beginning of the book, Montesquieu says the following:

> [I]t seems that human nature would rise up incessantly against despotic government. But, despite men's love of liberty, despite their hatred of violence, most peoples are subjected to this type of government. This is easy to understand. In order to form a moderate government, one must combine powers, regulate them, temper them, make them act; one must give one power a ballast, so to speak, to put it in a position to resist another; this is a masterpiece of legislation that chance rarely produces and prudence is rarely allowed to produce. By contrast, a despotic government leaps to view, so to speak; it is uniform throughout; as only passions are needed to establish it, everyone is good enough for that.[31]

Montesquieu claims to be stating the obvious. And it may sound obvious, especially to those of us who have been raised in a culture that celebrates checks and balances, and the separation of powers. But is it really true that passions alone are enough to establish a despotic government, and that anyone can do it? That does not seem obvious at all. And even if we assume that it is true, why does Montesquieu assert that moderate governments can be produced either by prudence or by chance? If it is so easy to establish despotism, while the alternative is so complex and delicately balanced, how could chance ever produce anything except despotism?

Montesquieu's response to this last question seems to come in his detailed analysis of the constitution of England, where he says that liberty will appear as in a mirror.[32] Although Montesquieu does not mention

30. Ibid.

31. Ibid., bk. 5, ch. 14, 63.

32. Ibid., bk. 11, ch. 5, 156.

the fact, the English constitution has no identifiable founder. There is no English Lycurgus or Moses, not even a James Madison or George Washington, and so this constitution may appear as a masterpiece of legislation produced by chance.

Before looking more closely at Montesquieu's discussion of the English constitution, let us pause to notice one more feature of the two passages I have quoted. In each one, "moderation" is offered as the appropriate goal for legislators, while "liberty" is presented as the goal of citizens. "Liberty" is a word with tremendous political appeal, which may help to explain why it is the very first word in Justice Kennedy's *Lawrence* opinion. But what, exactly, does it mean? Montesquieu begins with several examples of what "liberty" has meant to various people.[33] Some of the examples make intuitive sense. For instance, some people have thought that liberty is "the faculty of electing the one whom they were to obey." Others seem faintly ridiculous, such as "the usage of wearing a long beard."

The variety of examples may suggest that people's ideas of liberty are generally just a reflection of their prejudices. But then Montesquieu offers a very edifying definition of his own: "[I]n a society where there are laws," he says, "liberty can consist only in having the power to do what one should want to do and in no way being constrained to do what one should not want to do."[34] He then immediately replaces this formulation with a different one, namely, that "Liberty is the right to do everything the laws permit." Unlike the previous definition, which seems to imply the centrality of duty or obligation, this one seems bereft of any moral implications. Similarly bereft of moral content is Montesquieu's very striking statement a little later: "Philosophical liberty consists in the exercise of one's will or, at least (if all systems must be mentioned), in one's opinion that one exerts one's will."[35]

Perhaps these formulations are not necessarily inconsistent. But even on the assumption that they are consistent with each other, they beg the essential moral questions. What exactly should one want to do? Or, what exactly should the laws permit? Rather than answer these questions, Montesquieu makes a seemingly unrelated claim, saying that political liberty "is present only when power is not abused, but it has eternally

33. Ibid., bk. 11, ch. 2.

34. Ibid., bk. 11, ch. 3, 155.

35. Ibid., bk. 12, ch. 2, 188.

been observed that any man who has power is led to abuse it; he continues until he finds limits."[36]

And then, amazingly, Montesquieu adds the following remark: "Who would think it! Even virtue has need of limits."[37] The implication here seems to be that what one should want to do is something other than to be virtuous. With his use of the exclamation point, Montesquieu fairly shouts out that this is a surprising proposition, but he does not explain why it follows from the "eternal" observation that everyone with power is led to abuse it.

At this point, Montesquieu enters into a long discussion of how the abuse of power can be prevented. Reduced to its simplest possible terms, his answer is what we call checks and balances, or the separation of powers. This answer is presented primarily through what purports to be a description of the constitution of England. Several closely related features of this description are particularly important.

First, we suddenly get yet another new definition of liberty. "Political liberty in a citizen," says Montesquieu, "is that tranquility of spirit which comes from the opinion each one has of his security, and in order for him to have this liberty the government must be such that one citizen cannot fear another citizen."[38] This is the bourgeois understanding of the purpose of politics, expressed most vividly by Thomas Hobbes about a hundred years earlier. Montesquieu presents no argument in favor of this understanding. Instead, he offers a picture of one nation whose constitution has political liberty in this sense as its direct purpose, namely, England. The implication seems to be that we can look at England and see why this is the proper definition of political liberty.

Second, Montesquieu asserts that when legislative power and executive power are joined in the same hands, there can be no liberty because "one can fear that the same monarch or senate that makes tyrannical laws will execute them tyrannically."[39] This is the same point made by Locke—against Hobbes—when he argued that the legislative and executive powers ought to be separated in order to guard against the temptation to turn the law to the private advantage of the rulers.[40] Montesquieu's understanding of the separation of powers, however, turns out

36. Ibid., bk. 11, ch. 4, 155.
37. Ibid.
38. Ibid., bk. 11, ch. 6, 157.
39. Ibid.
40. John Locke, *Second Treatise of Civil Government*, ch. 12, § 143.

to be different from Locke's. Montesquieu implicitly contends that the bifurcation of powers that we find in Locke is deficient. Why? Because the power of judging must be separated from both the legislative and executive powers.

Much, though not all, of the ensuing description of the constitution of England focuses on the significance of this separated power of judging. Contrary to what we might expect, however, Montesquieu never even mentions what we Americans would think of as the independent judiciary. Instead, he claims that the power of judging in England lies entirely with juries, namely, ad hoc groups of citizens chosen temporarily, and partly by the parties themselves, to decide particular cases. "In this fashion," says Montesquieu, "the power of judging, so terrible among men, being attached neither to a certain state nor to a certain profession, becomes, so to speak invisible and null."[41] The claim here seems to be that the institution of the English jury completely removes the power of judging from politics. No political faction can get control of juries because the government does not choose their members. And, because they are evanescent bodies, they cannot acquire political interests or agendas of their own.

As a description of English legal practice, this is quite misleading. England had an enormously influential body of professional judges. Although appointed by the Crown, they had acquired over the course of history considerable independence and a profound power to shape the law. Judges, moreover, were generally uninhibited in pushing juries to arrive at the verdict favored by the judge, and some courts made no use of juries at all. In addition, the most senior judges had significant political positions (such as seats in the House of Lords) that went along with their judicial positions. In Montesquieu's presentation of the constitution of England, these judges are literally "invisible and null," for he gives virtually no hint of their existence.

But Montesquieu must have known about this prominent cadre of professional judges. He was himself a senior judge in Bordeaux, and he spent two years in England shortly before he began to compose *The Spirit of the Laws*. During this visit, he spent most of his time studying the English constitution, according to the biographer of his friend Lord

41. *The Spirit of the Laws*, bk. 11, ch. 6, 158.

Chesterfield.[42] The idea that a visiting judge from France, who was trying to learn about the English legal system, would have somehow not found out about his English counterparts is much too far-fetched to be given any credit.[43]

There is another reason to think that Montesquieu was not just ill-informed. *The Spirit of the Laws* became extremely influential among people who were themselves intimately familiar with the operation of the English legal system. The greatest example is William Blackstone, but we must also include the framers of the American Constitution. Montesquieu was one of the most frequently cited authors in American literature during the founding period.[44] And, although several philosophers are mentioned in the *Federalist Papers*, he is the only one invoked as an authority on the construction of constitutions. Indeed, in the *Federalist Papers,* Publius actually quotes Montesquieu for the proposition that judging must be separated from the legislative and executive powers, and for the proposition that of these three powers the judiciary is next to nothing.[45] Accordingly, I think we have to look for some explanation of Montesquieu's misrepresentation of English legal practice, without assuming that he was foolish or uninformed.

Montesquieu's description of the role of juries in the English constitution focuses entirely on criminal cases. This is consistent with a theme that runs throughout *The Spirit of the Laws* about the political importance of the criminal law. Indeed, at one point, Montesquieu goes so far as to say that "the citizen's liberty depends principally on the goodness of the criminal laws."[46] It is therefore worth noting that English judges played a relatively smaller role in the field of criminal law than they did in what we call civil litigation, such as suits about debts or monetary compensation for injuries. And it is also true that there was a right to

42. Robert Shackleton, *Montesquieu: A Critical Biography* (London: Oxford University Press, 1961), 125.

43. Some commentators have nonetheless thought that Montesquieu was unaware of the significant role of judicial magistrates in England. See, e.g., Laurence Claus, "Montesquieu's Mistakes and the True Meaning of Separation," *Oxford Journal of Legal Studies* 25 (Autumn 2005): 419–51.

44. Donald Lutz, "The Relative Influence of European Writers on Late Eighteenth-Century American Political Thought," *American Political Science Review* 78 (March 1984): 194, table 3.

45. *The Federalist,* no. 78, ed. Clinton Rossiter (New York: Mentor Books, 1961), 466.

46. *The Spirit of the Laws,* bk. 12, ch. 2, 188.

trial by jury in all of the most serious criminal cases. For that reason, one might argue that Montesquieu's exaggeration of the role of juries is not as egregious as it might at first appear.

But this defense of Montesquieu simply leads to a different problem. There are many indications in *The Spirit of the Laws* that Montesquieu is fully aware of the political importance of the noncriminal law, and in some places he clearly includes this form of law in discussions of the power of judging. I will give just one example. In a discussion of Roman law, Montesquieu describes a practice that he expressly likens to the English use of juries.[47] At that time, the Romans employed this device only for civil cases, not for criminal cases, and Montesquieu points out that the Romans restricted these jurylike tribunals to decisions about matters of fact. Questions of law or right were decided by specialists who were more analogous to the English judges who are left out of Montesquieu's discussion of the English constitution.[48]

The key to understanding what Montesquieu is up to, I would like to suggest, lies in his insight that it is both necessary and impossible to depoliticize the power of judging.

Think for a moment about what the function or power of judging is, especially in criminal cases. In the simplest possible terms, it is the power to decide whether the force of the government will be used to punish an individual because that individual engaged in some forbidden conduct. Again in the simplest possible terms, there are two kinds of mistakes that can occur. First, the government can forbid conduct that it should permit. In my opinion, this is what happened when the state of Texas outlawed homosexual sodomy. (And perhaps I should mention that Montesquieu argued against the criminalization of homosexual conduct.)[49] The second kind of mistake occurs when an individual is improperly convicted of engaging in conduct that the law makes criminal. (Interestingly, there is good reason to believe that this happened in the *Lawrence* case as well. There is considerable circumstantial evidence, which was never

47. Ibid., bk. 11, ch. 18, 179.

48. And, at another point, in the context of a discussion of kingship in the heroic period in Greece, he says that "the masterwork of legislation is to know where properly to place the power of judging" (ibid., bk. 11, ch. 11, 169). In context, there seems to be no distinction between civil and criminal matters.

49. Ibid., bk. 12, ch. 6.

presented to any of the courts that heard the case, suggesting that the defendants were prosecuted on the basis of false testimony by the police.)[50]

With respect to the second problem, any disinterested observer would agree that those who make judgments about guilt and innocence should be unbiased, with nothing to gain from a wrongful verdict. This seems to be the point of the English jury system as it was used in the eighteenth century, and Montesquieu presents the English jury as the model of depoliticized judging.[51]

But what about the first problem, namely, misguided laws like the Texas sodomy statute? English juries did have some power to moderate the effects of such laws, by refusing to return guilty verdicts even when the evidence showed that the defendant had violated the law. But this power of jury nullification seldom had significant or systematic manifestations. A much more important moderating force arose from the activities of those professional judges whom Montesquieu leaves out of the picture.

At this point, perhaps it will be useful to briefly describe the peculiar nature of English law. I mentioned earlier that the English constitution has no identifiable founder. The same is true of English law more generally. The primary source of the laws applied by the English courts of Montesquieu's time lay in ancient, unwritten customs. Through a gradual and extraordinarily complex historical process, this ancient customary law became the basis for a body of law peculiar to England. We call this the common law, and it is found primarily in a great stock of judicial opinions explaining how the law was applied in particular cases.

As time went on, judges increasingly began to look at prior decisions by other judges for evidence of what the ancient law required. And they

50. See Dale Carpenter, "The Unknown Past of *Lawrence v. Texas*," *Michigan Law Review* 102 (June 2004): 1464–1527.

51. The sense in which I am using the term "depoliticized" can be illustrated by contrasting the English jury with an example that Montesquieu later uses to show the horrible effects of putting the power to judge in a politically inappropriate place. At a certain point in Roman history, the power of judging was transferred to the class of people who were responsible for collecting taxes. The result, says Montesquieu, was that "they were rapacious, they heaped misfortune on misfortune and made public needs rise from public needs. Far from giving such people the power of judging, they should continually have been watched by judges" (*The Spirit of the Laws*, bk. 6, ch. 18, 183).

began to reason about new legal problems from starting points found in these judicial precedents. As one can imagine, there was thus an inherent tendency for the common law to change over time as it was subjected to the incessant pressure of judicial reasoning and changing social conditions. But these changes occurred almost imperceptibly, and many lawyers and judges in this common law tradition have believed that the most important elements of the common law never change at all (though some judicial decisions may have stated the law erroneously).

There was, of course, a second source of English law, namely, statutes, which by the eighteenth century were enacted by the joint consent of Parliament and the king. In principle, it was permissible for the legislature to change the common law by enacting a statute inconsistent with the decisions of the judges, and this principle put very real limits on the power of common law courts to impose their own policies on a reluctant nation. In practice, however, English judges had a strong tendency to interpret statutes so as to minimize conflicts with the existing common law. Thus, statutes underwent a gradual and largely unacknowledged interpretive evolution, just as the common law itself did.

I want to say that this evolution of law under the pressure of judicial reasoning is the political element in the power of judging in the English constitution. Whereas the decisions of juries really can be said to be "invisible and null" because they are unexplained and without precedential effects, the decisions of judges are more visible (because they are memorialized in reasoned opinions) and more influential (because they receive deference from future judges). To the extent that these decisions changed the law, I think we have to call them political acts. But because these legal changes were so gradual, and so disguised by their appearance as interpretations required in the resolution of particular disputes, their moderating effects can look like the work of a completely depoliticized judiciary.

As Paul O. Carrese has shown in a detailed study of *The Spirit of the Laws*, the separated and obscured power of judging seems to be the key element in Montesquieu's understanding of political moderation.[52] Montesquieu deliberately chose to hide the English judges in his description

52. Paul O. Carrese, *The Cloaking of Power: Montesquieu, Blackstone, and the Rise of Judicial Activism* (Chicago: University of Chicago Press, 2003).

of the English constitution because he quite reasonably believed that the beneficence of their political activities depended on those activities being largely unacknowledged by the judges, and largely unrecognized by the overtly political elements of English society.

If that understanding of Montesquieu is correct, it produces the following difficult interpretive problem. How, and to what extent, did Montesquieu believe that it was desirable—or even possible—for other nations to adopt the English model of judging? The difficulty arises from the fact that the English model appears to have grown up un-self-consciously, and so to speak by chance. Can prudence replicate this achievement elsewhere? Or would the transplantation of the English model require philosophers to rule as judges, or those called judges genuinely and adequately to philosophize?[53]

In order to illustrate the problem, let us take a very brief look at what would seem to be the most favorable conditions under which the English model could be adapted to a different country. The example, of course, is America.

V. MONTESQUIEU AND AMERICAN JUDICIAL REVIEW

The American legal system is in many ways a direct descendant of the eighteenth-century English legal system that Montesquieu purported to describe. Our use of juries is one obvious example. But even the common law that is still evolving in our state courts is built on the English law that the colonists brought with them to these shores. After our War of Independence, lawyers and courts continued to rely primarily on English common law precedents. And they still do so on occasion, though this has naturally become much less frequent as we have developed our own evolving body of common law decisions. The really big changes in America came at the constitutional level, and I want to focus on two changes that I think were particularly significant in altering the nature of our courts.

First, we adopted written constitutions, at the state level and then at the national level. Whereas Montesquieu was able to suggest that England was a republic hiding under the form of monarchy,[54] we threw off

53. Cf. Plato, *Republic* 473c–d.

54. *The Spirit of the Laws*, bk. 5, ch. 19, 70.

that form completely, and adopted the doctrine of the sovereignty of the people. That change had many important effects, but the one that is most relevant here has to do with the political character of courts.

The courts were now given a new kind of law to interpret and apply, and it seems to have been assumed that our traditional common law courts should and would continue to apply this new law in the same way that they applied ordinary statutes.[55] There was, however, this difference. Because the new constitutions were a form of law superior to acts of the legislature, we now had the possibility that courts would directly and openly invalidate laws enacted by the people's representatives, using a power that we call "judicial review." This dramatically increased the potential for American courts to become visibly powerful, and potentially very controversial, participants in serious political disputes.

In the *Federalist Papers,* proponents of the new federal constitution argued at length that the U.S. Supreme Court would not be able to usurp the legislative function of Congress, notwithstanding the Court's authority to declare congressional statutes void when they were inconsistent with the Constitution.[56] In that argument, Publius was responding to a straightforward objection from those who opposed the new Constitution. According to that objection, the power of judicial review would make unelected federal judges a kind of oligarchy, contrary to the principle of popular sovereignty. Why? Because whoever gets the last word is the effectual supreme ruler.

The core of the response in the *Federalist Papers* is that somebody always has to have the last word, and that the natural weakness and timidity of the judiciary makes it the safest repository of final decisions about the meaning of the Constitution. In support of his claims about the weakness of the judiciary, Publius twice invokes the authority of Montesquieu,[57] but this seems quite inapt when we recall that Montesquieu was talking about evanescent juries rather than life-tenured professional judges.

Whether or not Publius recognized that he was mis-citing Montes-

55. For further detail, see Philip Hamburger, *Law and Judicial Duty* (Cambridge, Mass.: Harvard University Press, 2008); and Nelson Lund, "Judicial Review and Judicial Duty: The Original Understanding," *Constitutional Commentary* 26 (Fall 2009): 169–82.

56. *The Federalist,* nos. 78–81.

57. Ibid., no. 78, 465–66.

quieu on this point,[58] there are indications that he was quite comfortable with what I am calling a politicized judiciary. At one point in his discussion, for example, Publius argues that an independent judiciary is valuable because the judges will "mitigate the severity and confine the operation" of unjust laws.[59] He does not explain just how they will do this, but he twice uses the Montesquieuian term "moderation," and the tenor of the passage suggests that this moderating activity is familiar to his readers from the long Anglo-American tradition of the common law.

Looking back from a distance of two centuries, I think it is fair to wonder whether Publius sufficiently appreciated the tension between the traditional moderating techniques of common law judges and the power of judicial review. But I also think that Publius may not have given sufficient attention to a feature of the new Constitution that made a powerful and self-confident Supreme Court especially desirable. The feature to which I am referring is dual federalism, which is the most truly novel feature in American constitutionalism.

The traditional federalist structure, discussed by Montesquieu and exemplified by our own Articles of Confederation, essentially involved alliances among small republics for the purpose of making a common defense against external threats.[60] The traditional balanced constitution, exemplified by England, involved an institutionalized sharing of political power among different orders of citizens, such as the commoners, the nobles, and a king.

America is different. We have two distinct governments, state and federal, each independently enacting and executing laws that directly regulate the citizenry in various aspects of life. Noting that this arrangement was so novel that there was no word to describe it, Tocqueville called what we have here an "incomplete national government."[61] The separation of powers between the state and national governments turns

58. *Federalist* 78 was written by Alexander Hamilton, who also wrote *Federalist* 9. The latter paper reflects a very careful and subtle reading of Montesquieu. I therefore think it unlikely that the incorrect citation of Montesquieu in *Federalist* 78 was inadvertent.

59. Ibid., 470.

60. *The Spirit of the Laws*, bk. 9, chs. 1–3.

61. Alexis de Tocqueville, *Democracy in America,* vol. 1, pt. 1, ch. 8, trans. Harvey C. Mansfield and Delba Winthrop (Chicago: University of Chicago Press, 2000), 149.

out, I think, to be no less important than the separation of powers among the legislature, the executive, and the judiciary. And especially with respect to the legal regulation of public morals.

Under the Constitution's original design, the federal government possessed only limited powers, leaving the states with most of the responsibility for setting social policy. Representative legislatures throughout the country made the hard decisions about the proper line between liberty and license, and these legislatures were generally left free by the Constitution to draw the line in light of the natural moral law as they understood it. The Constitution certainly did not assume, any more than it could possibly assure, that these judgments would be infallible. Unlike the Supreme Court, however, these legislatures are subjected to considerable market discipline because constitutional law protects the free movement of citizens and the free flow of information among the states.

Individuals can and do take advantage of this freedom, and state governments respond both to changing views among their citizens and to the threat of emigration. As the costs of transportation and information have fallen, moreover, geographic mobility has increased. Far from being an eighteenth-century anachronism, federalism has become an ever more effective device for promoting the kind of interjurisdictional competition that can promote the appropriate expansion of human liberty.[62]

There are, of course, no guarantees, but the genius of this kind of market competition is that the worst excesses, either in a libertine direction or its opposite, will tend to be self-correcting. Not always, as the examples of slavery and Jim Crow remind us. But even there the most effective responses have always come through the political processes rather than from the federal courts.[63]

There is, however, another aspect of competitive federalism that throws a different light on the federal courts. The division of powers between the state and national governments is a legal division created en-

62. For further detail, see Nelson Lund, "Federalism and Civil Liberties," *University of Kansas Law Review* 45 (July 1997): 1045–73; and Lund and McGinnis, "*Lawrence v. Texas* and Judicial Hubris." Interjurisdictional competition was apparently not an intended effect of the federalist structure. With respect to this effect, one might therefore say that our Constitution, like England's, is in some respects what Montesquieu would call "a masterpiece of legislation" produced by chance.

63. See, e.g., Nelson Lund, *Reforming Affirmative Action: How to Restore the Law of Equal Treatment*, Heritage Foundation Report to Congress (August 2, 1995), available online at http://mason.gmu.edu/~nlund/Pubs/HeritageAffirmativeAction.pdf.

tirely by a written document. It is therefore fundamentally different from the division of powers in a mixed regime like England's. Whereas there is a kind of natural (though imperfect) support for the balance among different orders of citizens, based on their distinct and common group interests, the balance entailed in our system of dual federalism was established by a legal fiat.

As Tocqueville recognized very clearly, this division is not a natural one, and political pressures will inevitably operate to upset the balance established by the Constitution. For that reason, he rightly stresses the importance of the U.S. Supreme Court in preventing the state and federal governments from encroaching on each other's jurisdiction.[64] I would add that this may be our Supreme Court's most important function. Not only is the maintenance of this allocation of powers a central feature of our constitutional order, no other institution is suited to protecting this allocation consistently and reliably.[65]

Over the course of our history, the federal government has proved to be the far more successful encroacher. Somewhat contrary to the expectations of Publius and Tocqueville alike, the Supreme Court has been quite rigorous and successful in stopping the states from exceeding the powers reserved to them by the federal Constitution. But the Court has been very lax about congressional usurpations against the states. And the Court itself has lately become a powerful usurping force in its own right.

The full story of those developments is long and complicated. I will close by using *Lawrence* to illustrate why I think we should be extremely skeptical about our Supreme Court's practice of substituting its moral or philosophic judgments for the more pedestrian task of applying the written law of the Constitution.

When one reads the *Lawrence* opinion, it appears that the Court may have created a constitutional right, not just to engage in sodomy, but to enjoy the government's respect for engaging in sodomy. This is the most obvious way to explain the opinion's reference to "the due process right to demand respect for conduct protected by the substantive guarantee of liberty."[66]

64. Alexis de Tocqueville, *Democracy in America*, vol. 1, part 1, ch. 8, 108.

65. See John O. McGinnis and Ilya Somin, "Federalism vs. States' Rights: A Defense of Judicial Review in a Federal System," *Northwestern Law Review* 99 (Fall 2004): 89–130.

66. 539 U.S. at 575 (emphasis added).

What would it mean to have a constitutional right to "demand respect" for protected conduct like sodomy? If the Court meant this seriously, it may presage a new jurisprudence in which governments are forbidden from doing anything that might convey disapproval of any sexual practices that five judges believe are somehow connected with efforts "to define one's own concept of existence, of meaning, of the universe, and of the mystery of human life."[67]

That would probably mean the abolition of all laws denying any of the benefits of marriage, including the dignitary benefits associated with the term "marriage," to homosexual couples. It would also seem to point toward the abolition of all laws that limit the number of people who can simultaneously be married to one another—so polygamy would become a constitutional right. And it is hard to see why laws against prostitution should survive, since this may be the only sexual outlet through which some people wish to, or even can, exercise "the right to define one's own concept of existence, of meaning, of the universe, and of the mystery of human life."

Of course, there are other ways to interpret the sloppy, self-indulgent language in the *Lawrence* opinion. Some of them are much less radical than this, but some are perhaps even more radical. Nowhere in the *Lawrence* opinion, for example, does the Court so much as entertain the possibility that state legislatures could have any valid reason for proscribing sodomy in general or homosexual sodomy in particular. Furthermore, the Court comes very close to implying that one obvious basis for such proscriptions—a desire to discourage behavior considered immoral by the majority—is inherently improper.

Even if we leave aside other possible rationales for the Texas statute, such as public health and promoting the institution of marriage, how is the desire to discourage putatively immoral behavior really different in any way marked out by the Constitution from the paternalistic desire to discourage other forms of putatively dangerous or self-destructive behavior?

When the government outlaws conduct that it regards as risky or unhealthy—such as the recreational use of drugs, or driving a motorcycle without a helmet—it is making a moral decision that assigns a higher val-

67. Ibid., 574 (quoting *Planned Parenthood v. Casey*, 505 U.S. 833, 851 [1992]).

ue to health and physical safety than to the spiritual insights that some people have said they get from hallucinogens, or to the mystical exhilaration of flirting with danger on the open road. Unless the Court were to distinguish without any guidance from the Constitution between the different moral judgments reflected in different forms of paternalistic legislation, it is hard to see how any regulatory statute could survive unless it is demonstrably necessary to prevent immediate injuries to people other than those who want to engage in the conduct.

I should stress that I do not believe the Court has actually embraced any such radically libertarian interpretation of the Constitution. In the end, the *Lawrence* opinion is so sloppy and lawless that it does not actually tell us much of anything about what the Court will decide in the future. Whatever new rights the Court may find, or refuse to find, among what Justice Kennedy calls "the components of liberty in its manifold possibilities"[68] (whatever that might mean), *Lawrence* will stand primarily for the proposition that due process jurisprudence has transcended the bounds of rational discourse. In other words, it is as though these Justices think that their role is to reveal hitherto unrecognized self-evident truths.

I do not believe it is entirely due to chance that when our Supreme Court Justices took upon themselves the role of philosopher-kings, they created a world in which morals regulation is deemed immoral, and philosophy—an activity now divorced by the Justices from reasoning—becomes the handmaiden of sodomy, abortion, and judicial self-satisfaction. Whether this Court is seen as the enforcer of its vision of the natural moral law or as an opponent of any enforcement of such a law, it is not too soon to declare that our philosopher-judges have been failures both as philosophers and as judges.

VI. CONCLUSION

St. Thomas argues that any human law that deviates from the natural law is to the extent of the divergence a perversion of law, and therefore not law.[69] The statutes enacted by our American legislatures are no doubt

68. Ibid., 578.
69. *Summa Theologica,* I–II, Q. 95, art. 2.

filled with provisions that are in this sense not law, and we will no doubt always have such statutes. Our Supreme Court has a long history of invalidating statutes that it regards as violations of the natural law, or of some other higher law, though it has almost always purported to appeal to the human law embodied in the U.S. Constitution. Some of the invalidated statutes may well have violated the natural law, and others almost certainly did not. In neither set of cases, I maintain, has the Court been justified in overriding the Constitution's requirement that it limit itself to enforcing human law.[70]

Our deeply rooted common law tradition, in which courts quietly moderated and updated the existing law, was an effective institutional device for addressing two problems that St. Thomas identified. First, reason sometimes suggests appropriate corrections to imperfect laws, and changed circumstances sometimes demand revisions in response to such changes.[71] Second, caution must be exercised lest the frequency and visibility of changes, even those salutary in themselves, undermine respect for the law.[72] One reason that this common law tradition worked reasonably well was that legislatures were always free to override the decisions of common law courts. When Supreme Court Justices arrogated to themselves the privilege of overriding legislatures without a warrant in the Constitution, this crucial safeguard was lost. Too often, the Justices have assumed that their own mutable and imperfect human reason,[73] or their mere unreasoned intuitions, is more reliable than the judgments reflected in the Constitution and statutes adopted by the people's elected representatives. The rancid and flaccid pseudophilosophy on display in recent judicial opinions dealing with sodomy and abortion confirms that these Justices cannot be trusted to discover and correct discrepancies between the natural law and the human laws they are charged with enforcing. They should stop trying.

70. For purposes of this essay, I leave aside a substantial academic debate in which some have argued that the Ninth Amendment or the Privileges or Immunities Clause of the Fourteenth Amendment enjoins the courts to strike down statutes on the basis of some sort of unwritten higher law. If that conclusion could be established, I agree that the courts would be bound to obey the mandate, but I have not yet seen persuasive arguments or evidence that this is the correct interpretation of those provisions. In any event, the Supreme Court has neither argued nor concluded that these constitutional provisions should be read this way, so its behavior cannot be explained by reference to such an interpretation.

71. *Summa Theologica*, I–II, Q. 97, art. 1.

72. Ibid., art. 2.

73. See ibid., art. 1, reply obj. 1.

John Rist

12 Aesthetics and Ethics

Some Common Problems of Foundationalism

This essay has a certain amount of historical content, though not enough. Not enough because in philosophy (as distinct from formal logic) there is no such thing as a naked argument: that is, an argument that appears in a timeless world, devoid of historical context. Philosophers think about the problems of their age and the answers their contemporaries have proposed for those problems. And often they say no more than is required for a possible solution of those particular problems, so that if we want to propose questions for them which they have not faced directly, we have to cooperate with them (as Ryle used to put it).

A basic problem in what, since Baumgarten in the mid-eighteenth century, we have agreed to call aesthetics,[1] has its apparent analogue in ethics: Is it possible or reasonable to avoid subjectivism, or, ultimately, nihilism? The problem is more difficult in aesthetics, for at least two reasons: first—and trivially—because it often seems safe to accept the cliché that beauty is in the eye of the beholder, in other words that it is all a matter of taste; second, because in aesthetics there seems to be no "ought." Yet one thing ethics and aesthetics have in common is the notion of inspiration (which is aesthetic as well as moral), and specifically, in the case of great beauties, whether of character, art, or nature, the pos-

A somewhat more developed version of this material is to be found in *What Is Truth?* (Cambridge: Cambridge University Press, 2009).

1. A. Baumgarten, *Meditationes Philosophicae de Nonnullis ad Poema Pertinentibus* (Halle, 1735).

sibility of lasting inspiration. In a godless context, however, the distinction between inspiration and instinct, or better mere *curiositas*—I shall return to the relevant sense of this ancient term—is easily lost, though the power of inspiration to perdure through many generations suggests that it appeals to something greater than the merely individualist, lustful or culture-bound. An artist possesses particular skills, and much discussion of art and beauty has enquired what those skills are, but "meta-aesthetics"—treating of the conditions for aesthetics—will consider what happens when the skills remain but the concept of beauty is neglected, set aside, or lost.

The Platonic tradition attempts to overcome subjectivism in aesthetics as in ethics, and in doing so to provide, in both its Christian and non-Christian forms, a justification for aesthetic assertions, a claim that there is a sense in which, like ethical assertions, they can be right or wrong. The key to that justification—which I believe can be determined more precisely in Christian than in non-Christian Platonism—lies not merely in the scriptural claim that the world reveals something of the splendor of God, but in an argument as to how it can be understood as doing so: an argument that physical beauty (both of nature and of human beings), as well as moral "beauty," can only be intelligibly claimed as beautiful insofar as it indicates the Beauty—not merely the power and goodness—of the God of Truth.

In the Old Testament the concept of beauty appears principally in derivative connection with God's "formless" splendor and glory *(kabod;* Greek: *doxa).* Beauty is the luminous revelation of that glory and majesty: "I will make my beauty pass before you" (Exodus 33:19; cf. 28:18). Yet God's beauty is a rare theme in the Old Testament. God himself is not identified as Beauty, but He is shown in Beauty and that Beauty is thought of as splendor, the revelation of His majesty and power rather than more "aesthetically." At the earthly level the beauty of the damsel Jerusalem was perfected by God's splendor (Ezekiel 16:14) and corrupted by human sinfulness, and in general physical beauty can be recognized in the beauty of a natural world that points back to its maker (Psalm 8).

This theme is particularly evident in the Greek books (Wisdom 13:5; Sirach 43:9–11) and in the Psalms, while the beauty of the human figure, especially the female figure, is emphasized in Psalm 44 (45) and above all in the Song of Songs—to which there is no need to attach an early allegorical understanding:[2] the tradition of Adam's delight in his new helpmeet is sufficient religious "justification" for this erotic (and perhaps courtly) poetry. All these texts certainly reaffirm a traditional emphasis on the desire of love, both for God and for woman,[3] yet generally and increasingly (despite the beauty of many of the matriarchs and of Lady Wisdom; see Wisdom 7:26, 8:2),[4] as we move into Hellenistic Judaism (Proverbs 6:25, 11:22, 31:30) female beauty is a snare and a delusion, liable to induce false worship: a theme to which the older language of Jerusalem the harlot "whoring after false Gods" (Jeremiah 3:3, etc.) certainly contributed.

In the New Testament there are a limited number of references to beauty, again normally revealed as "glory": in the account of the Transfiguration, in Hebrews 1:3 (Christ is the splendor of God's glory), and in Revelation 21:11.[5] In such cases glory promotes awe, but awe is overwhelming rather than inspirational. Gradually Christians came to pay beauty more attention, but in the "philosophical theology" of the early centuries of the Christian era beauty (especially the beauty of the human figure) was far more important among pagans, especially Platonists, than among Christians who inherited the Jewish distaste for images as idolatrous. They obviously regarded images of pagan gods as objects of idolatrous worship and probably evinced a more generalized concern that any physical beauty could lead to the worship of created objects, including the human form and the universe itself: a problem already foreshadowed in the wisdom literature (Wisdom 13:3, 13:7). The earliest Christian art, as in the Roman catacombs, seems to reflect neither canons of beauty nor even theological claims about glory; it is strictly "religious" and normally funerary, part of a personal and simple prayer for salvation: "Save me as you saved Daniel or Susannah."[6]

In the mid-third century, but before the advent of Neoplatonism,

2. See particularly G. Gerleman, *Ruth: Das Hohelied,* vol. 18 of *Biblischer Kommentar: Altes Testament* (Neukirchen-Vluyn: Neukirchener Verlag, 1965). Gerleman's claim was accepted by H. von Balthasar in *The Glory of the Lord,* vol. 6 (Edinburgh: T. & T. Clark, 1991), 130–37. Gerleman (51) notes that the first allegorical interpretation is as late as Rabbi Aqiba in the early second century A.D.

3. See G. Strola, *Il desiderio di Dio. Studio dei salmi 42–43* (Assisi, 2003).

4. Old Testament males are rarely described as beautiful: David is one of the few exceptions (1 Sam. 16:18).

5. See the comments of E. F. Osborn, *Irenaeus of Lyons* (Cambridge, 2001), 200.

6. P. Prigent, *L'art des premiers chrétiens* (Paris, 1995), 243–49.

Origen's *Commentary and Homilies on the Song of Songs* marks a major advance in Christian sensibility. Although "carnal" love is certainly "from Satan" (Homily 1), Origen's likening of all human souls to the Bride in her relationship with the divine Spouse is an unambiguous attempt to argue that the language of erotic love is an appropriate vehicle to describe progression in Christian holiness. For Origen, the soul, in seeking God, must become "beautiful" and female (*formosa;* Homily 1.3); that is, receptive (but not passive). But God's Word too, the object of the soul's love, is beautiful (Commentary, Prologue 2.17). The Word is the image and splendor of God, but this splendor is now to be understood not only as glory but as spiritual beauty; that is why *eros/amor* is the appropriate word to express the soul's love of Christ (2.20). The soul, as Wisdom 8.2 puts it, is a "lover of his form" *(decus);* there is nothing "indecorous" about the love of higher things, and those higher things are beautiful. Christ is not only splendor, the revealed majesty of God, but both Beauty itself *(pulchritudo, decus)* and the source of all other beauty, hence of the highest inspiration. Thus Beauty has been clearly and philosophically identified—without reduction to the more ambiguous "glory"—as a divine attribute. Origen's claim, in effect, is that there is a specifically Christian, and therefore correct, account of beauty, so that, in more modern parlance, a Christian aesthetic would be possible—or rather that any serious aesthetic must be a Christian aesthetic.

Origen could have provided no such account of his achievement. That should cause no surprise: it is an axiom of the history of ideas that new concepts are in use (often long in use) before they are recognized as such. No one in antiquity talks about "aesthetics"; "aesthetics" was a part of ethics, and in claiming that Christ is beautiful (and as such an object of desire) Origen is implying (but not asserting) in the first instance that moral or spiritual beauty is the focal reference point and cause of all forms of beauty, whether physical or spiritual. He can do that because he has accepted the Platonizing claim that beauty is what inspires us, that is, that it is the good in its affective aspect. We love the Good as beautiful—hence as the spur to creative action—while we recognize it as good.

"Erotic" love is a form of directed (or "intentional") desire, specifically for the beautiful. The problem with our handling of it, as Plato and Plotinus realized, is how to distinguish what is "really" beautiful from what is less beautiful and from what merely seems beautiful. On that discernment depends the kind of action promoted. If it is true, as I have argued elsewhere,[7] following another famous Platonic thesis, that we are multiple selves, at best moving in hope toward a simple and completed "soul," then so long as we are divided we shall have divided and diverse loves, because we shall find different and diverse things, often perversely, beautiful. Just as we have many "goods," so we shall strive for many "beauties," and since some of these "beauties" are in fact ugly to the good man, we shall find ourselves having an erotic desire not only for sexual excess but for more diversified "beauties" ("Money, lovely money"), as Plato had already pointed out in the *Republic*.

Even apart from obviously ugly "beauties," we shall have problems over choice: we shall have to prefer some beauties to others either because they are more beautiful, or because the others are for various good reasons "not for me." We cannot hope to make such choices if we have no standard, and Origen offers the standard of Christ. Nor perhaps can we always determine, in advance, what choices are to be made—though rules of thumb are available.

After Origen a rather obscure but perceptive bishop called Methodius also wrote a commentary on the Song of Songs, unfortunately lost, and also a *Symposium,* the very title of which indicates not merely a wish to use Platonic themes, but to appropriate and develop them in a deliberately Christian sense.

There is little specific discussion in Methodius's *Symposium* about the relationship between the beauty of Christ and the physical beauties of the world, but the whole setting of the dialogue is redolent of that theme. The Platonic thesis that physical beauties partake of the beauty of the divine, the basis for any Christian aesthetics, is fully present, and Methodius offers a reading of Platonic and Christian beauty even without any apparent reference to the specifically beauty-driven version of Platonism that is the philosophy of Plotinus and which undoubtedly enriched the views of beauty in the two Christians who set the tone for later Christian aesthetics in both East and West: Gregory of Nyssa and Augustine.

Plotinus's account of beauty is basically Platonic, but it is modified by pressing contemporary considerations and presented more systematically. Naturally, his first principles are metaphysical; the intelligibil-

7. J. M. Rist, *Real Ethics* (Cambridge, 2002).

ity of "aesthetics" in the strict sense, that is, of an account of the nature of a beauty recognizable through the senses, depends on related metaphysical and ethical claims about the existence of a transcendent world of forms, of Beauty and of Goodness. "Aesthetic" claims and values are set in the context of the moral and "spiritual" life and capabilities of the soul.

But considerations peculiar to his time and place affect both the substance and the emphases of Plotinus's position. Plato's original concerns had been twofold: to identify love of beauty and goodness as the necessary motor of the good life, and to devalue the beauty of the body in comparison with that of the soul. At this point we should recall that although we ourselves might distinguish three types of beauty (of art, nature, and intelligible reality), our own views of the relationships between these groups are not Plato's, nor those of the Greeks of the classical age in general. For the Greeks the most important of the natural beauties is that of the human (or divine) figure. The beauty of the landscape and of the details of nature is hardly considered,[8] and where it is, it is usually in the context of the success of the gods or of the Platonic demiurge in bringing order and proportion to the ugliness and shapelessness of unformed matter. Artists depicted natural beauties, but such representations were not high art; it was the Zeus of Pheidias or (later) the Aphrodite of Praxiteles who enjoyed such prestige: their bodies and souls.

Plotinus too distinguished the beauties of nature from the beauties of art, and the beauty of the human body as preeminent among natural beauties, but he had very specific reasons for being more concerned than was Plato with the beauty of the natural world. Chief among these was his hostility to "New Age" Gnosticism. Plotinus's major treatise against the Gnostics[9] was reasonably subtitled by his pupil Porphyry "Against those who think the maker of the universe and the universe are evil," and he was particularly concerned to argue that since the maker of the universe is good, his products must all be good and beautiful. Hence, as Plato had claimed in the *Phaedrus,* the form of beauty is specially clear to mankind because beautiful objects are visible in the material world.

8. Cf. J. M. Rist, "Why Greek Philosophers Might Have Been Concerned about the Environment," in L. Westra and T. M. Robinson, eds., *The Greeks and the Environment* (Lanham, Md., 1997), 19–32.

9. *Ennead* 2.9.

Contemporary problems in "aesthetics" revolve around the attraction of sense-perceptible "objects" or "targets." Properly Platonic theories all start from the premise that the beauty of the sensible world exists in some sort of dependence on "real" beauty which exists in the intelligible and immaterial world; otherwise true propositions in aesthetics, as in ethics, could not be sustained: choice, taste, or mere dictates of someone's will would prevail. Hence for Plotinus, as for Plato, sensible beauties are beautiful by participation or "imitation" of Beauty itself; material representation cannot be of the essence of real beauty, but material objects can be understood as possessing beauty. Among such material beauties we must distinguish between the beauty of natural objects, above all the human form, and the beauties of human artifacts or works of "art." In principle all material beauties can be evaluated and prioritized with reference to immaterial beauty.

Hence arise a number of typical problems, not all of which I shall discuss in any detail:

1. How can we measure the beauty of physical objects?
2. What use is such physical beauty?
3. If matter is unnecessary for beauty, what are beauty's essential elements?
4. In the universe of Plotinus, what is the relationship between the Form of beauty, and more generally the beauty of the intelligible world of immaterial forms, and the One or Good: in what sense is the One beautiful?

Questions 1 and 2 are comparatively straightforward. Physical beauty, as the *Symposium* had it, is measured by its approximation to immaterial beauty and its ability to lead the soul beyond itself. It first arouses love and has something to teach us about love's nature, for love cannot exist without a beautiful object. Its value is therefore obvious, but since there are higher loves than those of the physical world and the human figure, physical love, unless ordered, is also risky since it may resolve itself into a mere pathos, a sick and distracting obsession with the physical.

For Plotinus, the most beautiful physical object will presumably be that which properly attracts the soul without at the same time distracting it from higher goals, indeed which encourages the lover to transcend his immediate quest and go higher, acting, in Plato's language, as a stepping-stone.[10] If lower loves are not so treated as stepping-stones, it may happen that a lover, through a misuse of beauty, will fall into ugliness.[11] Which reopens the question (implicit in the *Symposium*) of whether physical loves are mere means to something higher—which is not a question of whether physical things are properly described as beautiful, which they certainly are by reference to the form, but of the attitude we should adopt toward them.

Without wholly rejecting the popular Stoic claim that beauty resides in some sort of symmetry of parts, with the addition of a good coloring,[12] Plotinus argues that this is insufficient. If beauty can only exist in composites, how can we explain the beauty of simple phenomena such as sunlight or a flash of lightening or the "simple beauty of color"[13]—or the more or less beautiful appearance of a similarly symmetrical face?[14] Rather than mere symmetry, the source of physical beauty is to be sought in the presence (as the *Phaedrus* had at least begun to suggest) of the splendor of life-giving light. Unless such "grace" plays on the symmetry of physical objects, we have a merely deathlike symmetry.[15] Thus in the case of a work of art beauty resides less in the constituted object (though it is there too) than in the active mind of the artist, just as the beauty of the natural world lies to a higher degree in its spiritual maker, the World Soul, and beyond that the living form of Beauty itself. And the beauty of the cause is always potentially more inspirational than that of the effect.

In such ideas much modern "aesthetics" is transcended: beauty is now to be evaluated not, of course, by a mere moralism measuring only short-term effects but in terms of its power to inspire to the purifications necessary if the "beautiful" soul is to pass through and beyond the world of sense to the world of the living Forms, then to the One, itself somehow both beautiful and the source of Beauty. A beauty higher than that of physical objects but also the cause of their genuine beauty is to be found first in the mind of the artist, who at his best—as Pheidias in sculpting his statue of Zeus—is aware not just of models available to the senses but of "what Zeus would be like if he wanted to make himself visible."[16]

10. *Symp.* 211C3; cf. Plotinus, *Enn.* 1.6.1.20.

11. Ibid., 3.5.1.63.

12. Plotinus, *Enn.* 1.6.1.21ff.; 6.7.22.25; cf. Cic., *Tusculan Disputations* 4.31, a well-known source probably cited, e.g., by Augustine in *De Civitate Dei* 22.19.

13. Plotinus, *Enn.* 1.6.1.31; 1.6.3.17.

14. Ibid., 1.6.1.37, 6.7.22.27.

15. Ibid., 6.7.22.22; cf. 5.8.1.32ff.

16. Ibid., 5.8.1.32–40.

Living spiritual beauty is the source of sensible beauty, and the nature of physical beauty can be neither understood nor justified without reference to it.

Plotinus thinks that Plato is the Master; where he is obscure, or appears to contradict himself from one dialogue to another, it is the duty of the Platonist to find a reconciliation. His treatment of the relationship between the Good (or more normally the One) and Beauty is a fine example of this. He knows that in the ascent passages of the *Symposium,* which provide him with much guidance for his own account of the return of the soul to the One, it is Beauty that is the object of love. Hence his "Neoplatonic" reconciliation: there is a sense in which we can identify the One as a special kind of beauty: a beauty *(kallos)* above beauty or a beauty in another mode.[17] Or he may use another and rarer word: *kallonē.*[18] Or he may introduce the archaic term *aglaia,* a word that means "splendor,"[19] and as a personification is the name of one of the Graces. This latter term is also applied to *Nous* and to the soul and seemingly indicates the One as seen by the aspirant to unity. The One shows itself as splendor (in the spirit of the *Phaedrus*), in that it is the "source" of beauty and maker of beauty *(kallopoion);*[20] it is what Plotinus and other Neoplatonists call the "flower of Beauty," the term "flower" marking ontological superiority.[21] Finally—and importantly—the effect of the beauty of the One on its lovers is to make them beautiful and lovable.[22] Inspirational love of the One shows us how lesser loves can be explained both as inspirational and as less inspirational.

Perhaps Plotinus has deluded himself into thinking that he has explained the relationship between beauty and the One, but at least what he seems to want to say is that the One is somehow revealed as Beauty, though the relationship between the One as beauty and the Form of Beauty is far from clear, especially as the two are for him at different ontological levels. But what if someone declared them to be at the same ontological level? What if God's goodness is beauty or His beauty goodness and hence, though below the Good love of Beauty will not always

17. Ibid., 6.7.32.26–29.

18. Ibid., 1.6.6.25; 6.2.18.1.

19. Ibid., 6.9.4.18.

20. Ibid., 6.7.32.

21. And perhaps, analogously, virginity, as the target of the *nous erōn* (6.7.35.19ff.); in general see J. M. Rist, "Mysticism and Transcendence in Later Neoplatonism," *Hermes* 92 (1964): 215–17.

22. *Enn.*1.6.7.

be identified with love of goodness, at its highest it will be so identified? Here we approach a move available to post-Nicene Christians. Here we would see Beauty as revelatory of the "first" God—to use antique language—but in no way inferior to it, though the exact relationship would still remain unclear.

Philosophically a fundamental problem remains; traditional Platonic aesthetics explains the nature of the beauties of the world, including and especially that of the human figure, in terms of the intelligible beauty of finite perfection recognized by intuitive thought. But in what sense—other perhaps than by a play on words—can the One's "splendor" properly be called beauty at all? Plotinus's answer is that the maker of beauty must in some sense be beautiful. But that still leaves it open as to what this beauty is. Plotinus knows that we recognize the One as beautiful; he says more than once that when we see it we know that it is beautiful.[23] But he has little to say beyond offering his principle that an effect is somehow better recognized in its cause to explain why it is appropriate—though it is—that the One is called beautiful. Although a "higher" beauty is basic to Neoplatonic metaphysics, in that without it a return to the One would be impossible, and although the Form of beauty is the supreme cause of the different "lower" kinds of beauty, physical and intelligible, its status remains ambiguous and incomplete. When Christians start to consider Neoplatonic notions of beauty, they are not confronted with an entirely coherent canvas; they can thus more easily pick and choose. They are told that in a sense the One is beauty, or is revealed as beauty, but they may be pardoned if they are puzzled as to the nature of that highest beauty to which they are urged to aspire. What they do know, however, is that it is available to all, and that it makes what would otherwise be unbeautiful beautiful.

Now it has always been puzzling to his readers how especially in the *Symposium* Plato moves the objects of *eros* so easily from the personal to the impersonal domain, and if (but only if) it is the case that the Form of the Good is never identified with any kind of mind, that problem remained unconsidered till the end of his life. Such hesitancy between a personal and an impersonal first principle persists in Plotinus, for although in adopting various pieces of Aristotle's account of the identity

23. Plotinus, *Enn.* 1.6.7.2ff., 6.9.9.47.

of knower and known, Plotinus is able to overcome the normal Platonic separation between the "personal" God and the impersonal Form, that solution itself both is and is not transcended in the "semipersonal" account he seems to give of the One. Yet until this ambiguity is resolved in favor of the "personal," we still wonder how the One (or its equivalent) can be a legitimate target for anything properly recognizable as inspirational *eros*. Or, to put it differently, when they think of an *eros* for the One, do Plato and Plotinus allow their theory of *eros* and of beauty to outrun their theory of the One itself? Plotinus has moved in the direction of personalizing the highest object of love, but he has failed to notice Plato's partial self-correction over another aspect of the "personalism" problem in the *Phaedrus*. In Neoplatonism mutuality between human lovers almost disappears (though a more personal relationship with the One seems to be achieved). Apparently Plotinus was so overimpressed by the dualism of the *Phaedo* as to overlook Plato's less disembodied account of even superior forms of human love in the *Phaedrus*.

At least he never overlooked the more physical aspects of beauty altogether; he never lost sight of the fact that for all its "seductiveness," bodily beauty still partakes of the beauty of the divine. Nor did he neglect another basic principle of Platonism: that all beauty (even seductive beauty) can be inspirational—not merely arousing—and that without beauty there is no honest inspiration, though there may be awe. That axiom, whether they liked it or not, was to be of inestimable value to Christians.

Of these Christians I would have preferred to turn to the two who (after Methodius's largely unsung efforts) revolutionized mainstream Christianity's attitude to beauty. The first of them was Gregory, bishop of Nyssa in what is now Turkey, who shares with his near-contemporary Augustine the apparent assumption that beauty, with many of its full Neoplatonic characteristics, is a divine attribute. Outside the Byzantine world, however, his influence has been far less than Augustine's, so for reasons of space I leave him aside in turning to Augustine himself. In thinking about "aesthetics" the bishop of Hippo had the opportunity to develop ideas gleaned from the philosophical writings of Cicero, then from the Platonists, not least in availing himself of Plotinus's insistence that God himself is an inspirational Beauty and the source of Beauty; beauty, we notice again, not simply splendor; inspiration, not simply awe.

Augustine dilates time and again on the beauty of God[24] who is "most just, most beautiful,"[25] and on the beauty of Christ who is the supreme form and beauty of God.[26] Especially in the *Confessions* he insists that it is this beauty so ancient and so new[27] that he has come to love, this beauty of "form" which gives us such delight, for as he tells us in Plotinian fashion, we can only love what is beautiful and delightful.[28] The highest beauty is a divine (and therefore necessary) attribute; God is simply beautiful because He exists as such. He exists by nature, that is, not by creation.[29] His existence, goodness, and beauty are one.

It was an essential part of Augustine's conversion to Christianity that he was converted to belief in an immaterial God. Hence for Augustine the highest beauty is immaterial, an idea which, despite claims that Jahwe is somehow "spiritual," is no necessary part of Old Testament and early Christian theology. So Augustine must offer a Christian version of how one can speak both of the "beauty" of an immaterial object, that is, of God, and also of the beauties of the physical world, whether natural objects (including human beings) or human constructs.

In his account of physical beauty Augustine offers us a thesis that is a curious blend of Stoicism and the anti-Stoicism of Plotinus. The Stoics accounted for beauty in terms of symmetry and proportion, and Augustine allows this more weight than might be expected of an ardent reader of Plotinus. Indeed he ignores some of the more pertinent criticism Plotinus makes of Stoic symmetry. Yet while retaining the Stoic language of symmetry and proportion, he reads it with Platonizing eyes. The physical beauty of an object is indicated by the proportion of its parts and a certain sweetness of color.[30] But then comes the Platonizing twist: the form of each thing is indicated by its unity, and every beautiful thing, insofar as it exists and is formed, possesses a certain unity,[31] a vestige of the divine unity.[32]

24. *Soliloquia* 1.1.3.

25. *De QuantitateAnimae* 36.80.

26. *De Musica* 6.17.56, etc.

27. *Confessiones* 10.27.38; cf. 7.17.23.

28. *De Mus.* 6.11.29–30, 6.13.38; cf. *Sermones.* 159.3; *Enarrationes in Psalmos* 118.10.6. The idea that only the truly beautiful can be loved is Stoic as well as Platonic; cf. *Stoicorum Veterum Fragmenta* 3.598: that which is worthy of love is *kalos.*

29. *De Vera Religione* 18.35–36.

30. *CD* 22.19.2; *Epistulae* 3.4.

31. *De Genesi contra Manichaeos* 1.12.18; *De Trinitate* 6.10.11.

32. *DVR* 32.59–60, 42.79.

But beauty is to be recognized not in a Plotinian world of impersonal (if living) realities, namely, the beauteous Forms, but in the living person of Christ. Like Gregory of Nyssa, Augustine is able to draw on the resources of Christianity to develop an account of the personal nature of true beauty: it is from the personal beauty of God in Christ that the nature of lesser beauties, especially those of God's image, man, is to be explained. And Augustine can still maintain the Platonic and Plotinian emphasis on the delight that both seeks and results from what is beautiful.[33]

Augustine cites the Platonic maxim, "We cannot love anything unless it is beautiful,"[34] but argues that it is the special virtue of the highest love that it makes the ugly, or the less than beautiful, beautiful and thus lovable.[35] Where Plotinus was already saying that the effect of the One on its lovers is to make them beautiful and lovable, Augustine (again like Gregory) goes further; it is the direct and deliberate act of God which makes those who love Him beautiful, for love (which is God) is the beauty of the soul.

By emphasizing that God, through Christ, is true beauty, Augustine has set himself problems in some ways precisely opposite to those of Plato. In Plato we find it puzzling how we can start from a love of human beings—bodies, then souls—and then move beyond the personal to the impersonal world of Forms. The problem is how can love, seemingly a relationship between persons, be transferred, without debasement, to the impersonal object—or at least to the less-than-personal in the case of Plotinus. In Augustine we have the opposite problem. Love is primarily of the primarily beautiful, that is, of God in Christ; the object of love is personal. Hence how can one explain the love not only of "lesser" persons, that is, our fellow human beings, but even of "beautiful" physical objects, themselves wholly impersonal? Would not such love be almost a perversion, and are not such beauties, as the ascetics and puritans had

33. *De Mus.* 6.11.29–30; *Conf.* 4.13.20; *De Diversis Quaestionibus ad Simplicianum* 1.2.22).

34. *De Mus.* 6.13.38.

35. *In Epistolam Ioannis ad Parthos* 9.9. See T. J. van Bavel, "The Double Face of Love in St. Augustine. The Daring Inversion: Love is God," *CIA* (Rome 1987): 69–80, and especially D. Dideberg, *Saint Augustin et la première Epitre de saint Jean: Une théologie de l'amour* (Paris, 1975). Following Hultgren, Dideberg (143–236) shows how Augustine's thought on the identification of Love with God develops from *De Fide et Symbolo* (A.D. 393) through the *Tractatus in Epistolam Ioannis* (407) to *Ep.*186 and *Serm.* 34 (of 418).

feared all along, whatever their appearance, merely shadows, hardly worthy of the title of beauty at all?

This may serve to introduce the idea that a sort of art is possible without beauty. An artist can create what is ugly for its own sake, or to make some point which has nothing to do with the direct expression of beauty,[36] but insofar as he is striving to represent beauty as the legitimate and inspirational ideal, his goal is only intelligible in the light of the existence of a beautiful God. All beauty implies structure, and the perfection of structure points toward the perfection (however limited) of the maker of structure. Insofar as I make a beautiful object, I am beautiful, and reflect God's beauty in that the word "beauty" makes sense and has a specific—if ultimate—point of reference. Without knowledge of God, beauty—in this like the moral good—would be recognizable but inexplicable. Our recognition of it would probably be specified as a conventional habit or a mere instinct like the instinct to eat, though less palpably goal-directed: in itself just a brute and primary fact. We could praise something as beautiful because we like it, or imagine we do, and our likes and dislikes would remain incomparable and impossible to evaluate or prioritize, thus inter alia generating a problem of the relationship between ethics and aesthetics.

We can now see how easy it is for Augustine to speak intelligibly of the beauty of self-sacrifice: God's self-sacrifice in Christ is the act of a beautiful soul, and the martyrs, though apparently ugly and deformed, are beautiful in imitation of that soul.[37]

The typical reader of Gregory or of Augustine feels no astonishment at the enormous emphasis they put on beauty, indeed on the beauty of God Himself, on beauty as a divine attribute. He finds no difficulty in seeing Gregory and Augustine identifying truth, goodness, and beauty.[38] Yet he should feel astonishment if while reading them he thinks of earlier Christian writers. For the first time Gregory and Augustine have more or less simultaneously placed beauty as well as awe at the center of mainstream Christianity and offered to explain and justify it.

In one sense, however, their solution plays for safety. The beauty of

36. He might, e.g., be trying to reveal an ugly truth or to show beauty in contrast to ugliness.

37. E.g., *EnPs.* 32.2.6.

38. E.g., at *De Libero Arbitrio* 2.13.35–38.

nature is a showing or revelation of the beauty of God, and the beauty of God, being personal, enables one to move easily between physical beauty (typified by the transfigured and resurrected Jesus) to beauty of character, thus to moral and spiritual beauty. But the "problem" of beauty, as of "love," was centered in antiquity—as now—on the seductive and hence ambivalent beauty of the human body, and, of course, on the painted and sculpted bodies of the gods. For these divine bodies might seem to offer the twin temptations of lasciviousness and idolatry, thus arousing criticism as promotors of both immorality and blasphemy. Perhaps here the fourth-century Christian retrieval of beauty would grind to a stop, ignoring any such "artistic" productions. Indeed the problem of the artistic depiction of the naked human body was later to become linked with the problem of (neo)paganism. Hence a reaction to anything judged to be neopagan entailed a blindness to various legitimate forms of artistic beauty, thus helping to engender, outside a Christianity weakened in the Renaissance and later, the development of "properly" artistic movements which Christianity found difficult to appropriate. By the time it had more or less done so, secular culture left Christian neoprudery behind in progressing toward an art and an account of art at first parallel with that possible within Christianity, then to more and more depersonalized forms, themselves ever harder to Christianize and indeed in more recent versions effectively, and often deliberately, anti-Christian. The problem of "pagan" art—or more properly the problem of a failure to distinguish between "true" and "false" inspiration—contributed historically to the contemporary phenomenon of a depersonalized art curiously appropriate to our mechanized, bureaucratic, and consumerist age.

Many think that it is possible to develop a serious ethical theory of obligation and responsibility within secular culture; I have argued elsewhere that the metaphysical foundations for such an edifice cannot be established: thus ethics will be reduced to post-Kantian formalism or to nihilism in the style of Nietzsche or to choice theory. Similarly in aesthetics: if human beauty is rejected by the godly and left to the secular world, that world will seem to develop an aesthetics of its own. Its foundations, however, will be flimsy, the ancient association of ethics and aesthetics will be lost, and we should be surprised neither at the current depersonalizations of art—entailing a corresponding decline in its inspirational power—nor at purely emotivist explanations of beauty.

I would like to add a little more on the depersonalization of art and the undue emphasis on what would traditionally be thought of as ugliness as "art" has developed in post-Christian societies. My claim is that in such societies beauty has as little defense against ugliness as has morality against nihilism: indeed that ugliness and nihilism can be expected to go hand in hand as both Christianity and its Platonic metaphysical features are whittled down. As I have already observed, my concern is not with the simple appearance of ugliness in art—any tragedy will display ugliness—but with its intent, with the emotions it tries to arouse, with the effects achieved when the sensed ugliness is no longer in the service of a deeper understanding of beauty and truth.

Classical and medieval theories of art identify the artist as the producer of what can somehow be called "beautiful" or "fine" (in Greek: *kalon*). Most earlier "aesthetics" is therefore concerned to identify the nature of the inspirationally "beautiful." Albert the Great offered a fairly typical definition: beauty subsists in the gleaming of substantial form over proportionally arranged parts of matter.[39] Most such definitions—themselves implying a further definition of the artist as the person capable of producing such beauty—are in some sense arbitrary. They suggest that "beautiful" work so defined will produce the proper inspiration which is the mark of the "aesthetic," but in such suggestions they also assume that the "right kind of person" will experience such inspiration. Just as in ethics, as Aristotle emphasized, the well-brought-up individual will delight in doing good, while the ill-brought-up individual will delight in doing harm, so in aesthetics the aesthetically well trained will be inspired by what is noble, others by what is in fact ugly. For just as Aristotelian ethics assumes it knows how the proper moral individual will behave, so traditional aesthetics (in some sense inseparable from ethics) knows what will inspire the aesthetically well formed.

That could be mere conventionalism. The meta-aesthetic question that is my present concern is: How do we know whether good taste in art is any better grounded than good taste in ethics? Most people are still inclined to believe—though not knowing why they believe—that in ethics taste may not always be the ultimate arbiter, while allowing that they

39. *Opusculum de pulchro et bono* 5.456, cited by R. Tatarkiewicz, *Mediaeval Aesthetics* (Warsaw, 1970), 243.

should give it its apparent due in aesthetics: beauty, but at least not all kinds of moral action, they will say, is in the eye of the beholder.

It is worth recalling how, in the eighteenth century in particular, the parallel between ethics and aesthetics worked itself out. To do that, we must return first to the historical question of the debate about artistic representations of the human body, then to the theoretical question of whether the production of beauty is the only function of the artist. For it can be argued that if Beauty exists, then in some sense Ugliness exists too (though not in a "perfect" form), and that the artist might enable us to expand our knowledge of the beautiful precisely by presenting what is not beautiful. But, as I have observed, he might also want to present the ugly not to show it up in contrast with the beautiful, but because he is fascinated by ugliness or because he has some ideological reason for presenting it "artistically" or "enticingly." He might, for example, want to corrupt someone's sexual morality. Here again, there might be a parallel with ethics. The good surgeon could be the good torturer; the good artist could be the good pornographer: it depends on the aim to which he chooses to dedicate his skill. Perhaps just as there are philosophers and sophists, there are "moral" philosophers and "moral" sophists, not to speak of practicing "aesthetic" philosophers and "aesthetic" sophists. "X is a good torturer" does not entail "X is a torturer" and "X is good" (unless you approve of torturers).

The new aesthetic canons of the early modern age had little effective foundation—at times that would be, as later, a matter of pride—and in the eighteenth century there developed in many quarters a tendency to fall back on a "value Aristotelianism" of taste. By that I do not mean that Aristotle would have approved of neoclassicizing taste, but that those who advocated it relied, as Aristotle had done in ethics, on the view that right-minded, "educated" people had the right taste in art and literature. The (particularly French) canonization of taste paralleled the development of theories of proper sentiments in English ethicists of the same period: first Shaftesbury, then more strikingly Hutcheson, even Hume. Such canons were open to attack not only from traditionalists appealing to (even poorly understood) Thomistic theories of beauty, but within the ever strengthening purely secular orbit by more determined students of "aesthetics."

The canonization of taste (or choice) is a conventional substitute for a metaphysical theory of art, indeed for precisely that Christian theory of art, developed from Platonism, which I have identified in Augustine and Gregory of Nyssa, whereby the beauty of Christ is the justifying metaphysical ground for both spiritual and physical beauties. In the absence of such grounding, we find the conventional, tasteful view of beauty, and it is only to be expected that this should be roughly contemporary with the "discovery" of aesthetics as a specific science by Baumgarten: "Art for art's sake" has now become inevitable, even apparently legitimate, though meaningless in an antimetaphysical context. The phrase itself appears to have been first used slightly later, by Théophile Gautier in *Mademoiselle de Maupin* (1835).

I race on to Kant, and it should come as no surprise that his moves in aesthetics parallel those in ethics. He has no time for an aesthetics of taste, nor for the idea that beauty can be understood by resort to the authority of Nature, whether or not underwritten by a deistic God or in more nearly pantheistic and effectively stoicizing versions. Kant remained a nominal, if rationalist, Christian, strongly imbued with the moralism of the Pietists, but his solution to the problems of meta-aesthetics—the shift from conventionalism or naturalism to resting supreme confidence in the artistic genius as such—carried forward the neopaganism of the Renaissance in a direction that led further and further from the original ancient paganism itself. For what chiefly distinguishes Renaissance Neoplatonism from the theories of Plotinus and Proclus is the centrality it places on "divine" man's role in the cosmos: a view clearly influenced by—and subversive of—the Christian doctrine of man, created in God's image and redeemed by Christ himself.

The influence of Rousseau on Kant (not least on his account of "genius") is generally acknowledged, and in later times it also contributed much to the drive, in art, toward "expressivism," a set of theories that sees the greatness of art in the opportunity it gives to man to express his (originally pure and noble) nature. At its most extreme this leads to the seemingly inevitable hyper-Renaissance thesis of Herder that the artist is to become a creator-god. That, however, might be read in different ways, depending on whether some vestige of the doctrine of original sin (still accepted by Kant) remains on the table to suggest its weaknesses as well as its strengths. Without it, there need be no limit to the powers and authority the creator-god might arrogate to himself. We have passed from personalism to the aesthetic superman as once from impersonal aesthetics to personalism.

There are many modern transformations of such views, often influenced directly or indirectly by Nietzsche. An especially informative one (by the American poet Wallace Stevens) is cited by Charles Taylor:[40] "After one has abandoned belief in God, poetry is the essence which takes its place as life's redemption." In this case the ambiguity surrounds the word "redemption." If Stevens means that at least something of a "vision" of a nonconsumerist, not mechanist, nonindustrial world is preserved by poetry, there is little difficulty in understanding what he wants to say. But if he thinks that such poetic language is self-explanatory, he is mistaken. Poetry as such cannot redeem; it can only point to phenomena such as would be redeeming and redeemed if there were a Redeemer, thus offering a "virtual" redemption. Once belief in God has been abandoned, any nonmetaphorical redemption has vanished; indeed even "metaphorical" has now become a substitute for "self-deluding." Stevens, in parallel with many ethical writers, is relying on a theology and a metaphysics that he has also explicitly rejected.

The "post-Kantian" artist is not merely a creator; he is also necessarily self-deceiving and hybristic, whether he thinks of himself as a virtual god or merely a seer or prophet. His premodern predecessors were members of a community rooted in transcendental values, and in however personal a vision they spoke out of the traditional values of that community. The reconstructed artist, to the contrary, tries to create his own community, and at its lowest that community consists of "groupies" (whether or not affiliated with the *Times Literary Supplement* or the *New York Review of Books*). In the absence of the divine, the artist—especially if self-conscious—can now only be a seer of himself, even of his self. Insofar as he expresses himself in such a spirit, he poses as a self-creator, as well as, to whatever degree, a creative artist. But though he is indeed a creator, and can be recognized as such, he cannot be a self-creator. If he thinks or implies that he is, he is producing art, however fine it may be, as a means of self-glorification *(ad maiorem gloriam mei)*—and thus of self-mutilation. The more general worship of the artist (at least by élites

40. C. Taylor, *Sources of the Self* (Cambridge, Mass., 1989) 493, citing Stevens's *Opus Posthumum.*

or would-be élites) then becomes a replacement of the worship of God. If Augustine is broadly right in his Christian account of art and beauty, the slogan "art for art's sake"—probably logically indefensible though confusingly suggesting the notion that a work of art, unlike a packet of cornflakes, is irreplaceable—also suggests the self-praise and self-worship of the self-creating artist who claims and embodies it.

The foregoing analysis enables us to face a more basic problem about the relationship between art and beauty and about the intelligibility of post-Christian artistic theory. Insofar as art is seen as the expression of the self, it will reflect the weaknesses of the self as well as its strengths, and the more unintelligible the ideology of the self, the more unintelligible (and beauty-free)—though not immediately the less clever—will be its expressions. The fate of such art is to become solipsistic; the groupies will have to understand less, pretend to understand more, and "at the end of the day" laud unintelligibility and ugliness for its own sake. Such ugliness, as I have noted, can be—but need not be—presented with great technical skill, though that skill need make no pretensions either to show up beauty or to present ugliness as a means to the better understanding of what it is for beauty to be absent.

We have now reached the postmodern turn, which calls for the disappearance of the self, of the artist or literary creator now unmasked as a competent piece of jetsam on the tide of social change. But I have argued that the comprehensibility of (inspirational) art depends on the recognition of the beauty of God which thus accounts, via the Incarnation, for both spiritual and physical beauties. In the postmodern worldview, however, while the superman may be absent, the role of the personal is still deliberately undercut; there can be no Incarnation, and therefore no possible explanation of beauty in the universe or in human beings. Outside Christian circles the return of a debased version of the impersonal can easily be recognized: an advent neither of the beauty of a transcendent God, nor of the immanently beautiful Nature of the seventeenth and eighteenth centuries, nor even of the self-created beauty of the expressivist. One can note the impersonal turn from the Absolute Spirit of Hegel—a form of depersonalized Christianity—to the more radical "being there" *(Dasein)* of Heidegger, from which all necessary moral as well as aesthetic content has been removed. Heidegger was a Nazi (as it happened), and the banality of Nazi art is well recognized. He could in other circumstances have been a Stalinist, finding in such a world the equally banal style of "Soviet realism."

In these all too rapid comments on the fate of nontranscendental art, I do not wish to be misunderstood. It would obviously be false to say that great technical improvements have not been made in recent art, literature, and poetry; it would be even more absurd to say that great works have not been produced. My thesis involves neither of these conclusions. It is that for all the technical advances, no coherent theory of the nature of beauty can be proposed in a world where it is impossible to distinguish beauty from ugliness inasmuch as each is an "authentic" expression of artistic skill. It is also that where works of great beauty have been achieved (usually on an immanent level, but sometimes where the immanent is a symbol for the transcendent, as with the French impressionists), the greatness achieved cannot be understood in terms of a nontranscendental, nonpersonal meta-aesthetic theory. Christian artists can learn from the techniques of the post-Christians, just as in ethics Christian philosophers can learn from the analytic skills of atheists, so long as they can separate the skills from the unintelligible, because foundationless, ideology, or, more precisely, banality.

Art, as I define it, is properly concerned (directly or indirectly) with beauty and the inspiration of beauty; that is the type of "art" I am trying to explain. But there is also parasitic or "sophistic" art—the product of skill without beauty and ultimately inexplicable except as what was once called *curiositas,* an enquiry into what should not be known or experienced and a desire for emotions that should not be aroused. No one is "inspired" to fornicate at a rock concert, though they may be aroused to fornicate, nor to masturbate after viewing a cleverly designed and "artistic" "skin-flick."

So my account, in the end, sees art as an ethical, or, better, as a spiritual phenomenon—necessarily subordinated to spiritual goals and the richness of man's capabilities. That means no *curiositas.* And it also refers us back to Plato's *Symposium* and the old question of the relationship between beauty and goodness. Theoretically, beauty is what later came to be called a "transcendental," but apparently it is not a distinct transcendental. Like awesome splendor (with which it is sometimes confused) it shows a facet of God, not His power as such, which might instill mere fear, but His creative and beautiful goodness, arousing and inspiring "erotic" longing.

In Greek times *kalon* could signify physical, moral, or spiritual beauty. Part of the enduring strength of that piece of linguistic good fortune is that it indicates a recognition that a proper foundation for ethics will ultimately have to be identical with a proper foundation for aesthetics. For the production of the "fine," as originally construed, involved an appeal to an "end" "seen" by the individual but beyond the individual. Just as in ethics neither emotivism nor formalism nor the cult of obligation nor utilitarianism can provide adequate defense against moral nihilism, so in aesthetics neither formalism, nor expessivism, nor mere engineering will defeat the Gadarene rush toward ugliness: ugliness seen as "authentic," "poignant," "deep," and so "beautiful."

In such aesthetics the key association between beauty and inspiration is lost. Inspiration is in a sense an emotion, but not all emotions, however skillfully aroused, call out an inspiration to the Good. Christian "meta-aesthetics" (broadly understood) is still able to discern whether emotions are inspirational or not, and by that discernment to advance our understanding of beauty, whether such beauty reveals the immanent or conceals (but symbolizes) the transcendent. But too much must not be claimed for it: no aesthetic theory can tell me whether the *Iliad* is more beautiful than *Hamlet,* let alone whether *Hamlet* is more inspirational than *Lear.*

Bibliography

LEGAL CASES

Brown v. Board of Education, 347 U.S. 483 (1954).
Griswold v. Connecticut, 381 U.S. 479 (1965).
Lawrence v. Texas, 539 U.S. 558 (2003).
Planned Parenthood v. Casey, 505 U.S. 833 (1992).
Roe v. Wade, 410 U.S. 113 (1973).
Scott v. Sandford, 60 U.S. 393 (1857).

OTHER PRINT MATERIALS

Aguirre, Maria Sophia. "The Family and Economic Development: Socioeconomic Relevance and Policy Design." In vol. 1, *The Family in the New Millennium,* edited by Scott Love and Thomas Holman. London: Praeger Perspectives, 2006.

———. "Family Dining, Diet and Food Distribution: Planting the Seeds of Economic Growth." *Economic Development and Cultural Change.* Forthcoming.

Anscombe, G. E. M. *Intention.* Cambridge, Mass.: Harvard University Press, 2000.

Appiah, Anthony. "Experimental Philosophy." Presidential Address, Eastern Division Meeting, American Philosophical Association, Baltimore, December 2007.

———. *Experiments in Ethics.* Cambridge, Mass.: Harvard University Press, 2008.

Aristotle. *Rhetoric.* Vol. 11 of *The Works of Aristotle,* translated by W. Rhys Roberts and edited by W. D. Ross. Oxford: Clarendon Press, 1924.

Armstrong, D. M. *What Is Law of Nature?* Cambridge: Cambridge University Press, 1983.

Arnhart, Larry. *Darwinian Natural Right.* Albany: State University of New York Press, 1998.

———. "Defending Darwinian Natural Right." *Interpretation* 27, no. 3 (Spring 2000): 263–77.

———. "Statesmanship as Magnanimity: Classical, Christian, and Modern." *Polity* 16 (Winter 1983): 263–83.

Audi, Robert. *The Good in the Right.* Princeton, N.J.: Princeton University Press, 2001.
Baumgarten, Alexander. *Meditationes Philosophicae de Nonnullis ad Poema Pertinentibus.* Halle, 1735.
Bedau, Mark. "Where's the Good in Teleology?" *Philosophy and Phenomenological Research* 2, no. 4 (December 1992): 781–806.
Bendersky, Joseph. "Interrogation of Carl Schmitt by Robert Kempner (I–III),""Carl Schmitt at Nuremburg, Appendix III." *TELOS* 72 (Summer 1987): 128.
Benedict XVI. *Deus Caritas Est.* Vatican City: Libreria Editrice Vaticana, 2005.
Bennett, Jonathan. *The Act Itself.* Oxford: Oxford University Press, 1995.
Berlin, Isaiah, and Beata Polanowska-Sygulska. *Unfinished Dialogue.* New York: Prometheus Books, 2006.
Berman, Paul. *Terror and Liberalism.* New York: Norton, 2003.
Bickel, Alexander M. *The Least Dangerous Branch.* Indianapolis, Ind.: Bobbs-Merrill, 1962.
Blanchette, Oliva. *The Perfection of the Universe According to Aquinas.* University Park: Pennsylvania State University Press, 1992.
Bloom, Allan. *The Closing of the American Mind.* New York: Simon & Schuster, 1987.
Blum, Lawrence. *Moral Perception and Particularity.* Cambridge: Cambridge University Press, 1997.
Boorse, Christopher. "Health as a Theoretical Concept." *Philosophy of Science* 44 (1977): 542–73.
———. "Wright on Functions." *Philosophical Review* 85, no. 1 (January 1976): 70–86.
———. "A Rebuttal on Health." In *What Is Disease?* edited by J. M. Humber and R. F. Almeder. Totowa, N.J.: Humana Press, 1997.
Brandt, Richard. "W. K. Frankena and the Ethics of Virtue." *Monist* 64 (1981): 271–92.
Brock, Steven. "The Legal Character of Natural Law According to St. Thomas Aquinas." Ph.D. diss., University of Toronto, 1988.
Budziszewski, J. *Written on the Heart: The Case for Natural Law.* Downers Grove, Ill.: Intervarsity, 1997.
Burnet, John, ed. *Platonis Opera.* 5 vols. Oxford: Clarendon Press, 1900–1907.
Carpenter, Dale. "The Unknown Past of *Lawrence v. Texas.*" *Michigan Law Review* 102 (June 2004): 1464–1527.
Carrese, Paul O. *The Cloaking of Power: Montesquieu, Blackstone, and the Rise of Judicial Activism.* Chicago: University of Chicago Press, 2003.
Casebeer, William. *Natural Ethical Facts.* Cambridge, Mass.: MIT Press, 2003.
Catechism of the Catholic Church. 2nd ed. Washington, D.C.: United States Catholic Conference and Libreria Editrice Vacticana, 1997.
Chang, Gene Hsin, and Guanzhong James Wen. "Communal Dining and the Chinese Famine of 1958–1961." *Economic Development and Cultural Change* 46, no. 1 (1997): 1–34.

Charles, David. "Aristotle on Hypothetical Necessity and Irreducibility." *Pacific Philosophical Quarterly* 69 (1988): 1–53.

Coleman, James. *Foundations of Social Theory.* Cambridge, Mass.: Belknap Press at Harvard University Press, 1990.

Congregation for the Doctrine of the Faith. "Doctrinal Note on Some Questions Regarding the Participation of Catholics in Political Life." Rome: CDF, 2002.

Cooper, John. "Hypothetical Necessity and Natural Teleology." In *Philosophical Issues in Aristotle's Biology,* edited by Allan Gotthelf and James Lennox. Cambridge: Cambridge University Press, 1987.

———. *Reason and Human Good in Aristotle.* Cambridge, Mass.: Harvard University Press, 1975.

Copleston, Frederick. *A History of Philosophy.* Vol. 2, *Medieval Philosophy from Augustine to Duns Scotus.* 1950. Reprint, New York: Image Books, 1993.

"Creation Reveals God and His Love, Says Benedict XVI: Comments on Psalm 135 (136) at General Audience." ZENIT, November 9, 2005, available online at www.zenit.org/english/visualizza.phtml?sid=79681.

Dante Alighieri. *Inferno.* Translated by John Ciardi. 1982. Reprint, New York: Penguin Books, 1954.

De Groot, Jean. "Form and Succession in Aristotle's *Physics.*" *Proceedings of the Boston Area Colloquium in Ancient Philosophy* 10 (1994): 1–23.

de Jouvenel, Bertrand. *The Pure Theory of Politics.* 1963. Reprint, Indianapolis, Ind.: Liberty Fund, 2000.

Delhaye, P. "Naturrecht." In vol. 7 of *Lexikon für Theologie und Kirche.* 2nd ed. Freiburg: Herder, 1957–1968.

Descartes, Réné. *Discours de la methode.* Paris: Vrin, 1970.

———. *Meditations on First Philosophy.* Edited by J. Cottingham, R. Stoothoff, and D. Murdoch. In vol. 2, *The Philosophical Writings of Descartes.* New York: Cambridge University Press, 1984.

———. *Meditations on First Philosophy: Sixth Meditation.* In *Descartes: Philosophical Writings,* translated and edited by Elizabeth Anscombe and Peter Thomas Geach. Edinburgh: Nelson, 1954.

———. *Oeuvres de Descartes.* Vol. 6. Edited by Charles Adam and Paul Tannery. Paris: Librairie Philosophique J. Vrin, 1983.

Des Chene, Dennis. *Physiologia: Natural Philosophy in Late Aristotelian and Cartesian Thought.* Ithaca, N.Y.: Cornell University Press, 1996.

Devins, Neal. "Judicial Matters." *California Law Review* 80 (1992): 1027, 1039–46.

Devlin, Patrick. *The Enforcement of Morals.* Oxford: Oxford University Press, 1960.

Dideberg, Dany. *Saint Augustin et la première Epitre de saint Jean: Une théologie de l'amour.* Paris: Editions Beauchesne, 1975.

Doris, John. *Lack of Character.* Cambridge: Cambridge University Press, 2002.

Ehrlich, Paul, and Anne Ehrlich. *The Population Explosion.* New York: Simon & Schuster, 1990.

———. *Population, Resources, Environment: Issues in Human Ecology.* San Francisco: W. H. Freeman, 1970.

Elders, Leo J. *The Ethics of St. Thomas Aquinas.* Frankfurt: Peter Lang, 2005.

Ellis, Brian. *Scientific Essentialism.* Cambridge: Cambridge University Press, 2001.

Engelhardt, H. T., Jr. *The Foundations of Bioethics.* 1st ed. New York and Oxford: Oxford University Press, 1986.

———. *The Foundations of Bioethics.* 2nd ed. New York and Oxford: Oxford University Press, 1996.

Fiedrowicz, Michael. *Apologie im frühen Christentum.* 2nd ed. Paderborn, Germany: Ferdinand Schoeningh, 2001.

Finnis, John. "Abortion, Natural Law, and Public Reason." In *Natural Law and Public Reason,* edited by Robert P. George and Christopher Wolfe. Washington, D.C.: Georgetown University Press, 2000.

———. *Aquinas: Moral, Political, and Legal Theory.* New York: Oxford University Press, 1998.

———. "Is Natural Law Theory Compatible with Limited Government?" In *Natural Law, Liberalism, and Morality,* edited by Robert P. George. Oxford: Clarendon Press, 1996.

———. "Law, Morality, and Sexual Orientation." *Notre Dame Journal of Law, Ethics, and Public Policy* 9 (1995): 11–39.

———. *Natural Law and Natural Rights.* Oxford: Clarendon Press, 1980.

———. "Natural Law Theories." *The Stanford Encyclopedia of Philosophy.* Available online at http://plato.stanford.edu/archives/spr2007/entries/natural-law-theories/.

———. "Public Good: The Specifically Political Common Good in Aquinas." In *Natural Law and Moral Inquiry: Ethics, Metaphysics, and Politics in the Work of Germain Grisez,* edited by Robert P. George. Washington, D.C.: Georgetown University Press, 1998.

———. "Questions about the Place of Natural Law." In *Natural Law and Contemporary Public Policy,* edited by David F. Forte. Washington, D.C.: Georgetown University Press, 1998.

Flanagan, Owen. *Varieties of Moral Personality.* Cambridge, Mass.: Harvard University Press, 1991.

Flannery, Kevin. *Acts Amid Precepts.* Washington, D.C.: The Catholic University of America Press, 2001.

Foot, Philippa. *Natural Goodness.* Oxford: Clarendon Press, 2001.

———. *Virtues and Vices.* Oxford: Oxford University Press, 1978.

Fortin, Ernest L. *Collected Essays.* Vol. 2. Edited by J. Brian Benestad. Lanham, Md.: Rowman & Littlefield, 1996.

Freeman, Derek. *Margaret Mead and Samoa: The Making and Unmaking of an Anthropological Myth.* Cambridge, Mass.: Harvard University Press, 1983.

Fried, Barbara. "Is There a Coherent Alternative to Cost-Benefit Analysis?" Harvard University Center for Ethics, Kennedy School of Government, December 2007.

Fukuyama, Francis. *The Great Disruption.* New York: Free Press, 1999.
Gallagher, David. "Person and Love in Aquinas." *Acta Philosophica* 4 (1995): 51–71.
Garcia, J. L. A. "Intention-Sensitive Ethics." *Public Affairs Quarterly* 9 (1995): 201–13.
Geach, Mary. "Marriage: Arguing to a First Principle in Sexual Ethics." In *Moral Truth and Moral Tradition: Essays in Honour of Peter Geach and Elizabeth Anscombe,* edited by Luke Gormally. Dublin: Four Courts Press, 1994.
———. *The Soul.* Ph.D. diss., Cambridge University, 1981.
Geach, Peter. *Truth and Hope.* South Bend, Ind.: University of Notre Dame Press, 2001.
Gelfand, Scott. "Hypothetical Agent-Based Virtue Ethics." *Southwest Philosophical Review* 17 (2000): 85–94.
George, Robert P. *In Defense of Natural Law.* Oxford: Clarendon Press, 1999.
———. "Recent Criticism of Natural Law Theory." *University of Chicago Law Review* 55 (1988): 1371–1429.
Gerleman, Gillis. *Ruth: Das Hohelied.* Vol. 18 of *Biblischer Kommentar: Altes Testament.* Neukirchen-Vluyn: Neukirchener Verlag, 1965.
Gilson, Etienne. *From Aristotle to Darwin and Back Again.* Translated by John Lyon. South Bend, Ind.: University of Notre Dame Press, 1984.
———. *History of Christian Philosophy in the Middle Ages.* 1922. Reprint, New York: Random House, 1955.
Goodin, Robert. *Protecting the Vulnerable.* Chicago: University of Chicago Press, 1985.
Gray, John. *Isaiah Berlin.* Princeton, N.J.: Princeton University Press, 1996.
———. *Two Faces of Liberalism.* New York: New Press, 2000.
Greenawalt, Kent. "How Persuasive Is Natural Law Theory?" *Notre Dame Law Review* 75 (2000): 1647–79.
———. "Natural Law and Public Reasons." *Villanova Law Review* 47 (2002): 531–52.
———. *Private Consciences and Public Reasons.* New York: Oxford University Press, 1995.
———. *Religious Convictions and Political Choice.* New York: Oxford University Press, 1988.
———. Review of *Natural Law and Natural Rights* by John Finnis. *Political Theory* 10 (1982): 133–36.
———. "What Are Public Reasons?" *Journal of Law, Philosophy, and Culture* 1 (2007): 81–82.
Grisez, Germain. "A Contemporary Natural Law Ethics." In *Normative Ethics and Objective Reason,* edited by George F. McLean. Washington, D.C.: Council for Research in Values and Philosophy, 1996.
———. *The Way of the Lord Jesus.* 3 vols. Quincy, Ill.: Franciscan Press, 1983–1997.
Grisez, Germain, John Finnis, and Joseph M. Boyle. "Practical Principles, Moral Truth, and Ultimate Ends." *American Journal of Jurisprudence* 32 (1987): 99–151.

Haldane, John. "Public Reason, Truth, and Human Fellowship: Going Beyond Rawls." *Journal of Law, Philosophy, and Culture* 1 (2007): 175–90.

Hamilton, Alexander, James Madison, and John Jay. *The Federalist Papers*. Edited by Clinton Rossiter. New York: New American Library, 1961.

Hare, R. M. "Health." *Journal of Medical Ethics* 12 (1986): 174–81.

Hart, H. L. A. *Law, Liberty, and Morality*. Stanford, Calif.: Stanford University Press, 1963.

Hassing, Richard. "Reply to Arnhart." *Interpretation* 28, no. 1 (Fall 2000): 35–43.

Havel, Václav. *Open Letters: Selected Writings, 1964–1990*. New York: Knopf.

Hegel, G. W. F. *Elements of the Philosophy of Right*. Edited by Allen W. Wood and translated by H. B. Nisbet. Cambridge: Cambridge University Press, 1991.

———. *Lectures on Natural Right and Political Science*. Translated by J. Michael Stewart and Peter C. Hodgson. Berkeley and Los Angeles: University of California Press, 1995.

———. *Philosophy of Right*. Translated by T. M. Knox. Oxford: Clarendon Press, 1953.

Hendin, Herbert. "Assisted Suicide, Euthanasia and Suicide Prevention: The Implications of the Dutch Experience." *Suicide and Life-Threatening Behavior* 25, no. 1 (Spring 1995): 193–203.

Hendin, Herbert, and Gerald Klerman. "Physician-Assisted Suicide: The Dangers of Legalization." *American Journal of Psychiatry* 150, no. 1 (January 1993): 143–45.

Hern, Warren D. "Is Pregnancy Really Normal?" *Family Planning Perspectives* 3, no. 1 (January 1971): 5–10.

Hittinger, Russell. *A Critique of the New Natural Law Theory*. South Bend, Ind.: University of Notre Dame Press, 1987.

Hobbes, Thomas. *De Cive*. In *Man and Citizen,* edited by Bernard Gert. New York: Doubleday, 1972.

———. *De Cive: The English Version*. Edited by Howard Warrender. Oxford: Clarendon Press, 1983.

———. *De Cive: The Latin Version*. Edited by Howard Warrender. Oxford: Clarendon Press, 1983.

———. *De Cive: The Latin Version*. In *Behemoth; or the Long Parliament*. Edited by Ferdinand Tönnies. London, 1889.

———. *The Elements of Law Natural and Politic*. Edited by Ferdinand Tönnies. Cambridge: Cambridge University Press, 1928.

———. *Leviathan*. Edited by Richard Tuck. Cambridge: Cambridge University Press, 1992.

———. *Leviathan*. In vol. 3 of *Opera Latina,* edited by William Molesworth. 1845. Reprint, Aalen: Scientia, 1961.

———. *On the Citizen*. Edited and translated by Richard Tuck and Michael Silverthorne. New York: Cambridge University Press, 1998.

———. *Thomas White's De Mundo Examined*. Translated by Harold Whitmore Jones. London: Bradford University Press in association with Crosby Lockwood Staples, 1976.

Hübner, Kurt. *Das Christentum im Wettstreit der Religionen.* Tübingen, Germany: J. C. B. Mohr (Paul Siebeck), 2003.

Hurka, Thomas. *Vice, Virtue, and Value.* Oxford: Oxford University Press, 2001.

Hursthouse, Rosalind. "Normative Virtue Ethics." In *How Should One Live?* edited by Roger Crisp. Oxford: Oxford University Press, 1996.

———. "Virtue Theory and Abortion." *Philosophy and Public Affairs* 20 (1991): 223–46.

———. "What Is Wrong with Virtue Ethics?" Unpublished manuscript.

Irwin, Terence. *Aristotle's First Principles.* Oxford: Clarendon Press, 1990.

Jaffa, Harry V. *Thomism and Aristotelianism: A Study of the "Commentary" by Thomas Aquinas on the "Nicomachean Ethics."* Chicago: University of Chicago Press, 1952.

Jefferson, Thomas. "Letter to Isaac H. Tiffany, August 26, 1816." In *Selected Writings of Thomas Jefferson,* edited by Harvey C. Mansfield Jr. Arlington Heights, Ill.: AHM Publishing Corp., 1979.

Jenkins, John I. "Expositions of the Text: Aquinas's Aristotelian Commentaries." *Medieval Philosophy and Theology* 5 (1996): 39–62.

John Paul II. Address to the Fiftieth General Assembly of the United Nations Organization, October 5, 1995. Available online at http://www.vatican.va/holy_father/john_paul_ii/speeches/1996/documents/hf_jp-ii_spe_05101995_address-to-uno_en.html.

Junker, Reinhard, and Siegfried Scherer, eds. *Evolution: Ein kritisches Lehrbuch.* 4th ed. Giessen: Weyel, 1998.

Kamtekar, Rachana. "Situationism and Virtue Ethics on the Content of Our Character." *Ethics* 114 (2004): 458–91.

Kant, Immanuel. *Immanuel Kant's Critique of Pure Reason.* Translated by Norman Kemp Smith. London: Macmillan, 1950.

———. *Kritik der reinen Vernunft.* Edited by Raymond Schmidt. Hamburg: Felix Meiner Verlag, 1952.

———. *The Metaphysics of Morals.* Translated by Mary Gregor. Cambridge: Cambridge University Press, 1991.

Kass, Leon. *The Hungry Soul: Eating and the Perfection of Our Nature.* Chicago: University of Chicago Press, 1999.

Kass, Leon, and James Q. Wilson. *The Ethics of Human Cloning.* Washington, D.C.: AEI Press, 1998.

Kennington, Richard. Review of *Lectures and Essays,* by Jacob Klein. *Review of Metaphysics* 41 (1987): 145.

Keys, Mary M. *Aquinas, Aristotle, and the Promise of the Common Good.* Cambridge: Cambridge University Press, 2006.

———. "Aquinas and the Challenge of Aristotelian Magnanimity." *History of Political Thought* 24, no. 1 (Spring 2003): 37–65. Reprinted in Keys, *Aquinas, Aristotle, and the Promise of the Common Good.*

Kisiel, Theodore. *The Genesis of Heidegger's Being and Time.* Berkeley and Los Angeles: University of California Press, 1995.

Klein, Jacob. *Lectures and Essays.* Annapolis, Md.: St. John's College Press, 1985.

Klemke, E. D. "Living Without Appeal." In *The Meaning of Life,* edited by E. D. Klemke. New York: Oxford University Press, 1981.

Koons, Robert. *Realism Regained: An Exact Theory of Causation, Teleology, and the Mind.* Oxford: Oxford University Press, 2000.

Korsgaard, Christine. *Sources of Normativity.* Cambridge: Cambridge University Press, 1996.

Kries, Douglas. "Thomas Aquinas and the Politics of Moses." *Review of Politics* 52 (1990): 84–104.

Kripke, Saul. *Naming and Necessity.* Oxford: Blackwell, 1980.

Larmore, Charles. "Visible Hand." Review of *Adam Smith and the Virtues of Enlightenment,* by Charles Griswold. *New Republic* 221, no. 16 (October 18, 1999): 42.

Laslett, Peter. Introduction to *Philosophy, Politics and Society, First Series.* New York: Macmillan, 1956.

Laslett, Peter, and James Fishkin. Introduction to *Philosophy, Politics and Society, Fifth Series.* New Haven, Conn.: Yale University Press, 1979.

Lefort, Claude. *Le travail de l'oeuvre Machiavel.* Paris: Gallimard, 1972.

Lennox, James. "Health as an Objective Value." *Journal of Medicine and Philosophy* 20 (1995): 499–511.

Lewis, V. B. "Can a Christian Be a Democrat? A (Devoted) Member of the *Polis*?" In *Love Alone Is Credible: Hans Urs von Balthasar as Interpreter of the Catholic Tradition,* edited by David L. Schindler. Grand Rapids, Mich.: Eerdmans, 2008.

———. "Plato's *Minos:* The Political and Philosophical Context of the Problem of Natural Right." *Review of Metaphysics* 60 (2006): 17–53.

Lincoln, Abraham. *Collected Works of Abraham Lincoln.* Edited by Roy P. Basler. New Brunswick, N.J.: Rutgers University Press, 1953.

Lisska, A. J. *Aquinas's Theory of Natural Law: An Analytic Reconstruction.* New York: Oxford University Press, 1996.

Lund, Nelson. "Federalism and Civil Liberties." *University of Kansas Law Review* 45 (July 1997): 1045–73.

———. *Reforming Affirmative Action: How to Restore the Law of Equal Treatment.* Heritage Foundation Report to Congress, August 2, 1995. Available online at http://mason.gmu.edu/~nlund/Pubs/HeritageAffirmativeAction.pdf.

———. "Rousseau and Direct Democracy (with a Note on the Supreme Court's Term Limits Decision)." *Journal of Contemporary Legal Issues* 13 (2004): 466–74.

Lund, Nelson, and John O. McGinnis. "*Lawrence v. Texas* and Judicial Hubris." *Michigan Law Review* 102 (June 2004): 1555–614.

Lutz, Donald. "The Relative Influence of European Writers on Late Eighteenth-Century American Political Thought." *American Political Science Review* 78 (March 1984): 189–97.

Macedo, Stephen. "Against the Old Sexual Morality of the New Natural Law." In *Natural Law, Liberalism, and Morality,* edited by Robert P. George. Oxford: Clarendon Press, 1996.

———. "In Defense of Liberal Public Reason: Are Slavery and Abortion Hard Cases?" In *Natural Law and Public Reason,* edited by Robert P. George and Christopher Wolfe. Washington, D.C.: Georgetown University Press, 2000.

———. "Liberal Civic Education and Religious Fundamentalism: The Case of God v. John Rawls?" *Ethics* 105 (1995): 468–96.

———. *Liberal Virtues.* Oxford: Clarendon Press, 1990.

Machiavelli, Niccolò. *Discourses on Livy.* Translated by Harvey C. Mansfield and Nathan Tarcov. Chicago and London: University of Chicago Press, 1996.

———. *The Prince.* Translated by Harvey C. Mansfield Jr. Chicago: University of Chicago Press, 1985.

———. *Il Principe.* In *Il Principe e Discorsi,* edited by Sergio Bertelli. Milan: Editore Feltrinelli, 1960.

MacIntyre, Alasdair. *After Virtue.* 2nd ed. South Bend, Ind.: University of Notre Dame Press, 1984.

———. *Dependent Rational Animals: Why Human Beings Need the Virtues.* Chicago and LaSalle, Ill.: Open Court, 1999.

———. "Politics, Philosophy and the Common Good." In *The MacIntyre Reader,* edited by Kelvin Knight. South Bend, Ind.: University of Notre Dame Press, 1998.

———. "Theories of Natural Law in the Culture of Advanced Modernity." In *Common Truths: New Perspectives on Natural Law,* edited by Edward B. McLean. Wilmington, Del.: ISI Books, 2000.

———. *Three Rival Versions of Moral Enquiry.* South Bend, Ind.: University of Notre Dame Press, 1990.

———. "Toleration and the Goods of Conflict." In vol. 2 of *Ethics and Politics: Selected Essays.* Cambridge: Cambridge University Press, 2006.

———. *Whose Justice? Which Rationality?* South Bend, Ind.: University of Notre Dame Press, 1988.

Madigan, Arthur. "What Happens to Aristotelian Teleology in the 20th Century?" Boston Colloquium in Medieval Philosophy, Boston, Fall 2005.

Makin, Stephen. "Aquinas, Natural Tendencies and Natural Kinds." *New Scholasticism* 63 (1989): 253–74.

Malcolm, Noel. "Hobbes' Theory of International Relations." In *Aspects of Hobbes.* Oxford: Clarendon Press, 2002.

Manent, Pierre. *The City of Man.* Translated by Marc A. LePain. Princeton, N.J.: Princeton University Press, 1998.

———. *Cours familier de la philosophie politique.* Paris: Fayard, 2000.

———. *Les libéraux.* Paris: Gallimard, 2001.

———. "Notre destin libéral." In *Carl Schmitt, Leo Strauss et la notion de politique,* edited by Heinrich Meier. Paris: Commentaire/Julliard, 1990.

———. *Tocqueville et la nature de la démocratie.* Paris: Fayard, 1993.

Maritain, Jacques. *Man and the State.* In *The Social and Political Philosophy of Jacques Maritain,* edited by J. W. Evans and L. R. Ward. London: Geoffrey Bless, 1956.

Martin, Christopher. "The Fact/Value Distinction." In *Human Values: New Essays on Ethics and Natural Law,* edited by D. S. Oderberg and T. Chappell. Basingstoke, U.K., and New York: Palgrave Macmillan, 2004.

McDonagh, Eileen L. *Breaking the Abortion Deadlock: From Choice to Consent.* Oxford: Oxford University Press, 1996.

McDowell, John. "Virtue and Reason." *The Monist* 62 (1979): 331–50.

McGinnis, John O., and Ilya Somin. "Federalism vs. States' Rights: A Defense of Judicial Review in a Federal System." *Northwestern Law Review* 99 (Fall 2004): 89–130.

McInerny, Ralph. *Characters in Search of Their Author: The Gifford Lectures, 1999–2000.* South Bend, Ind.: University of Notre Dame Press, 2001.

———. "What Do Communities Have in Common?" In *What Right Does Ethics Have? Public Philosophy in a Pluralistic Culture,* edited by Sander Griffioen. Amsterdam: VU University Press, 1990.

Meng, Jude Chua Soo. "To Close a Generation Gap: Thomists and the New Natural Law Theory." *Quodlibet: Online Journal of Christian Theology and Philosophy* 3, no. 2 (Spring 2001). Available online at http://www.quodlibet.net/meng-thomism.shtml.

Michael, Robert T., John H. Gagnon, Edward O. Laumann, and Gina Kolata. *Sex in America.* Boston: Little Brown, 1994.

Mill, J. S. "Nature." In *Nature, the Utility of Religion, and Theism.* Whitefish, Mont.: Kessinger, 2004.

Millikan, Ruth Garrett. "Biosemantics." *Journal of Philosophy* 86, no. 6 (1989): 281–297.

———. "In Defense of Proper Functions." *Philosophy of Science* 56, no. 2 (1989): 288–302.

———. *Language, Thought, and Other Biological Categories.* Cambridge, Mass.: MIT Press, 1984.

Monod, Jacques. *Chance and Necessity: An Essay on the Natural Philosophy of Modern Biology.* New York: Knopf, 1971.

Montaigne, Michel de. *Essais.* Edited by Maurice Rat. Paris: Éditions Garnier Frères, 1953.

———. "On Repentance." In *The Complete Essays,* translated by M. A. Screech. London: Penguin Books, 1991.

Montesquieu, Charles de Secondat, baron de. *The Spirit of the Laws.* Translated and edited by Anne M. Cohler, Basia Carolyn Miller, and Harold Samuel Stone. Cambridge: Cambridge University Press, 1989.

Murphy, Mark C. *Natural Law and Practical Rationality.* Cambridge: Cambridge University Press, 2001.

Nussbaum, Martha. *Aristotle's "De Motu Animalium": Text with Translation, Commentary, and Interpretive Essays.* Princeton, N.J.: Princeton University Press, 1978.

———. "Virtue Ethics: A Misleading Category?" *Journal of Ethics* 3 (1999): 163–201.

Oakes, Edward T. "The Achievement of Alasdair MacIntyre." *First Things* 65 (1996): 22–26.

Oakeshott, Michael. "Dr. Leo Strauss on Hobbes." In *Hobbes on Civil Association*. Indianapolis, Ind.: Liberty Fund, 1975.

———. *On Human Conduct*. Oxford: Clarendon Press, 1975.

O'Connor, D. J. *Aquinas and Natural Law*. London: Macmillan, 1967.

Oderberg, David. "Hylemorphic Dualism." In *Personal Identity*, edited by E. Paul, F. Miller, and J. Paul. Cambridge: Cambridge University Press, 2005. Originally published in *Social Philosophy and Policy* 22 (2005): 70–99.

———. *Moral Theory*. Oxford: Blackwell, 2000.

———. *Real Essentialism*. New York: Routledge, 2007.

———. "The Structure and Content of the Good." In *Human Values: New Essays on Ethics and Natural Law*, edited by D. S. Oderberg and T. Chappell. Basingstoke, U.K., and New York: Palgrave Macmillan, 2004.

Osborn, E. F. *Irenaeus of Lyons*. Cambridge: Cambridge University Press, 2001.

Pangle, Lorraine Smith. *Aristotle and the Philosophy of Friendship*. Cambridge: Cambridge University Press, 2002.

Pangle, Thomas L. *The Ennobling of Democracy*. Baltimore: Johns Hopkins University Press, 1992.

Parfit, Derek. *Reasons and Persons*. Oxford: Oxford University Press, 1984.

Peck, A. L., trans. *Parts of Animals*. In *Aristotle: Parts of Animals, Movement of Animals, Progression of Animals*, translated by A. L. Peck and E. S. Forster. Cambridge, Mass: Loeb Classical Library, Harvard University Press, 1968.

Pieper, Josef. *No One Could Have Known. An Autobiography: The Early Years*. Translated by Graham Harrison. San Francisco: Ignatius Press, 1987.

———. *On Hope*. Translated by Sr. Mary Frances McCarthy. 1949. Reprint, San Francisco: Ignatius Press, 1986.

Pinckaers, Servais. *Sources of Christian Ethics*. Translated by Sr. Mary Thomas Noble. Washington, D.C.: The Catholic University of America Press, 1995.

Pinker, Steven. *The Blank Slate: The Modern Denial of Human Nature*. New York: Viking Penguin Books, 2002.

Pippin, Robert B. *Idealism as Modernism*. New York: Cambridge University Press, 1997.

Popenoe, David, and Barbara Dafoe Whitehead. "Should We Live Together? What Young Adults Need to Know about Cohabitation Before Marriage." National Marriage Project, Rutgers University, 2000. Available online at http://marriage.rutgers.edu.

Prigent, Pierre. *L'art des premiers chrétiens*. Paris: Desclee de Brouwer, 1995.

Prufer, Thomas. "The Logic of Modernity." In *Recapitulations: Essays in Philosophy*. Washington, D.C.: The Catholic University of America Press, 1992.

Putnam, Robert D. *Making Democracy Work: Civic Tradition in Modern Italy*. Princeton, N.J.: Princeton University Press, 1993.

———. "Tuning In, Tuning Out: The Strange Disappearance of Social Capital in America." *PS: Political Science and Politics* 28, no. 4 (December 1995): 664–68.

Rabkin, Jeremy. "Continental Drift." *Claremont Review of Books* 5, no. 4 (Fall 2005): 47.

Rascoe, Burton. "A Bookman's Daybook." Review of *The Waste Land,* by T. S. Eliot. *New York Tribune,* November 5, 1922.

Ratzinger, Joseph Cardinal. *Glaube—Wahrheit—Toleranz.* Freiburg im Breisgau: Herder, 2003. Translated by Henry Taylor as *Truth and Tolerance: Christianity and World Religions.* San Francisco: Ignatius Press, 2004.

———. *Values in a Time of Upheaval.* Translated by Brian McNeil. San Francisco: Ignatius Press, 2006.

Rawls, John. "The Idea of Public Reason Revisited." *University of Chicago Law Review* 64 (1997): 765–807. Reprinted in the third edition of Rawls's *Political Liberalism* (see next entry).

———. *Political Liberalism.* 3rd ed. New York: Columbia University Press, 2003.

———. "The Priority of Right and Ideas of the Good." *Philosophy and Public Affairs* 17 (1988): 251–76.

———. *A Theory of Justice.* Cambridge, Mass.: Harvard University Press, 1971.

Reisman, Judith A., and Edward W. Eichel. *Kinsey, Sex, and Fraud: The Indoctrination of a People.* Edited by John H. Court and J. Gordon Muir. Lafayette, La.: Huntington House, 1990.

———. "Really, Dr. Kinsey?" *The Lancet* 337 (2 March 1991): 547.

Rhonheimer, Martin. *Natural Law and Practical Reason: A Thomist View of Moral Autonomy.* Translated by Gerald Malsbary. New York: Fordham University Press, 2000.

———. "The Political Ethos of Constitutional Democracy and the Place of Natural Law in Public Reason: Rawls's *Political Liberalism* Revisited." *American Journal of Jurisprudence* 50 (2005): 1–70.

Richardson, Henry. "Specifying Norms as a Way to Resolve Concrete Ethical Problems." *Philosophy and Public Affairs* (1990): 279–310.

Riedl, John O. "Thomas Aquinas on Citizenship." *Proceedings of the American Catholic Philosophical Association* 37 (1963): 159–66.

Rist, J. M. "Mysticism and Transcendence in Later Neoplatonism." *Hermes* 92 (1964): 215–17.

———. *Real Ethics.* Cambridge: Cambridge University Press, 2002.

———. "Why Greek Philosophers Might Have Been Concerned about the Environment." In *The Greeks and the Environment,* edited by L. Westra and T. M. Robinson. Lanham, Md.: Rowman & Littlefield, 1997.

Rodes, Robert E., Jr. *On Law and Chastity.* Durham, N.C.: Carolina Academic Press, 2006.

Rosenberg, Gerald N. *The Hollow Hope: Can Courts Bring about Social Change?* Chicago: University of Chicago Press, 1991.

Ross, W. D. *The Right and the Good.* Oxford: Oxford University Press, 1930.

Rousseau, Jean-Jacques. *Du contract social.* Vol. 3 of *Oeuvres complètes.* Paris: Éditions Gallimard, 1964.

Russell, Bertrand. "On the Definition of Virtue." In *Cambridge Essays 1888–1889,* vol. 1 of *Collected Papers of Bertrand Russell,* edited by Kenneth Blackwell. Winchester, Mass.: Allen & Unwin, 1983.

Schall, James V. "Friendship and Political Philosophy." *Review of Metaphysics* 50 (1996): 121–41.
Scheffler, Samuel. *Boundaries and Allegiances.* Oxford: Oxford University Press, 2003.
———. "Morality and Reasonable Partiality." Presentation, MIT Department of Linguistics and Philosophy, Spring 2007.
Schmitt, Carl. *Political Theology: Four Chapters on the Concept of Sovereignty.* Translated by George Schwab. Cambridge, Mass.: MIT Press, 1985.
Schneewind, Jerome. "Misfortunes of Virtue." *Ethics* 101 (1990): 42–63.
Shackleton, Robert. *Montesquieu: A Critical Biography.* London: Oxford University Press, 1961.
Shanley, Brian J. "Aquinas on Pagan Virtue." *The Thomist* 63 (1999): 553–77.
Simon, Julian. *The Ultimate Resource.* Princeton, N.J.: Princeton University Press, 1981.
———. *The Ultimate Resource 2.* Princeton, N.J.: Princeton University Press, 1996.
Simon, Yves. *The Philosophy of Democratic Government.* Chicago: University of Chicago Press, 1951.
Simpson, G. G. *The Meaning of Evolution.* New Haven, Conn.: Yale University Press, 1967.
Simpson, Peter L. Phillips. "Making the Citizens Good: Aristotle's City and Its Contemporary Relevance." *Philosophical Forum* 22 (1990): 149–66.
Slade, Francis. "Ends and Purposes." In *Final Causality in Nature and Human Affairs,* edited by Richard Hassing. Washington, D.C.: The Catholic University of America Press, 1997.
———. "On the Ontological Priority of Ends and Its Relevance to the Narrative Arts." In *Beauty, Art, and the Polis,* edited by Alice Ramos. Washington, D.C.: The Catholic University of America Press, 2000.
———. "Rule as Sovereignty: The Universal and Homogeneous State." In *The Truthful and the Good,* edited by John J. Drummond and James G. Hart. Boston: Kluwer Academic Publishers, 1996.
———. "Versions of Political Philosophy." Presentation, Fordham University, November 11, 2003.
Slings, S. R. *Platonis Republicam.* Oxford: Clarendon Press, 2003.
Slote, Michael. *Morals from Motives.* Oxford: Oxford University Press, 2001.
Smart, J. J. C., and Bernard Williams. *Utilitarianism: For and Against.* Cambridge: Cambridge University Press, 1973.
Smith, Michael. "From Metaethics to Normative Ethics." Lecture, Rutgers University Philosophy Department, New Brunswick, February 1999.
Smith, Thomas W. "Aristotle on the Conditions for and Limits of the Common Good." *American Political Science Review* 93 (1999): 628–31.
Sokolowski, Robert. "The Fiduciary Relationship and the Nature of Professions." In *Ethics, Trust, and the Professions: Philosophical and Cultural Aspects,* edited by E. D. Pellegrino, R. M. Veatch, and J. P. Langan. Washington, D.C.: Georgetown University Press, 1991. Reprinted in Robert Sokolowski,

Christian Faith and Human Understanding (Washington, D.C.: The Catholic University of America Press, 2006).
———. "Knowing Natural Law." In *Pictures, Quotations, and Distinctions.* South Bend, Ind.: University of Notre Dame Press, 1992.
———. "What Is Natural Law? Human Purposes and Natural Ends." *The Thomist* 68 (2004): 507–29. Reprinted in *Christian Faith and Human Understanding* (Washington, D.C.: The Catholic University of America Press, 2006).
Sowell, Thomas. *Black Rednecks and White Liberals.* San Francisco: Encounter Books, 2005.
Spaemann, Robert. "Weltethos als 'Projekt.'" *Merkur* 570, no. 71 (1996): 893–904.
Strauss, Leo. *Natural Right and History.* Chicago: University of Chicago Press, 1953.
Strola, Germana. *Il desiderio di Dio: Studio dei salmi 42–43.* Assisi: Citadella Editrice, 2003.
Swanton, Christine. "A Virtue Ethical Account of Right Action." *Ethics* 112 (2001): 32–52.
———. *Virtue Ethics: A Pluralistic View.* Oxford: Oxford University Press, 2003.
Tatarkiewicz, Wladyslaw. *Mediaeval Aesthetics.* The Hague/Paris/Warsaw: Mouton and PWN (Polish Scientific Publishers), 1970.
Taylor, Charles. *Sources of the Self.* Cambridge, Mass.: Harvard University Press, 1989.
Teachman, Jay D. "The Childhood Living Arrangement of Children and the Characteristics of Their Marriages." *Journal of Family Issues* 25, no. 1 (January 2004): 86–111.
Thatcher, Margaret. Convocation Address, Hofstra University, April 2000.
Thomas Aquinas. *Commentary on Aristotle's "De Anima."* South Bend, Ind.: Dumb Ox Books, 1994.
———. *Disputed Questions on the Virtues.* Translated by E. M. Atkins. Cambridge: Cambridge University Press, 2005.
———. *Summa Contra Gentiles: Book Four: Salvation.* Translated by Charles J. O'Neill. South Bend, Ill., and London: University of Notre Dame Press, 1975.
———. *Summa Theologiae.* Vol. 9. Translated by Kenelm Foster. New York: McGraw-Hill / London: Eyre & Spottiswoode, 1968.
Thomson, Judith. *Goodness and Advice.* Princeton, N.J.: Princeton University Press, 2001.
———. "On Some Ways in Which a Thing Can Be Good." In *The Good Life and the Human Good,* edited by E. Paul, F. Miller, and J. Paul. Cambridge: Cambridge University Press, 1992.
Thorp, J. M. Jr., K. F. Hartmann, and Elizabeth Shadigian. "Long-Term Physical and Psychological Health Consequences of Induced Abortion: Review of the Evidence." *Obstetrical and Gynecological Survey* 58, no. 1 (January 2003): 67–79.

Tinder, Glenn. *The Fabric of Hope: An Essay.* Atlanta: Scholars Press, 1999.
Tocqueville, Alexis de. *Democracy in America.* Vol. 2. Translated by Harvey C. Mansfield and Delba Winthrop. Chicago: University of Chicago Press, 2000.
Torrell, Jean-Pierre. *Saint Thomas Aquinas: The Person and His Work.* Washington, D.C.: The Catholic University of America Press, 1996.
Tucker, Aviezer. *The Philosophy and Politics of Czech Dissidence from Patočka to Havel.* Pittsburgh: University of Pittsburgh Press, 2000.
Urmson, J. O. *Emotive Theory of Ethics.* Oxford: Oxford University Press, 1969.
van Bavel, T. J. "The Double Face of Love in St. Augustine. The Daring Inversion: Love Is God." *Congresso Internazionale su S. Agostino nel XVI Centenario della Conversione Roma, 15–20 settembre. Atti* (1987): 69–80.
Veatch, H. B. "Natural Law and the 'Is'-'Ought' Question: Queries to Finnis and Grisez." In *Swimming Against the Current in Contemporary Philosophy.* Washington, D.C.: The Catholic University of America Press, 1990.
Velazco y Trianosky, Gregory. "Supererogation, Wrongdoing, and Vice: The Autonomy of Virtue Ethics." *Journal of Philosophy* 83 (1986): 26–40.
von Balthasar, H. *The Glory of the Lord.* Vol. 6. Edinburgh: T. & T. Clark, 1991.
Wallace, William. *Modeling of Nature.* Washington, D.C.: The Catholic University of America Press, 1996.
White, Kevin. "*Corpus tale:* The Development in St. Thomas Aquinas' Account of the Human Body's Specific Character." Unpublished manuscript.
———. "The Virtues of Man the Social Animal: Affabilitas and Veritas in Aquinas." *The Thomist* 57 (1993): 641–53.
Williams, Bernard. "Evolution, Ethics and the Representation Problem." In *Making Sense of Humanity.* Cambridge: Cambridge University Press, 1995.
Woodruff, Paul. *Reverence: Renewing a Forgotten Virtue.* Oxford: Oxford University Press, 2001.
Wright, Larry. "Functions." *Philosophical Review* 82, no. 2 (April 1973): 139–68.
———. *Teleological Explanation.* Berkeley and Los Angeles: University of California Press, 1976.
Wuellner, Bernard. *Summary of Scholastic Principles.* Chicago: Loyola University Press, 1956.
Zagzebski, Linda. *Virtues of Mind.* Cambridge: Cambridge University Press, 1996.
Zimmerman, Michael. *Nature of Intrinsic Value.* Lanham, Md.: Rowman & Littlefield, 2001.

Contributors

J. BUDZISZEWSKI is professor in the Departments of Philosophy and Government at the University of Texas at Austin.

JEAN DE GROOT is associate professor in the School of Philosophy at the Catholic University of America.

JORGE L. A. GARCIA is professor of philosophy at Boston College.

LUKE GORMALLY is honorary research fellow and director emeritus of the Linacre Centre for Healthcare Ethics, London.

MARY M. KEYS is associate professor in the Department of Political Science at the University of Notre Dame.

V. BRADLEY LEWIS is associate professor in the School of Philosophy at the Catholic University of America.

NELSON LUND is Patrick Henry Professor of Constitutional Law and the Second Amendment at George Mason University Law School.

DAVID S. ODERBERG is professor of philosophy in the Department of Philosophy at the University of Reading, U.K.

JOSEPH CARDINAL RATZINGER, BENEDICT XVI

JOHN RIST is emeritus professor of philosophy and classics at the University of Toronto.

FRANCIS SLADE is professor emeritus of philosophy at Saint Francis College, New York.

ROBERT SOKOLOWSKI is Elizabeth Breckenridge Caldwell Professor of Philosophy in the School of Philosophy at the Catholic University of America.

HOLGER ZABOROWSKI is assistant professor in the School of Philosophy at the Catholic University of America.

Index

abortion, 30, 40, 77, 95–97, 144, 205–7, 280, 287, 288, 292, 313, 314
absolute spirit, 334
aesthetics, 11, 71, 209, 315–36
Aguirre, Maria Sophia, 141, 166, 167
Andersen, Hans Christian, 293
Anscombe, G. E. M., 151
anthropology, 47, 128, 210
Appiah, Anthony, 129
Aquinas, Thomas, St., 7, 8, 10, 30, 36, 48, 65, 66, 68–74, 85, 89, 90, 93, 120, 124–26, 134, 161, 162, 170–94, 197, 206, 215, 217, 218, 220, 221, 230, 241, 245, 270, 272, 274–76, 278, 296, 313, 314
architecture, 32, 160, 280
Aristotle, 7, 11, 31, 32, 34, 35, 44, 48, 65, 66, 72, 119, 120, 124, 126, 134, 136, 141–95, 198, 206, 221, 224, 229, 231–33, 236, 237, 239, 240, 241, 247, 249, 250, 253, 254, 256–60, 262, 324, 330, 331
Armstrong, D. M., 57
Arnhart, Larry, 155, 189
Audi, Robert, 136
Augustine, St., 11, 74, 94, 319, 322, 325–28, 332, 334

Bacon, Francis, 33, 236
Basil the Great, St., 87
Baumgarten, Alexander, 315, 332
beauty, 11, 94, 315–36
Bedau, Mark, 152
Bennett, Jonathan, 106
Berlin, Isaiah, 212
Berman, Paul, 231
Bickel, Alexander M., 293, 294, 297
bigamy, 30
biology, 19, 44, 51, 52, 63, 75, 88, 97, 128, 142, 150, 152, 153, 155, 163, 164, 168, 265, 276, 278
Blanchette, Oliva, 146
Bloom, Allan, 59
Blum, Lawrence, 105, 133
Bodin, Jean, 243, 248, 250, 261
Boorse, Christopher, 153, 265, 266–68, 277, 278
Boyle, Joseph M., 5, 46, 47, 59, 60, 65–70, 72, 93
Brandt, Richard, 99, 100
Broad, C. D., 136, 137
Brock, Steven, 264, 276
Budziszewski, J., 5, 6, 93

Carpenter, Dale, 305
Carrese, Paul O., 306
Casebeer, William D., 155
Chang, Gene Hsin, 166, 167
chaos, 17, 51, 53–55
Charles, David, 157
Christian faith, 21, 23, 29, 30, 43, 173
Christianity, 2, 4, 11, 18–21, 23, 24, 26, 29–31, 40, 43, 76, 83, 115, 171, 173, 176, 182, 185, 186, 192, 290, 316–19, 324–30, 332, 334–36
Cicero, 47, 48, 178, 325
Cleanthes, 47, 48
Coleman, James, 165, 166
communism, 8, 167, 183, 225
conscience, 5, 6, 62, 70, 77, 83, 84, 86, 90, 91, 93, 95, 97, 190, 192
contraception, 30, 287
conventionalism, 330, 332
Cooper, John M., 141, 142, 150, 156, 157
cooperation, 165
Copleston, Frederick, 187

cosmic law, 47, 48, 56, 59, 75
creation, 2, 20, 24, 36, 76, 79, 80, 86, 89, 91, 125, 162, 186, 188, 189, 326

Dante Alighieri, 97
De Groot, Jean, 7, 154
de Jouvenel, Bertrand, 41
Delhaye, P., 20
democracy, 15, 182, 213, 231, 233, 239
Descartes, René, 9, 33, 34, 36, 37, 58, 59, 143, 236, 243, 244, 247, 268, 269, 273
Des Chene, Dennis, 34
Devins, Neal, 293
Devlin, Patrick, 210
Dideberg, Danny, 327
divorce, 41, 143, 144
Doris, John, 118, 119

economy, 7, 13, 49, 50, 165–67, 181, 202, 233, 290
education, 30, 41, 42, 119, 164, 165, 170, 183, 226, 287, 294
Ehrlich, Anne, 165
Ehrlich, Paul, 165
Eichel, Edward W., 211
Elders, Leo J., 36
Ellis, Brian, 56, 59, 61, 62
Engelhardt, H. T., Jr., 267, 268
epistemology, 9, 66, 67, 78, 246
essentialism, 5, 58–65, 68
Europe, 18, 22, 193, 239, 253
euthanasia, 30, 40, 73, 144
evolution, 7, 19, 44, 51, 127, 128, 138, 142, 152, 153, 155, 306

Fagothey, Austin, 136
family dinner, 167
fidelity, 105, 120, 121, 139, 145
Fiedrowicz, Michael, 22
final causality, 9, 34, 87, 152, 154, 186, 246, 270
Finnis, John, 5, 8, 36, 46, 47, 59, 60, 65–72, 93, 126, 136, 191, 197, 198, 204, 206, 207, 209, 214–22, 230, 231, 234
Fishkin, James, 196
Flanagan, Owen, 114
Flannery, Kevin, 156, 275, 277
flourishing, 5, 58, 64, 72, 92, 102, 131, 145, 155–57, 161, 165, 181, 190, 218, 223, 224, 233, 272, 274, 279, 283
food, 80, 141, 149, 151, 166, 167, 273, 282
Foot, Philippa, 129, 133, 267
Fortin, Ernest L., 185
freedom, 1, 9, 14, 17, 23, 24, 123, 143, 219, 229, 231, 241, 246, 247, 261, 286–88, 292, 310
Freeman, Derek, 211
Fried, Barbara, 123
Fukuyama, Francis, 165, 168

Gallagher, David, 134
Garcia, J. L. A., 6, 118
Garcia, Roman, 133
Geach, Mary, 271, 276
Geach, Peter, 88, 189
Gelfand, Scott, 109, 112, 122
generosity, 49, 117, 120, 163, 165
George, Robert P., 67, 68, 208, 210, 216, 217
Gerleman, Gillis, 317
Gilson, Etienne, 142, 187
God, 11, 17, 26, 27, 30, 34–37, 40, 51, 58, 61, 62, 76, 77, 79, 86, 89, 90–92, 94, 95, 109, 120, 125, 136, 184–88, 252, 296, 316–18, 320, 323–29, 332–35
Goodin, Robert, 137
Gormally, Luke, 9, 10
grace, 29–31, 35, 40, 80, 84, 94, 185, 322
gratitude, 139, 186, 187
Gray, John, 212
Greenawalt, Kent, 8, 198, 207, 213–17, 221, 223
Gregory of Nyssa, St., 319, 325, 327, 328, 332
Grisez, Germain, 5, 46, 47, 59, 60, 65–70, 72, 93, 136
Grotius, Hugo, 19, 197

Habermas, Jürgen, 12, 21, 22, 204, 205
Haldane, John, 222
Hamilton, Alexander, 249, 309
Hamlet, 336
happiness, 10, 72, 79, 111, 134, 141, 143, 144, 168, 169, 183, 188, 190, 201, 246, 250, 256, 258, 259, 295

Hare, R. M., 266–68
Hart, H. L. A., 206, 210
Hartmann, K. F., 144
Hassing, Richard, 155
Havel, Václav, 8, 188, 192–94
health, 9, 10, 59, 72, 144, 146–48, 151, 164, 167, 168, 210, 264–84, 312, 313
Hegel, G. W. F., 242, 244, 245, 250, 259, 260, 261, 334
Heidegger, Martin, 22, 247, 334
Hendin, Herbert, 144
Herder, Johann Gottfried, 332
Hern, Warren D., 96
Higgins, Thomas, 136
Hittinger, Russell, 30, 65, 66, 70, 81, 216
Hobbes, Thomas, 9, 25, 33, 35, 41, 42, 81, 86, 92, 173, 235, 237, 240–43, 245, 246, 248–50, 260–62, 301
honesty, 49, 105, 119, 121
Hübner, Kurt, 23
human goods, 7, 9, 63, 67, 68, 74, 142, 145–47, 160, 162, 163, 167, 169, 185, 209, 266, 274–77, 279, 280, 282, 283
human nature, 5, 7, 8, 30, 46–48, 60, 61, 65–72, 74, 75, 85, 125–29, 134, 141–46, 165, 169, 175, 182, 184, 190, 217, 299
humility, 172, 186, 188, 189, 192–94
Hurka, Thomas, 100, 138
Hursthouse, Rosalind, 108, 109, 111, 112

infanticide, 30
Irwin, Terrence, 153

Jaffa, Harry V., 172–78, 186, 187, 189–92, 194
Jefferson, Thomas, 253
Jenkins, John I., 173, 174, 178, 179
John Paul II, 24, 76, 128, 194
Junker, Reinhard, 19
justice, 14, 15, 18, 24, 39, 44, 58, 82, 116, 139, 174, 178, 180, 183, 188, 189, 196, 197, 199–204, 218–20, 226, 228, 231, 245, 273, 280, 282, 298

Kamtekar, Rachana, 118
Kant, Immanuel, 39, 46, 77, 102–4, 111, 116, 118, 133, 138, 196, 199, 201, 243, 245, 246, 329, 332, 333
Kass, Leon, 162–65
Kennington, Richard, 236
Keys, Mary M., 7, 8, 170, 186
Kisiel, Theodore, 247
Klein, Jacob, 236
Klemke, E. D., 50
Klerman, Gerald, 144
Koons, Robert, 87
Korsgaard, Christine, 102, 103, 135
Kries, Douglas, 188
Kripke, Saul, 60
Küng, Hans, 13

Larmore, Charles, 134, 135, 208
Laslett, Peter, 196
Lear, 336
Lefort, Claude, 244
Lennox, James, 150, 277
Lévi-Strauss, Claude, 22
Lewis, V. B., 8, 170, 226, 228, 232
liberalism, 8, 195–234, 251
Lincoln, Abraham, 203, 289, 290
Lisska, A. J., 65, 67
Locke, John, 62, 93, 173, 196, 197, 212, 297, 301, 302
Lund, Nelson, 10, 285, 289, 293, 297, 308, 310
Lutz, Donald, 303

Macedo, Stephen, 8, 198, 207–212, 216, 217, 221, 223–25, 233
Machiavelli, Niccolò, 9, 33, 35, 235, 236, 238, 240, 241, 244, 249–63
MacIntyre, Alasdair, 32, 136, 143, 147, 187, 190, 222, 224, 232
Madigan, Arthur, 99, 135, 136
Madison, James, 243, 253, 300
magnanimity, 170, 172, 186, 187, 189, 190, 194
Makin, Stephen, 270
Malcolm, Noel, 261
Manent, Pierre, 188, 231, 237, 248, 254
Maritain, Jacques, 66, 67, 69–72, 197, 204, 206
marriage, 24, 30, 41, 143, 144, 162, 163, 209, 276, 287, 312
Martin, Christopher, 45
martyrdom, 27

materialism, 273
McDonagh, Eileen, 95, 96
McDowell, John, 105, 133
McGinnis, John O., 285, 289, 310, 311
McInerny, Ralph, 180, 187
mechanism, 16, 18, 113, 273, 274, 280, 298
medicine, 9, 10, 32, 88, 264–84
Meng, Jude Chua Soo, 66, 67
Michael, Robert T., 211
Mill, J. S., 127
Millikan, Ruth Garrett, 152, 153
Monod, Jacques, 19
monogamy, 30
Montaigne, Michel de, 259
Montesquieu, Charles de, 10, 253, 285–314
moral philosophy, 5, 35, 44, 115, 139, 221, 259, 267, 331
More, Thomas, St., 240
murder, 28, 85, 86, 89, 106
Murphy, Mark C., 214, 216, 217

natural inclination, 36, 68–70, 73, 74, 79, 174, 190, 274–76
naturalism, 127, 273, 332
natural order, 29–31, 40
natural right, 8, 9, 40, 172, 173–80, 195–235, 247, 256, 296
natural sciences, 2, 3, 19, 236
neopaganism, 329, 332
Neoplatonism, 317, 325, 332
Neoscholasticism, 67
New Testament, 11, 317
norm, 4, 11, 20, 23, 56, 65, 86, 88, 89, 90, 102, 104, 130–32, 137, 168, 190, 193, 209, 214, 219, 223
normativity, 45, 56, 103
nourishment, 32, 41, 42
Nussbaum, Martha, 99, 136

O'Connor, D. J., 67
Oakes, Edward T., 143
Oakeshott, Michael, 235, 242
obligation, 4, 20, 27, 30, 33, 37–40, 43, 100, 101, 103, 104, 106, 133, 134, 136, 164, 286, 295, 300, 329, 336
Oderberg, David, 5, 45, 46, 56, 60, 63, 73, 128
Old Testament, 30, 316, 317, 326
Osborn, E. F., 317

paganism, 19, 26, 90, 173, 317, 329, 332
Pangle, Lorraine Smith, 191
Pangle, Thomas L., 193
Parfit, Derek, 46
Paul, St., 58, 90, 91
Pieper, Josef, 189, 247–49
Pinckaers, Servais, 173
Pinker, Steven, 75
Pippin, Robert B., 246
Platonism, 316, 319, 325, 332
Plotinus, 11, 318–27, 332
Polanowska-Sygulska, Beata, 212
political philosophy, 8, 9, 35, 171, 175, 183, 195–97, 229, 232, 235–63, 289, 294, 297
polygamy, 30, 312
Popenoe, David, 143
Prigent, Pierre, 317
prudence, 4, 29, 39, 42, 49, 83, 84, 111, 167, 168, 181–83, 222, 229, 273, 299, 307
Prufer, Thomas, 238
psychology, 59, 118, 174, 199, 210, 218, 293
public reason, 8, 26, 195–234
Pufendorf, Samuel von, 19
Putnam, Robert D., 165

Rabkin, Jeremy, 39
Rascoe, Burton, 236
rationality, 4, 20–23, 141, 148, 161, 211
Ratzinger, Joseph Cardinal/Benedict XVI, 3–5, 12, 19, 22, 24, 29, 76, 87, 206
Rawls, John, 8, 195–234
reasonableness, 71, 199, 208, 209, 217
regularity, 50, 52, 53, 57, 153
Reisman, Judith A., 211
Renaissance, 329, 332
Rhonheimer, Martin, 217, 223
Richardson, Henry, 104, 130–32, 137, 138
Riedl, John O., 184
Rist, John M., 11, 143, 319, 320, 323
Rodes, Robert E., Jr., 211
Rosenberg, Gerald N., 293
Ross, W. D., 102, 130, 139
Rousseau, Jean-Jacques, 60, 173, 196, 223, 243, 245, 247, 250, 297, 332
Russell, Bertrand, 101

Sakarov, Andrei, 193
Schall, James V., 191
Scheffler, Samuel, 139

Scherer, Siegfried, 19
Schmitt, Carl, 22, 247–50, 258
Schneewind, Jerome, 101, 124
Scholasticism, 92
secularization, 22
self-confidence, 165
sexuality, 7, 30, 32, 95, 143, 162–64, 209, 210, 285, 292, 304, 312, 319, 331
Shackleton, Robert, 302
Shadigian, Elizabeth, 144
Shanley, Brian J., 184
shelter, 41, 42, 282
Simon, Julian, 165
Simon, Yves, 67, 197, 214, 216, 231
Simpson, G. G., 51
Simpson, Peter L. Phillips, 232
Slade, Francis, 8, 9, 31, 32, 35, 274
Sling, S. R., 226
Slote, Michael, 107, 109, 112, 124
Smart, J. J. C., 75
Smith, Adam, 134
Smith, Michael, 113
Smith, Thomas W., 191
social sciences, 7, 128, 141, 143, 145, 165, 168, 169, 175, 187, 190, 210, 215
Sokolowski, Robert, 4, 5, 32, 141, 168, 274, 280
Solzhenitsyn, Aleksandr, 193
Somin, Ilya, 311
Soviet Union, 183, 192–94, 335
Sowell, Thomas, 290
Spaemann, Robert, 13
stem-cell research, 30, 37
Stevens, Wallace, 333
Strauss, Leo, 172, 173, 195, 198, 235, 248
Strola, Germana, 317
Swanton, Christine, 100, 104, 113, 114

Tatarkiewicz, Wladyslaw, 330
Taylor, Charles, 333
Teachman, Jay D., 143
teleology, 5, 7–9, 36, 62–65, 74, 93, 127, 136, 141–69, 235–63
Thatcher, Margaret, 260
theology, 1, 29, 36, 76, 79, 136, 156, 182, 186, 187, 189, 248, 249, 317, 326, 333
Thomism, 11, 36, 66, 173, 178, 185–87, 190, 195, 331
Thomson, Judith, 104, 115, 116, 123
Thorp, J. M., Jr., 144
Tinder, Glenn, 189
Tocqueville, Alexis de, 231, 290, 296, 309, 311
Torrell, Jean-Pierre, 173
torture, 106, 127, 331
truthfulness, 119, 145, 191
Tucker, Aviezer, 194

ugliness, 72, 94, 320, 322, 328, 330, 331, 334–336
United States, 37, 182, 183, 207, 214, 290, 291
Urmson, J. O., 133
utilitarianism, 74, 75, 99, 108, 111, 115, 118, 139, 140, 144, 199, 201, 221, 336

values, 4, 9, 15, 16, 20, 23, 24, 34, 36, 45–47, 49, 50, 52, 56, 65, 73, 76, 85, 95, 100, 102, 103, 113, 115, 130, 132, 133, 135, 137, 138, 192, 201, 203–7, 211, 217, 225, 264, 265, 267, 268, 274, 275, 297, 320, 321, 325, 331, 333
van Bavel, T. J., 327
Veatch, H. B., 65
Velazco y Trianosky, Gregory, 99
von Balthasar, H. U., 232, 317

Wallace, William A., 155
war, state of, 42, 258
well-being, 167, 180, 280
Wen, Guanzhong James, 166, 167
White, Kevin, 161, 184
Whitehead, Barbara Dafoe, 143
Wild, John, 136
Williams, Bernard, 74, 75, 104, 127, 128, 137, 138
Wilson, James Q., 163
wisdom, 83, 156, 163, 181–83, 189, 209, 247, 317
Woodruff, Paul, 188
world ethos, 13, 22
Wright, Larry, 153
Wuellner, Bernard, 54, 60

Zagzebski, Linda, 111–15
Zimmerman, Michael, 100, 138

Natural Moral Law in Contemporary Society was designed and typeset in Minion by Kachergis Book Design of Pittsboro, North Carolina. It was printed on 60-pound House Natural Smooth and bound by Sheridan Books of Ann Arbor, Michigan.